Printed in the United States
By Bookmasters

T0214326

Yiannis Papadopoulos · Koorosh Aslansefat ·
Panagiotis Katsaros · Marco Bozzano (Eds.)

Model-Based Safety and Assessment

6th International Symposium, IMBSA 2019
Thessaloniki, Greece, October 16–18, 2019
Proceedings

 Springer

Editors
Yiannis Papadopoulos (iD)
University of Hull
Hull, UK

Koorosh Aslansefat (iD)
University of Hull
Hull, UK

Panagiotis Katsaros
Aristotle University of Thessaloniki
Thessaloniki, Greece

Marco Bozzano (iD)
Fondazione Bruno Kessler
Trento, Trento, Italy

ISSN 0302-9743 ISSN 1611-3349 (electronic)
Lecture Notes in Computer Science
ISBN 978-3-030-32871-9 ISBN 978-3-030-32872-6 (eBook)
https://doi.org/10.1007/978-3-030-32872-6

LNCS Sublibrary: SL2 – Programming and Software Engineering

This Springer imprint is published by the registered company Springer Nature Switzerland AG
The registered company address is: Gewerbestrasse 11, 6330 Cham, Switzerland

Preface

This volume contains the papers presented at IMBSA 2019: the International Symposium on Model-Based Safety and Assessment, held during October 16–18, 2019, in Thessaloniki, Greece.

IMBSA focuses on model-based and automated ways of assessing safety and other attributes of dependability of complex computer systems. Since the first edition in Toulouse (2011), the workshop has evolved to a forum where brand new ideas from academia, leading-edge technology, and industrial experiences are brought together. The objectives are to present experiences and tools, to share ideas, and to federate the community.

This year a particular space was given to the assessment of open systems, autonomous systems, and systems that employ artificial intelligence (AI). There are specific challenges in the assessment of such systems which include unboundness, the infinity of possible configurations, uncertainty, and particularities related to the reasoning and operation of AI components.

To foster academic and industrial collaboration, in addition to more traditional talks reporting on novel advances on hot research topics, the program featured a poster and tutorial sessions, where speakers had the opportunity to present ongoing research and industrial experiences, and demonstrate their tool interactively.

We believe that a mixture of conventional talks about the newest achievements, the presentation of practical experiences, and interactive learning facilitates fruitful discussions, the exchange of information, as well as future cooperation. Therefore, following the previous edition of IMBSA in Trento (2017), an important focus of this year's edition in Thessaloniki was placed on tool tutorials and demonstrations. Nevertheless, the main scientific and industrial contributions were presented in traditional talks and are collected in this volume of LNCS.

For IMBSA 2019, we received 46 regular submissions from authors of 17 countries. Following rigorous review, the best 24 of these papers were selected by an international Program Committee to be published in this volume. As organizers, we want to extend a very warm thank you to all 50 members of the international Program Committee. Each submission was reviewed by at least three Program Committee members. The comprehensive review guaranteed the high quality of the accepted papers. We also want to thank the local organization team in Thessaloniki, and our fellow members of the Steering Committee: Leila Kloul, Frank Ortmeier, Antoine Rauzy, and Christel Seguin.

Finally, we wish you a pleasant reading of the articles in this volume. On behalf of everyone involved in this year's International Symposium on Model-Based Safety and Assessment, we hope you will be joining us at the next edition of IMBSA.

September 2019

Yiannis Papadopoulos
Koorosh Aslansefat
Panagiotis Katsaros
Marco Bozzano

Organization

General Chairs

Panagiotis Katsaros   Aristotle University of Thessaloniki, Greece
Yiannis Papadopoulos   University of Hull, UK

Program Committee Chairs

Marco Bozzano   FBK, Italy
Antoine Rauzy   Norwegian University of Science and Technology,
    Norway

Tools and Tutorials Chairs

Leila Kloul   Université de Versailles, France
Frank Ortmeier   Otto-von-Guericke University of Magdeburg, Germany

Industrial Chairs

Jean-Paul Blanquart   Airbus Defence and Space, France
Christel Seguin   ONERA, France

Organizing Committee

Yiannis Papadopoulos   University of Hull, UK
Koorosh Aslansefat   University of Hull, UK
David Parker   University of Hull, UK
Panagiotis Katsaros   Aristotle University of Thessaloniki, Greece

Program Committee

Ezio Bartocci   Technische Universität Wien, Austria
Stylianos Basagiannis   United Technologies Research Centre, Ireland
Saddek Bensalem   Universirsité Grenoble Alpes, France
Jean-Paul Blanquart   Airbus Defence and Space, France
Simon Bliudze   Inria Lille, France
Marc Bouissou   EDF, France
Marco Bozzano   FBK, Italy
Jean-Charles Chaudemar   ISAE, France
Lorenzo Bitetti   Thales Alenia Space, France
Jana Dittmann   Otto-von-Guericke University of Magdeburg, Germany
Marielle Doche-Petit   Systerel, France

Nicholas Matragkas	University of York, UK
Joxe Aizpurua Unanue	Mondragon University, Spain
Francesco Flammini	University of Naples, Italy
Lars Fucke	Diehl Aviation, Germany
Lars Grunske	Humboldt University Berlin, Germany
Matthias Güdemann	Input-Output Hong-Kong, China
Brendan Hall	Honeywell, USA
Kai Höfig	Siemens, Germany
Michaela Huhn	Ostfalia, Germany
Panagiotis Katsaros	Aristotle University of Thessaloniki, Greece
Tim Kelly	University of York, UK
Leila Kloul	Universite de Versailles, France
Agnes Lanusse	CEA LIST, France
Timo Latvala	Space Systems Finland, Finland
Till Mossakowski	Otto-von-Guericke University of Magdeburg, Germany
Jürgen Mottok	University of Regensburg, Germany
Thomas Noll	RWTH Aachen University, Germany
Frank Ortmeier	Otto-von-Guericke University of Magdeburg, Germany
Yiannis Papadopoulos	University of Hull, UK
Antoine Rauzy	Norwegian University of Science and Technology, Norway
Wolfgang Reif	Augsburg University, Germany
Jean-Marc Roussel	LURPA, ENS Cachan, France
Christel Seguin	ONERA, France
Ramin Tavakoli Kolagari	Technische Hochschule Nürnberg, Germany
Pascal Traverse	Airbus, France
Elena A. Troubitsyna	KTH, Sweden
Marcel Verhoef	European Space Agency, The Netherlands
Lijun Zhang	Chinese Academy of Sciences, China
Marc Zeller	Siemens, Germany

Steering Committee

Marco Bozzano	FBK, Italy
Leila Kloul	Universite de Versailles, France
Frank Ortmeier	Otto-von-Guericke University of Magdeburg, Germany
Yiannis Papadopoulos	University of Hull, UK
Antoine Rauzy	Norwegian University of Science and Technology, Norway
Christel Seguin	ONERA, France

Additional Reviewers

Sohag Kabir	University of Hull, UK
Youcef Gheraibia	University of York, UK
Alexander Knapp	University of London, UK
Viorel Preoteasa	Aalto University, Finland

Contents

Security Assessment

Safety Assessment in Automotive Industry

AI in Safety Assessment

Safety Models and Languages

Modeling Functional Allocation in AltaRica to Support MBSE/MBSA Consistency

Mathilde Machin[1(✉)], Estelle Saez[1], Pierre Virelizier[1], and Xavier de Bossoreille[2]

[1] IRT Saint-Exupéry, B612 3 rue Tarfaya, 31400 Toulouse, France
{mathilde.machin,estelle.saez}@irt-saintexupery.com,
pierre.virelizier2@safrangroup.com
[2] APSYS-Airbus, 36 rue Grimaud, 31700 Blagnac, France
xavier.debossoreille@apsys-airbus.com

Abstract. In order to ensure and maintain the consistency between the safety analyses and the system design definition during system development iterations, we propose to follow a model-based approach, using system architecture models (MBSE) and failure propagation models (MBSA). Most systems engineering methods define the functional architecture before defining the physical architecture. We developed a safety modeling method in accordance with this sequence, leading to perform safety analysis and consistency activities on the functional architecture first, then on the physical architecture. We therefore had to address the allocations of functions to physical elements.

This paper focuses on the modeling of functional architecture and allocations links to the physical architecture. We discuss how to model these concepts using AltaRica DataFlow proposing several alternatives, and present the difficulties we faced in the modeling of the allocation behavior, in particular the mapping of functional failure modes to physical failure modes.

Keywords: MBSE · AltaRica DataFlow · Allocation modeling · Consistency

1 Introduction

This paper is the continuity of our work to define a methodology, based on models capacities, to maintain the consistency between safety analyses and system design definition through the system development iterations [1]. These works handle the design and safety analysis models done during the preliminary design phase.

In the literature, two approaches emerge to link safety models with system architecture models: the use of a single model both describing the system architecture and including safety data and the use of two specific models for safety analysis and system description [2]. We choose the second alternative using system architecture models (MBSE) for system description and failure propagation models (MBSA) to support safety analyses [1]. We consider that the system model is the reference for the safety model, even though the two models remain independent. Consequently, our work aims at maintaining the consistency between both models by assisting the validation review of the dysfunctional model performed by the system architect.

© Springer Nature Switzerland AG 2019
Y. Papadopoulos et al. (Eds.): IMBSA 2019, LNCS 11842, pp. 3–17, 2019.
https://doi.org/10.1007/978-3-030-32872-6_1

Most systems engineering methods describe the functional architecture before defining the physical architecture. We developed a safety modeling method in accordance with this sequence. We perform the safety analysis and the consistency activities on the functional architecture first, and then extend them to the physical architecture. We propose to introduce in the safety model concepts defined by MBSE methods such as functions, allocations, physical elements. As a consequence allocations of functions to physical components have to be modeled in the safety model.

This paper focuses on the modeling of allocations links to the physical architecture. It is organized as follows. Section 2 presents the MBSE objects we consider and the functional architecture as previously modeled which is our starting point. Section 3 presents several alternatives to model this concept using AltaRica DataFlow and define selection criteria. Section 4 discusses the difficulties we faced in the application of the chosen alternative to a drone study case. Eventually Sect. 5 concludes the paper.

2 Context

Our methodology is based on MBSE and MBSA modeling characteristics detailed in the following sections. Note that in our experiment we have used Capella (with Arcadia) for architecture modeling and Cecilia OCAS for safety modeling.

2.1 System Description Models

The architecture description models we consider allow to hierarchically organize functions and physical elements, to describe exchanges between functions and physical elements, as well as corresponding allocation relations. In the following we qualify as "hierarchical" the functions and the physical elements that are decomposed in sub-

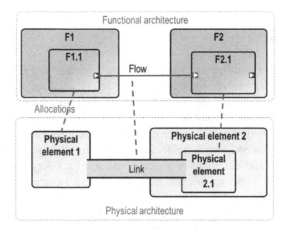

Fig. 1. MBSE model parts we consider. Functions (in green) are allocated (blue dashed) to physical elements (in yellow). Communication from a function to another is modeled by a functional flow and conveyed by a physical link. (Color figure online)

elements, as opposed to "leaf" functions or physical elements that are not refined in sub-elements. The Capella tool (following Arcadia method) or SysML editors provide the capacity of modeling the MBSE models as described in this section.

From a method and process point of view, we use an architecture description model that describes design at two levels (see Fig. 1): functional architecture on one hand and physical architecture on the other hand. In order to simplify the modeling activity we consider no intermediate layer between the functional and physical architecture. For instance this means that we do not model the "logical components" or the "behavioral components" from Arcadia [3].

2.2   Safety Assessment and Modeling

Within the ARP4754A [4] and ARP4761 [5] development processes, our work is positioned in the preliminary system safety analysis. In this framework, the safety assessment is used to show compliance with certification functional and safety requirements.

Early in the development, safety analysis at functional level allows to structure the architecture design by defining the functional independence requirements supporting the DAL (Development Assurance Level) allocation. Our proposition is to optimize the benefit of models by performing the safety assessment at functional level as soon as possible, and by reusing all related safety assessment, modeling, validation and consistency activities when addressing the physical architecture.

As far as safety modeling is concerned, we use the failure propagation modeling language AltaRica DataFlow. This language allows to create generic modeling bricks that can be seen as functions, physical elements or any other concept. Each leaf brick contains some behavior: failure modes occurring inside the function or physical element, dysfunctional logics defining how an upstream failure mode combines with the internal failure modes and functional logics defining how the system is designed to detect, mitigate or recover failure modes.

We organize AltaRica modeling of functional architecture as described in Fig. 2.

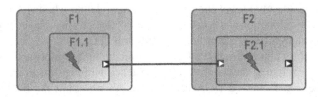

Fig. 2. MBSA modeling of functional architecture. Thunderbolts represent failure modes that are modeled inside functions.

Note that we limit the scope of the proposed safety modeling to failure modes of functions and physical elements. Even if components, such as wires, are likely to be modeled as physical links in MBSE (as defined in Fig. 1) and may have critical failure modes, we do not consider them in the following. The proposed method remains applicable at cost of modeling critical components as physical elements instead of links.

The functional model as shown in Fig. 2 supports safety analysis of functional architecture. Considering this functional model as a starting point, Sect. 3 addresses the step of modeling physical architecture inspired by allocation modeling methods taken from literature.

2.3   Related Work

This section presents other works dealing with modeling allocation in MBSA. This literature review is limited to the scope defined previously, notably the approach of using two specific models for safety and architecture, the preliminary system safety analysis and the use of AltaRica as MBSA language.

Our works share with the work proposed by Legendre [5] the overall objective of consistency of system description models and safety models. In the study case presented in [5], the architecture consistency is ensured in 4 steps: (1) functional breakdown, (2) physical breakdown, (3) physical links and (4) allocations. Contrary to our approach, the functional flows are not considered in the functional safety analysis. Consequently the function behavior is only constituted of internal failure modes, omitting how upstream failure modes combine to internal failure modes. Allocations are modeled by the inheritance feature of AltaRica 3.0. The physical element modeling is based on the function and thus inherits from the failure modes of the function. When defining the physical elements, it is possible to add some features: inputs and outputs, propagation logics and additional failure modes.

This approach does not share our objective of having a safety analysis based on the functional architecture and thus proposes a different modeling of functions. Nevertheless it offers an example of allocation modeling. The inheritance feature is specific to AltaRica 3.0 and has no graphical representation to our knowledge.

The French institution DGA proposes a MBSA method that includes a functional view and a physical view [7]. The functions are organized within a hierarchy that is more expressive than a simple breakdown: it includes logics. For example, it describes that the communication function is operational if its reception sub-function *and* its transmission sub-function are operational. Functions have no internal failure modes, they are linked to the outputs of the physical layer to define whether they are operational. Thus, these functions are used to observe the physical layer and combine observations to analyze the system failure conditions (FC).

This approach is characteristic of the use of functions by safety analysts for pure safety purposes, excluding any concern of consistency with the functional architecture from system designers. Indeed DGA uses models for assessing the final architecture design and not within a development process.

Back to design concerns, the works of Sagaspe [8] aims to generate allocations so as to ensure safety. Therefore both functional and physical layers are modeled without the objective of computing cutsets at functional level. Allocations are modeled as synchronizations, which is a modeling feature common to all versions of AltaRica (see [9] for more information about synchronization feature). This approach requires two steps of synchronizations: firstly the failure modes from all the functions allocated to one physical element are synchronized among themselves. Secondly this "functional" synchronization is synchronized with the failure mode of the allocated physical element. Let us note that some cases of physical links with failure modes are addressed by these works.

To conclude, even though several modeling features to model allocations of functions to physical element exist, there is neither dedicated work, nor comparison of modeling methods in literature. In the following we present several modeling alternatives and describe in detail the method we have experimented.

3 Several Alternatives and Criteria

Based on the functional modeling illustrated by Fig. 2, we present four alternatives to model allocations of functions to physical elements. To fulfill our objectives of consistency between system and safety models and of reuse of the functional layer, we focus on modeling solutions that contain both functional and physical failure modes. In addition, in order to have the same concepts as MBSE, we exclude methods that represent allocation not by a model element but by labeling functions (labels, known as attributes or user data, are used to post-process the cutsets).

To obtain results useful for development process, we need to generate cutsets that combine either functional failure modes or physical failure modes. We need two separated sets of cutsets. The corresponding generation feature is offered by the tool Cecilia OCAS. Otherwise, it could be done outside of the tool by post-processing the mixed set of cutsets, at cost of some computation time.

After a short presentation of each alternative, we compare their properties in Sect. 3.5.

3.1 The Functional Layer and the Physical Layer Linked by Synchronizations

This alternative comes from [8]. As shown in Fig. 3, the functional model is completely reused and allocations are modeled using the synchronization feature offered by AltaRica language.

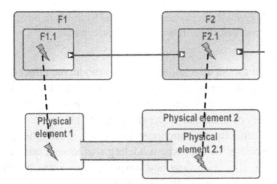

Fig. 3. The functional layer and the physical layer linked by synchronizations. Synchronizations are shown as dashed linked between failure modes.

Starting from an existing functional model, this alternative requires the following tasks to complete the physical model:

- Model fully the physical architecture, including behavior of failure propagation.
- Add synchronization of failure modes.

To our knowledge, synchronization is a feature that is graphically supported by none of the AltaRica tools. As a consequence, the usage of synchronization may make model difficult to read and debug.

Furthermore, computing separately functional and physical cutsets is not supported by Cecilia OCAS, as physical failure modes are synchronizations instead of simple events. Consequently, with this alternative and this tool, we are not currently able to recompute functional cutsets once the physical architecture is modeled.

3.2 The Functional Layer and the Physical Layer Linked by Flows

This alternative is an adaptation of the previous one (Sect. 3.1) taking inspiration from the DGA/TA method [7] to use flows for the modeling of allocation. As shown in Fig. 4, this alternative reuses completely the functional layer analysis model shown in Fig. 2.

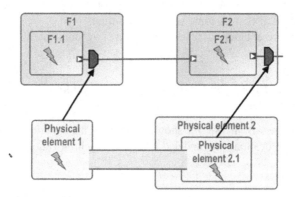

Fig. 4. The functional layer and the physical layer linked by flows. In blue, modeling artifacts to merge allocation flows and functional flows. (Color figure online)

The use of flows to model allocations require to model the effect of failure modes of allocation supports in the functional layer apart from the functional failure modes. Furthermore, changes required in functional layer have to be limited as far as possible. Thus, the failure modes of allocation supports are taken into account in functional layer outside of functions, directly on functional flows. To model the effects of physical failure modes on functional flows, some modeling artifacts are added: they contain the logics that define how allocation flow and functional flows are combined.

Starting from an existing functional model, this alternative requires the following tasks to complete the physical model:

- Model fully the physical architecture, including behavior of failure propagation.
- Add ports to input allocation flow in the functional layer.
- Add in the functional layer modeling artifacts to merge the allocation flows and the functional flows.

With respect to synchronizations, using flows to model allocations require more work, such as defining new ports, oblige to make some changes in functional layer. Nevertheless, it offers more flexibility in the way the failure modes from both layers can be combined.

3.3   The Functional Layer Using Physical Resources

As shown in Fig. 5, this alternative reuses completely the functional layer analysis model shown in Fig. 2 and uses flows to model allocations. Compared to the previous alternative, the behavior modeled in the physical layer is reduced: The physical layer provides to the functional layer the state of the physical elements but does not contain the information flows between physical elements. Yet physical layer can contain physical dependencies between physical elements, e.g., power supply (not shown in Fig. 5).

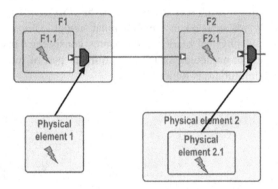

Fig. 5. The functional layer using physical resources

This alternative requires the following tasks to be built from the functional model:

- Model the physical architecture. The behavior modeled in the physical layer is limited to the impact of physical failures to allocated functions.
- Add ports to input allocation flows in the functional layer.
- Add in the functional layer modeling artifacts to merge the allocation flows and the functional flows.

Contrary to the previous two alternatives, physical layer is here "minimal". Each physical element only propagates its state as an allocation support to its allocated functions. The physical layer cannot be simulated or computed independently from the functional layer. The interest of "minimality" is twofold: the physical layer requires less effort to be modeled and, more important, the behavior information is modeled only once removing problems of behavior consistency between the one modeled in functional layer and the one modeled in the physical layer.

This alternative has some drawbacks. During a step-by-step simulation, the failure propagation is only visualized inside the functional layer as there is no flow in the physical layer. Furthermore this alternative cannot support any dynamic modeling (that includes deterministic events and may results in sequential behavior), e.g. aiming to model functional behavior that changes or reset physical behavior.

3.4   Functions Nested in Physical Layer

A commonplace practice in MBSA consists in modeling only the physical architecture with a rich behavior including reconfigurations, typically specified at functional level by the system architect. To match our objectives of reuse of functional model and consistency with MBSE, we adapt this practice as shown in Fig. 6. In this alternative, allocation is modeled as a containment of functions inside the physical element. Similarly to the allocation by flow, modeling artifacts are used to merge functional flow and physical state.

In all alternatives, modeling bricks such as functions are implemented in AltaRica DataFlow as classes. We use this feature to reuse the functional modeling. A function nested in the physical layer is the second instance of the class defined during functional modeling and already instanciated in the functional model. This avoids duplication between functional and physical models and ensures consistency between behaviors defined in both models in particular for the most difficult part of modeling that is the behavior such as reconfigurations logics.

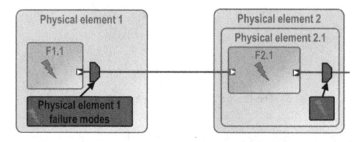

Fig. 6. Functions nested in physical layer

Starting from an existing functional model, this alternative requires the following tasks to complete the physical model:

– Model the physical architecture. The behavior is mainly contained in the new instances of existing function classes.
– Add modeling artifacts to merge the allocation flows and the functional flows.

Note that this alternative imposes that the functional model has at least the level of details required to model allocations. Indeed if several functions from MBSE are modeled as one MBSA model element and if these functions are allocated on different physical elements, this method is not applicable. This adds constraint on modeling structure.

3.5 Summary

Four methods of allocation modeling have been presented and are summed up in Table 1. We select the alternative described in Sect. 3.3 and named C in Table 1. This section summarizes our choice criteria.

Modeling Cost. As discussed previously modeling flows and logics in functional and physical layers raises issues of consistency between both layers and therefore is expensive in model edition and maintenance. For this reason we choose to discard the first two alternatives shown in Table 1 (A and B). Note that when renouncing to model flows and logics in both functional and physical layers, we also lose the capability of visualizing failures propagation in both layers during step-by-step simulation.

Structure Flexibility. In addition, our goal is to develop a method to keep MBSE and MBSA models consistent with minimal constraints on the safety model structure. That is why we choose the modeling of physical resources (C) against the nesting of functions (D).

Next section presents the issues raised by the application of the method of functional layer using physical resources to a study case.

Table 1. Properties of the four alternatives

Alternatives	Allocation modeling	Reuse of functional model	Flows in two layers?	Compliance static and dynamic modeling	Remarks
A - Two layers by synchronization	Synchronization	Breakdown and leaf functions	Yes	Static and dynamic	No graphical support for synchronizations
B - Two layers by flow	Flow (and flow merging)	Breakdown and leaf functions	Yes	Static and dynamic	
C - Functional layer using physical resources	Flow (and flow merging)	Breakdown and leaf functions	No	Static, difficult in dynamic	
D - Functions nested in physical layer	Nesting (and merging)	Leaf functions by class instanciation	No	Static and dynamic	Constraint on functional structure

4 The Functional Layer Supplied by the Physical Resources: Application

As in previous work [1], the study case is a remotely piloted drone named AIDA[1] (Aircraft Inspection Drone Assistant). The system is composed of a quadcopter drone, a control computer and a remote control. The system mission is to assist the pilot to inspect the aircraft before flight. The quadcopter drone can be piloted in automated or manual mode.

The system has been defined by a system architect through a MBSE model in Capella. The architecture definition focuses on avionics while modeling of actuation, sensing and body is coarse-grained. It contains 7 high level functions, 96 level-3 functions and 39 physical elements. Three FCs, whose one catastrophic and one hazardous have been analyzed.

The safety analyst has used the tool Cecilia OCAS to model of functional and physical layers applying the method from Sect. 3.3. The following sections detail some issues raised by allocation modeling and Sect. 4.4 gives an overview of lessons learnt by the case study.

4.1 Allocation of a Functional Flow to Physical Elements

When modeling the allocations, we face the case of a functional flow that is allocated to physical elements. As an illustration, let us consider in Fig. 7 the functional flow "Vertical speed consign". It is produced by the function SF2.2.4 (allocated to the physical element "Remote control") and sent to the function SF2.4.1 (allocated to the physical element "Main computer"). To make this communication physically feasible, the considered flow goes through several physical elements: communication of remote control, embedded radio controller and embedded network.

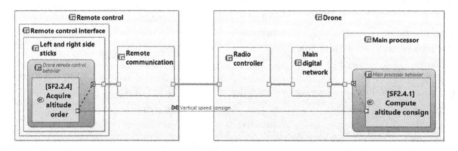

Fig. 7. Example of a functional flow allocated to several physical elements (extracted from our MBSE model)

---

[1] The MBSE and MBSA models are available under open source license at https://sahara.irt-saintexupery.com/.

From a dysfunctional point of view, if one of these physical elements fails, the functional flow is impacted. Consequently the dependency of the flow with the physical failures must be taken into account in the safety model. We enrich our allocation modeling method, by defining an intermediate object of allocation named *path* (taking inspiration from a Capella concept), as shown in Fig. 8.

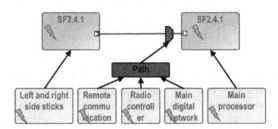

Fig. 8. Safety modeling of a functional flow allocated to several physical elements (For the sake of readability, this figure omits the hierarchy representation)

A path is a modeling artifact that does not contain any failure mode but embeds dysfunctional logics. For instance in Fig. 8 given the flow direction, the logics define that an erroneous "Radio controller" does not affect the speed consign if the "Main digital network" is lost.

Any modeling method dealing with functional allocations should address the need to allocate functional flows to physical elements. Even though our modelling proposition is inspired from Capella modelling, it is generic enough to be applied when using another MBSE tool.

4.2 Failure Modes More Detailed in Physical Layer than in Functional Layer

In order to model the physical layer from the functional layer model, we refine the functional failure modes. The functional layer is built with the generic failure modes "erroneous" and "loss". When modeling some components, we need to refine the erroneous failure mode, for instance, in:

- Higher value than expected ("HighErr")
- Lower value than expected ("LowErr")
- Other case of erroneous value ("Erroneous")

The three cases are distinguished because they have different safety effects, potentially impacting different FCs. As the information propagation is only modeled in the functional layer of the model, the functional layer must be enriched, adding new values to the flows (as illustrated in Fig. 9).

As the functional layer has been significantly updated, it is necessary to perform again the system validation of the corresponding dysfunctional model. Nevertheless the associated rework can be limited by formulating the logics in a way that the values of

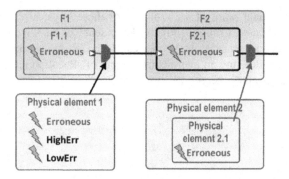

Fig. 9. Changes (shown in black) due to failure mode refinement. The domain of the functional flow from F1.1 to F2.1 contains the new values "highErr" and "lowErr" to propagate failure modes from the physical element 1. Consequently, the domain of F2.1 ports has changed so as to its logics. (For the sake of readability, this figure omits the failure modes of loss)

```
flow
        output : {ok, loss, erroneous, lowErr, highErr};
        input : {ok, loss, erroneous, lowErr, highErr};
state
        functionState : {ok, loss, erroneous};
assert
output = case { functionState = loss : loss,
                functionState = erroneous : erroneous,
                else input }
```

Fig. 10. Example of logics formulation to minimize changes to do when refining failure modes. The assertion formulation is valid whether input and output flows have "lower" and "higher" than possible values.

input and output flows are not explicitly mentioned, as illustrated in Fig. 10. In that case the logics are untouched and thus are still valid. Note that for functions whose behavior cannot be modeled following this formulation rule, the addition of physical layer and allocations requires a significant effort for revalidating the functional layer.

Even though the additional failure modes of our drone could have been identified before the physical step, the necessity of refining the failure modes can be found in industrial developments and therefore should be addressed by any allocation modeling method. The solution we present is generically applicable although it can become costly.

4.3   Failure Modes More Detailed in Functional Layer than in Physical Layer

Having different failure modes in the functional and physical layers raise several issues for modeling and validation. In Sect. 4.2, we have discussed the refinement of the failure modes at physical level. The opposite case can be found when one physical failure mode stands for several functional failure modes. In our experiment, we have encounter this case when dealing with control flows. We use this example in the following to illustrate the problematic.

In addition to many data flows, such as the speed consign mentioned in Sect. 4.1, our drone model contains a few control flows like the piloting mode. This mode can be set to auto or manual with significant impacts on system configuration. The mode selection function is allocated to the main processor whereas it is used in both main position control function (allocated to main processor) and monitoring position control function (allocated to monitoring processor).

During the first functional analysis, the failure modes of the "Selection" function failure modes were "Stuck to auto mode" and "Stuck to manual mode". In the physical analysis, this function was allocated to a computer whose failure modes were "Loss" and "Erroneous". Both functionally stuck failure modes were possible consequences of the physical failure mode "Erroneous" and this physical failure mode could not be refined to map the two functional failure modes.

To solve this issue, we relied on the fact that our drone has only two piloting modes and we made the assumption that the worst consequence of the physical erroneous was an inverted mode.

We used modeling artifacts that merge functional flow of piloting mode and physical failure mode. They inverse the piloting mode in case of an erroneous computer. Moreover, a flow is added in the functional layer to propagate the information that the piloting mode has been inverted due to a physical failure. Even if another physical failure occurs, the mode must not be re-inverted. Indeed, in our case, the failure of both main and monitoring computers should not result in a correct mode.

This modeling solution is specific to our case but it illustrates the difficulty to model functional failure modes more detailed than physical failure modes.

4.4   Discussion

Based on the application of "The Functional layer using physical resources" method (alternative (C) from Table 1), the last three sections have presented on the one hand modeling issues raised during application and on the other hand the modeling solutions we propose. In addition to the encountered modeling issues explanation and solution assessments provided in each section, in the following we discuss our alternative choice as a general lesson learnt.

When adding physical architecture and allocations, the leaf function structure from MBSE and MBSA models tends to get much closer than they were in the functional step. As an illustration, let us consider the typical case of several MBSE functions that are first modeled in one MBSA brick in the functional model. If, in a second time, these MBSE functions are allocated to different physical elements, the functions tend to be also modeled separately in the MBSA to ease allocation modeling. In that case the structure of the MBSE and MBSA models become closer than initially. Consequently the criteria of structure flexibility is not as clearly fulfilled by the chosen modelling alternative (C) as expected and the choice between the alternatives (C) and (D) becomes less definite.

In addition, the modeling and validation effort to address the differences between failure modes detail levels have a significant impact on modeling cost. Given the revalidation effort, the benefit of reusing the functional model is reduced to the capacity of re-computing the functional cutsets. Consequently, the cost of the alternative (C) is higher than expected and the cost of alternatives (A) and (B) should be re-assessed. Even if (A) and (B) do not solve the problem of functional failure modes more detailed than physical failure modes, they avoid to modify the functional modeling when detailed physical failure modes are needed.

As a lesson learnt, the capacity to model functional failure modes and physical modes needs to be added to the method choice criteria. The three criteria defined: modeling cost, structural flexibility and the capacity to link physical failure modes to functional failures need to be evaluated considering the size, complexity and expressivity of the system as well as the constraints from the system description modeling.

5 Conclusion

In this paper we have described several alternatives to model allocations in safety model. The chosen alternative has been successfully applied to a study case, with adaptations to unforeseen issues. We have presented modeling solutions to these issues and assessed their reusability. Based on lessons learnt from practice, we have qualified the criteria used for alternative choice, cost and structure flexibility, and found new properties, flow allocation on physical elements and especially, functional and physical failure mode conciliation.

Further work is required to complete possible modeling situations and find generic solutions to them. In particular, the application of several modeling alternatives on the same case would bring interesting lessons. To tackle the main difficulty we have faced, i.e., the discrepancy of detail level between functional and physical failure modes, combining both types of failure modes in cutset may be a track to assess, even if some quantification problems of functional failure modes will emerge.

The study of allocation of functional flows to physical links has not been addressed yet. In particular we did not analyze how to model and take into account the direction of physical link and of dysfunctional propagation. Further work will have to address this case in order to ensure a generic method. In addition we only have considered static models and it would be very interesting to extend our proposition to dynamic models. These methodological works will be continued in the project S2C (System and Safety Continuity), a collaboration between IRT Saint-Exupéry and IRT SystemX.

Acknowledgments. The authors thank all people and industrial partners involved in the MOISE project. This work is supported by the French Research Agency (ANR) and by the industrial partners of IRT Saint-Exupéry Scientific Cooperation Foundation (FCS).

References

1. Prosvirnova, T., Saez, E., Seguin, C., Virelizier, P.: Handling consistency between safety and system models. In: Bozzano, M., Papadopoulos, Y. (eds.) IMBSA 2017. LNCS, vol. 10437, pp. 19–34. Springer, Cham (2017). https://doi.org/10.1007/978-3-319-64119-5_2

2. Lisagor, O., Kelly, T., Niu, R.: Model-based safety assessment: review of the discipline and its challenges. In: The Proceedings of 2011 9th International Conference on Reliability, Maintainability and Safety, pp. 625–632 (2010)
3. Voirin, J.-L.: Model-Based System and Architecture Engineering with the Arcadia Method. Elsevier, Amsterdam (2017)
4. SAE, ARP4754A: Guidelines for development of civil aircraft and systems (2010)
5. SAE, ARP4761: Guidelines and methods for conducting the safety assessment process on civil airborne systems and equipment (1996)
6. Legendre, A.: Ingénierie système et Sûreté de fonctionnement: Méthodologie de synchronisation des modèles d'architecture et d'analyse de risques. Doctoral dissertation, Paris Saclay (2017)
7. Frazza, C.: Modélisation dysfonctionnelle des analyses de sécurité dirigées par les modèles (2016). http://projects.laas.fr/IFSE/FMF/J6/slides/P04_CF.pdf
8. Sagaspe, L.: Allocation sûre dans les systèmes aéronautiques: Modélisation, Vérification et Génération. Doctoral dissertation, Université Sciences et Technologies-Bordeaux I (2008)
9. Bozzano, M., et al.: Symbolic model checking and safety assessment of altarica models. In: Electronic Communications of the EASST, vol. 46 (2012)

Model Based Approach for RAMS Analyses in the Space Domain with Capella Open-Source Tool

Lorenzo Bitetti[1]([✉]), Régis De Ferluc[1], David Mailland[1],
Guy Gregoris[1], and Fulvio Capogna[2]

[1] Thales Alenia Space, Cannes, France
lorenzo.bitetti@thalesaleniaspace.com
[2] European Space Agency, Noordwijk, The Netherlands

Abstract. The objective of this paper is to evaluate the interest and applicability of a Model Based approach to support Dependability engineers in performing RAMS (Reliability, Availability, Maintainability and Safety) analyses.

In order to address the future challenges of the Space domain and to improve the co-engineering activities during the whole spacecraft design process, the open-source Capella tool, based on the Arcadia methodology, has been recently envisaged and evaluated in Thales Alenia Space.

Capella can already support Model Based System Engineering (MBSE) activities: from requirement specification to physical architecture definition, through functional and logical analyses. The MBSE approach has already demonstrated its benefits for System Engineering activities since it enhance the ability to capture, to analyze, to share, and to manage the information associated with the complete specification of a product.

Some features are currently being implemented in Capella in order to support also dependability activities. The Model Based RAMS approach with Capella is expected to improve the co-engineering activities between system engineers, equipment experts and dependability responsible. This will in turn improve the current Quality Assurance process, which is indispensable for the futures space missions.

The preliminary applications of the Model Based approach for RAMS analyses have shown some possible limitations and axes of improvements that will be addressed by future studies.

Keywords: Model based RAMS approach · Capella open-source tool · Arcadia methodology · Reliability and safety analyses

1 Introduction

1.1 Dependability Process in the Space Domain

The space domain is characterized by some specific needs and constraints which make the dependability process quite different compared to that of other engineering fields. Note that this paper is mainly focused on the satellite industry even if some aspects can be applicable also to launchers or crew missions.

© Springer Nature Switzerland AG 2019
Y. Papadopoulos et al. (Eds.): IMBSA 2019, LNCS 11842, pp. 18–31, 2019.
https://doi.org/10.1007/978-3-030-32872-6_2

The satellite industry is characterized by:

- No or very limited production in series, except for the expected new mega-constellations. In addition each satellite is quite unique, requiring therefore quite long development phases;
- No maintenance or repairing operations once the satellite is in orbit, even if on-orbit servicing missions are currently being studied and the corresponding technologies will be available in the future;
- High reliability and availability requirements, often specified for an extended period of time (e.g. 15 years of continuous operation for geostationary satellites);
- Very aggressive external environment and operating conditions (e.g. launch efforts, space radiations, extreme temperatures and thermal cycles, etc.);
- High autonomy of the satellite, especially in case of missions with limited ground visibility, and therefore nominal and failure scenarios have to be managed by the satellite itself, at the maximum extend.

In order to tackle all these needs and particularities of the space domain, several activities are performed during a typical dependability process [4–8]:

- **Feared Events Analysis (FEA)** is performed at the beginning of the project, it is a functional top-down analysis whose main objective is to identify the feared events leading either to interrupt the mission or even to lose the spacecraft. The main outcomes are the recommendations on how to recover and ideally to avoid these feared events;
- **Failure Mode and Effect Analysis (FMEA)** is a bottom-up analysis which is performed as soon as the design of the satellite is known. The results of the FMEA are used to improve the design and for the implementation of corrective actions or operational procedures to be executed, on-board or on ground, in case of failures;
- **Fault Tree Analysis (FTA)** is performed in order to ensure that the design conforms to the failure tolerance requirements even in case of multiple failures. This analysis is performed for some specific applications, like those linked to safety requirements or the investigation of in-orbit anomalies;
- **Failure Detection, Isolation and Recovery (FDIR)** analysis. Fault management strategies and mechanisms are chosen in order to ensure that availability, autonomy and failure avoidance or recovery requirements are fulfilled;
- **Reliability and Availability analyses** which are performed to demonstrate the compliance with the contractual requirements. Starting from this high level specification, reliability figures are allocated to the different systems. Then specific redundancy schemes are chosen for each equipment in order to guarantee an overall good reliability and availability of the system. Reliability Block Diagrams (RBD) and other models (e.g. Petri Nets, Markov chains, etc.) are usually used for these purposes.

There are some limits in the dependability approach currently followed in the space domain that could be ideally solved, or at least partially, with new and innovative approaches. Recent studies conducted by Thales Alenia Space have pointed out that:

– Graceful degradations are not, or not always, taken into account during the requirements specification and design phases. Redundancy schemes and fault management strategies are therefore chosen in order to guarantee a full success of the mission also in worst case scenario. This means that alternative and simpler architectures may probably exist in which the satellite is no longer fully redundant and cross-strapped;
– The allocation at lower levels (subsystem and equipment) of the satellite reliability and availability requirements is sometimes more linked to previously known or expected designs rather than to a real need at mission level. This can lead to a design where some functional chains may have a reliability higher or lower than the one really needed to guarantee performance and success of the mission. In addition, for some subsystems it may be more or less complex and costly to achieve a certain reliability figure. Therefore, the whole mass and cost of the satellite could be optimized by taking into account also this aspect during the allocation phase;
– Existing RAMS tools are sometimes not designed or at least not optimized for the first phases of the satellite development where multidisciplinary activities are performed iteratively in order to compare different designs and to choose the best solution. In fact these tools are not always linked, or at least not directly, to the ones used by system engineers. Therefore reliability aspects are taken into account later, and sometime too late, or the coherence between these models is not always guaranteed, especially when the hypotheses and designs change very frequently;
– Fault management process usually starts late in the development process since not enough information are available at the beginning. This could therefore lead to major design modifications and late changes that are usually costly and with a great impact on the planning;
– Main inputs for the dependability process are the analyses performed at lower level and the documents describing the whole functions and architectures. However these documents are not necessarily complete or not all detailed diagrams are available. The missing information are therefore to be found in specific documents, if available at the time of the analysis are done. The gathering of all the up-to-date information can become a time-consuming activity, especially in case of several re-issues of the documents or design modifications. Therefore the coherence with the current design and the correctness of the dependability analyses could be sometimes difficult to guarantee and especially to verify by a third party;
– Finally some analyses, like Fault Tree Analyses, are performed manually, which represents a high workload for the dependability responsible.

In order to address the future challenges of the space domain and to improve the co-engineering activities during the whole satellite lifetime, a Model Based approach has been considered as a good potential candidate to solve some of the aforementioned issues, or at least partially. The main goals and functionalities are described in the rest of this paper.

2 Model Based Approach with Capella Open-Source Tool

2.1 Arcadia Methodology and Capella Tool

Model Based System Engineering (MBSE) approaches have already been applied in different engineering domains and have demonstrated their interest and benefits. In fact, by enhancing the ability to capture, to analyze, to share and to manage the information associated with a whole product or system, MBSE approaches lead to:

- Improved communications among the different stakeholders (e.g. customer, managers, systems engineers, hardware and software developers, testers, and engineers of special disciplines);
- Increased ability to manage system complexity by enabling a system model to be viewed from multiple perspectives, and to analyze the impact of changes;
- Improved product quality by providing an unambiguous and precise model of the system that can be evaluated for consistency, correctness, and completeness;
- Enhanced knowledge capture and reuse of the information by capturing information in more standardized ways and leveraging built in abstraction mechanisms inherent in model driven approaches.

The open source Capella tool [1], based on the Arcadia methodology [2], has been used in the frame of on-going projects conducted by Thales Alenia Space.

Capella supports system engineering activities from requirements specification to the definition of the physical architecture, through the functional and logical analyses. In fact, different engineering steps and the corresponding models and concepts are defined in Arcadia to cover all these aspects:

- **Operational Analysis:** focused on the analysis of the user needs and goals, the expected mission phases and the operational scenarios of the system. It ensures the good adequacy of the system definition with regards to its real operational use;
- **System Analysis:** this level is used to model the system, viewed like a black box, by identifying its boundaries and external actors, and to clarify what the system is expected to do in the different phases of its whole mission to satisfy the former operational needs. At this stage the system actors, mission capabilities, functions and functional exchanges are defined;
- **Logical Analysis:** used to develop the logical architecture of the system and to identify the components and their interactions, but excluding the physical implementation or technical issues. The system is seen here as a white box by defining how it will work as to fulfill its expectations and by refining the previous system functions. In addition, the allocation of functions to components and the trade-offs between alternative architectures can be realized at this stage, before a specific physical architecture is defined in the next step;
- **Physical Analysis:** this final step of the Arcadia method aims at identifying the system physical components, their contents and relationships including the implementation or technical and technological aspects. It describes how the system will be developed and built, and makes the logical architecture evolve according to the final design.

2.2   Model Based Approach for RAMS Analyses

Several studies have been recently performed by Thales Alenia Space in order to evaluate the interest and applicability of a Model Based approach to support RAMS engineers in performing safety and reliability analyses and in producing the corresponding models and artifacts.

Some Capella viewpoints and interfaces with external tools, which were already available or that have been specifically developed by Thales Alenia Space, have been used for this purpose. The initial focus has been paid mainly on safety and reliability analyses for which some activities and studies have been performed, as presented below.

However it should be noted that in addition to these analyses, a more generic and global Model Based approach with Capella has been envisaged by Thales Alenia Space. As depicted in Fig. 1, the main dependability activities that are required to comply with the satellite Reliability, Availability, Maintainability and Safety (RAMS) requirements could be performed with or at least supported by this open-source tool.

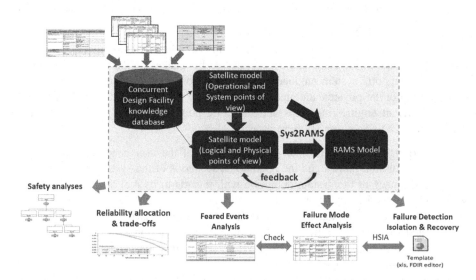

Fig. 1. Envisaged Model Based RAMS approach with Capella open-source tool

It should be noticed that this Model Based RAMS approach has not been fully implemented (yet) in Capella and that additional studies will be conducted in the future in order to develop all these features, to implement all the required interface with external RAMS tools and to provide at the same time some guidelines on the modeling strategy in Capella.

Safety Analyses. Several studies are currently performed at system, segment and equipment level in the frame of an internship and in collaboration with other Thales entities and external companies. Several existing tools allowing to perform safety analyses are evaluated in order to evaluate the interest of these tools and to derive some recommendations and suggestions leading to an improved and common MBSA approach.

While using MBSE tools for Safety applications it has been clearly demonstrated that, at least at that time, it was not possible to generate directly FTA, FMECA or other RAMS Analyses for the complex systems encountered in the space domain (e.g. navigation systems). MBSA tools based on AltaRica language [9] have also been tested. It was possible to perform fault tree analyses but some limitations have been found:

– It is not possible to make a model of a cold redundancy without introducing "fake" components in the fault tree. Contrary to other engineering domain, aeronautics for instance, cold redundancies are widely used in Space domain therefore this is an important aspect that has to be further addressed.
– A huge amount to time is spent by MBSA user to make his fault tree look like the expected one and this less time is left for the understanding of the system itself.
– It was not possible with old AltaRica versions to make a model of monitoring (it leads to a loop), being this latter an important feature of all Safety of Life system. This has been corrected recently in Alta Rica 3.0 but not tested yet in Thales Alenia Space.

Future studies will further address these points, eventually allowing MBSE and/or MBSA tools performing risk analysis of complex systems and supporting the (semi) automatic generation of FTA and FMEA (Fig. 2).

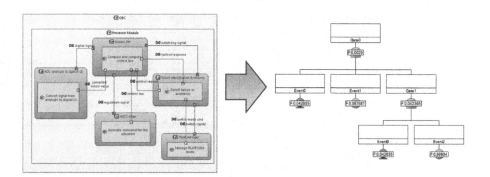

Fig. 2. Envisaged generation of fault trees starting from the model implemented in Capella.

Reliability Analyses. The already existing add-ons and viewpoints of Capella were not directly or not completely useful for reliability analyses. This is why a new viewpoint specifically dedicated to the reliability allocation and assessment has been implemented in Capella by Thales Alenia Space. The main aim is to compute the reliability figures of a functional chain or of a given system starting from the Capella model realized by system engineers. The main features and outputs of this viewpoint are described more in detail in the following section.

3   Examples of RAMS Analyses Performed with Capella

This section is mainly focused on the initial proof-of-concept of the Reliability viewpoint developed in Capella which represents a real innovation in the Model Based approach in the space domain. Here the steps to be followed to assess the reliability of a given system are described through the presentation of a practical example.

- The first step is to evaluate the completeness and validity of the Capella model versus the reliability model in order to derive the inputs, outputs and especially the level of details needed to have a direct link between them.

As an example, by comparing the Reliability model (a) and the Capella (b) one of the Electrical Power Subsystem (EPS) it has been derived that, as shown by the red blocks in Fig. 3, all the different items modeled in Capella are those needed in the Reliability model, and also with a similar level of details. This means that, in this particular case, there is no need to further refine the Capella model because of the reliability assessment purpose. On the other hand, in some cases the Capella model may have to be improved or even simplified.

A study that will be started in the next months will aim, among other goals, to define a modeling strategy and to provide some instructions and conditions to be respected for a successful utilization of the Reliability Viewpoint.

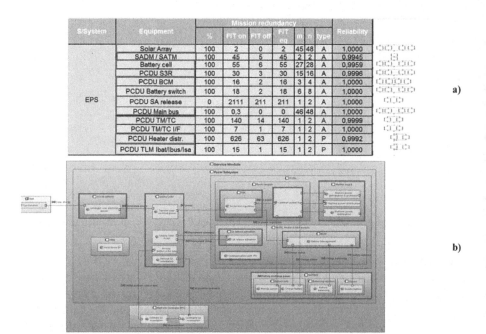

S/System	Equipment	Mission redundancy							Reliability	
		%	FIT on	FIT off	FIT eq	m	n	type		
	Solar Array	100	2	0	2	45	48	A	1,0000	
	SADM / SATM	100	45	5	45	2	2	A	0,9945	
	Battery cell	100	55	6	55	27	28	A	0,9959	
	PCDU S3R	100	30	3	30	15	16	A	0,9996	
	PCDU BCM	100	16	2	16	3	4	A	1,0000	
	PCDU Battery switch	100	18	2	18	6	8	A	1,0000	a)
EPS	PCDU SA release	0	2111	211	211	1	2	A	1,0000	
	PCDU Main bus	100	0,3	0	0	46	48	A	1,0000	
	PCDU TM/TC	100	140	14	140	1	2	A	0,9999	
	PCDU TM/TC I/F	100	7	1	7	1	2	A	1,0000	
	PCDU Heater distr.	100	626	63	626	1	2	P	0,9992	
	PCDU TLM Ibat/Ibus/Isa	100	15	1	15	1	2	P	1,0000	

b)

Fig. 3. Comparison of the Reliability model (a) and the Capella one (b) for the EPS subsystem (Color figure online)

- Then some additional information have to be filled by dependability engineers in the Capella model in order to be able to compute the reliability figures:
  - The duty cycle (d.c.): the ratio of functioning time over the total time for the identified element;
  - The intrinsic failure rates of the units at full duty cycle (FIT ON), expressed in failure per 10^9 h;
  - The intrinsic failure rates of the units when not operating (FIT OFF).
  - The quantity of units that are necessary to achieve a particular function (m);
  - The quantity of units that are available (n);
  - The redundancy type: cold, hot, warm or no redundancy;
  - Finally the user can also directly provide the reliability figure of one unit. This has been done especially for the mechanical items for which the reliability is assessed with the stress-strength method. In this case the probability is time independent and the failure rates are not defined (Fig. 5).

These values are those already presented in the Excel reliability model (see Fig. 3a) but with the proposed Model Based approach they are added directly into the Capella model. The user interface allowing to do that is depicted in Fig. 4.

Fig. 4. User interface allowing to enter the reliability information

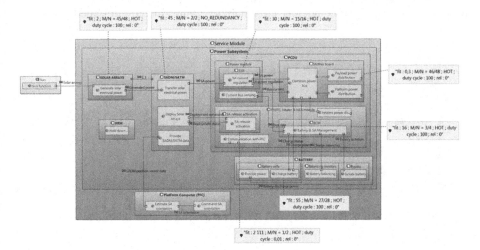

Fig. 5. Capella model with reliability inputs (Failure rates and redundancies schemes)

In the reliability viewpoint, as shown in Fig. 6, the user can also chose the classical relationship between two units (e.g. HW in series, fully cross-strapped, etc.) or define any particular link with more complex formulae (e.g. Bayesian expression for not fully cross-strapped items).

Fig. 6. User interface allowing to define the relationship between two hardware components

- Once all these reliability information are defined in Capella, the output of the reliability viewpoint is a table, like the one shown in Fig. 7, which can be easily imported in Excel where the reliability figures can be then computed.

Note that for this initial proof-of-concept it has been preferred to keep the two software separated instead of implementing the reliability formulae directly into Capella. This has been done for the purpose of compatibility with current analyses but also because it could be interesting in the future to have interfaces also with other external tools specifically focused on RAMS activities. Finally this has been done also to guarantee the coherence and quality of RAMS analyses, that could be performed also by non RAMS experts if everything is implemented directly in Capella, thus losing all the aforementioned benefits of a Model Based approach.

However this choice could be challenged and revised in the future, if needed, thus having the possibility of computing the reliability figures directly in Capella.

	Fit	M Number	N Number	Redundancy Type	Duty Cycle	Reliability
Power Distribution	88.0	1	2	HOT	100.0	0.0
Battery cells	55.0	27	28	HOT	100.0	0.0
SADM/SATM	45.0	2	2	NO_REDUNDANCY	100.0	0.0
S3R	30.0	15	16	HOT	100.0	0.0
SA release activation	2111.0	1	2	HOT	0.01	0.0
SOLAR ARRAYS	2.0	45	48	HOT	100.0	0.0
BCM	16.0	3	4	HOT	100.0	0.0

Fig. 7. Output of the Capella viewpoint and input of the Excel reliability model

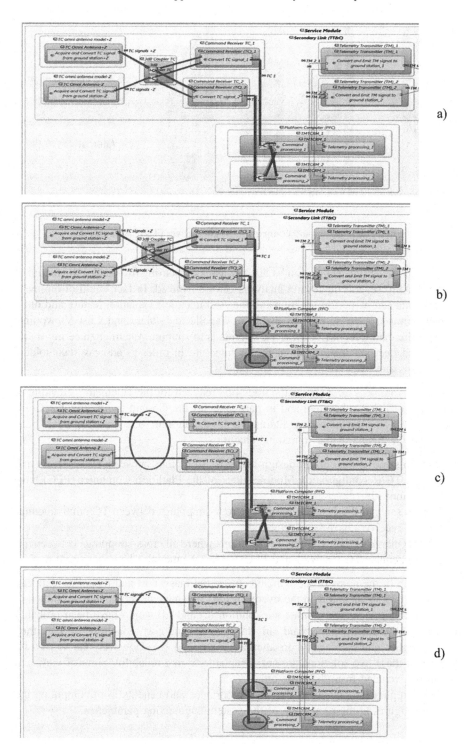

Fig. 8. Example of different TT&C architectures modeled in Capella

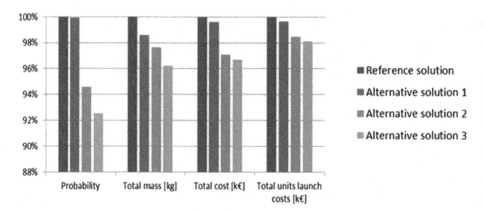

Fig. 9. Evaluation and comparison of alternative TT&C architectures

- Once the reliability figures can be directly assessed starting from a Capella model of the system, several interesting analyses can be realized. In fact, multi-disciplinary trade-offs can be performed by using the Architecture Evaluation feature and other viewpoints that are already available in Capella (e.g. Mass and Cost Viewpoints [3]). The main purpose of these viewpoints is to support system engineering trade-offs and decision making about the architecture in order to address stakeholders concerns and meet architecture expectations.

As an example, Fig. 8 shows the trade-offs realized for the Telemetry, Tracking & Command (TT&C) subsystem and in particular for the Ground to satellite TeleCommand link. Some architectures alternative to the current one (case a) have been envisaged for this particular functional chain:

- case (b) same as the current design but cross-strappings between TC receivers and the TM/TC/Reconfiguration Module blocs of the PlatForm Computer (PFC) have been removed;
- case (c) same as the current design but cross-strappings between TC omni antennas and TC receivers have been removed;
- case (d) merge of the two previous solutions where all cross-strappings between TC omni antennas, TC receivers and PFC TMTCRM modules have been removed.

For each of the items of these architectures, the mass, cost and reliability data can be defined in Capella and then the overall results obtained and compared, as shown in Fig. 9. In this particular example, the solution (c) and (d) would have been probably preferred if the attention was paid only to the mass and cost reductions. In fact, they lead to higher gains compared to alternative solution (b). However one can easily derive that these two solutions are not acceptable from a reliability point of view and should be excluded from the trade-off.

This simple example shows thus the importance and benefits from computing the reliability figures at the same time of the system engineering parameters.

4 Conclusion and Perspectives

The Model Based approach, by enhancing the ability to capture, to analyze, to share, and to manage the information associated with the complete specification of a product, has already demonstrated its benefits for System Engineering activities.

Several studies have been performed in recent years by Thales Alenia Space in order to evaluate the interest and applicability of a Model Based approach to support RAMS engineers in performing safety and reliability analyses and in producing the corresponding models and artifacts. The Capella open-source tool, based on the Arcadia methodology, has been used for this purpose.

Some Capella viewpoints and interfaces with external tools, which were already available or that have been specifically developed by Thales Alenia Space, have been used. The initial focus has been paid mainly on safety and reliability analyses for which some activities and studies have been performed.

The main outcomes and conclusions of these studies are that the Model Based RAMS approach is seen as a promising solution that could improve and solve some of the limitations identified for the current Quality Assurance process.

In fact, compared to the current and classic approach where RAMS analyses are "based on documents", several benefits are possible when the same tool is used and the same models are shared between all the stakeholders involved in the satellite development process:

- All information needed for the different activities, including RAMS ones, could be more easily captured and better structured and visualized;
- The coherence and validity of the different analyses can be guaranteed even during those phases when hypotheses and designs change frequently;
- Multi-disciplinary activities, including dependability aspects, can be performed since the early phases of the development process thus allowing to choose the best satellite architecture from both system engineering and dependability points of view at the same time;
- One can benefit of the computing power of the tools in order to generate complex analyses such as Fault Tree Analyses, to automatically check some design rules impacting the safety: such as the fault tolerance or to verify that no single failure could lead to catastrophic failure conditions;
- Some analyses and the corresponding artifacts can be automatically generated, or at least initialized, by the tool itself thus reducing the workload of the RAMS responsible who could be thus focused on those activities with a higher added value.

On the other hand, these preliminary evaluations have highlighted some classical open points and limitations of the Model Based approach:

- RAMS analyses often require dedicated and specific models which may differ from the ones implemented and used by system engineers. This is mainly due to their different points of view (functional versus dysfunctional behavior of the system, respectively) and because of the required granularity of the model: more or less detailed depending on the specific applications and goals;

- A good knowledge of the tools and good capabilities and experience in modeling are necessary to be able to fully take advantage of the aforementioned benefits of the Model Based approach and thus improving the efficiency and efficacy of the dependability process followed in the space domain;
- Sometimes the traditional functional approach and the currently used tools could be more powerful and efficient compared to a Model Based approach if the model of the system to be evaluated is too complex, meaning that is it composed of a very high number of elements and interactions between them;
- There is sometimes a tendency/psychological bias to develop the models in order to obtain the desired results, e.g. to demonstrate the validity and utility of a particular Model Based tool, without being too realistic and showing the existing limits of the approach;
- People (wrongly) think that, once all the single failures of the system are modeled in the tool, this latter could "magically" determine also all the propagation of these failures and/or the impact of multiple failures. In fact, the tools cannot add additional failure modes by themselves, there is no Artificial Intelligence or other features (for the time being) that could replace the analysis of RAMS engineers. Therefore we can only have, as an output of the tool, what has been modeled in it.
- Finally the models and the outputs (e.g. the fault trees generated by MBSA tools) could be sometimes not really "readable", they must be re-arranged and/or simplified in order to be understood and thus fully exploited.

For each of the aforementioned points, some dedicated activities and solutions have already been identified by Thales Alenia Space and are proposed for future studies (e.g. definition of guidelines and instructions on how to model the system, development of interface with commonly used RAMS tools, implementation of libraries and databases of failure rates and failure modes, identification of specific cases where the Model Based approach is more efficient than traditional one, etc.).

To conclude, the Model Based approach is thought to be a promising solution that can improve the co-engineering activities between system and RAMS engineers and thus the current Quality Assurance process followed in the space domain.

However current applications of the Model Based approach for RAMS analyses have shown also some possible limitations and improvements that need to be addressed by future studies.

Thales Alenia Space will evaluate further the Model Based approach in order to conclude on its interest and real benefits and then to use operationally these tools to improve the efficacy and efficiency of RAMS analyses.

References

1. Capella: Model based system engineering (MBSE) tool. https://www.polarsys.org/capella/index.html
2. Arcadia: Model based system engineering (MBSE) method. https://www.polarsys.org/capella/arcadia.html

3. Capella mass/cost/performance viewpoints. https://wiki.polarsys.org/Capella/Viewpoints/BasicViewpoints
4. ECSS-Q-ST-30C: Space product assurance – dependability
5. ECSS-Q-ST-30-02C: Space product assurance – failure modes, effect (and criticality) analysis
6. ECSS-Q-ST-30-09C: Space product assurance - availability analysis
7. ECSS-Q-ST-40C: Space product assurance – safety
8. ECSS-Q-ST-40-12C: Space product assurance - fault tree analysis
9. OpenAltaRica. https://www.openaltarica.fr/

Modeling Patterns for the Assessment of Maintenance Policies with AltaRica 3.0

Michel Batteux[1]([✉]), Tatiana Prosvirnova[2,3], and Antoine Rauzy[4]

[1] IRT SystemX, Palaiseau, France
`michel.batteux@irt-systemx.fr`
[2] Laboratoire Genie Industriel, CentraleSupélec, Gif-sur-Yvette, France
[3] ONERA/DTIS, UFTMiP, Toulouse, France
`tatiana.prosvirnova@onera.fr`
[4] Norwegian University of Science and Technology, Trondheim, Norway
`antoine.rauzy@ntnu.no`

Abstract. In this article, we present modeling patterns dedicated to the assessment of maintenance policies with AltaRica 3.0. From the analyst's perspective, these modeling patterns make models easier to design, to understand by stakeholders and to maintain. From a technical point of view, their design involves advanced features of AltaRica 3.0 that are worth presenting.

Keywords: Assessment of maintenance policies · AltaRica 3.0 · Modeling patterns

1 Introduction

AltaRica 3.0 is an object-oriented modeling language dedicated to probabilistic risk and safety analyses of complex technical systems [5]. It is of primary importance, in order to make the modeling process efficient (in AltaRica 3.0 as with any other modeling formalism), to reuse as much as possible modeling components. In AltaRica 3.0, reuse is mostly achieved by the design of modeling patterns, i.e. examples of models representing remarkable features of the system under study. Once identified, patterns can be duplicated and adjusted for specific needs. Patterns are actually pervasive in engineering, see e.g. [7,8]. Patterns are not only a mean to organize and to document models, but also and more fundamentally a way to reason about systems under study.

In this article we present modeling patterns to represent and to assess maintenance policies with AltaRica 3.0. We focus actually on corrective maintenance policies (components are repaired only when they are failed) taking into account that resources required to perform them (such as the number of repairmen or spare parts) may be limited. We show different modeling approaches, involving advanced features of AltaRica 3.0, such as the synchronization of events or the aggregation of prototypes.

© Springer Nature Switzerland AG 2019
Y. Papadopoulos et al. (Eds.): IMBSA 2019, LNCS 11842, pp. 32–46, 2019.
https://doi.org/10.1007/978-3-030-32872-6_3

The contribution of this article is thus twofold: first, it provides effective modeling patterns for the assessment of maintenance policies; second, it demonstrates the interest of AltaRica 3.0 advanced modeling constructs.

The remainder of this article is organized as follows. Section 2 introduces a case study that we use throughout the article to illustrate the presentation. Section 3 makes a brief description of the AltaRica 3.0 modeling language. Section 4 presents the maintenance policy modeling, according to three different modeling patterns. Section 5 provides some results on the three corresponding models. Finally, Sect. 6 concludes the article and discusses future works.

2   Illustrative Example

Figure 1 shows a system made of two subsystems: an equipment under control and a control system. We focus our study on the latter. This system is made of three sensors, a controller and two actuators. The controller is made of three data acquisition units (one per sensor) and a voter, also called a logic solver, which works according to a 2-out-of-3 logic. Each actuator is made of two components.

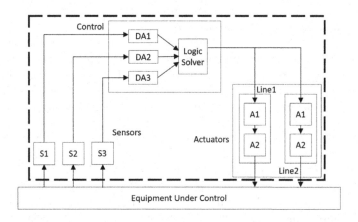

Fig. 1. An equipment under control and its control part.

All the components may fail in operation and be repaired. Failure rates (h^{-1}) are respectively 10^{-5} for sensors, 10^{-6} for data acquisition units, 10^{-8} for the logic solver and 10^{-6} for actuators. A maintenance operation is launched when the system as a whole is failed, i.e. if either two or more sensors are failed or two or more data acquisition modules are failed or the voter is failed or the two actuators are failed. All failed components are repaired during the maintenance operation and can be considered as good as new after. Failed components are repaired one by one. Mean times to repair components are one shift, i.e. 8 h for actuators, 4 h for sensors, data acquisition units and the logic solver. To accelerate maintenance operations, two repairers are involved (and can thus repair components in parallel).

The objective of this study is to calculate, for example, the system operational availability during its mission time, taking into account maintenance policies of the components.

3   AltaRica 3.0 Modeling

3.1   The AltaRica 3.0 Modeling Language

AltaRica 3.0 is an event-based and object-oriented modeling language dedicated to probabilistic risk and safety analyses of complex technical systems [9]. This language is the combination of two parts: the mathematical framework GTS, for Guarded Transition Systems ([4,10]) to describe the behavior of the system under study; the structuring paradigm S2ML, for System Structure Modeling Language ([3]), to organize the model.

The execution of an AltaRica 3.0 model, done by the mathematical framework GTS, is quite similar to other event-based formalisms. It means that when a transition is enabled, it is scheduled and will be potentially fired after its associated delay [6,12]. These delays can be deterministic or stochastic. For stochastic delays, AltaRica 3.0 provides usual probability distributions: exponential, Weibull, uniform or user defined ones.

To structure an AltaRica 3.0 model, S2ML provides the appropriate primitives. S2ML unifies the two main structuring paradigms for modeling languages: object-oriented and prototype-oriented. With S2ML, one can design the model in two ways. The 'top-down' approach: the system is considered at its highest level and modeling patterns are mainly used; it is the realm of prototype-oriented. The 'bottom-up' approach: the system is considered at its lowest level (the components) and libraries of components are mainly used: it is the realm of object-oriented.

Two main structural constructs can be used in AltaRica 3.0: a 'block' and a 'class'. A class is an "on-the-shelf", reusable modeling component. It is defined and then can be instanced in a model, or inherited by another class or block. A block is a modeling component with a unique instance, as opposed to a class which can have several instances. The definition of a block is also its (unique) instance. More information can be found in [3].

3.2   Modeling with AltaRica 3.0

To design the AltaRica 3.0 model of the system depicted Fig. 1, we start by modeling the main part. We only consider that this main part contains a set of hierarchically ordered components, without thinking about how these components are internally designed.

Main Part of the AltaRica 3.0 Model. The main part is given Fig. 2. It is defined with the block System, which contains two parts: one with the declaration of the different structural elements, the other defining the behavior.

```
block System
  // Declaration of elements
  Sensor S1, S2, S3;
  block Control
    DataAcquisition DA1, DA2, DA3;
    block LogicSolver
      extends RComponent (lambda = 1.0e-8, mu = 4);
      Boolean in1, in2, in3, out (reset = false);
      assertion
        out := if vs == WORKING
               then (in1 and in2) or (in1 and in3) or (in2 and in3)
               else false;
    end
    assertion
      LogicSolver.in1 := DA1.out;
      LogicSolver.in2 := DA2.out;
      LogicSolver.in3 := DA3.out;
  end
  block Actuators
    block Line1
      Actuator A1, A2;
      assertion
        A2.in := A1.out;
    end
    clones Line1 as Line2;
  end
  observer Boolean TE = (Actuators.Line1.A2.out == false) and
                        (Actuators.Line2.A2.out == false);
  // Definition of the behavior
  assertion
    S1.in := true; S2.in := true; S3.in := true;
    Control.DA1.in := S1.out;
    Control.DA2.in := S2.out;
    Control.DA3.in := S3.out;
    Actuators.Line1.A1.in := Control.LogicSolver.out;
    Actuators.Line2.A1.in := Control.LogicSolver.out;
end
```

Fig. 2. AltaRica 3.0 code for the main part.

The main part represents the hierarchy of declared components and the links between them (the behavioral part). It is composed of:

- Three instances S1, S2 and S3, of the class Sensor. We only assume that this class Sensor contains two flow variables in and out (we can see them in the second part defining the behavior).
- A block Control, which is a sub-block of the main block System. This block declares three instances DA1, DA2 and DA3 of the class DataAcquisition. It declares an internal block LogicSolver, which inherits from the class RComponent. We assume that the class RComponent represents reparable components and contains two parameters lambda and mu that we overload with the values 10^{-8} and 4. This inheritance means that the block LogicSolver

is a reparable component: it takes the features of the class RComponent. Furthermore, the block LogicSolver declares four flow variables in1, in2, in3 and out. These variables are used in the second part defining the behavior of the LogicSolver: the assertion defines the external behavior according to the internal behavior, i.e. the update of the variable out according to the other variables in1, in2, in3 and a state variable vs (an internal variable) coming from the inherited class RComponent. Finally the block Control specifies the external behavior of its sub-parts in the assertion.

– A block Actuator declaring a sub-block Line1. Line1 represents the first line of actuators. It is composed of two instances A1 and A2 of the class Actuator. These actuators are linked thanks to the assertion. The sub-block Line1 is cloned: a copy of Line1 is made and named Line2. One can notice that these two blocks Line1 and Line2 will independently live their own lives: changes into one block (e.g. the update of a variable, or the firing of a transition) has no impact on the other.

– Finally, a Boolean observer TE (Top Event) is declared. This observer observes if the two flow variables out, coming from the two actuators A2 of the two lines, are false.

After the first declarative part, the main block System defines the assertion, which describes how the sub-parts (the sensors, the control and the actuators) are linked together and with the environment. We assume here that the equipment under control cannot fail and the sensors always receive a correct value as input (i.e. the value true because we consider Boolean variables).

Library of Components. The main part of the AltaRica 3.0 model contains different components, which are instances of classes. These classes are defined in a dedicated library and are depicted Fig. 3. The class RComponentIO implements a generic reparable component with one input and one output. It inherits from another class RComponent, the same as the one inherited by the component LogicSolver of the block Control. This inheritance means that RComponentIO takes the features of RComponent. RComponentIO declares two flow variables in and out, which are used in the second part: the assertion defining the external behavior by updating the variable out, according to the variable in and the state (internal) variable vs, coming from the inherited class RComponent. Finally, the classes corresponding to the components Sensor, DataAcquistion and Actuator are defined. They inherit from the class RComponentIO and overload the values of the parameters lambda and mu.

4   Modeling Pattern for Maintenance

The (part of the) AltaRica 3.0 model, presented previously, does not integrate the behavioral description of a reparable component, as well as the maintenance policy according to the limited number of repairers. We start with the definition of two AltaRica 3.0 elements in Fig. 4: a domain and an operator. The domain

```
class RComponentIO
  extends RComponent;
  Boolean in, out (reset= false);
  assertion
    out := vs == WORKING and in;
end

class Sensor
  extends RComponentIO (lambda = 1.0e-5, mu = 4);
end

class DataAcquisition
  extends RComponentIO (lambda = 1.0e-6, mu = 4);
end

class Actuator
  extends RComponentIO (lambda = 1.0e-6, mu = 8);
end
```

Fig. 3. AltaRica 3.0 library of components.

```
domain SDomain {WORKING, FAILED, WAITING_REPAIR, REPAIR}

operator Integer IsNotFailed(SDomain aState)
  if (aState != FAILED) then 1 else 0
end
```

Fig. 4. AltaRica 3.0 code for the domain and operator.

SDomain defines four values, WORKING, FAILED, WAITING_REPAIR and REPAIR, which will be used after to define types of elements (e.g. variables, parameters or observers). The operator IsNotFailed returns an integer value (1 or 0) according to the value of the argument aState, of type SDomain.

4.1 Maintenance Policies

According to the European standard NF EN 13306 X 60-319, there are two main kinds of maintenance. The first one is the corrective maintenance, which is carried out after failure detection and is aimed at restoring an asset to a condition in which it can perform its intended function. This kind of maintenance implies an unavailability either of the overall or of a part of the system. The second one is the preventive maintenance, which aims at performing an intervention before the occurrence of a failure. Different kinds of preventive maintenance also exist. Planned maintenance is realized according to a specific bound reached by the system (e.g. date, time of running, distance travelled, etc.). Condition-based maintenance is realized according to a monitoring of the system. Finally, predictive maintenance uses sensor data to monitor a system, then continuously evaluates it against historical trends to predict failure before it occurs.

AltaRica 3.0 is a flexible and versatile tool. Maintenance policies can be taken into account with AltaRica 3.0, of course by realizing some kinds of abstraction. For example, [11] presents a modelling methodology for the assessment of preventive maintenance on a compressor drive system. In the following, we focus on the corrective maintenance policy at the component level. We introduce some condition at system level, to realize maintenance actions, i.e. when a sufficient number of components are failed: at least two sensors are failed, or two data acquisition units or the logic solver unit or one actuator per lines. Furthermore we consider only two repairers to repair failed components.

In Fig. 5, two transitions representing the maintenance policy are added to the main part of the AltaRica 3.0 model.

```
block System
  // Declaration of elements
  ...
  event maintenanceReq (delay = Dirac(0.0), hidden = true);
  event maintenance (delay = Dirac(0.0));
  // Definition of the behavior
  transition
    maintenanceReq: (IsNotFailed(S1.vs) + IsNotFailed(S2.vs)
                          + IsNotFailed (S3.vs)) <= 1
              or ...
              // The maintenance policy involving all components
              -> skip;
    maintenance: !maintenanceReq
            & ?S1.maintenance & ?S2.maintenance & ? ...
            // All transitions 'maintenance' of all components
  assertion
    ...
end
```

Fig. 5. Main part of the AltaRica 3.0 model with the maintenance policy.

The two events `maintenanceReq` and `maintenance` are defined with an instantaneous delay, represented by the distribution `Dirac(0.0)`. It means that the transitions, labelled by these instantaneous events, are fired as soon as they are enabled. In the following, we will associate the transition and its label, if there is no ambiguity.

The transition `maintenanceReq` specifies the maintenance policy in the guard, by using the operator `IsNotFailed` with the states of the components: at least two sensors are failed. This transition is hidden (the attribute `hidden` of the labelling event is set to `true`), meaning it will never be fired alone, it must be synchronized with other transitions. Furthermore, no action is associated to this transition: the instruction `skip`. By defining the two events, and their associated transitions, `maintenanceReq` and `maintenance`, we totally separate the definition of the maintenance policy (in the guard of the transition `maintenanceReq`) and the action of maintenance (in the transition `maintenance`).

The transition `maintenance` synchronizes the transition `maintenanceReq` and all the transitions `maintenance` of the components. The symbol ! means that the transition `maintenanceReq` is mandatory: to fire this transition `maintenance`, the guard of the transition `maintenanceReq` must be true. Conversely, the symbol ? means that the transitions `maintenance` of the components are optional: the transition can be fired if its guard is true, but it is not required. When the transition `maintenance` of a component is fired, it changes its state from `FAILED` to `WAITING_REPAIR`: it has to wait the availability of a repairer.

The behavior of a reparable component `RComponent` is described according the state machine depicted Fig. 6. Nodes represent the different states of the component, which are from the domain `SDomain`. Edges represent transitions between states. It is a generic behavior which will be adapted according to the considered modeling pattern.

In the following we present how to model the availability of a repairer to repair a component, with three different patterns: by propagation of flow variables, by synchronizing events, or by using the virtual aggregation.

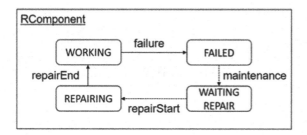

Fig. 6. State machine of a reparable component.

4.2   Repair by Propagation of Flow Variables

Figure 7 represents the reparable component used for the pattern propagation of flow variables. The component is initialized to the state `WORKING`: the attribute `init` of the state variable `vs` is set to `WORKING`. The event `maintenance` is synchronized at system level: its attribute `hidden` is set to `true`. Two flow variables are defined. `rUsed` indicates that a repairer repairs the component. `rAvailable` takes the value of the availability of a repairer, and is used in the guard of the transition `repairStart`, i.e. to launch the repair of the component.

Figure 8 shows the additions to the main part of the AltaRica 3.0 model, which are needed for the pattern by propagation of flow variables. The parameter `repairer` defines the number of repairers (i.e. 2). The flow variable `rUsed` provides the number of used repairers to repair components. This variable is updated in the assertion by adding all flow variables `rUsed` of the components.

```
class RComponent
  SDomain vs (init = WORKING);
  Integer rUsed (reset = 0);
  Boolean rAvailable (reset = false);
  parameter Real lambda = 1.0e-5;
  parameter Real mu = 2.0;
  event failure (delay = exponential(lambda));
  event maintenance (delay = Dirac(0.0), hidden = true);
  event repairStart (delay = Dirac(0.0));
  event repairEnd (delay = Dirac(mu));
  transition
    failure: vs == WORKING -> vs := FAILED;
    maintenance: vs == FAILED -> vs := WAITING_REPAIR;
    repairStart: vs == WAITING_REPAIR and rAvailable -> vs := REPAIR;
    repairEnd: vs == REPAIR -> vs := WORKING;
  assertion
    rUsed := if vs == REPAIR then 1 else 0;
end
```

Fig. 7. AltaRica 3.0 code of the reparable component for the pattern by propagation of flow variables.

Finally the flow variable `rAvailable` provides the information that a repairer is available. It is updated according to the value of `rUsed` and `repairer`. Then, it is used to update all the variables `rAvailable` of the components.

```
block System
  // Declaration of elements
  ...
  parameter Integer repairer = 2;
  Integer rUsed (reset = 0);
  Boolean rAvailable (reset = false);
  // Definition of the behavior
  transition
    ...
  assertion
    ...
    rUsed := S1.rUsed + S2.rUsed + S3.rUsed + Control.DA1.rUsed + ...
    // All flow variables 'rUsed' of components
    rAvailable := rUsed < repairer;
    S1.rAvailable := rAvailable;
    S2.rAvailable := rAvailable;
    S3.rAvailable := rAvailable;
    Control.DA1.rAvailable := rAvailable;
    ...
    // All flow variables 'rAvailable' of all components
    // take the value of the variable 'rAvailable'
end
```

Fig. 8. Main part of the AltaRica 3.0 model with the pattern by propagation of flow variables.

```
class RComponent
  SDomain vs (init = WORKING);
  parameter Real lambda = 1.0e-5;
  parameter Real mu = 2.0;
  event failure (delay = exponential(lambda));
  event maintenance (delay = Dirac(0.0), hidden = true);
  event repairStart (delay = Dirac(0.0), hidden = true);
  event repairEnd (delay = Dirac(mu), hidden = true);
  transition
    failure: vs == WORKING -> vs := FAILED;
    maintenance: vs == FAILED -> vs := WAITING_REPAIR;
    repairStart: vs == WAITING_REPAIR -> vs := REPAIR;
    repairEnd: vs == REPAIR -> vs := WORKING;
end
```

Fig. 9. AltaRica 3.0 code of the reparable component for the pattern by synchronizing events.

4.3 Repair by Synchronizing Events

Figure 9 represents the reparable component used for the pattern by synchronizing events. The three events **maintenance**, **repairStart** and **repairEnd** have their attributes **hidden** set to **true** in order to synchronize them at the system level.

Figure 10 represents the additions to the main part of the AltaRica 3.0 model used for the pattern by synchronizing events. A new block **Repairer** is added. It defines the behavior of the repairer crew according to dedicated events. It is basic: it defines the start and stop of a repair if one of the two repairers is available. Then two new events **repairStartC** and **repairEndC** are defined for all components C. These events are used in the transition part to synchronize the own events **repairStart** and **repairEnd** of the component C, with the events **repairStart** and **repairEnd** of the block **Repairer**.

4.4 Repair by Virtual Aggregation

For the pattern with the virtual aggregation, the class defining the component is represented Fig. 11. This class is the same as the one defined in Fig. 9. In addition, it virtually aggregates a new element of type T, which is used in the class with the alias t. This virtually aggregated element is used in the class within the two transitions **repairStart** and **repairEnd**, by synchronizing them with two events of t. When the class is instantiated (i.e. when an object with this class as type is declared), this aggregation is resolved by indicating a real object (an instance of a class or a block to be used instead of T). This object must be compatible according to the use of it in the declared class.

Figure 12 represents the additions to the main part of the AltaRica 3.0 model used for the pattern by virtual aggregation. A new block **Repairer** is defined. It is the same as for the previous pattern by synchronizing events. This block is used when all classes are instantiated, inheriting from the class **RComponent**, to resolve

```
block System
  // Declaration of elements
  ...
  block Repairer
    parameter Integer repairer = 2;
    Integer rAvailable (init = repairer);
    event repairStart, evRepairEnd (delay = Dirac(0.0), hidden = true);
    transition
      repairStart: rAvailable > 0 -> rAvailable := rAvailable - 1;
      repairEnd: true -> rAvailable := rAvailable + 1;
  end
  event repairStartS1 (delay = Dirac(0.0));
  event repairEndS1 (delay=exponential(S1.mu));
  event repairStartS2 (delay = Dirac(0.0));
  event repairEndS2 (delay=exponential(S2.mu));
  ...
  // For all components, two new events 'repairStart' and 'repairEnd'
  // Definition of the behavior
  transition
    ...
    repairStartS1: !S1.repairStart & !Repairer.repairStart;
    repairEndS1: !S1.repairEnd & !Repairer.repairEnd;
    repairStartS2: !S2.repairStart & !Repairer.repairStart;
    repairEndS2: !S2.repairEnd & !Repairer.repairEnd;
    ...
  // All events previously defined are used to synchronize the events
  // of the considered component with the events of the block
  //     'Repairer'
  assertion
    ...
end
```

Fig. 10. Main part of the AltaRica 3.0 model with the pattern by synchronizing events.

the virtually aggregated element. The resolution of the virtual aggregation is done by the attribute (`virtual T = main.Repairer`). It means that the virtual element T, used in the class with the alias `t`, is equal to the block `Repairer`. The keyword `main`, preceding the word `Repairer` with a dot between them, indicates that the object `Repairer` is declared at the main hierarchical level of the model, i.e. the block `System`.

5   Experiments

Table 1 shows different quantitative features of the models for these three patterns: the model `Mf` for the pattern propagation of flow variables, the model `Me` for the pattern synchronizing events, and the model `Mv` for the pattern virtual aggregation. The first two features are done for the designed models, whereas the others are done for the compiled models. The difference between models `Mf` and `Me` concerns the number of flow variables and their updates in the assertion: more important in the model `Mf`. Nevertheless, this result hides the additional

```
class RComponent
  embeds virtual T as t;
  SDomain vs (init = WORKING);
  parameter Real lambda = 1.0e-5;
  parameter Real mu = 2.0;
  event failure (delay = exponential(lambda));
  event maintenance (delay = Dirac(0.0), hidden = true);
  event repairStart (delay = Dirac(0.0));
  event repairEnd (delay = Dirac(mu));
  transition
    failure: vs == WORKING -> vs := FAILED;
    maintenance: vs == FAILED -> vs := WAITING_REPAIR;
    repairStart: !t.repairStart & vs == WAITING_REPAIR -> vs := REPAIR;
    repairEnd: !t.repairEnd & vs == REPAIR -> vs := WORKING;
end
```

Fig. 11. AltaRica 3.0 code of the reparable component for the pattern by virtual aggregation.

events, per components, defined in Me; which is not indicated in this table but can be found thanks to the number of lines. Furthermore models Me and Mv seem to be equal when compiled. More precisely, they are equal and it is totally normal because the virtual aggregation pattern considers synchronization of events, but from a generic way: by including it directly into the class. The main difference is thus according to the size of the designed models. In the following, especially with the assessment tools, these two models are used equally. Finally it is recommended to use the pattern by virtual aggregation. On the one hand, fewer errors are made at the design phase. On the other hand, it defines fewer flow variables, than the pattern by propagation of flow variables, which has a cost when the model is evaluated by the assessment tools: these variables are updated in the assertion and there is a computational cost for that at runtime.

Table 1. Quantitative features for the three patterns.

Features	Mf	Me	Mv
Number of lines, *at design*	143	177	130
Number of lines of the main block (System), *at design*	84	124	66
Number of state variables	11	12	12
Number of flow variables	48	24	24
Number of events	34	34	34
Number of lines of the assertion	48	24	24

Some experiments are also realized in order to evaluate the Boolean observer TE. This observer indicates when the values of the two flow variables out, of the two actuators A2 of the two lines, are false. It means that the system is failed.

```
block System
  // Declaration of elements
  block Repairer
    parameter Integer repairer = 2;
    Integer available (init = repairer);
    event repairStart (delay = Dirac(0.0), hidden=true);
    event repairEnd (delay = Dirac(0.0), hidden=true);
    transition
      repairStart: available > 0 -> available := available - 1;
      repairEnd: true -> available := available + 1;
  end
  Sensor S1, S2, S3 (virtual T = main.Repairer);
  block Control
    DataAcquisition DA1, DA2, DA3 (virtual T = main.Repairer);
    block LogicSolver
      extends RComponent (lambda = 1.0e-8, mu = 4.0,
                          virtual T = main.Repairer);
      ...
    end
    ...
  end
  block Actuator
    block Line1
      Actuator A1, A2 (virtual T = main.Repairer);
      ...
    end
    ...
  end
  ...
  // Definition of the behavior
  ...
end
```

Fig. 12. Main part of the AltaRica 3.0 model with the pattern by virtual aggregation.

We used the AltaRica 3.0 stochastic simulator of the OpenAltaRica platform ([1]) to perform the experiments.

Table 2 shows the means of fired transitions for the following number of generated histories: 10^5, 10^6 and 10^7, for a mission time equal to 20 years (175200 units of time). The execution time, to generate these histories, has not been taken into account. On the one hand, it is quick: 1–2 min for 10^7 histories on a personal laptop. On the other hand, our interest does not focus on performance analysis of the tool. Elements can be found in [2] or [1].

Table 2. Means of fired transitions.

Number of histories	10^5	10^6	10^7
Mv	22.9015	22.9089	22.9002
Mf	22.9133	22.8936	22.8997

Table 3 shows statistics provided by the stochastic simulator, on the observer TE, for 10^7 generated histories. The considered mission time was 20 years and we also considered different time instants: 5, 10 and 15 years. We focused on the two following statistics. 'had-value' (denoted h-v) is equal to 1 if the observer took the value true for a non-null period at least once from time 0 to time d (with d equals to 5, 10, 15 or 20 years), and 0 otherwise. 'number-of-occurrences' (denoted n-o) is equal to the number of dates the observer started taking the value true over the time period $[0, d]$ (with d equals to 5, 10, 15 or 20 years). The obtained results are quite similar.

Table 3. Statistics on the observer.

		Mf	Mv
5 years	h-v	0.315882	0.315438
	n-o	0.343274	0.343362
10 years	h-v	0.646718	0.646189
	n-o	0.848165	0.849419
15 years	h-v	0.830037	0.829901
	n-o	1.35688	1.3594
20 years	h-v	0.919748	0.920068
	n-o	1.86367	1.86752

6 Conclusion

In this article, we presented three different modeling patterns with the AltaR-ica 3.0 modeling language to represent a corrective maintenance policy on a set of components, with a limited number of repairers. A main modeling part of the system has first been proposed. This part is common to the three modeling patterns and was realized with a 'top-down' approach. Behaviors of the components were not directly defined. Furthermore we included the maintenance policy into this main part.

Regarding the limited number of repairers, meaning their assignment to failed components according to their availability, the three different patterns were presented. The first one uses the propagation of flow variables. This pattern is not difficult but error prone. In addition it could be less efficient during execution. In fact it duplicates the number of flow variables, thus the number of elements to update in the assertion. The second and third patterns use the synchronization of events. The second one defines these synchronizations by hand, for all the components. The third one uses the virtual aggregation to integrate these synchronizations into a generic class. This third pattern is more easy to design models, and thus less error prone.

These modeling patterns for maintenance policies with AltaRica 3.0 open the way to new opportunities. On the one hand, modeling patterns allow engineers to model simply and efficiently classical safety features: e.g. periodically tested component, (warm) redundancies, shared resources, common cause failures, etc. Some of these patterns are defined in libraries. For the others, it is possible, in an easy way, to design tools helping engineers to create models with such patterns. On the other hand, it is possible to extend the use of AltaRica 3.0 modeling language to study other performance indicators than those for safety, e.g. scheduling maintenance policies.

References

1. Aupetit, B., Batteux, M., Rauzy, A., Roussel, J.M.: Improving performance of the AltaRica 3.0 stochastic simulator. In: Podofillini, L., Sudret, B., Stojadinovic, B., Zio, E., Kröger, W. (eds.) Proceedings of Safety and Reliability of Complex Engineered Systems, ESREL 2015, pp. 1815–1824. CRC Press, September 2015
2. Aupetit, B., Batteux, M., Rauzy, A., Roussel, J.M.: Vers la définition d'un kit d'évaluation pour les simulateurs stochastiques. In: Actes du Congrès Lambda-Mu 20 (actes électroniques). Institut pour la Maîtrise des Risques (IMdR), Saint-Malo, France (2016). https://doi.org/10.4267/2042/61811
3. Batteux, M., Prosvirnova, T., Rauzy, A.: From models of structures to structures of models. In: 4th IEEE International Symposium on Systems Engineering, ISSE 2018, Rome, Italy, October 2018
4. Batteux, M., Prosvirnova, T., Rauzy, A.: AltaRica 3.0 assertions: the why and the wherefore. J. Risk Reliab. (2017, article accepted)
5. Batteux, M., Prosvirnova, T., Rauzy, A.: AltaRica 3.0 in 10 modeling patterns. Int. J. Crit. Comput.-Based Syst. 9(1–2), 133–165 (2018). https://doi.org/10.1504/IJCCBS.2019.098809
6. Cassandras, C.G., Lafortune, S.: Introduction to Discrete Event Systems. Springer, New-York (2008). https://doi.org/10.1007/978-0-387-68612-7
7. Gamma, E., Helm, R., Johnson, R., Vlissides, J.: Design Patterns - Elements of Reusable Object-Oriented Software. Addison-Wesley Professional Computing Series. Addison-Wesley, Boston (1994)
8. Maier, M.W.: The Art of Systems Architecting (2009)
9. Prosvirnova, T., et al.: The AltaRica 3.0 project for model-based safety assessment. In: Proceedings of 4th IFAC Workshop on Dependable Control of Discrete Systems, DCDS 2013, pp. 127–132. International Federation of Automatic Control, York, September 2013
10. Rauzy, A.: Guarded transition systems: a new states/events formalism for reliability studies. J. Risk Reliab. **222**(4), 495–505 (2008). https://doi.org/10.1243/1748006XJRR177
11. Zhang, Y., Barros, A., Rauzy, A., Lunde, E.: A modelling methodology for the assessment of preventive maintenance on a compressor drive system. In: Haugen, S., Barros, A., van Gulijk, C., Kongsvik, T., Vinnem, J.E. (eds.) Safe Societies in a Changing World, Proceedings of European Safety and Reliability Conference (ESREL 2018), pp. 915–922. CRC Press, Trondheim, June 2018
12. Zimmermann, A.: Stochastic Discrete Event Systems. Springer, Heidelberg (2008). https://doi.org/10.1007/978-3-540-74173-2

A Domain Specific Language to Support HAZOP Studies of SysML Models

Arut Prakash Kaleeswaran[1,3(✉)], Peter Munk[1], Samir Sarkic[2], Thomas Vogel[3], and Arne Nordmann[1]

[1] Bosch Corporate Sector Research, 71272 Renningen, Germany
{ArutPrakash.Kaleeswaran,Peter.Munk,Arne.Nordmann}@de.bosch.com
https://www.bosch.com/research/
[2] Bosch Automotive Electronics Software Campus, 71701 Schwieberdingen, Germany
Samir.Sarkic@de.bosch.com
[3] Humboldt-Universität zu Berlin, Berlin, Germany
thomas.vogel@informatik.hu-berlin.de

Abstract. To deal with the rising system complexity, Model-Based System Development (MBSD) approaches are becoming popular due to their promise to improve consistency between different views of the system model. For dependable systems, safety analysis is one of the important views. Model-Based Safety Analysis (MBSA) can partially automate the generation of safety artifacts and provide traceability between the system model and the generated safety artifacts. Thus, MBSA not only supports the safety analysis of the system, it also eases an impact analysis of model changes and hence supports an iterative and agile development of safety-critical systems. This paper presents an MBSA approach for the Hazard and Operability (HAZOP) studies using a Domain-Specific Language (DSL) for guidance and establishing strong links to the system model and requirements for consistency and traceability. The combination with the DSL and features like auto-completion and consistency checks that we implement in our tool help to detect flaws in the safety analysis at early design stages, when elimination of such flaws is typically cheap as opposed to later development stages. Our approach is evaluated based on a SysML model of Bosch's Boost Recuperation System (BRS).

1 Introduction

The complexity of modern, software-intensive systems continues to increase due to the rising number of features and functionalities [2]. When complex software-intensive systems are used in safety-critical domains such as automotive, robotics, and avionics, their malfunction might lead to severe damages or even loss of lives. Consequently, safety of these systems is of paramount importance. To ensure safety, these systems have to be developed according to safety standards such as IEC 61508 or ISO 26262 in the automotive domain. These standards require safety analysis methods such as Failure Mode and Effects Analysis (FMEA), Fault Tree Analysis (FTA), or Hazard and Operability (HAZOP),

© Springer Nature Switzerland AG 2019
Y. Papadopoulos et al. (Eds.): IMBSA 2019, LNCS 11842, pp. 47–62, 2019.
https://doi.org/10.1007/978-3-030-32872-6_4

all of which inherently require a model of the system. Thus, these methods analyze the safety of a system based on a model of the system [5,6,13,14], focusing, e. g., on FMEA [15] or FTA [8].

In previous work, we presented Model-Based Safety Analysis (MBSA) methods for FMEA [11] and FTA [12] by combining and linking both with Model-Based System Development (MBSD) methods and artifacts. However, a systematic integration of HAZOP is missing. Without links between HAZOP study elements and MBSD artifacts, there is a high risk that the safety analysis and the system model become inconsistent, potentially leading to forgotten hazards as well as incomplete and inconsistent risk evaluations.

In this paper, we present an approach that uses a Domain-Specific Language (DSL) with strong links to a System Modeling Language (SysML) model to support HAZOP studies with features like traceability and consistency checks. In this work, we do not attempt to fully automate the HAZOP study because as per Taylor [18], "to be able to accept the responsibility for risk reduction recommendations the HAZOP team requires full understanding of the problems and the basis for analysis. This cannot be achieved via a purely computer generated HAZOP". Instead, we implemented our DSL with its metamodel in a tool and provide the user with auto-completion and context menus to ease HAZOP studies. Thus, our main contribution is to provide comprehensive automated support based on a DSL that assists users in conducting HAZOP studies while automatically maintaining consistency with a SysML model and system requirements. We show the applicability of the proposed approach in a case study of an industrial automotive product, the Boost Recuperation System (BRS) from Bosch.

2   Background and Related Work

The Hazard and Risk Analysis (HARA) is fundamental for ensuring the safe design and operation of a system and it is the precondition for both FTA and FMEA. Success of a HARA relies on identifying and subsequently analyzing possible scenarios that can cause hazardous events with different degrees of severity. Several techniques are available to identify these hazardous events, all of which require rigorous, thorough, and systematic application. One particular technique typically used as part of the HARA is the HAZOP study.

A HAZOP study is a structured and systematic technique for examining a defined system with the objective to identify potential hazards and their causes [1]. For an examined hazard, a solution or an action is provided to change the system design in order to avoid the hazard. The HAZOP study is structured in a tabular format. In each column, the hazard examination is made for an element or attribute of the system. An example for a coolant transfer system is provided in Table 1 while a more detailed explanation and more examples can be found in IEC 61882:2016 [1]. The standard columns of a HAZOP table based on [1] and [16] are given in the following. Please note that in the remainder of this paper we enumerate each HAZOP Column by **HCn**.

Table 1. Example for a HAZOP Table [1].

Element (HC1)	Guide word (HC2)	Deviation (HC3)	Consequences (HC4)	Cause (HC5)	Action required (HC6)
Transfer Coolant	No	No transfer of coolant takes place	Pump stopped	Explosion (Due to the temperature greater than 900 °C)	Consider low-level alarm for flow of coolant

Element (HC1): The design intent for a given part of a system is expressed in terms of elements.

Guide word (HC2): A word or phrase which expresses and defines a specific type of deviation from an element's design intent.

Deviation (HC3): A deviation is a way in which the process conditions may depart from their design/process intent.

Consequences (HC4): The results of the deviation, in the case that the deviation actually occurs. Several consequences may follow from one cause and, in turn, one consequence can have several causes.

Cause (HC5): The reason(s) why the deviation could occur. Several causes may be identified for one deviation.

Action Required (HC6): The actions required for addressing uncertainties (or) recommendations for mitigation of the hazard.

Performing a complete and consistent HAZOP study can be a difficult, time-consuming, and labor-intensive activity [4]. Therefore, several researchers have attempted to develop expert systems to resolve these drawbacks. Dunjó et al. [4, Sect. 3.5] discuss the efforts made towards this goal. Most of the surveyed approaches are rule-based and apply expert systems to suggest guide words or potential deviations based on the analyzed system elements [7,10]. Only a very limited number of approaches are model-based or leverage the benefits of a DSL. However, Völter et al. [19] propose and justify the use of DSLs in safety-critical environments in order to introduce rigor, consistency, and traceability. Yet, to the best of our knowledge, no comprehensive model-based approach supporting HAZOP studies by the use of a DSL exists.

For example, Lhannaoui et al. [9] provide a conceptual HAZOP metamodel to describe business-related risk analysis. However, they do not provide any implementation and tool support for their metamodel as they focus mainly on improving business processes rather than engineering processes, which are the focus of our work. Guiochet [7] and Hansen et al. [10] both provide rule-based approaches that suggest appropriate HAZOP guide words based on the selected UML (Unified Modeling Language) element and attribute. Guiochet additionally demonstrates the integration of the HAZOP study with the system model. Both need to be modeled in the same standalone HAZOP tool, which allows establishing consistency of HAZOP study results and the UML system model as well as checking for completeness of all possible failures for the modeled elements. Thus, both approaches rely on the standard general-purpose UML metamodel.

Attasara-Mason [3] provides an integrated system and HAZOP metamodel, expressed in the open-source database management system *ConceptBase*. To the best of our knowledge, this is the only approach that facilitates a metamodel to ensure traceability and consistency between the HAZOP study and the system model. Their approach imports the system model and the HAZOP study into the *ConceptBase* and is able to check dependencies as well as consistency based on the Object Constraint Language (OCL). However, in contrast to our approach, changes in the system model that break the consistency with the HAZOP study cannot be detected automatically. Furthermore, our implementation provides the user with auto-completion and context help. Thus, our approach is more comprehensive in terms of providing traceability and automated support for users conducting HAZOP studies.

3   Approach

Our approach targets machine support for and during a HAZOP study, mainly based on a strong link to a system model to ensure consistency of the HAZOP study with the system. As large parts of the automotive domain as well as several Bosch business units use SysML models, we want to provide HAZOP support for SysML models and their respective system requirements that are stored separately in a requirement management tool. We designed a DSL that is capable of formalizing HAZOP study results and link them with SysML elements of all SysML diagram types.

3.1   Metamodel

Figure 1 shows the main concepts of the metamodel of the proposed HAZOP-DSL that will later be arranged in the concrete language syntax.

The main concept of the HAZOP-DSL is the `Analysis`, which captures the results of a HAZOP study as shown in Table 1 with an arbitrary number of `Statements`. A `Statement` consists of three parts: (1) One `ColumnType` that defines the column (**HC3–HC6**), so either `Deviation`, `Consequence`, `Cause`, or `ActionRequired`. (2) One `Element` that references the SysML model element the statement is targeting, which is **HC1**. (3) An arbitrary number of `Utilities` that specify the actual <u>content</u> of the HAZOP table cell. Note that since the guide word (**HC2**) is already part of the `Deviation` (**HC3**), we do not express it separately again but provide them as part of the `Utility` and highlight them visually with red color as illustrated by the example in Fig. 2.

The different `Utilities` that structure the content of HAZOP table cells are described in the following. Please note that we enumerate them with (**U***m*) for later use. The `GuideWord` (**U1**) provides a reference to one guide word from a given list and the guide word's description collected from [7]. The `Element` (**U2**) allows referencing elements from a SysML system model, e. g., SysML blocks

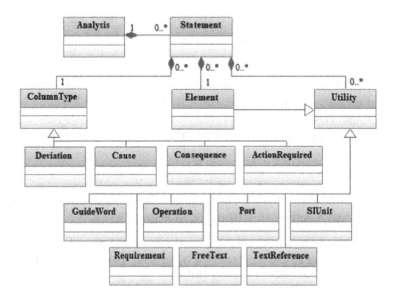

Fig. 1. Simplified metamodel of the proposed HAZOP-DSL.

and activities. The `Operation` **(U3)** allows referencing SysML operations of system model elements. The `Port` **(U4)** allows referencing ports of system model elements. The `Requirement` **(U5)** allows referencing system requirements. The `FreeText` **(U6)** allows input of arbitrary text strings. The `TextReference` **(U7)** allows re-use of previously defined `FreeText` **(U6)**, text snippets from a user-defined list of commonly used HAZOP phrases, and user-defined lists of short terms instead of longer sentences. The `SIUnit` **(U8)** allows the use of SI units that can be looked up by name for convenience and consistency.

3.2 Constraints

Depending on the `ColumnType`, certain utilities are mandatory or not allowed, as listed in Table 2. The columns **HC3–HC6** do not use the utility `Requirement` **(U5)** because these columns focus only on deviation from the original design, failure cause due to deviation, consequences to the system due to the failure, and actions required to overcome the failure. Therefore, references to requirements are not required for these columns. The column **HC3** uses the utility `Guide-Word` **(U1)** to find out possible deviations or failures. Therefore, utility **U1** is used in column **HC3** and restricted for columns **HC4–HC6**.

3.3 Concrete Syntax

The concrete syntax of the HAZOP-DSL provides a fixed structure for `State-ments` expressing **HC3–HC6**, as defined by the grammar shown in Listing 1.1 and expressed in the Extended Backus-Naur form (EBNF). Each `Statement`

Table 2. Constraints for usage of `Utilities` depending on the `ColumnType`. Note that **U5** is used in Sect. 5 as an extension of the HAZOP study for the BRS example.

ColumnType	Utility constraints
Deviation (**HC3**)	U1 | U2 | U3 | U4 | ~~U5~~ | U6 | U7 | U8
Consequences (**HC4**)	~~U1~~ | U2 | U3 | U4 | ~~U5~~ | U6 | U7 | U8
Cause (**HC5**)	~~U1~~ | U2 | U3 | U4 | ~~U5~~ | U6 | U7 | U8
Action required (**HC6**)	~~U1~~ | U2 | U3 | U4 | ~~U5~~ | U6 | U7 | U8

starts with the `ColumnType`, followed by the `Element` of interest, and an arbitrary number of `Utilities`, i. e., text snippets, references to system elements or requirements, and SI units (cf. metamodel in Sect. 3.1).

Listing 1.1. Grammar of the proposed HAZOP-DSL in EBNF.

```
Statement = ColumnType , "for" , Element , ":" , Utilities;
ColumnType = HC3 | HC4 | HC5 | HC6;
Element = HC1;
Utilities = { Utility };
Utility = U1 | U2 | U3 | U4 | U5 | U6 | U7 | U8;
```

Figure 2 shows four exemplary `Statements`, one per line, in the proposed DSL, expressing columns **HC3–HC6** from Table 1. These `Statements` are (i) the `Deviation` (**HC3**) statement ("No/none Transfer of coolant takes place") emphasizing the `GuideWord` (**U1**) utility ("No/None"), (ii) the `Consequences` (**HC4**) statement with the `TextReference` (**U7**) utility ("Pump is stopped"), (iii) the `Cause` (**HC5**) statement with the `SIUnit` (**U8**) utility ("°C") used with a `FreeText` (**U6**) utility ("Explosion (Due to . . .)"), and (iv) the `ActionRequired` (**HC6**) statement with the `Port` (**U4**) utility ("coolant") in combination with the `FreeText` (**U6**) utility ("Consider the low-level alarm..."). All four statements refer to the same `Element` called "Transfer_Coolant".

Author: Arut , **Version:** V1

Deviation for *TransferCoolant* : No/none Transfer of coolant takes place
Consequences for *TransferCoolant* : Pump is stopped
Cause for *TransferCoolant* : Explosion (Due to the temperature greater than 900 °C)
Action Required for *TransferCoolant* : Consider the low-level alarm for flow of coolant

Fig. 2. Screenshot of HAZOP-DSL statements describing the example of Table 1.

4   Implementation

We implemented the proposed approach in a language workbench that has been shown to be beneficial for safety-critical applications [19]. The proposed

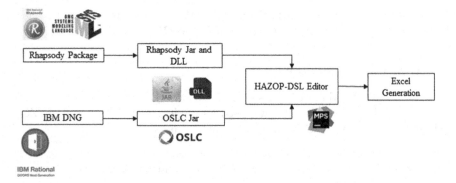

Fig. 3. Integration of the DSL with the system model and requirements.

HAZOP-DSL is developed using the language workbench *Meta Programming System* (MPS) from Jetbrains for its flexibility as well as for integrating the HAZOP-DSL with our previous model-based FMEA [11] and FTA [12]. In our approach, the SysML model to be analyzed is imported from IBM's system modeling tool *Rational Rhapsody* and the system requirements are imported from IBM's requirements tool *DOORS Next Generation* (DNG). Several Bosch business units and other automotive companies use Rhapsody and SysML to model the automotive system architectures and DNG to manage requirements.

The following sections introduce our implementation of integrating the system model and requirements, and of the DSL in MPS. A technical overview of the integration of the DSL with the system model and requirements is given in Fig. 3. The required system model and system requirements are imported, the HAZOP study is performed using the DSL referring to the imported model and requirements, and finally the analysis results are exported in the Excel format.

4.1 System Model and Requirements Import

SysML model elements from Rhapsody can either be imported via XMI export or by directly accessing the Java-based Rhapsody API. System requirements are imported using DNG's *Open Services for Lifecycle Collaboration* (OSLC) API. The primary motive of referencing system model elements and requirements in our DSL is to detect inconsistencies between references and HAZOP study.

Inside our language workbench, we provide options to manually trigger the import of the system model from Rhapsody and requirements from DNG. If the system model or the requirements changed, a pop-up is raised for each of the changes for the user to either accept or neglect the specific change, e.g., a changed `Element`, `Operation`, or `Port`. To avoid false positives based on renaming, the system model and requirements imports are based on their unique IDs as provided by both, Rhapsody and DNG. The imported system model and the requirements are stored inside the language workbench next to the DSL to be referenced by the respective `Utilities`. From this list, the user manually selects the `Element` and `Requirement` for column **HC3–HC6**.

4.2 DSL Implementation

DSLs are implemented in MPS by so-called *language aspects*. In the following, we discuss the relevant aspects that we used to implement the proposed HAZOP-DSL and to integrate it with the system model and system requirements.

Structure. The *structure* aspect of MPS defines the metamodel of the language, i. e., its concepts, their properties, dependencies, and relations. The MPS structure aspect supports extension and inheritance among concepts, so that, following Sect. 3.1 and Fig. 1, the `ColumnType` concept is extended by `Deviation`, `Cause`, `Consequences`, and the `ActionRequired` concepts. Similarly, the specific utilities **(U1–U8)** extend the `Utility` base concept.

Editor. The *editor* aspect of MPS allows to provide the concrete syntax of the DSL. MPS supports projectional editors, i. e., for each concept of the language's *structure* aspect, a *projection* can be provided. Due to stakeholder demands, the HAZOP-DSL was implemented as a textual DSL, i. e., the *editor* aspect provides a textual projection for all concepts. Similarly, tabular, mathematical, and graphical notations can be provided as projections, or a mix of those [19].

The projections of the `Statement` concept realize the grammar presented in Sect. 3.3. The projection of the `Analysis` concept realizes a document that contains an `author`, a `version`, and an arbitrary number of `Statements`. Figure 2 shows an example of an `Analysis` in the textual editor of our HAZOP-DSL.

In the `Analysis` editor, once the user starts typing `ColumnType`, auto-completion for all possible `ColumnTypes` is provided. Furthermore, the editor displays the according `Statement` editor, where the `Element` and the `Utilities` have to be filled in. Since a *textual* editor in MPS is just a textual *projection* of the language structure, i. e., an abstract syntax tree (AST), auto-completion is automatically provided by MPS. For example, in all places in the editor where `Elements` are allowed in the syntax, MPS will automatically provide a list of all legal instances, i. e., all elements from the imported system model. Figure 5 shows an example of the editor, show-casing the introduced auto-completion.

Constraints and Type System. The constraints discussed in Sect. 3.2 are implemented using the *constraints* aspect of MPS. Additional constraints are realized using the *type system* aspect, which allows to implement inference rules that check the model for constraints and annotate errors and warnings inside the editor. In our DSL, we provide checks for redundant `Statements`, i. e., multiple `Statements` that refer to the same `Element` and `ColumnType`. In this case, a warning is raised as shown in Fig. 5. Similarly, checks for missing `Statements` and, as mentioned in Sect. 4.1, broken links to the system model and requirements are in place and raise errors. Furthermore, an error is raised for a missing `GuideWord` **(U1)** in the `Deviation` statement as shown in Fig. 5.

Intentions. The MPS *intentions* aspect allows to provide context help options as shown in Fig. 5. For example, we provide intentions on `Statements` that will, upon selection, add missing `Statements` for system model elements, i. e., `Statements` with the specific `ColumnTypes` that have not been specified yet for the `Element` of the selected `Statement`.

Plug-In Action. The *plug-in* aspect of MPS allows to provide actions that the user can trigger, e. g., through buttons or menu options. The imports of the system model and requirements, including handling of system model changes as described in Sect. 4.1, are realized with this *plug-in* aspect.

5   Application Example

This section introduces an industrial case study based on the Bosch Boost Recuperation System (BRS) to demonstrate the feasibility of our proposed approach.

5.1   Boost Recuperation System

The BRS is a 48 V electrical machine integrated with the internal combustion engine of a car using a belt drive. BRS uses recuperation to recover energy for use of vehicle acceleration. The BRS consists of a 48/12 V DC/DC converter, a 48 V lead-acid battery, a DC electric motor, and a combustion engine [17]. The BRS system is modeled in SysML activity diagrams. Figure 4 shows a simplified BRS activity diagram, the phase-current measurement, on which we will focus in the following. Within this diagram, the *PhaseCurrentControl* provides the calculated pulse-width modulation (*PWM*) signal that is applied to the DC motor. The *PhaseCurrentControl* depends on the measured phase-current, rotor speed, and angle of the motor.

The top left of the diagram contains the package name and the diagram name. The three columns are known as *swim lanes*, the blocks inside the swim lanes are called *call operation actions*. Figure 4 shows three swim lanes, namely, *CAN* with one, *SystemControl* with two, and *PhaseCurrent* with two call operation actions. Such actions are connected by activity edges via their pins.

Making changes in the system becomes harder with time to analyze all the deviations and their impact on each iteration by using standard spreadsheet-based HAZOP analysis. The activity diagram in Fig. 4 was modeled in Rhapsody. The BRS model comprises 35 main packages, 57 swim lanes, and 123 call operation actions of hardware and software functions. With 1–3 deviations per swim lane and call operation action, there is a need to analyze 320 deviations.

5.2   HAZOP Study for BRS

Table 3 shows an exemplary row of the BRS HAZOP study for the call operation action *PhaseCurrentMeasurement* in the swim lane *PhaseCurrent*. The `Deviation` for this swim lane and call operation action is represented based on the GuideWord "more", i. e., a quantitative increase. Thus, the Deviation is "too high voltages (greater than 48 V) are measured in one or all phases".

For the BRS, the process followed for the HAZOP study is the same as introduced in Sect. 2 and given by IEC 61882:2016 [1]. However, the resulting Table 3 differs from the standard HAZOP table in several aspects, cf. Table 1. The required adoptions and extensions to the metamodel in order to support the BRS HAZOP flavor are explained in the following.

A first adoption to our metamodel is the Element that is used in **HC1**. While it was a reference to a generic SysML model element in the generic approach, Element is now a reference to the combination of a *swim lane* and one of its *call operation action*. Column **HC1** is represented in the BRS HAZOP table by the first two columns (see columns **BC1** and **BC2** in Table 3). Columns 3–6 and 8 in Table 3 (**BC3–BC6** and **BC8**) are unchanged with respect to columns **HC2–HC6** in the standard HAZOP. Columns 7, 9 and 10 in Table 3, namely, **BC7**, **BC9** and **BC10** are additional columns added for the BRS HAZOP study:

SG Violation (BC7): The list of affected safety goals (SGs) due to the deviation and consequences. SGs are a collection of safety requirements.

Derived SA Requirement (BC9): Based on the proposed solution in ActionRequired (**BC8**), the necessary changes in the system architecture (SA) are added as requirements in DNG and their requirement IDs are referenced.

Impact Verification (BC10): Analyzing the impact of the Cause (**BC6**) on the system using techniques such as verification or simulation.

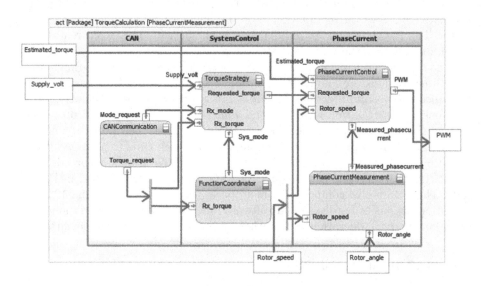

Fig. 4. Activity diagram of the BRS torque calculation, simplified for intellectual property reasons.

Table 3. One exemplary row of the BRS HAZOP study, split into two rows for lay-outing purpose. (SG = safety goal, SA = system architecture).

#	Element (BC1)	Function (BC2)	Guide Word (BC3)	Deviation (BC4)	Consequences (BC5)	...
1	PhaseCurrent	PhaseCurrent-Measurement	More/too high	too high voltages (greater than 48 V) are measured in one or all phases	HW related failures, e.g., ageing or random failure of control unit	...

...	Cause (BC6)	SG Violation (BC7)	Action Required (BC8)	Derived SA Requirement (BC9)	Impact Verification (BC10)
...	wrong measurement of current could lead to wrong torque generation	SG01, SG02, SG03	Add Phase-current plausibility check component with ASIL-B	16634, 17444	Simulated and verified with fault injection

Table 4. Constraints for the usage of `Utilities` for the additional columns.

ColumnType	Utility constraints
SG violation (**BC7**)	~~U1~~ | ~~U2~~ | ~~U3~~ | ~~U4~~ | U5 | ~~U6~~ | U7 | ~~U8~~
Derived SA requirement (**BC9**)	~~U1~~ | ~~U2~~ | ~~U3~~ | ~~U4~~ | U5 | ~~U6~~ | ~~U7~~ | ~~U8~~
Impact verification (**BC10**)	~~U1~~ | U2 | U3 | U4 | ~~U5~~ | U6 | U7 | U8

The constraints on the utilities for the additional columns are listed in Table 4. The columns **BC7** and **BC9** use the utility `Requirement` (**U5**) to refer to imported system requirements from DNG. Additionally, column **BC7** uses the utility `TextReference` (**U7**) to refer to user-defined short terms for a collection of system requirements. The column **BC10** does not use the utilities `GuideWord` (**U1**) and `Requirement` (**U5**) because it refers only to information from the verification or simulation.

5.3 Development Workflow

This section presents the envisioned development workflow when performing a HAZOP study with support of the proposed HAZOP-DSL. The steps to perform the analysis expressed in Table 3 with the HAZOP-DSL are the following:

1. The HAZOP-DSL document is started by entering the author's name and the version number of the analysis.
2. After the header, HAZOP statements are added line by line by selecting the `ColumnType`. Selection of the `ColumnType` will create a sentence structure that leaves two placeholders: element and content.
3. In the first placeholder, the `Element` of the system model is selected from the auto-completion option and causes the function name to appear in the second

placeholder. In the example shown in Fig. 5, the element is *PhaseCurrent* and the function is *PhaseCurrentMeasurement*.

4. In the second placeholder, the user fills the analysis content by concatenating utilities, e.g., guide words, text, and references. In the example shown in Fig. 5, the utilities selected for `Deviation` **(BC4)** are a `GuideWord` **(U1)** ("too high"), `FreeText` **(U6)** ("voltages..."), and `SIUnit` **(U8)** ("V").

5. As shown in Fig. 5, the context help can be used to add more columns **(BC5–BC10)** to the same element, or to auto-populate the analysis with all remaining columns for this element.

6. For the remaining `ColumnTypes`, the statements use the `TextReference` **(U7)** utility from a user-defined list in `Consequences` **(BC5)** and another `TextReference` **(U7)** utility from a user-defined short term for a safety goal requirement in `SG Violation` **(BC7)**, as well as a `Requirement` **(U5)** utility in `Derived SA Requirement` **(BC9)**. The listed utilities are combined with the `FreeText` **(U6)** utility.

7. In Fig. 5, the last statement appears with an error and warning. The error indicates that no `GuideWord` **(U1)** utility is selected for the `Deviation` **(BC4)** statement, and the warning indicates that there is an existing `Deviation` statement with same element and function name.

8. In the second to last statement for `Impact Verification` **(BC10)**, the function name is highlighted to indicate a broken link to the system model.

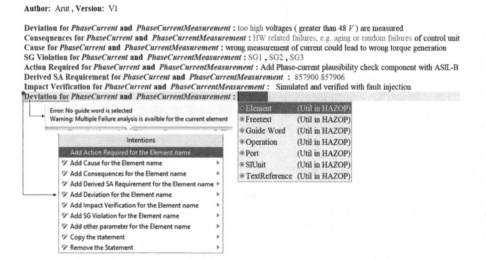

Fig. 5. HAZOP study row from Table 3 expressed in the proposed HAZOP-DSL with an context help, auto-completion, error and warning example.

6 Discussion

The first advantage to mention is introducing structure into the HAZOP study results, i.e., a metamodel and clear syntax for the content that otherwise is just prose text in a standard spreadsheet-based HAZOP analysis. This already improves readability, increases consistency among HAZOP statements, and reduces the potential for errors. HAZOP statements written in the proposed DSL are in parts already *correct by construction* as they have to follow the structure given by the syntax shown in Sect. 3.3 and restrict the use of GuideWords to a fixed set that was agreed on beforehand for a particular analysis. Further utilities raise consistency even more, e.g., by ensuring consistent use of text modules and physical units. All of these features enforce rigor in HAZOP studies, which is required for safety analysis of high quality.

A second and—from our point of view—a more important advantage of the proposed approach is the established link between the system model and the HAZOP study. While the features above ensure consistency *among* HAZOP study results, the system link ensures traceability and consistency *between the HAZOP studies and the system model*. This feature is a strong help during system design and system evolution, in particular:

1. During initial system design, when doing the HAZOP study in early design phases of the project, support by our approach is provided for consistency and completeness. **Consistency** is ensured through the import of the system models and Utilities **(U2–U4)** referring not just to the correct Element names, but to unique identifiers that will remain consistent during further updates and imports of the system model. The constraints introduced in Sect. 3.2 ensure **Completeness** to the extent that analysis of the Elements of interest is complete.
2. An even stronger support is provided during the naturally occurring system evolution. In standard spreadsheet-based HAZOP analysis, ensuring consistency of the HAZOP study with the system model is extremely time-consuming and error-prone, demanding strict processes and a large amount of discipline from all team members. Since the Utilities **(U2–U5)** refer to unique identifiers of system elements and requirements, HAZOP-DSL Statements remain valid even during renaming. However, if Statements refer to Elements that were deleted, replaced, or structurally changed (changed Operations or Ports), Statements referring to deprecated Elements will immediately be invalidated and the analyst is pointed to parts of the HAZOP study that need to be checked or reworked.

Our main motivation to provide a DSL for what is usually prose text in a standard HAZOP study, is to support the user during the analysis. The main advantages of our approach are delivered to the user, the HAZOP analyst, by features provided in the MPS-based editing environment, namely:

Traceability and Impact Analysis. If the system model changes, e.g., in the course of a regular system design evolution, when the user triggers the system import as explained in Sect. 4.2, she is presented with the changes and may accept or reject them. Based on the accepted changes, `Statements` that comprise a system model reference **(U2–U4)** can automatically be checked and invalidated if out-of-date, raising a warning or an error at the according `Statement`; see Fig. 5 for an illustration. Additionally, all HAZOP study results regarding a certain system model element can be aggregated automatically and consistently as opposed to text-based matches in a classical text-based HAZOP.

Auto-Completion. Most parts of a `Statement` are supported by auto-completion, when potential candidates for the respective `Utility` are known. This is trivial for the concepts that have a fixed set of candidates, namely `ColumnType` and the utility `GuideWord` **(U1)**. It is also implemented for the `Element`, as candidates are known from the imported system model, as well as all utilities referencing the system model and requirements **(U2–U5)**. Auto-completion of the utility `SIUnit` **(U8)** relies on a static lookup table. For example, when using the utility `Element` **(U2)**, all available elements of the system model are provided and the appropriate `Element` can be selected. For utility `SIUnit` **(U8)**, the user can select the unit notation by typing its complete or partial name, which leads to the correct unit notation through a SI unit lookup table, e.g., $\frac{m^2}{s}$.

Context Help. All `Statements` can be manually typed or they can be added using context help as described in Sect. 4.2. For example, this allows adding *all remaining* `ColumnTypes` for a certain `Element`, ensuring completeness of the analysis for the according `Element`. In addition, the user has an option to auto-generate only one particular of the missing `ColumnTypes` for the `Element` of the currently selected `Statement`.

7 Conclusion

To the best of our knowledge, the proposed approach is the first to explore the use of a DSL to establish strong links between a HAZOP study and the analyzed system model. The presented DSL supports the user during analysis with auto-completion, context help, consistency, and traceability to the system model and requirements. Through linking the HAZOP study with a system model, the impact of changes in the system model on the analysis results can be detected and the user is pointed to required changes in the analysis. Thereby, consistency is increased while manual effort of dealing with system evolution is decreased. Our approach was evaluated with an industrial system and we successfully adapted it to support the extended HAZOP study with additional columns.

As next steps, we consider providing the standard HAZOP table format, which in MPS leaves the DSL largely unchanged by providing an additional tabular projection. To enhance HAZOP-DSL's usability, we plan to present our tool to safety engineers and evaluate our tool with further real-world use-cases. While we currently provide a standard set of HAZOP guide words, suggesting guide words based on the properties of the selected element following the approach by Guiochet [7] is another potential extension point.

References

1. IEC 61882:2016: Hazard and Operability studies (HAZOP studies) - Application guide (2001)
2. Amarnath, R., Munk, P., Thaden, E., Nordmann, A., Burton, S.: Dependability challenges in the model-driven engineering of automotive systems. In: IEEE International Symposium on Software Reliability Engineering Workshops (ISSREW) (2016)
3. Attasara-Mason, P.: Safety critical computer systems: an information management perspective on their development. In: International Conference on Management of Innovation and Technology, pp. 1271–1276, September 2008
4. Dunjó, J., Fthenakis, V., Vílchez, J.A., Arnaldos, J.: Hazard and operability (HAZOP) analysis. A Lit. Review. J. Hazard. Mater. **173**, 19–32 (2010)
5. Fenelon, P., McDermid, J.A.: An integrated tool set for software safety analysis. J. Syst. Softw. **21**(3), 279–290 (1993)
6. Grunske, L.: Towards an integration of standard component-based safety evaluation techniques with SaveCCM. In: Hofmeister, C., Crnkovic, I., Reussner, R. (eds.) QoSA 2006. LNCS, vol. 4214, pp. 199–213. Springer, Heidelberg (2006). https://doi.org/10.1007/11921998_17
7. Guiochet, J.: Hazard analysis of human-robot interactions with HAZOP-UML. Saf. Sci. **84**, 225–237 (2016)
8. Joshi, A., Vestal, S., Binns, P.: Automatic generation of static fault trees from AADL models. In: DSN 2007 Workshop on Architecting Dependable Systems (2007)
9. Lhannaoui, H., Kabbaj, M.I., Bakkoury, Z.: A conceptual metamodel approach to analysing risks in business process models. J. Theor. Appl. Inf. Technol. **80**, 211–220 (2015)
10. Marius Hansen, K., Wells, L., Maier, T.: HAZOP analysis of UML-based software architecture descriptions of safety-critical systems. In: Proceedings of NWUML 2004: 2nd Nordic Workshop on the Unified Modeling Language, number 35 in TUCS General Publication (2004)
11. Munk, P., et al.: Semi-automatic safety analysis and optimization. In: 55th ACM/ESDA/IEEE Design Automation Conference (DAC) (2018)
12. Nordmann, A., Munk, P.: Lessons learned from model-based safety assessment with SysML and component fault trees. In: Proceedings of the 21th ACM/IEEE International Conference on Model Driven Engineering Languages and Systems, pp. 134–143 (2018)
13. Ortmeier, F., Thums, A., Schellhorn, G., Reif, W.: Combining formal methods and safety analysis – the ForMoSA approach. In: Ehrig, H., et al. (eds.) Integration of Software Specification Techniques for Applications in Engineering. LNCS, vol. 3147, pp. 474–493. Springer, Heidelberg (2004). https://doi.org/10.1007/978-3-540-27863-4_26
14. Papadopoulos, Y., McDermid, J., Sasse, R., Heiner, G.: Analysis and synthesis of the behaviour of complex programmable electronic systems in conditions of failure. Reliab. Eng. Syst. Saf. **71**(3), 229–247 (2001)
15. Papadopoulos, Y., Parker, D., Grante, C.: Automating the failure modes and effects analysis of safety critical systems. In: Proceedings of the 8th International Symposium on High Assurance Systems Engineering, pp. 310–311. IEEE (2004)
16. Rausand, M.: Risk Assessment: Theory, Methods, and Applications (2011)

17. Robert Bosch GmbH: The BRS boost recuperation system: increased power, enhanced comfort and lower fuel consumption. https://www.bosch-presse.de/pressportal/de/media/migrated_download/de/BRS_Broschuere_RZ_en.pdf
18. Taylor, J.: Automated HAZOP revisited. Process Saf. Environ. Prot. **111**, 635–651 (2017)
19. Völter, M., et al.: Using language workbenches and domain-specific languages for safety-critical software development. Softw. Syst. Model. **18**, 2507–2530 (2018)

Integrating Existing Safety Analyses into SysML

Kester Clegg[1(✉)], Mole Li[2], David Stamp[2], Alan Grigg[2], and John McDermid[1]

[1] University of York, York YO10 5DD, UK
{kester.clegg,john.mcdermid}@york.ac.uk
[2] Rolls-Royce (Controls) PLC, Derby, UK
{mole.li,alan.grigg,david.stamp}@rolls-royce.com

Abstract. Migrating systems and safety engineering (often with legacy processes and certified tools) towards a model based systems engineering (MBSE) environment is a socio-technical problem. Establishing a common conceptual framework requires agreement on modelling artefacts and the integration of existing tool chains to minimise disruption. We discuss our experience integrating a SysML Safety Profile to model fault trees but which has the prerequisite requirement to continue the analysis of those models by existing tools. We demonstrate a lightweight profile that minimally captures the fault logic for a Rolls-Royce gas turbine engine controller and provides specific in-house extensions for both fault tree and engine dispatch analysis by exporting model entities and relationships from the SysML fault trees. During integration we realised a more fundamental need to reconcile the systems engineers' functional view with the safety engineers' focus on failure modes and fault logic in order to maximimse the longer term benefits of MBSE development.

Keywords: SysML · Fault Tree Analysis · Failure modes

1 Introduction

Systems engineers have traditionally used separate models of the system functions from those used for safety analysis. Part of this stems from the need to consider the system from a functional perspective on one hand and on the other hand how it will fail. As failures frequently cut across functional boundaries and model very different things, system and safety models can be difficult to reconcile and verify for consistency. While it can be argued that maintaining two models from a single set of system specifications can act as an independent check that the system will behave as expected under failure, the differences between the system and safety models is often a source of inefficiency and misinterpretation.

In this paper we document our experience that trying to reconcile system and safety perspectives is not simply a question of sharing a single data repository captured in a modelling language such as SysML (Systems Modelling Language). Support for different perspectives requires alignment not only of artefacts, but of

© Springer Nature Switzerland AG 2019
Y. Papadopoulos et al. (Eds.): IMBSA 2019, LNCS 11842, pp. 63–77, 2019.
https://doi.org/10.1007/978-3-030-32872-6_5

how the system should be modelled to gain a common understanding across the company's engineers. The context of this work is as part of Rolls-Royce's Ultra-Fan engine demonstrator program,[1] which has elected to trial SysML during system development.

1.1 Paper Structure

Section 1.2 gives some background to safety critical and systems modelling using SysML perspective and previous work. Section 1.3 describes the specific requirements for the ENCASE (Enabling Novel Controls and Advanced Sensors for Engines) project. Section 2 looks at our implementation of the fault tree SysML profile. Section 3 details our bespoke SysML profile that provides support for modelling fault logic both within SysML and through the use of export scripts to existing fault tree analysis tools. Section 4 gives a summary of engine dispatch analysis.[2] The issue of gradually introducing MBSE through integration with the existing analytical toolchain is covered in Sect. 5. In Sect. 6 we discuss some of the problems and solutions to reconcile different modelling viewpoints with respect to the functional specification and derived safety requirements. Finally Sect. 7 concludes our experience and outlines the work going forward.

1.2 Background and Previous Work

Model Based Systems Engineering (MBSE) brings different modelling viewpoints and tool chains under the umbrella of a single model repository that forms the basis of all development and analytical effort. Various flavours of MBSE have been proposed over the last two decades [12] that targeted the needs of systems development. The references listed here are mostly pertinent to safety critical civil aerospace development as to cover all topic domains within MBSE would require a more extensive review. However, even within the more restricted remit of safety critical aerospace systems and safety modelling there is a wide variety of approaches, with many based around particular languages (AltaRica [3,5, 13], SCADE/Lustre [10]), or around a modelling environment such as Matlab Simulink [15] in combination with other tools, such as HiP-Hops [16] or physical simulation environments such as Modelica or Simscape ([14,15]. The decision to adopt SysML as the modelling language for UltraFan was taken prior to our work starting on ENCASE.

SysML is an extension of the Unified Modelling Language (UML) that focuses on systems modelling. SysML supports the specification, analysis, design, verification and validation of a broad range of systems and systems-of-systems.[3]

---

[1] Part of Innovate UK's ENCASE (Enabling Novel Controls and Advanced Sensors for Engines) project.

[2] Dispatch refers to the engine's ability to carry a fault for given time before maintenance action is taken.

[3] This paper refers to the current Object Modelling Group (OMG) SysML v1.5, not the upcoming 2.0 standard. See http://www.omgsysml.org/.

However, 'support' in this sense is intended to mean a well-defined specification to describe the system, so that development and analysis can be performed using tools that take their data from a single model repository. This allows existing (perhaps certified) tools to be used provided that a means to export the data from the repository into a format the tool can use is made available. In order to do that, an input method must be provided that allows the critical information and knowledge capture of both system and safety concerns. Unfortunately while a graphical interface for system modelling is widely supported by tool vendors for SysML, a similar environment for safety analysts to model fault logic is rarely provided. Fault logic is typically modelled using a graphical representation of logic gates that traces the fault from base event to effect and which can contain additional information, such as failure rate, dispatch information and descriptive failure modes. A typical example is shown in Fig. 1 and the technique is defined in standards like IEC 61025 [9].

In 2017 the OMG issued a Request for Proposals on how to represent fault trees in SysML as part of the Safety and Reliability Analysis Profile for UML, which will extend the SysML language with "the capability to model safety information, such as hazards and the harms they may cause, model reliability analyses, including Fault Tree Analysis (FTA) and Failure Mode and Effects Analysis (FMEA), and use structured argument notation to organise the model and specify assurance cases" [2]. As part of this, an early profile for Fault Tree Analysis (FTA) and Failure Mode and Effects Analysis (FMEA) has been developed and published [2] and is likely to form part of SysML 2.0. However, while the new profile is moving in the right direction, it isn't sufficiently defined to be adopted for use on the development of UltraFan within Rolls-Royce and neither is it likely to support the specific requirements for Rolls-Royce to model engine dispatch availability. Our work attempts to bridge this current gap in SysML capability by providing a bespoke SysML profile to support Rolls-Royce's Fault Tree and Time Limited Dispatch (TLD) analyses.

1.3   ENCASE Project

ENCASE's initial starting point to model fault trees in SysML was an early paper from the National Aeronautics and Space Administration (NASA)'s Jet Propulsion Laboratory on fault protection modelling, which captured fault logic using UML (Unified modelling language) activity diagrams [6]. We investigated the potential of this approach but found issues with it. Firstly, while it is possible to model OR logic gates on activity diagrams using nodes, there is no provision for AND gate representation. The nature of the system redundancy provided by a dual channel FADEC (Full Authority Digital Engine Control) [11] means that modelling fault logic requires the use of AND gates (due to the possibility of the same function on both channels failing). Secondly activity diagrams were never intended to model fault trees, and trying to use them for that purpose inevitably brings compromises. At Rolls-Royce Controls, system engineers are already using activity diagrams to model system functions and incorporating safety model artefacts like fault logic gates using activity diagram notation would cause confusion and the potential for misunderstood syntax/semantics. Furthermore, at least as implemented in PTC's Integrity Manager, activities on activity diagrams become Call Behaviour Actions, which semantically seems an over specification for fault logic that is minimally expressed as set of fault propagation paths containing logic gates. Although there are other potential diagram types within SysML, none offer specific support for fault tree analysis and we decided we could best meet our needs by creating a bespoke diagram type.

There is also recent work investigating the formal translation of activity diagrams in UML/SysML to fault trees [7]. While this is a rigorous method, that entails a one to one correspondence between the two models, at this stage in the ENCASE project a more pragmatic approach is required due to the variety of ways engineers model activities. For example there are parts of activity diagrams, such as Join Nodes, that are semantically ambiguous and can be used/interpreted differently by users which would make automated translation difficult. However there is a more fundamental problem with attempting a direct translation, in that traditional fault logic models often contain quite abstract failure modes that will not have a corresponding entity in a functional model. For example system engineers may model functional behaviour that mitigates against a known hazard, but they are unlikely to model the *loss* of that function and its effect on the system. Therefore the fault tree may contain fault logic that cannot be linked to or directly translated from entities within activity diagrams. It may be possible to do a partially automated translation if both models were carefully constructed to reflect the same functional hierarchy and channel implementation. We discuss this possibility in more detail in Sect. 6.

The primary practical concern for the safety team was that the SysML fault tree models should be capable of modelling the system fault logic as it had been done historically and exporting it in a format where it could be analysed by their existing tools such as FaultTree+ (part of Isograph's Reliability Workbench suite). Their requirements were that the graphical user interface should be as close as possible to FaultTree+ and that the information kept in the SysML model should be the minimum required to export the fault logic for analysis. This made adapting some existing approaches, such as Component Based Fault Trees [1] unsuitable as they were felt to be too complex for what was needed, despite the requirement for modular fault trees. Being able to compose sub fault trees that can be joined to existing branches of fault logic for specific forms of analysis, such as time limited dispatch analysis, is supported via transfer gates and in this respect mirrors the functionality offered by FaultTree+.

2   Implementation

The current modelling environment for UltraFan is provided by PTC's Integrity Modeler (formerly Artisan) using SysML extended to aid efficient modelling of gas turbine controllers. A typical screenshot is shown in Fig. 2 and to date the software is mostly used to capture system specification through activity diagrams. In the left hand panel, below the activity diagrams in the package

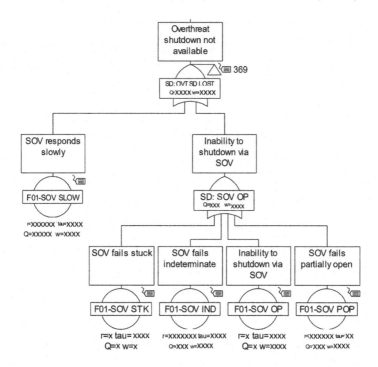

Fig. 1. Lower level of a fault tree showing base events with FMES (Failure Mode and Effects Summary) identifiers unique names as rendered by RWB's FaultTree+.

hierarchy can be seen the fault tree structures. Our initial trials showed that there are some user interface issues with very large fault trees being represented in a 'file browser' type format, as the user can quickly get lost scrolling through hundreds of gates. However, there are tools within PTC IM that allow a quick search between entities on the fault tree diagrams and their location with the package browser.

In order to bridge the gap between traditional safety engineering that uses separate models from the system engineers' models, and in a similar spirit to the OMG RFP mentioned earlier, we have drafted the first stage of our Model Based Safety Assurance (MBSA) profile that will in time allow the full integration of safety analysis models with existing system models. Our profile remains a work in progress and this part is sufficient to start to migrate the existing fault tree models into the SysML repository. Similar to SysML extensions in UML, the proposed Fault Tree Profile reuses a subset of UML 2.5 and provides a bespoke diagram type (an extension of structured diagram) and additional gate definitions to aid specific types of Fault Tree and dispatch analysis for Rolls-Royce. The initial version of our profile is detailed in [4] and the profile's entities and linkages are described in detail there. However, we have since released a new version with substantive changes, in particular the removal of 'failure modes' as

68   K. Clegg et al.

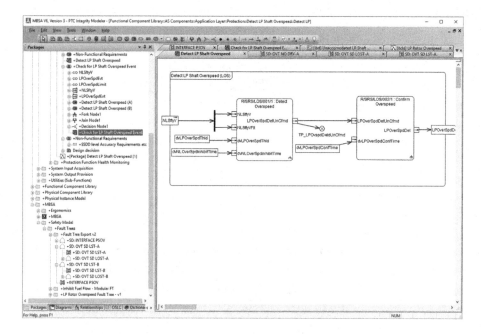

Fig. 2. Example of activity diagram modelled in PTC Integrity Modeler (formerly Artisan).

a first class entity, due to issues with the user interface and ease of export to analytical tools (see Sect. 3).

The main aim of the profile was to capture the minimum information needed to accurately export the fault logic to FaultTree+ and to ensure that a single specification was used to drive both safety and systems modelling. Using as lightweight a profile as possible means much of the FMES (Failure Modes and Effects Summary) base event and dispatch information does not need to be kept in the SysML model.[4] Instead, the events and gates have unique identifiers that is sufficient for the information associated with them to be extracted from the FMES database. The reason for this is that the FMES is quite large ($>$3K rows with many columns) and there has to be an explicit case made for bringing that information into the SysML model where it is less easy to keep it maintained and checked.

Therefore it is easiest when a new analysis is to be run to extract the summary failure rate data directly from the databases, while keeping the fault propagation logic, base and dispatch events within the SysML model. This is in keeping with our belief that the SysML model represents a knowledge repository, whereas the FMECA and FMES databases are designed to handle, import and export large amounts of data efficiently and are able to interface with a wide range of

---

[4] The FMES is a derived summary of the Failure mode, effects and criticality analysis (FMECA) database ($>$25K rows) which is maintained with the latest failure rates.

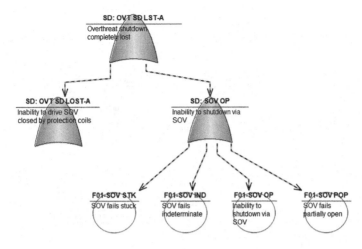

Fig. 3. Lower level of H01 (this is a top level hazard for turbine overspeed) fault tree showing OR gates and base events with FMES identifiers, as rendered by PTC Integrity Modeler using our Fault Tree SysML profile.

analytical tools. Figure 3 shows an example fault tree modelled using our profile in PTC Integrity Modeler. Removing the FMES data (which is not used by the safety analysts when modelling the fault logic—it is added by FaultTree+ by combining the failure rates of base events) gives a much cleaner interface. The gate descriptions or 'failure modes' are tags on both events and gates.

3   Changes to the Previous Fault Tree Profile for SysML

Version 1 of our profile is shown in [4] which describes in detail the profile's entities. However, due to user experience studies, we have had to make some fundamental changes to the profile and have further extended it with transfer gates, null gates and dispatch events (see Fig. 4) in order to accommodate the types of analysis for engine dispatchability that are specific to Rolls-Royce (civil aerospace). As engine dispatch analysis is a complex topic, we give a short summary in Sect. 4.

Our changes to the profile centre around the removal of 'failure modes' as a first class entity that could be linked to other parts of the SysML specification (see Fig. 3 that shows using gate descriptions as 'failure modes'). The motivation for having them as first class entities in the profile was to enable a more flexible traceability to derived safety requirements and to enable verification checks so that each failure mode was associated with a function and every function was associated with at least one failure mode. Unfortunately, user tests revealed that users would often 'copy and paste' failure mode instances when modelling dual channel functions (instead of creating unique failure modes for each channel). The effect of this was that the model would link that failure mode instance to both logic gates, so that it would end up with two inputs (one from each

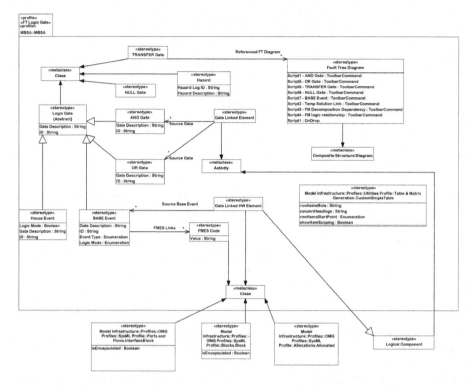

Fig. 4. Meta model of the proposed Fault Tree Profile, which will form part of a larger MBSA profile. The Fault Tree Diagram scripts are not part of the profile but serve to recreate a familiar user interface for safety analysts in PTC Integrity Modeller (PTC IM). The export script is not shown.

channel).[5] While the fault tree diagrams looked fine to the user, on exporting the fault tree logic to Reliability Workbench, it was realised that these failure modes had the wrong number of inputs to the next gate. Although this issue could perhaps have been addressed by suitable user training, it was felt that this was not particularly user friendly due to the linked inputs being effectively 'hidden' from the user (i.e. the additional links were not visible on the fault tree diagram).

The solution was to remove failure modes and instead consider them as 'human readable' descriptions of the logic gates in the fault tree. This simplified the model parsing for export and removed some of the 'clutter' of the fault tree diagrams. As most gates have a unique identification with respect to their channel, this reduced the possibility of the user creating 'hidden' links

---

[5] As explained later, a single gate with two inputs from either channel is possible where both channels access the same hardware component and therefore share the same fault logic. However, that is a specific case and is definitely not correct in the case of a duplicate control function running on each channel.

in the model by using an existing gate defined for another channel. There are exceptions to this, as there are hardware components that both channels use (such as the fuel shutoff valve) and for which there is a single set of associated base events and fault logic. In this case, the user must take care to define the gates and events that represent the shared hardware above the split in the fault tree branch that models the implementation of a specific channel's fault logic, so that both channels can have access to an instance of the gate or event on their respective branches of the fault tree. This ability to model the shared hardware for either channel or repeated instances of hardware is particularly important for common cause analysis.

3.1 Additional Extensions to the Profile

The rationale for creating a bespoke fault tree SysML profile is so that in-house modelling techniques and practices can be maintained with as little disruption or additional training as possible as the transition is made to MBSE. In the case of Rolls-Royce, a specific gate called a *TRANSFER gate* is used for linking sub trees (often stored in separate files) to branches of an existing fault tree. This means that sub fault trees that model shared system resources (such as hardware or network buses) can be built up into libraries and added to models as required. This has the advantage that if change needs to be made to a sub tree, it can be made once and the change will be reflected wherever that sub tree is used.

The second type is a variant of a base event termed a *House event* and this is used to model the presence of dispatch faults in certain configurations needed for dispatch analysis (see next section). House events as implemented in FaultTree+ are base events except that their logic mode is restricted to either true or false. Selecting them to TRUE (logic mode) incorporates the event into the analysis. Selecting the house event to FALSE removes it from the analysis. House events can be modelled under an OR gate or an AND gate dependent upon the system effect being modelled.

At Rolls-Royce Controls *NULL gates* are sometimes used above a house event as a type of neutral interface. NULL gates do nothing except pass the input onward, however they are more flexible than a direct input from a base event if changes are needed, as NULL gates can take an input another gate or subtree, whereas a base or house event cannot. House events are primarily of interest for engine dispatch analysis in order to satisfy the requirements of CS-E 1030 and the process is briefly described in the following section.[6]

4   Modelling Time Limited Dispatch

A FADEC system is designed to be fault tolerant so that many single faults lead to loss of redundancy rather than functionality. This enables airlines to

---

[6] See [8] for a detailed discussion on the Time Limited Dispatch requirements for more-electric gas turbine engines with respect to CS-E 1030.

operate engines with faults in the control system until a convenient place and time of repair is reached. At the end of each flight the on-condition maintenance ensures that the system provides a record of known faults (if any) and determines whether the faults within the system are sufficient to prohibit dispatch. If departure is allowed with known faults then in many cases a time limit is set for the repair to be carried out.

With respect to base event models and time limited dispatch, there are two types of maintenance policy:

– On-condition maintenance requires that a fault be repaired within a fixed period of time after a fault is detected. This is modelled using the time at risk model with all faults conservatively assumed repaired at the end of the allowable period.
– Fixed interval maintenance only repairs faults at one of a number of scheduled maintenance slots. When a fault is detected it is repaired at the next slot. This is modelled with the 'dormant' model with repair rate set to zero and the inspection interval set to the period between maintenance slots. Note, zero repair time is used since the safety models only consider flight time and the repairs effectively take no flight time (no repairs in flight!) regardless of the actual repair time on-ground.

Certain events do not have an associated control systems dispatch period and instead have an immediate effect. These are modelled as Do Not Dispatch (DND) faults and may be designated as initiating events. A number of event groups have been defined and these include an event group for each of the main exposure periods (i.e. DND, Short Time Dispatch (STD), Long Time Dispatch (LTD), Unlimited Dispatch (ULD), and Dormant) along with additional groups for any exposure periods that may arise that do not fall within the main categories. In general the dispatch period used for a base event should be that set by the dispatch status generated by that fault when it occurs while the system is in a 'full-up configuration'. This strategy gives the correct results for one or two fault cut sets. Issues may occur with three fault cut sets. The dispatch information is not kept in the SysML model, in keeping with our principle that the profile should be as lightweight as possible and that information is easier to maintain and manage via the FMES and FMECA databases.

There are three main aspects to the Fault Tree Analysis for Time limited Dispatch (TLD):

1. Fleet average rate calculation.
2. Specific rates for individual dispatchable configurations.
3. Cut set analysis to demonstrate that no hazardous event can be caused by a single control system fault in any dispatchable configuration.

The first is covered by setting exposure periods for base events. The second is covered by modelling dispatchable configurations using House Events. The house events are added for each Dispatchable Fault (DF) identified in the dispatch summary. These are added both to the individual main and sub-models, and their logic mode set FALSE. Each house event in turn is selected to TRUE and the model run, giving results for each dispatchable configuration. The third also uses the dispatchable fault house events. It involves setting their logic mode to basic to ensure they appear in cut sets and then examining the cut sets for all Hazardous events to ensure that there are no cut sets where both a dispatchable fault and a single control system fault occur. If such a cut set existed it would indicate that there is a dispatchable configuration where a single control system fault results in a hazardous event.

In FaultTree+ a base event can take three values for its logical mode—basic, true or false. A house event can only take either true or false, and therefore it is either part of tree as a dispatch fault that is 'on' or excluded as an input. This is a tool specific extension we include in profile so that export to FaultTree+ will support existing methods of analysis. If a different tool was being used for analysis, it would be possible to create a profile that extended the base event class to create a dispatchable fault that contained a simple boolean tag to indicate if it should be part of dispatchable configuration for analysis. The ability to extend profiles in this way to match the export needs of specific analytical tools is one of the great advantages of SysML.

In order to demonstrate compliance to the requirements of CS-E 1030 it is required to calculate the top event rates of the various hazards in each of the declared dispatchable configurations. To facilitate this analysis requires the addition of a number of dispatchable events to the fault trees in order to model degraded configurations. Previously this analysis was performed manually through the use of NULL gates that 'switched' house events to TRUE. However, as we discuss in the following section, thanks to the extensive automation interface provided with PTC IM, it will in future be possible to largely automate this configuration of this task using export scripts.

5   Using Scripts to Integrate Analytical Tools

Bringing together different engineering perspectives under the SysML umbrella is complicated by the established traditions and processes for those disciplines. Engineers get used to particular tool idiosyncrasies and work arounds, but more fundamentally they establish a level of trust through methods of working with the tools. In order that the migration process towards MBSE retains these trusted methods, accommodating existing analytical tools is essential. Fortunately, many tools allow import and export of data into spreadsheets or CSV (comma separated values) files. The current environment for modelling SysML at Rolls-Royce Controls is PTC's Integrity Manager (Fig. 5).

PTC's IM comes with an extensive automation interface that can use Visual Basic (VB) scripts to provide customisations to the user interface, to edit and change models and to export data via formats such Microsoft's Excel database. This facility has been of great benefit when creating the user interface for our bespoke fault tree diagram. For example, it was possible to replicate to a large extent the look and feel of FaultTree+, so that users could use familiar icons

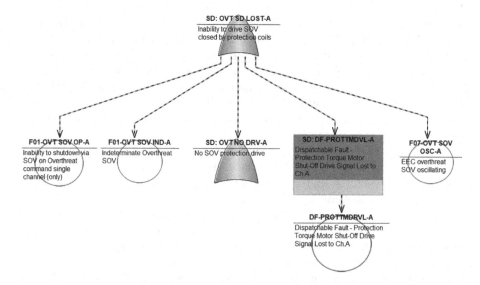

Fig. 5. Dispatch event shown with NULL gate. Export scripts can identify these events through Rolls-Royce's naming convention and enable them by setting their logical mode to TRUE and then exporting the fault logic for that dispatch configuration.

and graphic symbols in their diagrams. An example of additional functionality is to enable them to create new branches of the fault tree by double clicking on a gate with no inputs. This opens a new fault tree diagram if one does not already exist and the user can use the same gate instance on the new diagram to help readability. Furthermore the use of scripts can limit the types of action allowed on fault tree diagrams by prohibiting the wrong 'links' between entities or warn the user if the cardinality between entities is exceeded, it is even possible to perform look ups to match gate names against the FMES database. But the real value of scripts in the SysML model is allow exports to analytical tools.

5.1   Exporting Fault Tree Logic

By choosing a minimal capture of fault logic for the fault tree profile, the information required to extract for import into FaultTree+ is relatively easy to obtain. FaultTree+ requires fault logic imports to summarise two worksheets, one for base events and one for the gates and their inputs. Due to the automation interface, the data repository can easily parse all classes belonging to a package. In our case, the gates and events are extensions of classes and so these can be filtered from the data dictionary. The complexity comes from maintaining and identifying the dependents and dependees for each gate. The dependent relationship is the output of that gate into another gate. The dependee relationship is the inputs to that gate from other gates or events. A typical output is shown in Fig. 6. Once the fault logic has been imported, the analysis can be run as usual. The probability and exposure data behind the fault logic remains in the FMES and FMECA databases and can be extracted as needed into the SysML model or FaultTree+.

	Name	Type	Description	Input 0 Type and Name	Input 1 Type and Name	Input 2 T
1	Name	Type	Description	Input 0 Type and Name	Input 1 Type and Name	Input 2 T
2	SD: OVT SD LOST-A	OR	Inability to drive SOV closed by protection coils	E:F01-OVT SOV OP-A	E:F01-OVT SOV IND-A	G:SD: OV1
3	INT: SOVHSS OP-A	TRANSFER	SOV drive High Side Switch open due to EEC fault affecting multiple signals			
4	SD: OVT SOV OP-A	OR	Inability to energise SOV protection drive	E:F07-OVT SOV DRV OFF-A	G:INT: SOVHSS OP-A	G:INT: SO'
5	SD: OVT NO DRV-A	OR	No SOV protection drive	G:CON: PSOV INV-A	G:SD: OVT SOV OP-A	
6	CON: PSOV INV-A	TRANSFER	protection SOV drive signal lost due to harness / connector faults			
7	SD: OVT SD LOST-B	OR	Inability to drive SOV closed by protection coils	E:F01-OVT SOV OP-B	E:F01-OVT SOV IND-B	G:SD: OV1
8	INT: SOVHSS OP-B	TRANSFER	SOV drive High Side Switch open due to EEC fault affecting multiple signals			
9	SD: OVT SOV OP-B	OR	Inability to energise SOV protection drive	E:F07-OVT SOV DRV OFF-B	G:INT: SOVHSS OP-B	G:INT: SO'
10	SD: OVT NO DRV-B	OR	No SOV protection drive	G:CON: PSOV INV-B	G:SD: OVT SOV OP-B	
11	CON: PSOV INV-B	TRANSFER	protection SOV drive signal lost due to harness / connector faults			
12	SD: SOV OP	OR	Inability to shutdown via SOV	E:F01-SOV STK	E:F01-SOV IND	E:F01-SO'
13	SD: DF-PROTTMDVL-A	NULL	Dispatchable Fault - Protection Torque Motor Shut-Off Drive Signal Lost to Ch.A	E:DF-PROTTMDRVL-A		
14	SD: DF-PROTTMDRVL-B	NULL	Dispatchable Fault - Protection Torque Motor Shut-Off Drive Signal Lost to Ch.B	E:DF-PROTTMDRVL-B		
15	INT: SOVLSS OP-A	TRANSFER	SOV drive Low Side Switch open due to EEC fault affecting multiple signals			
16	INT: SOVLSS OP-B	TRANSFER	SOV drive Low Side Switch open due to EEC fault affecting multiple signals			
17	SD: INTERFACE PSOV	OR	Protection SOV	G:SD: OVT SD LST-A	G:SD: OVT SD LST-B	
18	SD: OVT SD LST-A	OR	Overthreat shutdown completely lost	G:SD: SOV OP	G:SD: OVT SD LOST-A	
19	SD: OVT SD LST-B	OR	Overthreat shutdown completely lost	G:SD: SOV OP	G:SD: OVT SD LOST-B	

Fig. 6. Export of gate logic to Excel worksheet. The fault logic is represented by the inputs to each gate (up to 17, including whether it came from an event or another gate) and the dependent gate (the gate that receives the output). The failure modes in the previous profile were replaced as descriptions of the gate. Although 25 columns in the worksheet for the gates are specified (and a similar number for events), the gate and base event unique IDs are sufficient for extracting additional information from the FMES/FMECA as needed to analyse dispatch configurations.

5.2   Automating the Dispatch Analysis

As explained in Sect. 4, dispatch analysis is carried out by selecting house events and setting them to TRUE in the fault tree and running the analysis. To date this has been a manual task, and quite a substantial one given the combination of dispatch configurations and events. However, now that information is in the SysML model, it can be parsed by scripts that can generate a set of dispatch configurations for export into FaultTree+. The dispatch status of each event is maintained in the FMES (Failure Mode and Effects Summary) database and can be extracted to create a list of dispatch configurations. The script loops through each configuration, and selectively generates an export containing each enabled dispatch event integrated into the fault logic as needed. These are then passed on to FaultTree+ and the analysis run as usual. Being able to automate the generation of fault logic for the different dispatch configurations represents a considerable saving of man hours.

6   Alignment of Safety and System Models

Advocates of MBSE are quick to point out the improved fidelity and efficiency of maintaining a single development model. However, as safety engineers have traditionally modelled their understanding of the system's fault logic with respect to a hazard independently of other system models, some abstract failure conditions may have little obvious connection to system functions. In such cases, a realignment and reassessment of failure modes may be necessary. For example safety engineers often model a system with respect to its redundancy and mitigation against a hazard, thus an analysis for a dual channel control system might query why the mitigation provided by the redundant channel has failed in addition to the channel in control. Contrast this with the system engineer's perspective, which is to consider an engine protection feature in its abstract specification first, then its implementation and finally how it is implemented on a respective channel. In the move towards using a single SysML model for all system development and analysis, little benefit is going to be gained unless concept and viewpoints on the system share a common understanding and reference points. For example, rather than the top level fault logic models starting by querying channel redundancy, they could follow where possible the functional hierarchy provided by the system engineers and instead consider redundancy at the level of channel implementation. Fault trees are often "richer" than system models in that they may have to include physical or external factors that lie outside the system's functional specification but are required to understand how that function could fail. In such cases it can seem there is little correspondence between the system and safety models, but such differences can be overcome by ensuring a flexible profile that allows links to hardware and activity models alike from the fault logic. Visibility of the associated fault logic for functions can then be provided to the system's engineers without the unnecessary addition of unrelated events that are present in the full fault tree.

7   Conclusions

In this paper we have sought to identify some of the benefits and problems when migrating system and safety modelling under the MBSE SysML umbrella. Through the use of lightweight bespoke profiles and user interface scripts, analysts gain familiar means to input their models into the SysML repository. The short term benefits are that analysts are able to continue with tried and trusted analytical methods by exporting data to existing tools, with the additional benefit of potentially time saving auto-generation of certain analyses such as dispatch configurations. However, longer term benefit requires a more significant shift towards a common understanding of how the system should be specified and analysed, so that system and safety engineers can cross-reference each others models and ensure better traceability from derived safety requirements. Looking longer term still, we can expect to see the OMG's SysML 2.0 safety profile solidify to give stricter semantics within meta-models, leading to the possibility that large parts of the fault logic could be auto-generated from system functions and hardware models.

References

1. Adler, R., et al.: Integration of component fault trees into the UML. In: Dingel, J., Solberg, A. (eds.) MODELS 2010. LNCS, vol. 6627, pp. 312–327. Springer, Heidelberg (2011). https://doi.org/10.1007/978-3-642-21210-9_30

2. Biggs, G., Juknevicius, T., Armonas, A., Post, K.: Integrating safety and reliability analysis into MBSE: overview of the new proposed OMG standard. In: INCOSE International Symposium, vol. 28, pp. 1322–1336, July 2018

3. Boiteau, M., Dutuit, Y., Rauzy, A., Signoret, J.P.: The AltaRica data-flow language in use: modeling of production availability of a multi-state system. Reliabil. Eng. Syst. Saf. **91**(7), 747–755 (2006). https://EconPapers.repec.org/RePEc:eee:reensy: v:91:y:2006:i:7:p:747-755

4. Clegg, K., Li, M., Stamp, D., Grigg, A., McDermid, J.: A SysML profile for fault trees-linking safety models to system design. In: Romanovsky, A., Troubitsyna, E., Bitsch, F. (eds.) SAFECOMP 2019. LNCS, vol. 11698, pp. 85–93. Springer, Cham (2019). https://doi.org/10.1007/978-3-030-26601-1_6

5. David, P., Idasiak, V., Kratz, F.: Automating the synthesis of AltaRica Data-Flow models from SysML. In: Proceedings of ESREL 2009, vol. 1, November 2009

6. Day, J., Murray, A., Meakin, P.: Toward a model-based approach to flight system fault protection. In: 2012 IEEE Aerospace Conference, pp. 1–17. IEEE (2012)

7. Dickerson, C.E., Roslan, R., Ji, S.: A formal transformation method for automated fault tree generation from a UML activity model. IEEE Trans. Reliab. **67**(3), 1219–1236 (2018)

8. Fletcher, S., Norman, P., Galloway, S., Burt, G.: Impact of engine certification standards on the design requirements of More-Electric Engine electrical system architectures. SAE Int. J. Aerosp. **7**(1), 24–34 (2014)

9. IEC 61025: Fault tree analysis (FTA): Standard, International Electrotechnical Commission, Geneva, CH, August 2006

10. Joshi, A., Heimdahl, M.P.E.: Model-based safety analysis of simulink models using SCADE design verifier. In: Winther, R., Gran, B.A., Dahll, G. (eds.) SAFECOMP 2005. LNCS, vol. 3688, pp. 122–135. Springer, Heidelberg (2005). https://doi.org/10.1007/11563228_10

11. Li, M., Batmaz, F., Guan, L., Grigg, A., Ingham, M., Bull, P.: Model-based systems engineering with requirements variability for embedded real-time systems. In: 2015 IEEE International Model-Driven Requirements Engineering Workshop (MoDRE), pp. 1–10, August 2015. https://doi.org/10.1109/MoDRE.2015.7343874

12. Lisagor, O., Kelly, T., Niu, R.: Model-based safety assessment: review of the discipline and its challenges. In: The Proceedings of 2011 9th International Conference on Reliability, Maintainability and Safety, pp. 625–632, June 2011. https://doi.org/10.1109/ICRMS.2011.5979344

13. Rauzy, A., Blériot-Fabre, C.: Model-based safety assessment: rational and trends. In: 2014 10th France-Japan/8th Europe-Asia Congress on Mecatronics, MECA-TRONICS 2014, Tokyo, pp. 1–10, November 2014. https://doi.org/10.1109/MECATRONICS.2014.7018626

14. Schallert, C.: Automated safety analysis by minimal path set detection for multi-domain object-oriented models. Math. Comput. Model. Dyn. Syst. **23**(3), 341–360 (2017). https://doi.org/10.1080/13873954.2017.1298624

15. Shao, N., Zhang, S., Liang, H.: Model-based safety analysis of a control system using Simulink and Simscape extended models. In: MATEC Web of Conferences, vol. 139, p. 00219 (2017). https://doi.org/10.1051/matecconf/201713900219

16. Sorokos, I., Papadopoulos, Y., Azevedo, L., Parker, D., Walker, M.: Automating allocation of development assurance levels: an extension to HiP-HOP. IFAC-PapersOnLine **48**(7), 9–14 (2015). 5th IFAC International Workshop on Dependable Control of Discrete Systems

FDS-ML: A New Modeling Formalism for Probabilistic Risk and Safety Analyses

Liu Yang[(⊠)] and Antoine Rauzy

Department of Mechanical and Industrial Engineering (MTP),
Norwegian University of Science and Technology (NTNU),
Trondheim, Norway
liu.yang@ntnu.no

Abstract. In this article, we present FDS-ML, a new modeling formalism dedicated to probabilistic risk and safety analyse. FDS-ML relies on the notion of finite degradation structures, an algebraic framework recently introduced by the authors. FDS-ML provides a simple and clear way to design combinatorial models.

The assessment of FDS-ML models relies on the decision diagram technology. Classical concepts defined for fault trees, such as those of minimal cutsets, availability, reliability and importance measures, can be lifted up to finite degradation structures and computed by means of decision diagram algorithms.

The article aims at presenting the most important ideas underlying FDS-ML and its implementation. It illustrates the practical interest of the proposed approach by means of a case study stemmed from the ISO/TR 12489 standard.

Keywords: Probabilistic risk and safety analyses · Modeling language · Finite degradation structures · Combinatorial models · Decision diagrams

1 Introduction

Probabilistic risk and safety analyses are used in virtually all industries to determine whether the risk of operating complex technical systems (aircraft, nuclear power plants, offshore platforms...) is low enough to be socially acceptable. A large number of modeling formalisms have been proposed to carry out these analyses. They can be roughly split into two categories: combinatorial formalisms and stochastic discrete event systems. The first category gathers Boolean formalisms such as fault trees [11], reliability block diagrams [4] as well as so-called multistate systems [12]. In combinatorial formalisms, the state of the system is described as a combination of the states of its components. The second category gathers formalisms such as Markov chains, stochastic Petri nets, stochastic automata networks as well as high level modeling languages such as AltaRica 3.0 [1]. They provide analysts with a much higher expressive power than the former,

© Springer Nature Switzerland AG 2019
Y. Papadopoulos et al. (Eds.): IMBSA 2019, LNCS 11842, pp. 78–92, 2019.
https://doi.org/10.1007/978-3-030-32872-6_6

but the price to pay is a dramatic increase of the computational complexity of assessments.

Finite degradation structures (FDS) have been recently introduced by the authors as a unified algebraic framework for combinatorial models [13,14]. FDS generalize existing combinatorial formalisms (both for Boolean and multistate systems) at no algorithmic cost. Classical concepts defined for fault trees— minimal cutsets, availability, reliability, importance measures,... —can be lifted up to FDS.

FDS-ML is a small domain specific modeling language designed on top of FDS. It makes it possible to define domains (finite degradation structures), operators, variables, formulas and eventually sets of equations.

We developed a prototype assessment engine for FDS-ML models. Algorithms implemented in this prototype rely on the decision diagram technology. As fault trees, the assessment process works in two steps: first, a decision diagram is built for the (equivalent of the) top event of the model. Second minimal cutsets and probabilistic indicators are calculated by traversing this diagram.

This article aims at presenting theoretical foundations of FDS-ML, as well as the current version of the language. It describes also assessment algorithms. Finally, it shows the interest of the proposed approach by means of a use case stemmed from the ISO/TR 12489 standard [6].

The remainder of this article is structured as follows. Section 2 introduces the use case we shall throughout the article to illustrate the concepts and algorithms. Section 3 presents FDS. Section 4 presents the language FDS-ML. Section 5 describes assessment algorithms and the data structures they rely on. Section 6 presents some experimental results obtained on the case study. Finally, Sect. 7 concludes the article.

2 Illustrative Use Case

2.1 Presentation

Safety instrumented systems (SIS) are designed to keep an equipment under control in a safe state when some abnormal conditions occur. As illustrative use case, we shall consider the TA4 system of ISO/TR 12489 [6], which pictured Fig. 1.

The objective of this SIS is to protect a pipe section from overpressures. It involves seven main components: three sensors (S1, S2 and S3), two logic solvers (LS1 and LS2) and two actuators (the isolation valves V1 and V2) which are activated via the solenoid valves (SV1, SV2 and SV3). When the sensors detect an overpressure in the protected section, the logic solvers send a control signal to the solenoid valves which close isolation valves so to release the pressure. The logic solver LS2 works according to a 1-out-of-2 logic, i.e. that it sends the order to close the valves if at least one out of two sensors S2 and S3 detects an overpressure.

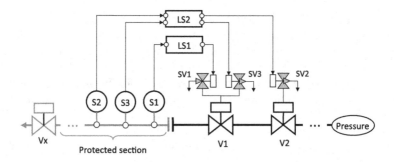

Fig. 1. Architecture of the safety instrumented system in TA4 of ISO/TR 12489

According to the standard IEC61508 [5], failure modes of the components of a SIS can be classified along two directions: safe versus dangerous failure modes and detected versus undetected failure modes.

In our example, safe failure modes are those which contribute to close the isolation valves, even though there is no overpressure (spurious triggers), while dangerous faire modes are those which contribute to keep the isolation valves open, even though there is an overpressure. Logic solvers embed autotest facilities so that their failures are immediately detected. On the contrary, failure of valves remain undetected between two maintenance interventions. Failures of sensors may be detected or not.

ISO/TR 12489 makes the additional following assumptions.

- The three solenoid valves are perfectly reliable.
- All other components may fail (independently). Their probabilities of failure follow negative exponential distributions. The parameters of these distributions are given Table 1. Safe failures are always detected.
- The system is maintained once a year (once in 8760 h). The production is stopped during the maintenance. Components are as good as new after the maintenance.

Table 1. TA4 reliability parameters

Parameter	Sensor	Logic solver	Isolation valve
Dangerous undetected failure rate	$3.0 \times 10^{-7}\,h^{-1}$	NA	$2.9 \times 10^{-6}\,h^{-1}$
Dangerous detected failure rate	$3.0 \times 10^{-5}\,h^{-1}$	$6.0 \times 10^{-7}\,h^{-1}$	NA
Safe failure rate	$3.0 \times 10^{-5}\,h^{-1}$	$3.0 \times 10^{-5}\,h^{-1}$	2.9×10^{-4}

It is not possible to compare safe failures and dangerous failures, because the risk they represent, both in terms of frequency of occurrence and severity of consequences, are very different On the one hand, spurious triggers of SIS have a strong economic impact, but indeed no impact on safety. On the other hand, dangerous failures have an impact on safety. If they remain undetected, they may lead to a catastrophic accident.

2.2 Modeling

According to what precedes, we shall consider three failure modes: safe-failure, dangerous-detected-failure and dangerous-undetected-failure.

Usually, the different failure modes are analysed one-by-one. In our case, this means that one would design a dedicated fault tree to describe safe-failures of the system, another one for dangerous-detected-failures and a third one for dangerous-undetected-failures.

The modeling framework presented in this article makes it possible to study different failure modes by means of a unique model. This model makes in turn possible to study, for instance, the combination of a safe-failure of a sensor and a dangerous-detected-failure of a valve. To the best of authors' knowledge, such combinations have not been formally defined in the standard nor in any other previous work.

We can read Fig. 1 as a block diagram. Each component can be seen as a basic block, with an internal state, some input and some output flows. Failures propagates through the block diagram. Therefore, both states and flows may take one of the four values: W (working), safe-failure (Fs), dangerous-detected-failure (Fdd) and dangerous-undetected-failure (Fdu).

Two fundamental operations are performed on states and flows: series composition, denoted by $\ominus$, and parallel composition, denoted by $\|$. These operators are defined Table 2.

Table 2. Definition of $\ominus$ and $\|$

$u \ominus v$		v			
		W	Fs	Fdd	Fdu
	W	W	Fs	Fdd	Fdu
u	Fs	Fs	Fs	Fdd	Fdd
	Fdd	Fdd	Fs	Fdd	Fdd
	Fdu	Fdu	Fs	Fdd	Fdu

$u \| v$		v			
		W	Fs	Fdd	Fdu
	W	W	Fs	W	W
u	Fs	Fs	Fs	Fs	Fs
	Fdd	W	Fs	Fdd	Fdu
	Fdu	W	Fs	Fdu	Fdu

It is easy to verify that the series operator $\ominus$ is not commutative but associative and that the parallel operator $\|$ is both commutative and associative.

Using $\ominus$ and $\|$, the model for the whole SIS could be as sketched Fig. 2.

In the remaining part of this article, we shall study how to implement the above ideas in the framework of FDS-ML.

$S1.in := W$	$S1.out := S1.in \ominus S1.state$
$S2.in := W$	$S2.out := S2.in \ominus S2.state$
$S3.in := W$	$S3.out := S3.in \ominus S3.state$
$LS1.in := S1.out$	$LS1.out := LS1.in \ominus LS1.state$
$LS2.in := S2.out \parallel S3.out$	$LS2.out := LS2.in \ominus LS2.state$
$V1.in := LS1.out \parallel LS2.out$	$V1.out := V1.in \ominus V1.state$
$V2.in := LS2.out$	$V2.out := V2.in \ominus V2.state$
$SIS := V1.out \parallel V2.out$	

Fig. 2. Model for the SIS TA4 of ISO/TR 12489

3   Finite Degradation Structures

3.1   Definition

Finite degradation structures rely on the algebraic notion partially ordered sets.

A *partially ordered set* (poset) is pair $\langle D, \sqsubseteq \rangle$, where D is a set and $\sqsubseteq$ is a binary relation over D, such that $\forall a, b, c \in D$:

- $a \sqsubseteq a$ (*Reflexivity*);
- if $a \sqsubseteq b$ and $b \sqsubseteq c$, then $a \sqsubseteq c$ (*Transitivity*);
- if $a \sqsubseteq b$ and $b \sqsubseteq a$, then $a = b$ (*Antisymmetry*).

A *finite degradation structure* is such poset $\langle D, \sqsubseteq \rangle$. The elements in D represent the states of a component, while the partial order $\sqsubseteq$ represents the *degradation order* amongst these states, interpreted informally as "less or equally degraded than". For instance, a working state W is less degraded than the failed state F, therefore $W \sqsubset F$.

We require moreover the poset $\langle D, \sqsubseteq \rangle$ to have a unique least element, denoted $\bot$, that represents the initial working state. In other words, a finite degradation structure is a *(meet-)semi-lattice*.

Four FDS are graphically represented Fig. 3. These diagrams are called Hasse diagrams. Vertices represent states and the relation $a \sqsubset b$ is represented by drawing as a line segment that goes upward from a to b. For simplicity, we name the FDS in (a), (b), (c) and (d) by **WF**, **WDF**, **SWF** and **W3F**.

W3F is essentially the FDS we used Sect. 2. Its least element is the working state W. The degradation order is described by the inequalities $W \sqsubset Fs$, $W \sqsubset Fdd$ and $Fdd \sqsubset Fdu$. Fs is incomparable with Fdd and Fdu since they correspond to radically different situations. We have $Fdd \sqsubset Fdu$ because an undetected failure is always more dangerous than a detected one.

W3F is indeed not the only way to describe the states of SIS.

3.2   Products and Abstractions

Let $\mathcal{S} : \langle D_S, \sqsubseteq_S, \bot_S \rangle$ and $\mathcal{T} : \langle D_T, \sqsubseteq_T, \bot_T \rangle$ be two FDS. Then the product $\mathcal{S} \otimes \mathcal{T}$ of $\mathcal{S}$ and $\mathcal{T}$ is the FDS $\langle D, \sqsubseteq, \bot \rangle$ such that,

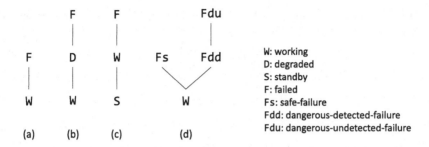

Fig. 3. Graphical representation of FDS.

- $D = D_S \times D_T$, where $\times$ stands for the Cartesian product.
- $\forall \langle x_S, x_T \rangle, \langle y_S, y_T \rangle \in D, \langle x_S, x_T \rangle \sqsubseteq \langle y_S, y_T \rangle \Leftrightarrow x_S \sqsubseteq_S y_S \wedge x_T \sqsubseteq_T y_T$.
- $\perp = \langle \perp_S, \perp_T \rangle$.

Let $\mathcal{R}, \mathcal{S}, \mathcal{T}$ be three FDS. It is easy to check that $\mathcal{R} \otimes \mathcal{S}$ and $\mathcal{S} \otimes \mathcal{R}$ on the one hand, $\mathcal{R} \otimes (\mathcal{S} \otimes \mathcal{T})$ and $(\mathcal{R} \otimes \mathcal{S}) \otimes \mathcal{T}$ on the other hand are equal up to an isomorphism. In this sense, the product of FDS is commutative and associative.

Let $\mathcal{S} : \langle D_S, \sqsubseteq_S, \perp_S \rangle$ and $\mathcal{T} : \langle D_T, \sqsubseteq_T, \perp_T \rangle$ be two FDS, then $\mathcal{T}$ is an *abstraction* of $\mathcal{S}$, which is denoted $\mathcal{S} \twoheadrightarrow \mathcal{T}$, if there exists a surjective structure preserving mapping from $\mathcal{S}$ to $\mathcal{T}$, i.e. a function $\varphi : \mathcal{S} \rightarrow \mathcal{T}$ such that:

- $x \sqsubseteq_S y \Rightarrow \varphi(x) \sqsubseteq_T \varphi(y)$ for all $x, y \in D_S$.
- $\varphi(\perp_S) = \perp_T$.
- $\forall y \in D_T, \exists x \in D_S$ such that $\varphi(x) = y$.

Let $\mathcal{R}, \mathcal{S}, \mathcal{T}$ be three FDS. It is easy to check that if $\mathcal{R} \twoheadrightarrow \mathcal{S}$ and $\mathcal{S} \twoheadrightarrow \mathcal{T}$ then $\mathcal{R} \twoheadrightarrow \mathcal{T}$ (the composition of abstraction is an abstraction).

Taken together products and abstractions make possible to define the state of a system as a combination of the states of its component.

3.3 Finite Degradation Models

Let **O** be a set of operators defined over finite degradation structures and let **V** be a set of variables. We assume that each variable v of **V** takes its value into some finite degradation structure, called the domain of v and denoted dom(v).

Formulas over **O** and **V** are built as usual, verifying that they are well-typed, i.e. that each operator has the correct number of arguments and that its arguments are of the correct types.

We denote by var(f) the set of variables showing up in the formula f.

From now, we shall assume that **V** is decomposed into two distinct subsets **S** and **F**, i.e. $\mathbf{V} = \mathbf{S} \uplus \mathbf{F}$. Variables of **S** and **F** are called respectively state and flow variables. State variables play the role of basic events in fault trees while flow variables play the role of intermediated events.

A *finite degradation model* (FDM) ϕ over $\mathbf{O}$ and $\mathbf{V}$ is a set of equations of the form:

$$\phi : \left\{ \begin{array}{l} w_1 := f_1 \\ w_2 := f_2 \\ \quad \vdots \\ w_n := f_n \end{array} \right\} \tag{1}$$

such that:

- the w_i's are variables of $\mathbf{F}$;
- the f_i's are well-typed formulas over $\mathbf{O}$ and $\mathbf{V}$;
- for any $w \in \mathbf{F}$, there is exactly one equation $w := f$ in the set whose left hand side member is w. We say that this equation defines w and that f is the definition of w.

Let w be a flow variable defined by the equation $w := f$ and let v be a variable. We say that f depends on the variable v if either $v \in \text{var}(f)$ or there is a flow variable $u \in \text{var}(f)$ such that u depends on v.

A finite degradation model is data-flow if no variable depend on itself. In the sequel, we shall only consider data-flow models.

The set of equations presented Fig. 2 is thus a finite degradation model. The variables $X.state$ are state variables and the variables $X.in$ and $X.out$ are flow variables. All of the variables of this model take their values into the finite degradation structure $\mathbf{W3F}$.

A finite degradation model over $\mathbf{O}$ and $\mathbf{V} = \mathbf{S} \uplus \mathbf{F}$ can thus be interpreted as a function from $\bigotimes_{v \in \mathbf{S}} \text{dom}(v)$ into $\bigotimes_{w \in \mathbf{F}} \text{dom}(w)$ (the data-flow property warranties that this construction is possible and uniquely defined).

If operators are correctly chosen, i.e. if they are abstractions, then the model itself is an abstraction.

It is easy to verify that both operators $\oslash$ and $\parallel$ are abstractions. Therefore the model presented Fig. 2 can be seen as an abstraction $(\mathbf{W3F})^7 \twoheadrightarrow (\mathbf{W3F})^{15}$, as it involves 7 state variables and 15 flow variables.

3.4   Minimal Cutsets

Let $\mathbf{M}$ be a finite degradation model built over $\mathbf{O}$ and $\mathbf{V} = \mathbf{S} \uplus \mathbf{F}$.

Conventionally, we call the flow variable on which the current analysis is focused on the *observer* of the analysis. Observers play the role of top-events in fault trees.

Let $w \in \mathbf{F}$ be the observer of the analysis. According to w, the model $\mathbf{M}$ can be interpreted as an abstraction $\phi|_w : \bigotimes_{v \in \mathbf{S}} \text{dom}(v) \twoheadrightarrow \text{dom}(w)$. Then, $\forall\, y \in \text{dom}(w)$, we define the set of *cutsets* of w for y, denoted by $\mathbf{CS}(w, y)$, as follows.

$$\mathbf{CS}(w, y) \stackrel{def}{=} \{\overline{v} | \overline{v} \in \bigotimes_{v \in \mathbf{S}} \text{dom}(v), \phi|_w(\overline{v}) = y\} \tag{2}$$

A cutset $\mathbf{CS}(w, y)$ represents a combination of the states of components that leads the state of the observer w to be y. Therefore, the set of *minimal cutsets*, denoted by $\mathbf{MCS}(w, y)$, is defined as follows:

$$\mathbf{MCS}(w, y) \stackrel{def}{=} \{\overline{\mathbf{v}} \in \mathbf{CS}(w, y), \nexists \overline{\mathbf{u}} \in \mathbf{CS}(w, y), \overline{\mathbf{u}} \sqsubset \overline{\mathbf{v}}\} \tag{3}$$

The minimality of cutsets is captured by the degradation order defined in $\bigotimes_{v \in \mathbf{S}} \mathrm{dom}(v)$. In this sense, a minimal cutset of w and y represents one of the least degraded composition of components' states that degrades the state of the observer w from its least element $\bot$ to y. The extension of the concept of minimal cutsets from Boolean systems into multistate systems is one of the most important contributions of FDS.

3.5 Probabilistic Indicators

Let $\mathcal{S} : \langle D, \sqsubseteq, \bot \rangle$ be a FDS. We can equip $\mathcal{S}$ with a probability measure p, i.e. a function $p : D \to [0, 1]$ such that $\sum_{d \in D} p(d) = 1$.

The probability measure could also be a function of time, i.e. $p : D \times \mathbb{R}^+ \to [0, 1]$, where $p(d, t)$ represents the probability of being in the state $d \in D$ at time $t \in \mathbb{R}^+$. However, as it makes no difference in terms computationally speaking, we keep the above simplest definition.

Now, let $\mathcal{S} : \langle D_S, \sqsubseteq_S, \bot_S \rangle$ and $\mathcal{T} : \langle D_T, \sqsubseteq_T, \bot_T \rangle$ be two FDS equipped respectively with probability measures p_S and p_T.

Then, their product $\mathcal{S} \otimes \mathcal{T}$ can be equipped with the natural probability measure p defined as follows. $\forall \langle x, y \rangle \in D_S \times D_T$,

$$p(\langle x, y \rangle) \stackrel{def}{=} p_S(x) \times p_T(y)$$

It is easy to verify that p is actually a probability measure on $\mathcal{S} \otimes \mathcal{T}$. Its construction assumes indeed that the events represented by $\mathcal{S}$ and $\mathcal{T}$ are statistically independent.

Let $\mathcal{S} : \langle D_S, \sqsubseteq_S, \bot_S \rangle$ and $\mathcal{T} : \langle D_T, \sqsubseteq_T, \bot_T \rangle$ be two FDS. Assume that $\mathcal{S}$ is equipped with p_S and that $\mathcal{T}$ is an abstraction of $\mathcal{S}$. Then, the natural probability measure p_T is defined as follows. $\forall y \in D_T$

$$p_T(y) = \sum_{x \in \varphi^{-1}\{y\}} p_S(x)$$

The above two natural constructions make it possible to lift-up probabilistic indicators defined for fault trees to finite degradation models.

4   FDS-ML

FDS-ML stands for Finite Degradation Structures - Modeling Language. In its current version, which is purely textual, this small domain specific modeling language provides constructs to declare domains (finite degradation structures) and operators on the one hand, state and flow variables and equations on the other hand. We shall review these constructs in turn.

4.1 Domains and Operators

The syntax of FDS-ML is rather straightforward and is strongly inspired from the one of AltaRica 3.0 [1]. Therefore, we shall present it on example.

Figure 4 shows the FDS-ML code that declares the FDS **W3F** and the operators $\ominus$ and $\parallel$ involved in the model described Fig. 2.

```
 1  domain W3F {W, Fs, Fdd, Fdu} (W<Fs, W<Fdd, Fdd<Fdu)
 2
 3  operator series(W3F, W3F) return W3F
 4       *, W -> *
 5       *, Fs -> Fs
 6       *, Fdd -> Fdd
 7       W, Fdu -> Fdu
 8       Fs, Fdu -> Fdd
 9       Fdd, Fdu -> Fdd
10       Fdu, Fdu -> Fdu
11  end
12
13  operator parallel(W3F, W3F) return W3F
14       W, * -> W
15       Fs, * -> Fs
16       *, Fs -> Fs
17       *, W -> W
18       Fdd, Fdd -> Fdd
19       Fdd, Fdu -> Fdu
20       Fdu, Fdd -> Fdu
21       Fdu, Fdu -> Fdu
22  end
```

Fig. 4. Declarations of the FDS **W3F** and the operators $\ominus$ and $\parallel$.

The declaration **W3F** is self-explanatory.

The declaration of operators is just a bit more tricky. The first part consists in giving a name to the operator, and to declare the type of its arguments and its output. In the current version of FDS-ML, operators can return only one value.

The body of the declaration is a list of statements that are read in order. The first one that matches the values of the argument is taken. * matches any value.

Declarations of domains and operators can be reused from model to model. One of our objectives is to develop domain specific libraries of such declarations.

4.2 Variables and Equations

In FDS-ML, a model is declared as a **block**, i.e. a prototype in the sense of object-oriented theory.

```
1   block TA4
2       W3F S1.state, S2.state, S3.state (W=..., Fs=..., Fdd=...)
3       W3F S1.in, S1.out, S2.in, S2.out, S3.in, S3.out
4       ...
5       assertion
6           S1.in := W
7           S1.out := series(S1.in, S1.state)
8           ...
9           SIS := parallel(V1.out, V2.out)
10      observer top = SIS
11  end
```

Fig. 5. Model of the SIS TA4 of ISO/TR 12489 written in FDS-ML.

This block is made of two parts: first variables are declared, then equations are given. Figure 5 sketches the model of the SIS.

The FDM for the SIS, as written in FDS-ML, is given in Fig. 5. The domains (i.e. FDSs) and the operators should be defined separately before use. The model is written in the part of **block**, where state variables should be declared and assigned with probabilities in parentheses (W=..., Fs=..., Fdd=...). Formulas are written in the part of **assertion** and the **observer** should be declared right after.

5 Algorithms

The implementation of FDS-ML is programmed in Python. Only the main algorithms are presented in this section.

In the implementation, formulas are encoded by binary trees, which is the same as fault trees. The leaves of a formula tree are state variables. Each internal node $(\Diamond, f_l, f_r)$ encodes the formula $f_l \Diamond f_r$.

The *decision diagram* (DD) used in this article is a particular type of binary decision diagrams (BDD) that represent multi-valued functions in binary way [7,8]. Algorithms presented in this article is similar to those for BDD.

In the DD in this article, each internal node (s, v, n_d, n_r) is labelled with state s, variable v, down-child n_d and right-child n_r. The terminal node $(s, /, /, /)$ is only labelled with state s.

The DD is built for the top of a formula.

If the formula contains only a variable v without any operator, its DD is called a one-level DD. The one-level DD of v such that $dom(v) = \mathbf{W3F}$ is shown in Fig. 6. For every $s \in dom(v)$, we create an internal node (s, v, n_d, n_r) where n_d represents the resulting node if $v = s$. These internal nodes are connected successively by their right-child n_r in a chain. We fix the order of states in such chain for a given variable v.

The algorithms of building DD for formulas are given in Fig. 7. The input of BuildDD is the node of formula tree. The function n.IsTermi() returns true if n is a terminal node while n.IsInter() is true if n is a internal node.

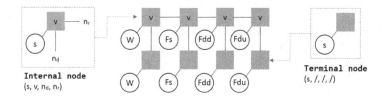

Fig. 6. The one-level DD of v such that $\mathrm{dom}(v) = \mathbf{W3F}$.

Note that the `Combine` algorithms, as well as the `Prob` algorithms in Fig. 9, use caching [3]. Caching makes it possible to not redo an operation that has been already done.

$\texttt{BuildDD}(v)$	$\leftarrow \texttt{One-Level-DD}\ v$	if v is a state variable
$\texttt{BuildDD}((\Diamond, f_1, f_2))$	$\leftarrow \texttt{Operate}(\Diamond, n_1, n_2)$	
	$n_1 \leftarrow \texttt{BuildDD}(f_1)$	
	$n_2 \leftarrow \texttt{BuildDD}(f_2)$	
$\texttt{Operate}(\Diamond, n_1, n_2)$	$\leftarrow \texttt{Combine}(\Diamond, n_1, n_2)$	if $n_1.\texttt{IsInter}()$ and $n_2.\texttt{IsInter}()$
	$\leftarrow \texttt{Value}(\Diamond, n_1, n_2)$	if $n_1.\texttt{IsTermi}()$ and $n_2.\texttt{IsTermi}()$
	$\leftarrow (n_1.s, n_1.v, n_d, n_r)$	if $n_1.\texttt{IsInter}()$ and $n_2.\texttt{IsTermi}()$
	$n_d \leftarrow \texttt{Operate}(\Diamond, n_1.n_d, n_2)$	
	$n_r \leftarrow \texttt{Operate}(\Diamond, n_1.n_r, n_2)$	
	$\leftarrow (n_2.s, n_2.v, n_d, n_r)$	if $n_1.\texttt{IsTermi}()$ and $n_2.\texttt{IsInter}()$
	$n_d \leftarrow \texttt{Operate}(\Diamond, n_1, n_2.n_d)$	
	$n_r \leftarrow \texttt{Operate}(\Diamond, n_1, n_2.n_r)$	
$\texttt{Combine}(\Diamond, n_1, n_2)$	$\leftarrow \texttt{Combine}(\Diamond, n_2, n_1)$	if $v_2 \prec v_1$
	$\leftarrow (n_1.s, n_1.v, n_d, n_r)$	otherwise
	$n_r \leftarrow \texttt{Operate}(\Diamond, n_1.n_r, n_2)$	
	$n_d \leftarrow \texttt{Operate}(\Diamond, n_1.n_d, n')$	
	$\quad n' \leftarrow n_2 \quad$ if $v_1 \prec v_2$	
	$\quad \leftarrow n_2.n_d$ if $v_1 = v_2$	
$\texttt{Value}(\Diamond, n_1, n_2)$	$\leftarrow (s, /, /, /)$	
	$s \leftarrow \Diamond(n_1.s, n_2.s)$	The value assignment by $\Diamond$

Fig. 7. Recursive algorithm of building DD for formulas.

The symbol $\prec$ in the algorithm represents the variable ordering of DD. It is worth noting that if all the operators used in the model are commutative, then the variable ordering is arbitrary. Otherwise, for instance $u \ominus v$, the local ordering of u, v should be $u \prec v$. Note that only the state variables in the model need to be ordered.

Figure 8 shows the DD built for $u \ominus v$, where $\text{dom}(u) = \text{dom}(v) = \textbf{W3F}$.

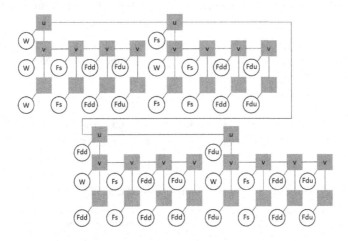

Fig. 8. DD of the formula $u \ominus v$, where $\text{dom}(u), \text{dom}(v) = \textbf{W3F}$.

Once the DD is built, we can calculate the probabilistic indicators for the flow variable defined by the formula associated to this DD. The algorithms are given in Fig. 9. For any internal node $n = (s, v, n_d, n_r)$, $p_n = p(s) \in [0, 1]$ where $s \in \text{dom}(v)$ and p is the probability measure defined in $\text{dom}(v)$.

$\texttt{Prob}(n, y) \leftarrow 0$	if $n.\texttt{IsTermi}()$ and $n.s \neq y$
$\leftarrow 1$	if $n.\texttt{IsTermi}()$ and $n.s = y$
$\leftarrow p_n \times \texttt{Prob}(n.n_d, y) + \texttt{Prob}(n.n_r, y)$	if $n.\texttt{IsInter}()$

Fig. 9. Algorithms of calculating probabilities from DD.

6   Experiments

In this section, we provide the assessment results of the model of SIS presented in Sect. 2.

The flow variable SIS of the model in Fig. 2 is selected as the observer of the analysis.

The variable ordering in this case is not arbitrary as $\ominus$ is not commutative. According to the model in Fig. 2, we select a valid variable ordering: $S1.state \prec LS1.state \prec V1.state \prec S2.state \prec S3.state \prec LS2.state \prec V2.state$.

As inputs, the state probabilities of each type of the components are calculated according to the failure rates given in Table 1. For those with NA (not applicable), the probability is set to be zero.

The calculation results of the number of cutsets $|\textbf{CS}(SIS, y)|$ and the number of minimal cutsets $|\textbf{MCS}(SIS, y)|$ for each state $y \in \text{dom}(SIS)$ are given in Table 3.

As illustration, the seven minimal cutsets in **MCS**(SIS, Fdd) are listed in Table 4, which are the least degraded scenarios that SIS is degraded from W to Fdd.

Table 3. The number of cutsets $|\mathbf{CS}(SIS, y)|$ and minimal cutsets $|\mathbf{MCS}(SIS, y)|$ for each state $y \in dom(SIS)$.

y	W	Fs	Fdd	Fdu
$|\mathbf{CS}(SIS, y)|$	433	9623	4169	2159
$|\mathbf{MCS}(SIS, y)|$	1	7	7	17

Table 4. The minimal cutsets in **MCS**(SIS, Fdd).

$S1.state$	$LS1.state$	$V1.state$	$S2.state$	$S3.state$	$LS2.state$	$V2.state$
Fdd	W	W	W	W	Fdd	W
W	W	Fdd	W	W	W	Fdd
Fdd	W	W	Fdd	Fdd	W	W
W	Fdd	W	W	W	Fdd	W
W	Fdd	W	Fdd	Fdd	W	W
W	W	Fdd	W	W	Fdd	W
W	W	Fdd	Fdd	Fdd	W	W

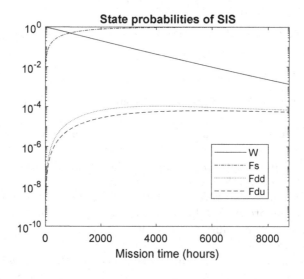

Fig. 10. The results of the probability of each state in $dom(SIS)$.

For probabilistic indicators, the results of the state probabilities in $dom(SIS)$ are pictured Fig. 10. Numerically, the average probabilities P_{avg} within the mission time (8760 h for each state are: $P_{avg}(W) = 1.449 \times 10^{-1}$, $P_{avg}(Fs) = 8.550 \times 10^{-1}$, $P_{avg}(Fdd) = 7.6916 \times 10^{-5}$ and $P_{avg}(Fdu) = 4.6073 \times 10^{-5}$.

7   Conclusion

In this article, we introduced a new modeling formalism, so-called FDS-ML, dedicated to the design of combinatorial probabilistic risk assessment models. We presented decision diagram based algorithms to assess FDS-ML models and we showed by means of a use case stemmed from ISO/TR 12489 standard the interest of the proposed approach.

FDS-ML relies on the notion of finite degradation structures. Finite degradation structures can be seen as the most general mathematical framework to design combinatorial probabilistic risk assessment models. As of today, the language is rather simple: it just provides constructs to define domains (finite degradation structures) and operators as well as to declare variables and equations. This is necessary and sufficient for basic uses, but our ambition is to make FDS-ML a full object-oriented language, using the S2ML+X paradigm [2,10]. Here X would stand for the current FDS-ML. Object-orientation, in the sense of S2ML, is a key enabler for the design of reusable modeling patterns, as demonstrated with AltaRica 3.0 [1]. The design of such patterns for finite degradation models is of primary importance for their industrial deployment as it makes it possible to hide, to some extent, the mathematical difficulties: with suitable, domain-specific libraries of modeling patterns, analysts can design their models by copying existing ones and adjusting them to their particular needs.

Regarding the implementation, much remains also to do. So far, our prototype is implemented in Python, which is indeed not ideal in terms of efficiency. We plan to move to C++ as soon as concepts and methods will be sufficiently stable. Decision diagram algorithms are now relatively mature. We plan to implement also bottom-up algorithms generalizing those designed for fault tree assessment [9].

References

1. Batteux, M., Prosvirnova, T., Rauzy, A.: Altarica 3.0 in 10 modeling patterns. Int. J. Crit. Comput.-Based Syst. **9**(1–2), 133–165 (2018). https://doi.org/10.1504/IJCCBS.2019.098809
2. Batteux, M., Prosvirnova, T., Rauzy, A.: From models of structures to structures of models. In: IEEE International Symposium on Systems Engineering, ISSE 2018. IEEE, Roma, October 2018. https://doi.org/10.1109/SysEng.2018.8544424. Best paper award
3. Brace, K.S., Rudell, R.L., Bryant, R.S.: Efficient implementation of a BDD package. In: Proceedings of the 27th ACM/IEEE Design Automation Conference, pp. 40–45. IEEE, Orlando (1990). https://doi.org/10.1145/123186.123222

4. Guo, H., Yang, X.: A simple reliability block diagram method for safety integrity verification. Reliab. Eng. Syst. Saf. **92**(9), 1267–1273 (2007). https://doi.org/10. 1016/j.ress.2006.08.002
5. International IEC standard IEC61508 - functional safety of electrical/electronic/programmable safety-related systems (E/E/PE, or E/E/PES). Standard, International Electrotechnical Commission, Geneva, Switzerland, April 2010
6. ISO/TR 12489:2013 petroleum, petrochemical and natural gas industries - reliability modelling and calculation of safety systems. Standard, International Organization for Standardization, Geneva, Switzerland, November 2013
7. Minato, S.I.: Zero-suppressed BDDs for set manipulation in combinatorial problems. In: Proceedings of the 30th ACM/IEEE Design Automation Conference, DAC 1993, pp. 272–277. IEEE, Dallas (1993). https://doi.org/10.1145/157485. 164890
8. Minato, S.I.: Binary Decision Diagrams and Applications for VLSI CAD. Kluwer Academic Publishers, Dordrecht (1996)
9. Rauzy, A.: Anatomy of an efficient fault tree assessment engine. In: Virolainen, R. (ed.) Proceedings of International Joint Conference PSAM 2011/ESREL 2012, June 2012
10. Rauzy, A., Haskins, C.: Foundations for model-based systems engineering and model-based safety assessment. J. Syst. Eng. (2018). https://doi.org/10.1002/sys. 21469
11. Ruijters, E., Stoelinga, M.: Fault tree analysis: a survey of the state-of-the-art in modeling, analysis and tools. Comput. Sci. Rev. **15**, 29–62 (2015). https://doi.org/ 10.1016/j.cosrev.2015.03.001
12. Ushakov, I.: Probabilistic Reliability Models. Wiley, Hoboken (2012)
13. Yang, L., Haskins, C., Rauzy, A.: Finite degradation structures: a formal framework to support the interface between MBSE and MBSA. In: IEEE International Symposium on Systems Engineering, ISSE 2018. IEEE, Roma, October 2018. https:// doi.org/10.1109/SysEng.2018.8544411
14. Yang, L., Rauzy, A.: Reliability modeling using finite degradation structures. In: Proceedings of the 3rd International Conference on System Reliability and Safety (ICSRS), pp. 168–175. IEEE, Barcelona, November 2018. https://doi.org/10.1109/ ICSRS.2018.00035

Integrating Safety Design Artifacts into System Development Models Using SafeDeML

Tim Gonschorek[1]($\boxtimes$) (iD), Philipp Bergt[2], Marco Filax[1](iD), and Frank Ortmeier[1](iD)

[1] Otto von Guericke University, Universitätsplatz 2, 39106 Magdeburg, Germany
{tim.gonschorek,marco.filax,frank.ortmeier}@ovgu.de
[2] Xitaso Engineering GmbH, Werner-Heisenberg-Straße 1, 39106 Magdeburg, Germany
philipp.bergt@xitaso.com

Abstract. Applying a safety artifact language as Safety Design Modeling Language SafeDeML integrates the generation of the safety design into the system modeling stage – directly within the system architecture. In this paper, we present a modeling process and a prototype for the CASE tool Enterprise Architect for SafeDeML. The goal is to support the system designer in developing a standard (in this paper Iso 26262) conform system and safety design containing all relevant safety artifact within one model. Such integration offers several modeling guarantees like consistency checks or computation of coverage and fault metrics. Since all relevant information and artifacts are contained within the model, SafeDeML and the prototype can help to decrease the effect of structural faults during the safety design and further supports the safety assessment. To give an idea to the reader of the complexity of the approach's application, we present an exemplary implementation of the safety design for a brake light system, a real case-study from the Iso 26262 context.

Keywords: Safety design for critical systems ·
Model-based safety assessment for ISO 26262 · Safety design integration

1 Introduction

Modeling and developing the safety design of a complex system is a challenging task. One major challenge is, in our point of view, that the modeling of relevant artifacts, e.g., fault or failure definitions, are not integrated within the original system architecture. Therefore, a task like ensuring that all relevant random hardware faults have been covered or the structured analysis of the failure propagation behavior, based on the system structure, can be error-prone.

We thank Dr. Thorsten Piper from Continental Automotive GmbH and Jan von Hoyningen-Hüne from the Conti Temic microelectronic GmbH for providing the case study and their intensive support in the development of the SafeDeML metric.

© Springer Nature Switzerland AG 2019
Y. Papadopoulos et al. (Eds.): IMBSA 2019, LNCS 11842, pp. 93–106, 2019.
https://doi.org/10.1007/978-3-030-32872-6_7

In this paper, we present a way of integrating the failure modeling and all artifacts generated while developing the safety design into the system development. Therefore, we defined the modeling formalism *Safety Design Modeling Language* (SafeDeML), which integrates into SYSMLdevelopment models.

Since modeling using SafeDeML is integrated into the system architecture, safety-relevant information are directly derivable from the model including random hardware faults common for specific hardware parts according to a standard or interdependencies between connected components. This implies two major features: the safety design, which is derived from the system design (e.g., component structures and interconnections), is directly connected with the design artifacts without any break of the medium also enabling easy consistency checks between system and safety design. Further, since all relevant artifacts of the design are placed within the system model, decisions taken for the safety design get more traceable and the interoperability with other design teams, the maintainability, and the comprehensibility of the design increases.

Based on this theoretical concept we developed a structured modeling and analysis process guiding the developer through the stages of modeling fault and failure behavior in a local and in a global scope. Further, it supports the analysis of failure propagation of defined failure through the system architecture and helps the designer in ensuring that relevant faults are covered by the safety design. SafeDeML and the corresponding design process are implemented in the prototype SafeDeTool as a plugin for the CASE-tool Enterprise Architect. We applied this prototype for validating SafeDeML and the process on a real case study from the ISO 26262 context, a brake light system driver.

The improvements we see in applying SafeDeML and the prototype SafeDeTool are the following:

- Direct integration of the safety design into the system modeling.
- Integration of underlying artifacts from which design decisions were derived.
- Separation of the design into hardware and system level.
- An extendable fault library providing automatically fault import.
- A modeling process guiding the designer for decreasing structural faults.

In the following, we present the process integration and its benefits in more detail. Before, we give a short introduction into fault modeling with ISO 26262 and SafeDeML in Sect. 3 and provide an overview over existing modeling schemata in Sect. 3. After that we investigate the modeling process in more detail and present its applicability on a real case study (*cf.* Sect. 4). In the last section (Sect. 5), we conclude the paper and give an outlook on possible future work.

2   Background

2.1   Error Modeling and Iso 26262 in a Nutshell

In general, the scope of the ISO 26262[1, 17, 22] is the development of an *item*, i.e., the vehicle part under development. This item consists of several *(sub) systems.*

Further, an item defines *functions* that are provided by the item and are realized by the systems it consists of. The system is also defined as an abstraction of *components* which are again an abstraction containing both *hardware parts* and *software units*.

Safety Goals are top-level safety requirements for the item under development, leading to the functional requirements that must be concerned for avoiding a hazardous event. These safety requirements must be traceable to the design element (e.g., component, software, or function) implementing it. To be compliant with the defined safety goals, the design must ensure that no safety goal could be violated by the malfunction of any element. Such a malfunction is in general defined as failure.

A *Failure* is the termination of the ability of an element of an item under development to perform a function as required (in particular regarding the set of safety goals). They are often defined as the inability of performing a required function or service, required on the outside of the element. The internal state causing the failure is often referred to as error. An *Error* is a discrepancy between a computed, observed or measured value or condition, and the true, specified, or theoretically correct value or condition. Such an error can occur subsequent to an unforeseen condition during operation or to a fault within an element. A *Fault* (e.g., a random hardware fault) is an abnormal condition that can cause an element or the complete item to fail.

Further, according to [3], we assume that not every error occurring within an element leads to an observable failure and therefore not every fault has the potential of leading to a violation of the safety goal. The goal of our modeling method is to support the designer in concerning all relevant faults. For preventing that a safety goal relevant fault leads to a failure and eventually to a potential hazard, safety measures are defined.

A *Safety Measure* is an activity or technical solution to avoid or control systematic failures and to detect or control random hardware failures or to mitigate their harmful effects. Especially while modeling the safety design, a designer can apply a specialization of safety measures, safety mechanisms. A *Safety Mechanism* is a technical solution implemented to detect, or mitigate, or tolerate faults or to control or avoid failures in order to maintain intended functionality or a safe state.

2.2   Safety Design Modeling Language

The *Safety Design Modeling Language* (SafeDeML) was first published in [13]. SafeDeML is intended to be a modeling extension for system models which integrates the basic fault/failure modeling concepts within the actual system architecture model. We developed the language itself as a SYSML extending UML-profile, so it can be adapted to be used within several CASE tools. This UML-profile is presented in Fig. 1.

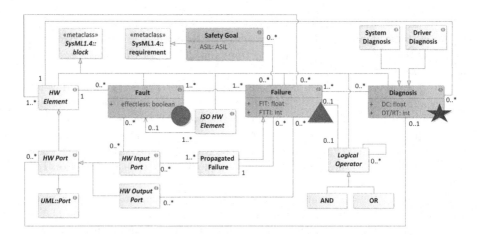

Fig. 1. UML-profile as SysML extension for the language SafeDeML. (Color figure online)

For SafeDeML the basic elements are Faults (blue circle), Failure (red triangle), and Diagnosis (blue star)[1]. Faults in that context represent random hardware faults. Such hardware faults can either be «effectless» or can be connected to a failure element via a «results in» relation, depending on whether the fault leads to a recognizable failure at the border of the corresponding hardware component. If a failure is not introduced by single but multiple faults, logical operators can be used. Further, a modeler can define FIT and FTTI values for each failure and, in addition, which safety goal is directly linked to that particular fault. This is especially useful if the current model-based systems engineering (MBSE) approach of a company not yet includes the connection of safety goals, corresponding safety requirements and the model components which are derived from these safety requirements.

To model a possible failure diagnosis and further mitigation, we introduced the diagnosis element. These are connected to a failure using a «detected by» relation. A diagnosis can either be a diagnosis detected on the hardware component or by a corresponding software implementation (System Diagnosis) or defined a diagnosis perceivable by the user of the system (Driver Diagnosis).

SafeDeML also implements atomic hardware elements (HW Element) taken from the Iso 26262 standard. An assignment of such a hardware element, e.g., a power supply or a simple clock, automatically introduces all corresponding possible hardware faults into this particular component. Further, it is also possible that a failure is not directly diagnosed on a specific hardware component and therefore propagates its erroneous behavior over particular hardware ports (HW Port, HW Input Ports, HW Output Ports) to adjacent components connected via a link in the system model.

---

[1] For reasons of space, for a visualization of the model elements and their connections, we refer the reader to the implementation images in Sect. 4, Fig. 5.

For the verification and validation of the system we say that a safety goal is violated if a failure exists that is marked as relevant for that safety goal but is not covered by any measure, i.e., a diagnosis element.

3   Related Work

The essential idea of SafeDeML and SafeDeTool is the integration of fault – failure – safety mechanism modeling into the standard system architecture development and derive information like failure propagation directly from the system model. In the literature, there also exist several works on the synthesis of system and safety design and also further safety analysis.

HipHops [15,20,21], for example, provides a language and tool integration for failure modeling and propagation analysis. From a given system architecture HipHops generates a parallel model used for failure definition and propagation analysis. This model, however, must again be kept up to date with the system model and does also not support the definition of related safety mechanisms for the system and generated artifacts are not integrated back into actual system models. This is the same for the Marte UML extension [23] which together with the DAM profile [5] provides a framework of defining dependability analysis specific extensions to the modeling language. Unfortunately, it is not provided to model the intended Fault – Failure – Diagnosis chain as it is desirable when executing a fault related safety measure.

The Component Fault Tree (CFT) [2,16] methodology is another work, focusing on the fault modeling and analysis. It provides an extended failure propagation and analysis mechanism based on the system component structure. Even a tool integration, the SafeT toolbox [18], exists. This methodology, however, again focus rather on the safety analysis than on the safety design.

Another related work to SafeDeML is SafeML [7,8]. SafeML provides an UML-profile extending standard SysML, too. This integration, however, has another focus that SafeDeML. It rather focuses on a static safety design artifact elements like faults, failures, and hazards, but they are not used to support the design process by means of propagation analysis or decreasing the effect of structural faults. They are instead used for integrating safety design results in the system model. However, if SafeML would be integrated into SysML (*cf.* [6]), it could be conceivable to define a relation between SafeML and SafeDeML.

The work [19] from the Chess framework [9,24] also presents an approach to model the fault – failure relations on a system model. Further, they also provide propagation analysis based on the model structure [12]. This model, however, is intended to be used for the safety analysis rather than for the direct design purpose and therefore does not integrate essential design elements, e.g., the definition of safety mechanisms, into the model. Moreover, the model containing the failure definitions is defined in a separated modeling language and framework that must again be kept up to date with the system design.

What, in our point of view, are still open problems are (i) the propagation analysis of potentially critical faults with respect to defined safety and diagnosis mechanisms (directly within the system model) and (ii) the support of the designer in validating that all necessary faults have been addressed during the safety design process.

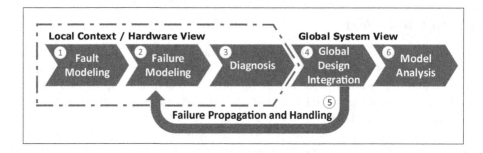

Fig. 2. A schema of the proposed safety design analysis and development process.

4   A Modeling Process for the Safety Design Integration

One integral step of the safety design definition is analyzing the error behavior of the system. This, in general, includes the analysis of the hardware component faults, i.e., which fault (combination) leads to a hazardous behavior and thereby violates a safety goal.

The normal system model is, in the context of complex systems, not designed by a single engineer. There are experts responsible for designing particular hardware components, often connected, in a higher abstraction level, with several other hardware elements to form the complete overall system. We split, therefore, the safety design modeling into two different views, the *Local Context/Hardware View* and the *Global System View*. In the *Hardware View*, we define the failure behavior of single hardware components. Here, the hardware designer can define a specific failure behavior or only a specific failure reaction at the component's borders. This includes the propagation of component failure not covered on the particular hardware component or the handling of faults. In the *Global System View*, the failure behavior of the single components is integrated into the system architecture and global failure properties like the failure propagation can be analyzed using already defined interconnections between adjacent components from the system architecture.

Figure 2 presents the general process for the failure modeling workflow consisting of 6 different steps. These are in the *Local Context* the *Fault Modeling* ① providing all information about possible random hardware faults, the *Failure Modeling* ② where it is defined whether an existing fault leads to an erroneous behavior at the component's border and which failure is connected to which safety goal, and *Diagnosis* ③ where appropriate safety mechanisms or propagation strategies are defined for possible failure elements.

In the *Global System View* during the *Global Design Integration* ④ the interconnections between the hardware components are analyzed and the failure propagation is simulated. *Failure Propagation and Handling* ⑤ represents the refinement of a components failure mitigation strategy, i.e., extending diagnosis and propagation strategies, when additional propagated failures must be handled. After the global system model is defined, during *Model Analysis* ⑥ consistency checks like fault analysis rate, safety goal violations by unhandled failures or measures like diagnostic coverage are executed.

4.1 A Brake Light Case Study

To provide an impression on the applicability of our method, we present the developed process and prototype at a lightweight real-world case study – a brake light controller[2] (Fig. 3). This includes a mechanical interface (*ME*) directly passing the outputs from the electrical engineering component (*EE*) to the LED elements. The *EE* itself consists of four brake light drivers (*BLD*) responsible for transforming the digital signal from the main controller (*MaC*) to an analog output signal for the LED. We have four *BLD* each responsible for a specific brake light (left/right and trunk lid/bumper). As a fallback for the *MaC* and the *BLD* the system contains a hardware part co-controller (*CoC*) directly generating an analog output signal for the brake light LED.

MaC and *BLD* are connected via a serial/parallel interface and the *BLD* passes the signal form the *MaC* using daisy chaining. The *CoC* is connected to each *BLD* via a parallel line and each *BLD* implements one outgoing connection to the corresponding LED.

4.2 ① Fault Modeling

In this stage, the goal is to define the random hardware faults which must be taken into account for the safety-related system analysis. The improvement is that we define the faults integrated into the system design, i.e., we embed the fault definition into the SYSML component instantiation and heredity idea. This results in two different modeling contexts. On the one hand, all faults defined for a superclass are also passed to the inherited to the child class. On the other hand, we derive the relevant faults by the atomic hardware types contained on a hardware component. Such atomic types are components that are, in normal situations, not extra modeled, e.g., a clock, a power supply, or specific memory registers. To be compliant with the ISO 26262, we defined the atomic components and the related faults according to Table D.1 of part 5 of the standard.

An example for such a definition is given by the **Element Fault Diagrams** presented in Fig. 4. Here the atomic hardware parts are assigned to the particular components *MaC*, *CoC*, and *BLD*. Further, the *MaC* get assigned to additional fault elements for the serial/parallel interface output, which could not been directly derived from the atomic parts. *MaC* and *CoC* also inherit all atomic hardware parts from their supercomponent *HW Part Controller*.

---

[2] For complexity and space reasons we only provide the physical architecture part of the system model.

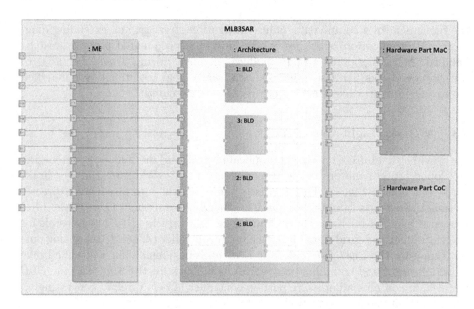

Fig. 3. Cases study architecture of the Brake Light Systems visualizing the relevant elements: Brake Light Driver 1–4 (*BLD*) within the electrical engineering block (*EE*), the hardware main controller (*hardware part MaC*), and hardware part co-controller (*hardware part CoC*). The mechanical interface (*ME*) represents the connection to the outer system context, i.e., pins and plugs.

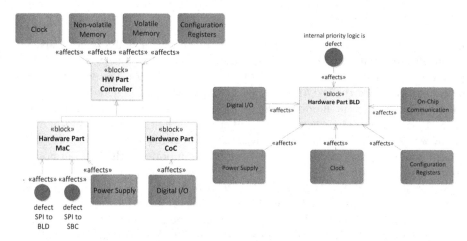

Fig. 4. Element Fault Diagram of the *MaC* and *BLD* component definition with assigned Iso 26262 atomic hardware parts.

This fault modeling concept offers the possibility of building up a fault library that can be extended during a single and across multiple projects. Thereby, the applied reuse of already proven in use system elements supports the designer in several situations, but in particular for the system analysis, verification, and validation.

4.3 ② Failure Modeling

After the fault modeling ① all defined and derived faults are imported into the component specific **Internal Fault Diagram**. During this phase we define per fault element whether it introduces a component failure. If it does, we connect the fault to a corresponding, newly created, failure element. This connection can either be direct or via a logical junction in connection with one or more additional faults. During this phase of the process, the tool-guided approach ensures that each defined fault has been under investigation at least once and has been classified whether it leads to a failure or is marked as «effectless». This step is shown in Fig. 5 for the *MaC* and one of the *BLD*.

Thereby we reduce the possibility of systematic faults related to the overseeing a fault or a missing recording whether a fault has already been handled. Further, we assign to each failure properties like FIT or FTTI. If it is not possible to derive safety goal dependencies of the hardware components, e.g., because the safety requirements are not linked within the model, we offer the possibility to directly link a failure to a safety goal. In this setting, however, we lose the possibility of deciding whether a corresponding fault is a Single Point Fault

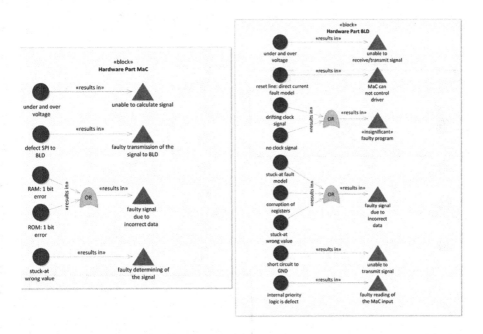

Fig. 5. Internal Fault Diagram of the *MaC* and *BLD* component containing the additional failure definitions.

(SPOF) or a Multi Point Fault (MPOF). Therefore the designer must decide if the specific failure alone is sufficient to violate a safety goal or if multiple must occur.

4.4 ③ Diagnosis

One important aspect within the standards for handling faults and failures is the definition of appropriate safety mechanisms, in our context depicted as diagnoses elements. Such diagnosis elements can either be implemented directly in hardware but also linked to a specific software functionality, responsible for that diagnosis. During the process execution, the tool guides the user through each open failure element and for each the designer must decide whether the element will be diagnosed on the particular hardware element.

The diagnosis definition for our case study is presented in Fig. 6. Elements outside the *Global Context* frame are directly defined and intended to be implemented on the hardware component. If a failure is not diagnosed at the initial hardware, the failure can also be deployed over the connections of the system design further to other adjacent components (*cf.* Global Context of *MaC* in Fig. 6). The propagation simulation and the according import handling are discussed in the following section.

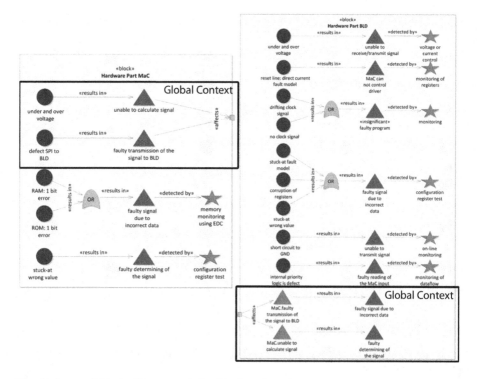

Fig. 6. Internal Fault Diagram of the *MaC* and *BLD* component containing all diagnosis elements and relevant for the global context propagated failure and their import.

4.5 ④ Failure Propagation and ⑤ Refinement

An error-prone part of the system safety design is the tracing of propagated failures through complex system design, especially if the analysis is not executable within the actual system architecture. Without appropriate support within the system model, overseeing a relevant failure effect is quite likely. In this context, the process and tool implementation provide automatic failure propagation mechanism derived from the actual system architecture. Therefore, all failures not diagnosed are propagated regarding the defined propagation schema through the system model.

Failure Propagation ④. If a failure element is not diagnosed at all or connected to a specific outport, it is propagated. For the case a non-diagnosed failure is not connected to a specific outport, it is propagated through all available ports and connections. On the other side, a propagated failure can also be imported through an inport. In the *Global Context* of the *BLD* in Fig. 6 we see such an import of the failures *unable to calculate signal* and *faulty transmission of the signal to BLD* of the *MaC*.

Handling of Propagated Failure Elements ⑤. The SafeDeTool prototype supports the designer by pointing to these propagated failures and demanding a reaction. Either these failures are again propagated or they get connected to a new hardware failure in the importing component. If nothing, in particular, is defined, the failure simply gets propagated further of all available outports of the component. This breadth style propagation is indeed an over-approximation. If required, also a default propagation defining failure form which import a propagated via which outport, e.g., according to the physical implementation and wiring on the component, is also provided.

During this stage, the designer is automatically guided by the tool such to not handled failure component-wise such that at least all failure could be analyzed once without overseeing a single one. If a failure in a propagation change is diagnosed in a later step, all following propagations are removed.

4.6 ⑥ Model Analysis: Consistency and Further Analysis

After having implemented the system's failure behavior and safety design following the process, we can execute several qualitative checks:

- *Fault and Failure Modeling Consistency:* Since all necessary fault elements are derived from, e.g., a hardware part library or additional standard elements, it can be validated whether all faults have at least been once processed by the designer. The same processing coverage metric applies to failure elements.
- *Safety Goal Violation:* During the modeling process, we connected the safety goals via their requirements, either by existing links between requirements and system model elements or by defining the affected safety goals using the failure properties. By utilizing this connection, we can compute whether there exists a not diagnosed or mitigated fault, possibly violating a connected safety goal.

- *Computation of the Diagnostic Coverage*: Having the connection of the defined Iso 26262 hardware parts, the corresponding faults, and the direct implementation in the model we can compute the diagnostic coverage of the diagnosis elements for a specific component.
- *Single Point and Latent Fault Metric*: During the modeling, we defined whether a possible failure is a single point or latent failure. Analyzing this information and the derived diagnostic coverage for a specific component, we can compute and evaluate single point and latent point fault metric.

In addition to these metrics, we could (not implemented yet) also use external tools to evaluate our system. Therefore, we interpret the extended system model as a starting point for further analysis. The idea is to have all relevant information within one specific model and transform the system architecture, behavior and injected fault and failure definitions into the corresponding input language of an analysis tool. From the full static architecture and, if logical computation and corresponding computing time are of interest, from a set of corresponding state machines, a formal model can be generated as presented in [10, 11]. Having the formal model and the additional information, e.g., FFTI or FIT values, it is possible to apply a formal verification tool or IDE (e.g., [4, 14]) and parse the results back into the given model. The benefit of this approach, in comparison with simply modeling several models by hand containing only the information relevant for the verification scopes, are: (i) Generated models are consistent since they are always generated from one specific model and (ii) if the model generation process is automated, also the trust in the consistency and the traceability of the results increases (especially during an assessment).

Further, from the information contained in a SafeDeML mode, necessary information is given to execute inductive verification techniques, e.g., Failure Mode and Effect Analysis (FMEA) [25].

5   Conclusion

In this paper, we presented a process and a prototypical implementation for integrating SafeDeML into the normal system design and applied it one a real case study. What can be seen is that the integration of the fault analysis artifacts into the system modeling eases the analysis of the global failure behavior when failure propagation is of interest.

When following the presented process in addition to the provided prototype, the occurrence of systematic faults can be prevented or at least mitigated. This is induced by the fact that defined process presents a structured approach defining libraries for error-prone tasks like failure definition or the resulting handling of fault and failure elements were for complex systems single elements can easily be overseen. Further, these failures can be mitigated by the fact that we have all relevant information and artifacts that are generated during the analysis and provide the base for specific safety design decisions, are within one single model. In addition, implemented change management and consistency checks must focus only on one particular model rather than on many, not necessarily traceable consistent models.

Moreover, the artifacts generated by the presented process contribute to the following safety artifacts, defined by part 4 of the ISO 26262. This contribution is given for the *Technical Safety Concept and System design specification* by the generation of the fault propagation and mitigation artifacts, for *Hardware-software interface specification* by the connection between the defined diagnosis elements and the implementing function and software definitions, and for the *System verification report* and *Safety analysis report* by the consistency checks, computed coverage metrics, and also by the generation of the inductive analysis artifacts (e.g., for an FMEA).

All in all, we think that applying SafeDeML and the prototype SafeDeTool could decrease the effort of the safety design modeling and analysis and provide a first step for integrating all different design document within one system model for applying model-based system design and safety assessment.

References

1. Road vehicles - functional safety: part(x): standard
2. Adler, R., et al.: Integration of component fault trees into the UML. In: Dingel, J., Solberg, A. (eds.) MODELS 2010. LNCS, vol. 6627, pp. 312–327. Springer, Heidelberg (2011). https://doi.org/10.1007/978-3-642-21210-9_30
3. Avižienis, A., Laprie, J.-C., Randell, B.: Dependability and its threats: a taxonomy. In: Jacquart, R. (ed.) Building the Information Society. IIFIP, vol. 156, pp. 91–120. Springer, Boston, MA (2004). https://doi.org/10.1007/978-1-4020-8157-6_13
4. Behrmann, G., et al.: Uppaal 4.0. In: Proceedings of QEST, pp. 125–126 (2006)
5. Bernardi, S., Merseguer, J., Petriu, D.C.: A dependability profile within MARTE. Softw. Syst. Model. **10**(3), 313–336 (2011)
6. Biggs, G., Juknevicius, T., Armonas, A., Post, K.: Integrating safety and reliability analysis into MBSE: overview of the new proposed OMG standard. In: INCOSE International Symposium, vol. 28, no. 1, pp. 1322–1336 (2018)
7. Biggs, G., Sakamoto, T., Kotoku, T.: 2A2-I06 SafeML: A model-based tool for communicating safety information (robotics with safety and reliability). Proc. Robomec **2013**(0), _2A2-I06_1-_2A2-I06_4 (2013)
8. Biggs, G., Sakamoto, T., Kotoku, T.: A profile and tool for modelling safety information with design information in SysML. Softw. Syst. Model. **15**(1), 147–178 (2016)
9. Cicchetti, A., et al.: CHESS: a model-driven engineering tool environment for aiding the development of complex industrial systems. In: Goedicke, M., Menzies, T., Saeki, M. (eds.) Proceedings of ASE, p. 362. IEEE, Piscataway (2012)
10. Filax, M., Gonschorek, T., Ortmeier, F.: Correct formalization of requirement specifications: a V-model for building formal models. In: Lecomte, T., Pinger, R., Romanovsky, A. (eds.) RSSRail 2016. LNCS, vol. 9707, pp. 106–122. Springer, Cham (2016). https://doi.org/10.1007/978-3-319-33951-1_8
11. Filax, M., Gonschorek, T., Ortmeier, F.: Building models we can rely on: requirements traceability for model-based verification techniques. In: Bozzano, M., Papadopoulos, Y. (eds.) IMBSA 2017. LNCS, vol. 10437, pp. 3–18. Springer, Cham (2017). https://doi.org/10.1007/978-3-319-64119-5_1

12. Gallina, B., Javed, M.A., Muram, F.U., Punnekkat, S.: A model-driven dependability analysis method for component-based architectures. In: Proceedings of Euromicro DSD/SEAA, pp. 233–240 (2012)

13. Gonschorek, T., Bergt, P., Filax, M., Ortmeier, F., von Hoyningen-Hüne, J., Piper, T.: SafeDeML: On integrating the safety design into the system model. In: Romanovsky, A., Troubitsyna, E., Bitsch, F. (eds.) SAFECOMP 2019. LNCS, vol. 11698, pp. 271–285. Springer, Cham (2019). https://doi.org/10.1007/978-3-030-26601-1_19

14. Gonschorek, T., Filax, M., Lipaczewski, M., Ortmeier, F.: VECS - verification enviroment for critical systems - tool supported formal modeling and verification. In: IMBSA 2014: Short & Tutorial Proceedings. Otto von Guericke University, Magdeburg (2014)

15. Grunske, L., Kaiser, B., Papadopoulos, Y.: Model-driven safety evaluation with state-event-based component failure annotations. In: Heineman, G.T., Crnkovic, I., Schmidt, H.W., Stafford, J.A., Szyperski, C., Wallnau, K. (eds.) CBSE 2005. LNCS, vol. 3489, pp. 33–48. Springer, Heidelberg (2005). https://doi.org/10.1007/11424529_3

16. Kaiser, B., Liggesmeyer, P., Mäckel, O.: A new component concept for fault trees. In: Proceedings of SCS, pp. 37–46 (2003)

17. Langenhan, T.: Still Basic Guide to Automotive Functional Safety, 2nd edn. Epubli, Berlin (2016)

18. Moncada, V., Santiago, V.: Towards proper tool support for component-oriented and model-based development of safety critical systems. In: Commercial Vehicle Technology 2016, pp. 365–374. Shaker Verlag, Aachen (2016)

19. Montecchi, L., Lollini, P., Bondavalli, A.: Dependability concerns in model-driven engineering. In: Proceedings of ISORC, pp. 254–263. IEEE (2011)

20. Papadopoulos, Y., McDermid, J.A.: Hierarchically performed hazard origin and propagation studies. In: Felici, M., Kanoun, K. (eds.) SAFECOMP 1999. LNCS, vol. 1698, pp. 139–152. Springer, Heidelberg (1999). https://doi.org/10.1007/3-540-48249-0_13

21. Papadopoulos, Y., et al.: Engineering failure analysis and design optimisation with HiP-HOPS. Eng. Fail. Anal. **18**(2), 590–608 (2011)

22. Ross, H.L.: Functional Safety for Road Vehicles. Springer, Cham (2016). https://doi.org/10.1007/978-3-319-33361-8

23. Selic, B., Gérard, S.: Modeling and Analysis of Real-Time and Embedded Systems with UML and MARTE: Developing Cyber-Physical Systems. Elsevier, Amsterdam (2013)

24. Mazzini, S., Favaro, J.M., Puri, S., Baracchi, L.: CHESS: an open source methodology and toolset for the development of critical systems. In: EduSymp/OSS4MDE@MoDELS (2016)

25. Stamatis, D.H.: Failure Mode and Effect Analysis: FMEA from Theory to Execution. ASQ Quality Press, Milwaukee (2003)

Dependability Analysis Processes

A Conceptual Framework to Incorporate Complex Basic Events in HiP-HOPS

Sohag Kabir, Koorosh Aslansefat[(✉)][ID], Ioannis Sorokos,
Yiannis Papadopoulos, and Youcef Gheraibia

Department of Computer Science and Technology, University of Hull, Hull, UK
{s.kabir,k.aslansefat-2018,i.sorokos,y.gheraibia,
y.i.papadopoulos}@hull.ac.uk

Abstract. Reliability evaluation for ensuring the uninterrupted system operation is an integral part of dependable system development. Model-based safety analysis (MBSA) techniques such as Hierarchically Performed Hazard Origin and Propagation Studies (HiP-HOPS) have made the reliability analysis process less expensive in terms of effort and time required. HiP-HOPS uses an analytical modelling approach for Fault tree analysis to automate the reliability analysis process, where each system component is associated with its failure rate or failure probability. However, such non-state-space analysis models are not capable of modelling more complex failure behaviour of component like failure/repair dependencies, e.g., spares, shared repair, imperfect coverage, etc. State-space based paradigms like Markov chain can model complex failure behaviour, but their use can lead to state-space explosion, thus undermining the overall analysis capacity. Therefore, to maintain the benefits of MBSA while not compromising on modelling capability, in this paper, we propose a conceptual framework to incorporate complex basic events in HiP-HOPS. The idea is demonstrated via an illustrative example.

Keywords: Fault tree · Markov Process · Model-based safety analysis · HiP-HOPS · Reliability · Real time analysis

1 Introduction

By performing safety and reliability analysis of systems, it is possible to know how they can fail and what is the probability that they will operate without any failure for a specific time period. Fault Tree Analysis (FTA) [32] is a widely used top-down deductive approach for reliability analysis. Using FTA, it is possible to understand the potential causes of system failure and the probability of that failure.

Although FTA is primarily performed manually by analysts, the emergence of model-based safety analysis (MBSA) [26] has greatly reduced required manual effort by proposing ways for automating FTA. Among different available MBSA approaches, Hierarchically Performed Hazard Origin and Propagation Studies

© Springer Nature Switzerland AG 2019
Y. Papadopoulos et al. (Eds.): IMBSA 2019, LNCS 11842, pp. 109–124, 2019.
https://doi.org/10.1007/978-3-030-32872-6_8

(HiP-HOPS) [22] offers multiple state-of-the-art functionalities, supported by a tool. HiP-HOPS can automatically generate fault trees and Failure Mode and Effects Analyses (FMEAs) from system models. HiP-HOPS also supports multi-objective optimisation of system models and semi-automatic allocation of safety requirements to system components in the form of Safety Integrity Levels (SILs). These features automate some of the processes for the ASIL allocation specified in ISO 26262 [24].

Safety analysis through traditional FTA cannot model dynamic behaviour of systems by taking into account the complex interactions and dependencies between system components. To model complex dependencies and dynamic system behaviour, classical static fault trees are extended as dynamic fault trees by introducing dynamic gates. However, this approach is rarely used in industry due to the complexity associated with the analysis of such models and lack of training [35]. Moreover, there is lack of support for model-based analysis of DFTs.

Generally, during reliability analysis via a static or dynamic fault tree, system components are assumed to have various states of nominal operation or of failure. Component failure behaviours are defined accordingly either as probability of failure or failure rate or distribution of time of failure. However, components in practical systems can operate in multiple states and can have complex failure behaviour. For instance, in [17,25,31], Trivedi et al. illustrated the concepts of reliability and availability analysis of systems by considering the complex failure behaviour of components. In doing so, they utilised the modelling capability of Markov chains and used exponentially distributed data.

In [1,4], Markov chain-based complex behaviour modelling of system components were considered and basic events of fault trees were proposed to be substituted by such state-space models. Zixian et al. [36] combined a Markov model and fault tree for the analysis of time-independent and dependent failure behaviour of components in medical industry. In their approach, failure of all medical equipment was modelled using a single type of Markov model and the human error was modelled using another type of Markov model. This implies that all physical components are assumed to have same failure behaviour, however, this may not be true in all practical applications. Recently, Zeller and Montrone [35] proposed a component-oriented concept of Markov chains to incorporate the Markov chain-based model of basic events in Component Fault Trees. At the same time, Nguyen et al. [20] used stochastic reward nets instead of Markov chains to model the complex behavior of basic events in fault trees. Note that none of the above concepts was proposed in the context of MBSA and they are only applicable to exponentially distributed data. Moreover, all the approaches focus only on design time (offline) analysis, hence there is no provision for incorporating runtime evidence about components' states in the analysis to update the belief about system reliability and/or availability.

Currently, reliability analysis through HiP-HOPS lacks an appropriate component concept that would allow to model the complex failure behaviour of a component as a Basic Event (BE) in the form of a separate subgraph. HiP-HOPS neither offers the modelling of multi-state components nor can the annotation of the BEs incorporate complex degradation behaviour and repair actions. Therefore, considering the advantages provided by HiP-HOPS, and MBSA in general, in this paper we propose a conceptual framework to incorporate the concept of complex basic event in the HiP-HOPS. Note that our goal is not to model the state-space-based failure behaviour of a system due to complex interactions between its components. Instead, we aim to model the behaviour of some selected components of the system using state-space-based methods. As part of reliability analysis using HiP-HOPS, in the proposed framework, firstly we identify the components that have complex failure behaviour. Subsequently, we propose to model the failure behaviour of the basic events associated with such components using a Semi-Markov Process (SMP). Then, offline reliability analysis is performed based on the parameters available at design time. The framework can also perform real-time analysis during system operation by monitoring and providing evidence in the state-space models of the basic events. In summary, our work is different from other existing works and is advantageous because:

- It considers component-level complex behaviour modelling in the context of model-based safety analysis.
- Via the use of SMP, the proposed framework could analyse systems with both exponentially and non-exponentially distributed data.
- In addition to performing design time offline analysis, the approach has the capability to perform runtime analysis.

2   Background

2.1   Reliability Analysis in HiP-HOPS

Hierarchically Performed Hazard Origin and Propagation Studies (HiP-HOPS) is a state-of-the-art software reliability analysis method. The tool and the surrounding methodology [21] have evolved as a body of work over the past decade, incorporating further techniques for design [23] and dependability requirement optimization [27,28], temporal fault tree analysis [13], integration with the EAST-ADL [5] and AADL [19] modeling languages, uncertainty analysis [14] and more.

At the core of the HiP-HOPS approach is its ability to perform semi-automatic Fault Tree Analysis (FTA). FTA is a deductive, top-down analysis approach, applied extensively across numerous industries involved in dependability-critical systems development. See [18] for an extensive but older review and [11] for a more recent one. In FTA, system-level 'failures' (undesirable events, depending on the context) are modeled as the root of tree structures, whose leaf nodes represent basic events which cannot be further analyzed in the context of the analysis. Between the root (aka 'top-event') and the leaves of the tree, logic gates link and propagate the logic that governs the tree. Traditionally, gates used have been Boolean AND and OR gates, however more advanced options have also been explored in the literature e.g. temporal [33] and fuzzy logic events and operators, first seen in [29].

In HiP-HOPS, the user begins by annotating a model of the system architecture with mostly local (per system element) failure behaviour information. This information describes any basic events associated with the given element and the logic with which they are propagated from the element's inputs to its outputs. As the information is limited to the boundaries of this black-box view of each element, users do not need to break their modeling workflow to cross-reference potentially complex relationships with other, distant elements in the system architecture hierarchy. In addition to the qualitative failure logic, HiP-HOPS allows to associate failure and repair rates with basic events, which can be used for reliability analysis in later stages. It is important to note that, in HiP-HOPS, all the quantitative information provided is under the assumption that the failure a BE represents can either occur or not. In other words, the state of a BE is binary and can thus only represent up to one failure class per BE.

Once the annotation of a system model is complete, the HiP-HOPS tool can be invoked, automatically synthesizing local fault trees for each system element. The algorithm combines the local fault trees into a merged one, which is then minimized using logical rules to eliminate redundant sub-trees and so forth. Once the resulting minimal fault tree is complete, it can be analysed qualitatively and quantitatively. In the former case, the necessary and sufficient combinations of basic events, known as the minimal cut set, can be determined. Minimal cut sets are useful for directly identifying single points of failure as single-member cut sets as well as other critical combinations of low-level failures that can cause systemic failure. For quantitative analysis, the basic events of the fault tree can be assigned probabilities in various forms, most often failure rates according to some assumed distribution. The logical operators found in the fault tree structure can be used to combine the probabilities of linked basic events. For instance, AND and OR gates would combine, respectively, via multiplication and addition, the probability of basic events occurring, assuming the events are considered independent.

2.2 Complex Failure Behaviour Modelling of a System

In traditional fault-tree-based reliability analysis, systems and their components are usually considered to have two types of states: *working* and *failed*. To facilitate reliability analysis, each of such elements can have their probability of failure or failure rate or distribution of time of failure or steady-state or instantaneous (un)availability defined. At the same time, if a component/system can be repaired then a repair rate is defined. However, modern large-scale complex systems have the capacity to work in different states and have complex repair processes. A component in such a system can work as a primary at a particular point in time, and in another instance the same component can work as a secondary or spare. Moreover, if a component acts as a spare, it can be in different modes of spare such as cold, warm, and hot spares.

A component does not necessarily transition directly from a working state to a failed state, and vice versa. The complete failure of a component may occur following a complex degradation process and recovery from failure may also involve complex repair processes. For instance, a battery, when fully charged, may be considered as a fully operational component. From this mode, the battery can fail directly. The battery may be discharged to different levels over the course of operation. Consider each of the distinct charged levels such as 75%, 50%, and 25% as a distinct mode of operation. From each of these modes the battery can transition to the failed mode. The battery can also shift from one mode of operation to another mode either through further discharging or by recharging.

Such multi-modal operation capability of systems and their components gives rise to different dynamic failure characteristics like priorities among events and functionally dependent events. However, using the classical fault tree approach, it is not possible to model such complex dynamic behaviour. Expressiveness of traditional fault trees has been enhanced through different extensions of fault trees such as Dynamic Fault Trees [8] and State/Event Fault Trees [16]. These approaches are mostly useful in modelling dependencies and priorities among events. For a quantitative analysis, these models are usually transformed to state-space-based models like Markov chains or Semi Markov Process and [3] Petri Nets [15]. This leads to a state-space explosion problem, which limits their applicability to large-scale industrial systems. In addition to this, Markov models, the most widely used approach for dynamic reliability analysis, are applicable only to systems consisting of components with exponentially distributed lifetime.

2.3   Reliability Modelling Using Semi Markov Process

Semi-Markov Process (SMP) has been widely used in reliability evaluation of industrial systems [30]. The SMP has the ability to consider non-exponential probability distributions that can be counted as an advantage in comparison to other state-space methods. In this paper, three SMP parameters of $(p, P, F(t))$ are considered, where: p is the initial probability distribution vector, P is conditional transition probabilities matrix and $F(t)$ describes matrix of distribution functions of sojourn times in state i^{th}, when j^{th} state is next.

Considering X_i, $\forall_i = 0, 1, 2, \ldots$ as random variables, the time-homogeneous SMP X is determined by a vector of initial state probabilities $p(0) = \lceil P\{X_0 = i\} \rceil = \lceil 1, 0, \ldots, 0 \rceil$ and the matrix of conditional transition probability $P(t) = \lceil P_{ij}(t) \rceil$ is computed by Eq. (1).

$$P_{ij}(t) = P\{X(t) = j | X(0) = i\} \quad i, j \in States \tag{1}$$

The $P_{ij}(t)$ matrix provided in previous equation can be satisfied by Kolmogorov-Feller's equation in Eq. (2) [34].

$$P_{ij}(t) = \delta_{ij}[1 - G_i(t)] + \sum_{k \in S} \int_0^t P_{kj}(t - x) dQ_{ik}(x) \tag{2}$$

where $\delta_{ij} = 1$ if $i = j$ and $\delta_{ij} = 0$ otherwise, G_i is the distribution of the sojourn time in state i described by Eq. (3) [6], and $Q_{ij}(t)$ describes the kernel matrix by Eq. (4) [9].

$$G_i(t) = P\{S_i \leq t \mid X_0 = i\} = \sum_{j=1}^{i} Q_{ij}(t) \tag{3}$$

where $S_i, i = 0, 1, 2, \ldots$ is the state of the system at time t.

$$Q_{ij}(t) = P\{X_1 = j, S_i \leq t \mid X_0 = i\} \tag{4}$$

The solution of Eq. (2) can be found by applying the Laplace Stieltjes Transformation (LST) in Eq. (5) [10]. Note that for non-exponential failure distributions such as Weibull and Gamma, some approximation algorithm is needed (refer to [2, 7, 34]).

$$\tilde{p}_{ij}(s) = \delta_{ij}[1 - \tilde{g}_i(s)] + \sum_{k \in S} \tilde{q}_{ik}(s)\tilde{p}_{kj}(s) \tag{5}$$

Equation (5) in matrix form can be rewritten as follows:

$$\tilde{p}(s) = \lceil 1 - \tilde{g}(s)\rceil + \tilde{q}(s)\tilde{p}(s) \tag{6}$$

Hence, it can be rewritten as Eq. (7).

$$\tilde{p}(s) = \lceil 1 - \tilde{q}(s)\rceil^{-1}\tilde{g}(s)) \tag{7}$$

In the above Eq. (7), the inverse of $1 - \tilde{q}(s)$ can be replaced by the summation of powers of $\tilde{q}(s)$. Equation (7) can then be rewritten as Eq. (8). This equation is useful for singular kernel matrices.

$$\tilde{p}(s) = \left(\sum_{n=0}^{\infty} \tilde{q}(s)^n\right)\tilde{g}(s) \tag{8}$$

Having solved Eq. (8) with taking the inverse LST of $\tilde{p}(s)$, the unconditional state probabilities in time domain are determined as follows:

$$P(t) = P(0)P(t) \tag{9}$$

Finally, the reliability of a system can be achieved through summation of probability of operational state in the SMP.

3 Proposed Approach

Figure 1 shows the framework of the proposed approach. As seen in the framework, the Annotation, Synthesis, and Analysis phases of the HiP-HOPS methodology are extended with new activities. Additionally, a new phase for real-time evaluation is added in the new approach. In this new approach, the annotation phase of the HiP-HOPS is extended by introducing an additional check. If, for quantitative analysis, the failure rate and repair rate are not sufficient to model

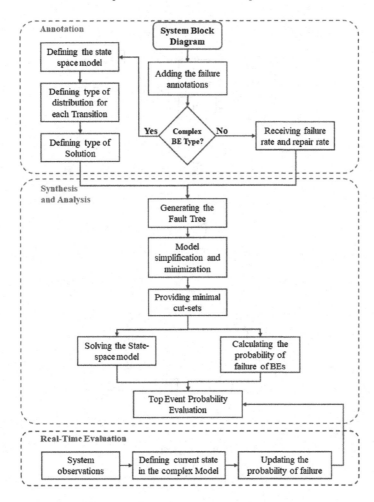

Fig. 1. Framework of the proposed approach

a BE, then a complex BE must be defined instead. In that case, a suitable state-space based model is selected to model its behaviour. As a result of this, the logical annotations of the components do not change.

Consider the architecture of a system in Fig. 2. Each component is annotated with its failure behaviour according in HiP-HOPS' format. For instance, the annotation of component C3 is: O-C3 = O-C1 OR I-C3. This means that the component C3 will fail to produce any output ('O' stands for the 'Omission' failure class) if there is no output from C1 (O-C1) or if there is an internal ('I') failure of C3 (I-C3). As mentioned earlier, the annotation would remain the same in the current approach. For quantitative analysis, HiP-HOPS uses λ_{C1} and μ_{C1} as the failure and repair rates of component C1. However, if the component C1 has a complex failure behaviour then this kind of data cannot be used. For this

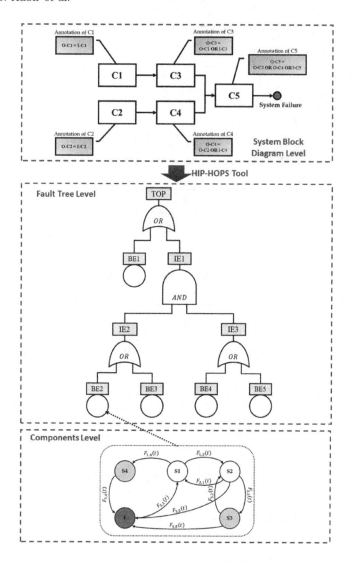

Fig. 2. An example system architecture with failure annotations

reason, the proposed approach would use a state-space-based model to represent the failure behaviour of C1. For instance, Fig. 2 shows a semi-Markov process based complex failure behaviour of component C1's.

The synthesis and analysis steps would produce both qualitative and quantitative results. For qualitative results, following the procedure described in Sect. 2.1, fault trees would be generated first and minimal cut sets would be generated next. However, as we currently have a Semi-Markov (SM) model for the complex BEs, we cannot perform the quantitative analysis as described in Sect. 2.1 until we solve the SMP models. Therefore, the first step of quantitative analysis in the proposed approach is to solve the SMP-based models of the complex BEs to obtain the failure probability of the BEs. The process of solving SMP-based models are discussed in Sect. 2.3. Afterwards this data will be used to obtain the probability of the top event of the fault tree. Additional analysis such as criticality analysis of BEs can also be performed.

Note that all the above analyses are performed at design time. However, the proposed framework also introduces real-time analysis via HiP-HOPS. For real-time analysis, fault trees created during design time and the observations about system operation are used to update the knowledge about the system failure probability and criticality of BEs. As the complex BEs have state-space models of failure behaviour, the basic idea of this phase is to utilise the real-time operational knowledge of the system to place observations in the state-space models. Thus, during run-time, the approach can identify in which state a BE is in, which was not possible to determine at design time. Based on this new knowledge, the probability of each complex BE will be updated, which will eventually be propagated to update the belief about system failure probability.

Consider the failure behaviour model of component C1 in Fig. 2. At design time, it is not possible for analysts to know in which state the component will work during operation. As a result, the design time analysis will calculate the probability of the BE associated with this component by solving the state-space of the model of Fig. 2. However, at run-time, based on the observation of the system operation, the analysts may find that the component is working in state **S4**. Due to this new knowledge, a modified state-space would be solved for the model to obtain a new failure probability of the BE.

4   Illustrative Example

To illustrate the idea of safety analysis of systems with complex BEs via HiP-HOPS, we use a simplified version of the oxygen sensing and generation unit of an Automatic Pond Oxygen Management System first presented in [12], and shown in Fig. 3. The role of this system is to continuously sense the oxygen level of a pond and if the oxygen level falls below certain level then the system will automatically generate oxygen. The system contains two oxygen level sensing blocks, A and B. Each of these blocks contains a battery and an oxygen sensor. The battery keeps the sensor alive and the sensor senses the pond's oxygen level. Readings from both blocks are fed to the Decision Making (DM) block. Based on these readings, the DM can decide whether to generate oxygen or not. Note that although both block A and B work simultaneously, input from at least one of them is necessary to make a decision by the DM. When the DM finds that it is necessary to generate oxygen, it uses the oxygen generator (OG) unit to generate oxygen. During operation the OG draws power from the power supply.

For a model-based analysis of this system using HiP-HOPS, the architecture of the system was annotated by taking into account the failure behaviour of each of the system components. A fault tree was automatically generated based on this annotated architecture and shown in Fig. 4. Table 1 shows the ID and

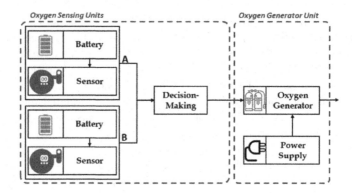

Fig. 3. An example system

description of the basic and intermediate events of the fault tree. In this study, basic events 1, 4, and 6 were considered as complex basic events. The SMP-based failure behaviour models of these BEs are shown in Fig. 5. Parameters associated with these models and failure rates of other BEs are shown in Table 2.

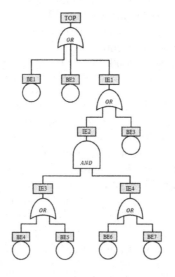

Fig. 4. Fault tree of the system in Fig. 3

Without loss of generality we evaluate the reliability of the system of Fig. 3 for a mission time of 500 h. To illustrate the effectiveness of proposed framework, we have created some scenarios as shown in Table 3. As can be seen, at time interval [0, 100] no observation has been provided for the states of the system components. As a result, analysis performed within this interval is like an offline analysis. At time interval [101, 200], it is observed that the battery system is in

Table 1. ID and description of the basic and intermediate events of the fault tree

Event ID	Event description
TE	No oxygen generated when required
IE1	No outputs from decision making block
IE2	No output from oxygen level sensing blocks
IE3	No output from oxygen level sensing block A
IE4	No output from oxygen level sensing block B
BE1	Power supply failure
BE2	Internal failure of oxygen generator
BE3	Internal failure of decision making block
BE4	Battery in oxygen level sensing block A failed
BE5	Sensor in oxygen level sensing block A failed
BE6	Battery in oxygen level sensing block B failed
BE7	Sensor in oxygen level sensing block B failed

Table 2. Parameters for the BEs and their SMP-based models in Fig. 5

BEs	Parameters	BEs	Parameters
BE1	$F_{1,2}(t) = 1 - e^{-0.00065t}$	BE2	$\lambda = 0.00023$
	$F_{2,1}(t) = 1 - e^{-0.00073t}$	BE3	$\lambda = 0.00023$
	$F_{2,3}(t) = 1 - e^{-0.00633t}$	BE4, BE6	$\alpha(t) = 1 - e^{-0.00078t}$
	$F_{2,5}(t) = 1 - e^{-0.00044t}$		$\beta(t) = 1 - e^{-0.00082t}$
	$F_{3,2}(t) = 1 - e^{-0.00075t}$		$D(t) = 1 - e^{-0.00064t}$
	$F_{3,5}(t) = 1 - e^{-0.00044t}$		$F_{Power}(t) = 1 - e^{-0.00285t}$
	$F_{1,4}(t) = 1 - e^{-0.00860t}$	BE5	$\lambda = 0.00015$
	$F_{4,5}(t) = 1 - e^{-0.00088t}$	BE7	$\lambda = 0.00091$

Table 3. Experimental settings

Mission time	Real time observation
$t = [0, 100]$	No observation
$t = [101, 200]$	State D2 in the SMP of battery has been observed
$t = [201, 500]$	State S4 in the SMP of power system has been observed

state D2 and at time interval [201, 500], the power system has been observed to be in state S4. Figure 6 shows the reliability of the battery and power systems with and without observation. The changes in reliability of these systems due to real time monitoring is clearly reflected in the figure. For instance, for battery system and the power system, the reliability declined steadily until 100 h and 200 h, respectively. After 100 h and 200 h, respective reliability per each system

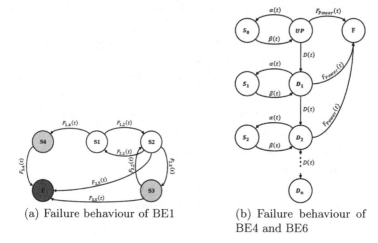

(a) Failure behaviour of BE1

(b) Failure behaviour of BE4 and BE6

Fig. 5. State-based behaviour of BEs 1, 4, and 6

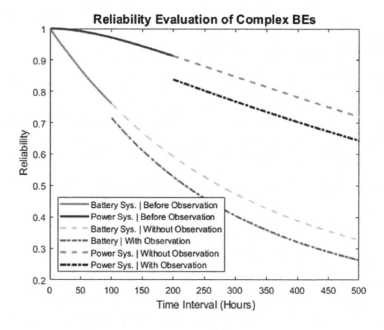

Fig. 6. Reliability of Battery and Power systems with and without observation

drops sharply and then continue to decline steadily again. That means because of our real time observation of the battery and power system states, our knowledge about the reliability of these systems is updated accordingly, which is not possible with design time analysis. Figure 7 shows the reliability of the whole system for 500 h mission time. The effects of the observing the operating states of battery

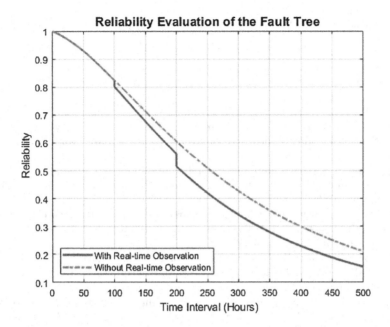

Fig. 7. Reliability of the whole system with and without observation

and power system on the reliability of the whole system is clearly visible in the figure. This real-time analysis feature not only helps us to update our belief about the system reliability, but also allows us to perform a meaningful analysis by taking into account the real operational status of the system.

5   Conclusion

In this paper, we have presented a framework for incorporating the concept of SMP-based complex behaviour modelling of system components in HiP-HOPS. The framework retained all the functionality provided by HiP-HOPS while offering a simple way for modelling the failure behaviour of complex systems. Thus, it enables fast, modular and compositional MBSA of such complex systems. The SMP-based basic event modelling supports distribution-independent analysis of system. Moreover, the proposed framework enables us to perform evidence-based runtime systems analysis.

The current approach focuses solely on the quantitative analysis part of the HiP-HOPS approach. In the future, we plan to explore the qualitative analysis aspects by considering the complex behaviour of basic events. Currently, the effectiveness of the approach is evaluated via a small illustrative example. In future work, more detailed evaluation using large-scale industrial systems will be pursued to illustrate the advantage of our proposed framework in MBSA of complex systems.

Acknowledgements. This work was supported by the DEIS H2020 Project under Grant 732242.

References

1. Adler, R., Forster, M., Trapp, M.: Determining configuration probabilities of safety-critical adaptive systems. In: 21st International Conference on Advanced Information Networking and Applications Workshops (AINAW 2007), vol. 2, pp. 548–555. IEEE (2007)
2. Aslansefat, K.: A novel approach for reliability and safety evaluation of control systems with dynamic fault tree. M.Sc. thesis, Abbaspur Campus, Shahid Beheshti University (2014)
3. Aslansefat, K., Latif-Shabgahi, G.: A hierarchical approach for dynamic fault trees solution through semi-Markov process. IEEE Trans. Reliab. 1–18 (2019). https://doi.org/10.1109/TR.2019.2923893
4. Bouissou, M., Bon, J.L.: A new formalism that combines advantages of fault-trees and Markov models: Boolean logic driven Markov processes. Reliab. Eng. Syst. Saf. **82**(2), 149–163 (2003)
5. Chen, D., Mahmud, N., Walker, M., Feng, L., Lönn, H., Papadopoulos, Y.: Systems modeling with EAST-ADL for fault tree analysis through HiP-HOPS. IFAC Proc. Vol. **46**(22), 91–96 (2013)
6. Cochran, J.: Wiley Encyclopedia of Operations Research and Management Science. Wiley, Hoboken (2010)
7. Distefano, S., Longo, F., Trivedi, K.S.: Investigating dynamic reliability and availability through state-space models. Comput. Math. Appl. **64**(12), 3701–3716 (2012)
8. Dugan, J.B., Bavuso, S., Boyd, M.: Dynamic fault-tree models for fault-tolerant computer systems. IEEE Trans. Reliab. **41**(3), 363–377 (1992)
9. Fricks, R., Telek, M., Puliafito, A., Trivedi, K.S.: Markov renewal theory applied to performability evaluation. Technical report, North Carolina State University, Center for Advanced Computing and Communication (1996)
10. Insua, D., Ruggeri, F., Wiper, M.: Bayesian Analysis of Stochastic Process Models, vol. 978. Wiley, Chichester (2012)
11. Kabir, S.: An overview of fault tree analysis and its application in model based dependability analysis. Expert Syst. Appl. **77**, 114–135 (2017)
12. Kabir, S., Azad, T., Walker, M., Gheraibia, Y.: Reliability analysis of automated pond oxygen management system. In: 18th International Conference on Computer and Information Technology (ICCIT), pp. 144–149. IEEE (2015)
13. Kabir, S., Walker, M., Papadopoulos, Y.: Dynamic system safety analysis in HiP-HOPS with Petri nets and Bayesian networks. Saf. Sci. **105**, 55–70 (2018)
14. Kabir, S., Walker, M., Papadopoulos, Y., Rüde, E., Securius, P.: Fuzzy temporal fault tree analysis of dynamic systems. Int. J. Approx. Reason. **77**, 20–37 (2016)
15. Kabir, S., Yazdi, M., Aizpurua, J.I., Papadopoulos, Y.: Uncertainty-aware dynamic reliability analysis framework for complex systems. IEEE Access **6**(1), 29499–29515 (2018)
16. Kaiser, B., Gramlich, C., Förster, M.: State/event fault trees-a safety analysis model for software-controlled systems. Reliab. Eng. Syst. Saf. **92**(11), 1521–1537 (2007)

17. Kim, D.S., Ghosh, R., Trivedi, K.S.: A hierarchical model for reliability analysis of sensor networks. In: 2010 IEEE 16th Pacific Rim International Symposium on Dependable Computing, pp. 247–248, December 2010
18. Lee, W.S., Grosh, D.L., Tillman, F.A., Lie, C.H.: Fault tree analysis, methods, and applications a review. IEEE Trans. Reliab. **34**(3), 194–203 (1985)
19. Mian, Z., Bottaci, L., Papadopoulos, Y., Biehl, M.: System dependability modelling and analysis using AADL and HiP-HOPS. IFAC Proc. Vol. **45**(6), 1647–1652 (2012)
20. Nguyen, T.A., Min, D., Choi, E., Tran, T.D.: Reliability and availability evaluation for cloud data center networks using hierarchical models. IEEE Access **7**, 9273–9313 (2019)
21. Papadopoulos, Y., Maruhn, M.: Model-based synthesis of fault trees from Matlab-Simulink models. In: 2001 International Conference on Dependable Systems and Networks, pp. 77–82. IEEE (2001)
22. Papadopoulos, Y., McDermid, J.A.: Hierarchically performed hazard origin and propagation studies. In: Felici, M., Kanoun, K. (eds.) SAFECOMP 1999. LNCS, vol. 1698, pp. 139–152. Springer, Heidelberg (1999). https://doi.org/10.1007/3-540-48249-0_13
23. Papadopoulos, Y., et al.: Engineering failure analysis and design optimisation with HiP-HOPS. Eng. Fail. Anal. **18**(2), 590–608 (2011)
24. Papadopoulos, Y., et al.: A synthesis of logic and bio-inspired techniques in the design of dependable systems. Ann. Rev. Control **41**, 170–182 (2016)
25. Ramezani, Z., Latif-Shabgahi, G.R., Khajeie, P., Aslansefat, K.: Hierarchical steady-state availability evaluation of dynamic fault trees through equal Markov model. In: 2016 24th Iranian Conference on Electrical Engineering (ICEE), pp. 1848–1854. IEEE (2016)
26. Sharvia, S., Kabir, S., Walker, M., Papadopoulos, Y.: Model-based dependability analysis: state-of-the-art, challenges, and future outlook. In: Software Quality Assurance, pp. 251–278. Elsevier (2016)
27. da Silva Azevedo, L., Parker, D., Walker, M., Papadopoulos, Y., Araujo, R.E.: Assisted assignment of automotive safety requirements. IEEE Softw. **31**(1), 62–68 (2014)
28. Sorokos, I., Papadopoulos, Y., Azevedo, L., Parker, D., Walker, M.: Automating allocation of development assurance levels: an extension to HiP-HOPS. IFAC-PapersOnLine **48**(7), 9–14 (2015)
29. Tanaka, H., Fan, L., Lai, F., Toguchi, K.: Fault-tree analysis by fuzzy probability. IEEE Trans. Reliab. **32**(5), 453–457 (1983)
30. Trivedi, K.S., Bobbio, A.: Reliability and Availability Engineering: Modeling, Analysis, and Applications. Cambridge University Press, Cambridge (2017)
31. Trivedi, K.S., Kim, D.S., Ghosh, R.: System availability assessment using stochastic models. Appl. Stochast. Models Bus. Ind. **29**(2), 94–109 (2013)
32. Vesely, W., Dugan, J., Fragola, J., Minarick, J., Railsback, J.: Fault tree handbook with aerospace applications. Technical report, NASA Office of Safety and Mission Assurance, Washington, DC (2002)
33. Walker, M., Papadopoulos, Y.: Qualitative temporal analysis: towards a full implementation of the fault tree handbook. Control Eng. Pract. **17**(10), 1115–1125 (2009)

34. Zajac, M., Kierzkowski, A.: Attempts at calculating chosen contributors with regard to the semi-Markov process and the Weibull function distribution. J. Pol. Saf. Reliab. Assoc. **2**, 217–222 (2011)

35. Zeller, M., Montrone, F.: Combination of component fault trees and Markov chains to analyze complex, software-controlled systems. In: 2018 3rd International Conference on System Reliability and Safety (ICSRS), pp. 13–20. IEEE (2019)

36. Zixian, L., Xin, N., Yiliu, L., Qinglu, S., Yukun, W.: Gastric esophageal surgery risk analysis with a fault tree and Markov integrated model. Reliab. Eng. Syst. Saf. **96**(12), 1591–1600 (2011)

Compositionality of Component Fault Trees

Simon Greiner[(✉)], Peter Munk, and Arne Nordmann

Robert Bosch GmbH, Corporate Sector Research, Renningen, Germany
{simon.greiner,peter.munk,arne.nordmann}@bosch.com

Abstract. In order to deal with the rising complexity of safety-critical systems, model-based systems engineering (MBSE) approaches are becoming popular due to their promise to improve consistency between different views of the system model. Component Fault Trees (CFTs) are one particular technique to integrate the well-known Fault Tree Analysis (FTA) with a model of the system. CFTs decompose the specification of fault propagation on component level, which results in smaller, easier to manage models and leads to a safety analysis view that is consistent with the system model. However, although CFTs gain more and more popularity, their semantics is not well defined and the compositionality of CFTs is not formally proven to the best of our knowledge.

In this paper, we provide a formal basis for CFTs, formalize semantics of CFTs and formally prove compositionality of CFTs by mapping them to information flow semantics, which is well-researched in the security analysis domain. Our results allow insights in the compositionality of CFTs, showing a high potential for validation techniques of CFTs and discuss these consequences in detail. We claim that this proof is crucial for the use of CFTs in assurance cases for safety-critical systems and one fundamental approach to integrate safety and security engineering.

1 Introduction

With systems becoming increasingly complex, analyzing and assuring their dependability becomes more and more challenging, e.g., in the domain of highly-automated driving [2]. Since safety is a system property, component tests are not sufficient. Hence, analysis has to be done on system level, requiring potentially large safety artifacts to be reviewed. With growing complexity, the number of test cases and size of analysis results to be reviewed grows exponentially.

The challenge of the growing size of a particular safety artifact, the fault tree, led to the proposal of Component Fault Trees (CFT) by Kaiser et al. [17,18]. CFTs decompose the fault tree of a system and link its parts to system elements. This allows specification and review of fault propagation on component level and

This work was partially funded within the project SecForCARs by the German Federal Ministry for Education and Research with the funding ID 16KIS0792. The responsibility for the content remains with the authors.

Y. Papadopoulos et al. (Eds.): IMBSA 2019, LNCS 11842, pp. 125–140, 2019.
https://doi.org/10.1007/978-3-030-32872-6_9

analysis on system level after automatically generating the system's fault tree based on the CFTs and the system architecture. This automation speeds up the impact analysis of a system's safety properties after changes. However, to the best of the authors' knowledge, the composability property of CFTs has not been formally proven so far.

We argue that a proof of the composability of CFTs is key to allow their usage in assurance cases of safety-critical systems. This paper presents such a formal proof, resulting in two main contributions: First, we provide formal semantics for CFTs and a formal proof that the correctness of CFTs is compositional. This is shown by mapping CFTs to the formalization of non-interference [8], a well-known property from the security engineering domain. We discuss consequences of our formalization and compositionality of CFTs for event types, component reuse, and validation. Second, we show that this mapping is one fundamental approach to integrate safety and security engineering.

2   Components and Component Fault Trees

CFTs are a compositional way to describe the propagation of faults through a system in Model-based Systems Engineering (MBSE). Depending on the point of view of the user of a CFT, it either represents the description of the actual behavior of the component in case of a fault, or it represents the specification of the fault behavior the component is supposed to implement. While both use cases are valid, the intended meaning of when a component is consistent with a CFT is the same. In the remainder, we consider CFTs to be the description of the actual fault propagation of a component.

In this section, we formally define the semantics of CFTs. In Sect. 2.1 we introduce the formal computational model of components. In Sect. 2.2 we formally define CFTs and what it means for a CFT to correctly describe the fault propagation of a component.

2.1   Components

In the remainder of this work we take the formalization of components from Greiner and Grahl [8] and reuse their notation for better comparability of further results in this paper.

A component has an internal state, input ports, and output ports. A component can receive messages via input ports and send messages via its output ports. Received messages can trigger the component to change its internal state. Formally, we consider components as Input-Output Labeled Transition Systems (see [26] for a formal definition of IOLTS). A port has a name and a signature, i.e. names and types of variables that can be communicated via the port. For a message m communicated via an input port with name p with value v, we write $m = p?v$, for a message n communicated via an output port with name q with value w, we write $n = q!w$. We refer to the set of all messages communicated via an input port as inputs, and the set of all messages communicated via an output port as outputs. If it does not matter whether a message is an input or an output, we write $m = p.v$ or $n = q.w$ respectively. We write $c \xrightarrow{m} c'$ for a component c communicating message m and transitioning to a component c'. You can consider c' to have a changed internal state. If c' is irrelevant, we write $c \xrightarrow{m}$, if there exists some c' such that $c \xrightarrow{m} c'$.

The behavioral definition of a component limits the sequence of messages a component can communicate. We refer to a sequence of messages as a trace. We use $\frown$ as the concatenation operator for traces and $\varnothing$ to refer to the empty trace. The length of a trace is defined as the amount of messages in a trace. We write $c \xrightarrow{t} c'$ if a component c transitions to component c' while communicating the trace t. A component c can communicate a trace $t \frown m$ while transitioning to component c', if there exists a component c'' such that $c \xrightarrow{t} c''$ and $c'' \xrightarrow{m} c'$. We again write $c \xrightarrow{t}$, if there exists some c' such that $c \xrightarrow{t} c'$. We refer to all possible traces as $\mathcal{T}$. Finally, we explicitly define environments in which components can run. Environments model the entities providing inputs to a component after observing the behavior of the component.

Definition 1 (Environment). *An environment ω is a function $\mathcal{T} \mapsto \mathcal{P}(\mathcal{I})$, where $\mathcal{P}(\mathcal{I})$ is the powerset of all inputs.*

Environments limit the traces components can communicate while running in environments to those traces, where the environment provides necessary inputs.

Definition 2 (Communication under Environment). *A component c can communicate a trace t under an environment ω, written $\omega \models c \xrightarrow{t}$, iff $c \xrightarrow{t}$ and for all $t_1, t_2, p?v$ with $t = t_1 \frown p?v \frown t_2$, it holds that $p?v \in \omega(t_1)$.*

2.2 Component Fault Trees (CFTs)

Following the definition of Kaiser et al. [17,18], we consider a CFT as a visual description for a given component that tells which output events are caused by which combinations of input events and basic events.

An event, as used in a CFT, belongs to a port of a component, over which a message is communicated in a erroneous way. The type of an event states in which way the communicated message deviates from a correct one. We introduce the examples ex and val as types of events later in this section.

Definition 3 (Event). *An event E is a tuple (p, t), where p is port and t is a type. If p is an input (output) port, E is an input (output) event.*

Herein, we distinguish between input events (or input errors), output events (or output errors), and basic events (or internal faults). Basic events are caused by internals of the component, e.g., the breaking of hardware, glitches in a clock, and similar. Hence, basic events are happening independent from the modeled interfaces. For a concise presentation in this paper, we consider basic events in a CFT to be communicated by the environment as a message via an implicit

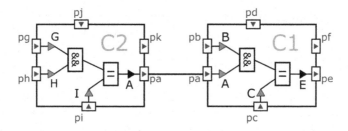

Fig. 1. Two simple CFTs, where output events (black triangle) depend on input events (yellow triangles). (Color figure online)

special port into the component. In the remainder, we thus treat basic events analogously to input events.

For each output event, the CFT describes the logical combination of input events and basic events that lead to the output event by means of chained AND and OR gates. Together, input events, basic events, AND gates, and OR gates describe a formula in propositional logic where the events are the literals which only appear non-negated in the formula.

Please note that general fault tree standards such as the IEC 61025 [14] define more complex gates such as a voter gate. We neglect these in this work since they can be transformed into combinations of AND and OR gates. Additionally, the IEC 61025 [14] defines a NOT gate (and a derived XOR gate) together with the hint that it "is advised that this gate be used carefully by an experienced analyst to avoid unwanted results". This hint and the lack of use cases might be the reason why we are unaware of industrial fault trees that use NOT gates, except for mimicking behavior that is inherent to CFTs, namely exchanging subtrees depending on variants used. For this reason, we neglect NOT gates and derived gates as well, assuming literals to occur non-negated in the resulting propositional formula. We can thus formally define a CFT as a tuple of a propositional formula of input (and basic) events and an output event.

Definition 4 (CFT). *A CFT is a tuple* (P, E), *where* P *is a propositional logic formula, where each literal in* P *is an input event, and each input event only appears non-negated in* P. E *is an output event.*

A CFT describes which combinations of input and basic events lead to which output events. Figure 1 (right) shows the exemplary component $C1$ with input ports p_a, p_b, p_c, and p_d, and the output ports p_e and p_f. The CFT shows the events A, B, and C on the respective ports and the output event E on port p_e.

Example 1. The CFT (P, E) shown in Fig. 1 (right) defines $P = (A \sqcap B) \sqcup C$. The semantics of the specification given by the CFT is that E may happen, if either an event A and an event B happen or the event C happens. In other words, the CFT states: if E happened, then previously either the events A and B happened, or the event C happened (or both). In our example, the complete propositional logic formula of the CFT is $E \Rightarrow P$, i.e. $E \Rightarrow ((A \sqcap B) \sqcup C)$.

Please note that a CFT does not state that event E has to happen (equivalence instead of implication), if the other events happen, i.e. a CFT describes a worst-case fault propagation.

We consider two types of events:

1. A timing event (p, ex) describes for a correct message communicated over the port p that in the erroneous case, this message is not communicated (i.e., commission error); or in the correct case a message is not communicated over p, while it is communicated in the erroneous case (omission error).
2. A value event (p, val) describes that in the correct case a message is communicated over p with value v, while in the erroneous case a message on the port is communicated with a value v', different from v.

Example 2. Reconsidering our example in Fig. 1, we assume the events (in the sense of Definition 3 describing a deviation from correct behaviour) to be defined as $A = (p_a, ex)$, $B = (p_b, val)$, $C = (p_c, val)$, and $E = (p_e, val)$. Assume the component for which the CFT provides a specification can communicate the following traces:

$$t_c = p_a?1, p_b?2, p_c?3, p_d?4, p_e!5 \qquad t_2 = p_b?2, p_c?3, p_d?4, p_e!6$$
$$t_1 = p_b?2, p_c?3, p_d?4, p_e!5 \qquad t_3 = p_b?3, p_c?3, p_d?4, p_e!6$$

Let t_c above be a correct execution without any input events occurring. For t_1, the CFT correctly describes the behavior of the component: Here, only a timing event happens on port p_a, i.e. the message is not received. The CFT states that the component still sends the correct output message ($E = (p_e, val)$), since no value event occurred at port b (p_b, val) and $P = (A \sqcap B) \sqcup C$.

However, the behavior in t_2 is a counterexample for the correctness of the CFT w.r.t. the component's behavior, because the timing event A happened in the form of not communicating $p_a?1$, while the value event B does not happen. Yet E occurred and the component sends the wrong output value.

The component's behavior in trace t_3 would again be correctly described by the CFT, since additionally to A the value event B happened, and thus the value event E happens.

We will see in the following that it is easier to provide a formal definition of the semantics of a CFT in terms of when an event must not happen. So, instead of expressing when a output event may happen, we rephrase the semantics of a CFT such that it describes when an output event must not happen. For a CFT describing $E \Rightarrow P$, we consider the contrapositive of the formula and gain $\overline{P} \Rightarrow \overline{E}$. The resulting formula states that if P is not satisfied, i.e., if a respective combination of input events does not happen, then the event E must not happen.

Example 3. For our example, the reformulation is as follows:

$$\overline{((A \sqcap B) \sqcup C)} \Rightarrow \overline{E} \equiv ((\overline{A} \sqcup \overline{B}) \sqcap \overline{C}) \Rightarrow \overline{E} \equiv ((\overline{A} \sqcap \overline{C}) \sqcup (\overline{B} \sqcap \overline{C})) \Rightarrow \overline{E}$$

In other words: If neither event A nor event C happens, then event E must not happen. Also, if neither event B nor C happens, then event E must not happen.

For every propositional formula P, with literals only appearing non-negated, the formula $\overline{P}$ is a propositional formula with literals only appearing negated. For $\overline{P}$ we can find a disjunctive normal form with clauses $\overline{P_1}, \ldots \overline{P_n}$, such that $\overline{P} = \overline{P_1} \sqcup \ldots \sqcup \overline{P_n}$. $\overline{P} \Rightarrow \overline{E}$ then holds, iff for all clauses $\overline{P_i}$ it holds that $\overline{P_i} \Rightarrow \overline{E}$.

Definition 5 (Clause). *A clause $\overline{P_i}$ is a propositional formula, where each literal only appears negated and $\sqcap$ is the only logical operator in the formula.*

A clause $\overline{P_i}$ only considers events on particular ports. Let for a given CFT: $\overline{P_i} = \overline{A_1} \sqcap \ldots \sqcap \overline{A_n}$ and $\overline{F}$ be the negated output event, where $A_i = (q_i, t_i)$ and $F = (q_f, t_f)$. So in Example 3, $\overline{A} \sqcap \overline{C}$ and $\overline{B} \sqcap \overline{C}$ are two separate clauses.

For this specification, messages on ports other than q_i and q_f are irrelevant to the specification. We can now define when messages at most differ from each other according to an event or a clause.

Definition 6 (Message Event-Equivalence). *A message $m = q.v$ is irrelevant w.r.t. an event $A_i = (q_i, t_i)$, if $q \neq q_i$. For a message m that is irrelevant, we write $m \approx_{\overline{A_i}} \square$.*
Two messages $m_1 = q_1.v_1$ and $m_2 = q_2.v_2$ are event-equivalent w.r.t. an event $A_i = (q_i, t_i)$, written $m_1 \approx_{\overline{A_i}} m_2$, if

$$m_1 \approx_{\overline{A_i}} \square \text{ and } m_2 \approx_{\overline{A_i}} \square \text{ or}$$

$$q_i = q_1 = q_2 \text{ and } t_i = ex \text{ or}$$

$$q_i = q_1 = q_2 \text{ and } t_i = val \text{ and } v_1 = v_2$$

Two messages $m_1 = q_1.v_1$ and $m_2 = q_2.v_2$ are event-equivalent w.r.t. a clause $\overline{P_i} = \overline{A_1} \sqcap \ldots \sqcap \overline{A_n}$, written $m_1 \approx_{\overline{P_i}} m_2$, if $m_1 \approx_{\overline{A_i}} m_2$ for all $0 < i \leq n$
Two messages $m_1 = q_1.v_1$ and $m_2 = q_2.v_2$ are event-equivalent w.r.t. a clause $\overline{P_i}$ and an event E, written $m_1 \approx_{\overline{P_i}, E} m_2$, if $m_1 \approx_{\overline{P_i}} m_2$ and $m_1 \approx_E m_2$.

Example 4. Revisiting Example 2, $\approx_A$ is defined as

$$q_1.v_1 \approx_{\overline{A}} \square \qquad \text{if } q_1 \neq q_a \text{ and}$$
$$q_1.v_1 \approx_{\overline{A}} q_2.v_2 \qquad \text{if } q_1 = q_2 = q_a \text{ or } q_1.v_1 \approx_{\overline{A}} \square \text{ and } q_2.v_2 \approx_{\overline{A}} \square$$

Analogously $\approx_{\overline{C}}$ is defined as

$$q_1.v_1 \approx_{\overline{C}} \square \qquad \text{if } q_1 \neq q_c \text{ and}$$
$$q_1.v_1 \approx_{\overline{C}} q_2.v_2 \qquad \text{if } q_1 = q_2 = q_c \text{ and } v_1 = v_2 \text{ or } q_1.v_1 \approx_{\overline{C}} \square \text{ and } q_2.v_2 \approx_{\overline{C}} \square$$

Given event equivalence of messages, we can canonically define equivalence of traces. Two traces are equivalent w.r.t. an event, if both traces at most differ on irrelevant messages and other messages in the traces are equivalent.

Definition 7 (Trace Event-Equivalence). *Two traces t_1, t_2 are event-equivalent w.r.t. an event A_i, written $t_1 \approx_{\overline{A_i}} t_2$, iff*

$$t_1 = \varnothing \text{ and } t_2 = \varnothing \text{ or}$$
$$t_1 = m_1 \frown t_1' \text{ and } m_1 \approx_{\overline{A_i}} \square \text{ and } t_1' \approx_{\overline{A_i}} t_2 \text{ or}$$
$$t_2 = m_2 \frown t_2' \text{ and } m_2 \approx_{\overline{A_i}} \square \text{ and } t_1 \approx_{\overline{A_i}} t_2' \text{ or}$$
$$t_1 = m_1 \frown t_1' \text{ and } t_2 = m_2 \frown t_2' \text{ and } m_1 \approx_{\overline{A_i}} m_2 \text{ and } t_1' \approx_{\overline{A_i}} t_2'$$

Event-equivalence of traces w.r.t. a clause is defined analogously.

Example 5. For the clause $\overline{B} \sqcap \overline{C}$ the trace t_c from Example 2 is equivalent to traces t_1 and t_2. However, t_c is not equivalent to t_3, since $p_b?2 \approx_{\overline{B} \sqcap \overline{C}} p_b?3$ does not hold. For the clause $\overline{A} \sqcap \overline{C}$, t_c is not equivalent to any of the traces t_1, t_2, t_3, since $p_a?1 \approx_{\overline{A}} \square$ does not hold, but no message on p_a is communicated in one of the traces t_1, t_2, or t_3.

To provide formal semantics of the specification of a CFT for a component, we compare correct runs of the component with runs where erroneous inputs are provided to the component. Given an environment ω, we define erroneous environments ω_f w.r.t. a clause $\overline{P_i}$ and an output event E such that ω_f can provide input messages that deviate from correct messages according to $\overline{P_i}$. ω_f, however, may provide arbitrary input messages after observing an output from the component, which is not specified by E. In that case, the CFT is not correct w.r.t. the component.

Definition 8 (Erroneous Environment). *ω_f is an erroneous environment for ω w.r.t. a clause $\overline{P_i}$ and an output event E, written $\omega_f \approx_{\overline{P_i}, \overline{E}} \omega$, iff for all $t_1 \approx_{\overline{P_i}, \overline{E}} t_2$ it holds that*

$$\forall p?v \in \omega(t_1) \quad \bullet (p?v \approx_{\overline{P_i}, \overline{E}} \square \text{ or } \exists q?u \in \omega_f(t_2) \bullet p?v \approx_{\overline{P_i}} q?u) \text{ and} \quad (1)$$
$$\forall q?u \in \omega_f(t_2) \quad \bullet (q?u \approx_{\overline{P_i}, \overline{E}} \square \text{ or } \exists p?v \in \omega(t_1) \bullet p?v \approx_{\overline{P_i}} q?u) \quad (2)$$

Definition 8 limits how the inputs provided by a correct and an erroneous environment may differ, after observing behaviors of the component which differ in the correct and the erroneous run at most according to the specification provided by P_i and E. Line 1 defines that the erroneous environment must not omit a message, which is provided by the correct environment, unless the correct message is irrelevant. However, the messages may differ according to the clause $\overline{P_i}$ and the output event E. Line 2, states that the erroneous environment must not provide messages, which are not provided by the correct environment, except irrelevant messages. Again, the messages may, however, differ according to the fault specification.

Erroneous environments describe all possible environments, which a component can run in, such that *at most* input events according to a clause are provided. Therefore, an environment should be an erroneous environment to itself (i.e. no input events happen at all). We extend the definition of environments from above.

Definition 9 (Environment (extd.)). *A function ω is an environment w.r.t. a clause $\overline{P_i}$ and an event E, iff it is an environment according to Definition 1, and ω is an erroneous environment to itself according to Definition 8 (i.e., $\omega \approx_{\overline{P_i},\overline{E}} \omega$).*

We can now define correctness of a CFT w.r.t. a component. A clause $\overline{P}$ and an output event E are correct w.r.t. a component, if for every execution in an erroneous environment, there is also an execution in the respective correct environment, such that the correct and the erroneous execution at most differ on input messages allowed by $\overline{P}$ and output messages allowed by $\overline{E}$.

Definition 10 (Clause correctness w.r.t. a component). *Given the relation $\approx_{\overline{P},\overline{E}}$ for the clause $\overline{P}$ and the output event E. $\overline{P}$ and E are correct w.r.t. a component c, if*

$$\forall \omega_f, \omega_c \forall t_f \bullet \omega_f \approx_{\overline{P},\overline{E}} \omega_c \wedge \omega_f \models c \xrightarrow{t_f} \implies \exists t_c \bullet \omega_c \models c \xrightarrow{t_c} \wedge t_f \approx_{\overline{P},\overline{E}} t_c$$

Finally, we can define for the complete CFT when it is correct w.r.t. a component c, if all clauses defined by the CFT are correct w.r.t c.

Definition 11 (CFT correctness w.r.t. a component). *Given a component c, a CFT (P, E) with $\overline{P} = \overline{P_1} \sqcup \ldots \sqcup \overline{P_n}$. (P, E) is correct w.r.t. c, iff $\overline{P_i}$ and E are correct w.r.t. c for all $0 < i \leq n$.*

In this section we have formalized CFTs and CFT correctness w.r.t. a component. In the following section we formally discuss CFT composition and show that CFT correctness is compositional.

3   Compositionality of Component Fault Tree Correctness

The core idea of components is to compose them to larger, typically more complex systems. When composing components, we also have to compose their CFTs to a CFT for the composition. In this section, we formally prove that the correctness of CFTs is compositional. The formalization of the semantics of CFTs in Sect. 2 is equal to the formalization of non-interference, a well-known security property that describes information flow through a system. For details on non-interference, we refer to Sect. 5. For proving compositionality of CFT correctness, we re-use results compositionality of non-interference from [8].

In Sect. 3.1 we formally define CFT composition and discuss in Sect. 3.2 compositionality of correctness of composed CFTs w.r.t. composed components. In Sect. 3.3 we show that some restrictions we made in this paper for presentation purposes can be relaxed without violating the core of our results.

3.1   CFT Composition

The composition of components in a model is defined by connectors between one output port of one component and an input port of the other component, see Fig. 1. These connectors are implicitly directed, with the direction from an output port to an input port. We assume that the composition of components is acyclic. This means that we assume that if an output port of component a is connected to an input port of component b, then there is no output port of component b, which is connected to an input port of component a (and analogously for compositions). For sake of simplicity of the presentation in this paper, we assume that connectors only connect ports with the same name. For two components c and d each providing the ports p_a, we write $c.p_a$ and $d.p_a$ to distinguish them. Also, for simplicity of the presentation, we assume that an output event is at most connected to one input port.

For the CFTs of composed components, we assume, for a simpler presentation, that two ports connected by a connector define the same events, i.e. if a connector connects $c.p_a$ and $d.p_a$, and for $c.p_a$ an event (p_a, t) is defined, then an event (p_a, t) is also defined for $d.p_a$ and vice versa.

Two CFTs can be composed, if the output event of one CFT is the same as an input event of the other CFT. If (P_c, E) is a CFT of component c and (P_d, A) is a CFT of component d, and c and d are composed via a connector on the port which has defined event A, then we can also compose the CFTs. The CFT of the composition $comp$ is (P'_c, E), where P'_c is the formula P_c where each occurrence of A is replaced by the formula P_d.

Definition 12 (CFT composition). *Let c and d be components, $p_1 \ldots p_n$ ports, which are input ports of c and outputs ports of d, $A_1^1 \ldots A_{m_1}^1, \ldots A_1^n \ldots A_{m_n}^n$ events with A_j^i being an event on port p_i, i.e. an input event of c and an output event of d. Let further be (P_c, E) be a CFT of c and (P_j^i, A_j^i) the CFTs of d for the output events A_j^i.*

We define the CFT of the composition of c and d for output event E as $(P_{c,d}, E)$, where $P_{c,d}$ is formula P_c with each occurrence of A_j^i is replaced by P_j^i.

Note that by assumption, compositions of components are acyclic. Therefore for all compositions of c and d it is clear in which direction messages are passed. The composition of two CFTs thus itself is a CFT according to Definition 4. As such, we can discuss the correctness of a composed CFT w.r.t. a component.

3.2 Compositionality of CFT Correctness

If two CFTs (P_c, E) and (P_d, A) are correct w.r.t. the components c and d respectively, it is not obvious that their composition $(P_{c,d}, E)$ is correct w.r.t. the composition of c and d. We consider here the composition of two components as the interleaving composition of their LTS.

For the following proofs, we assume components to (1) accept inputs only depending on the port, not the communicated value (no discrimination on inputs over the same port), (2) not to produce indeterministic output and (3) not to have indeterministic internal behavior.

Definition 13 (Deterministic components). *A component c is determin-istic, if*

$$c \xrightarrow{p?v} \qquad\qquad\qquad \implies c \xrightarrow{p?v'} \text{ for all } v \text{ and } v' \text{ and}$$
$$c \xrightarrow{m_1} \text{ and } c \xrightarrow{m_2} \text{ and } m_1 \neq m_2 \implies m_1 \text{ and } m_2 \text{ are inputs, and}$$
$$c \xrightarrow{m} c_1 \text{ and } c \xrightarrow{m} c_2 \qquad\qquad \implies c_1 = c_2$$

In the remainder, we assume all components to be deterministic.

We can now show that the composed CFT is also correct w.r.t. the composition of the components.

Theorem 1 (Composed CFT correctness w.r.t. composition). *Given components c and d, CFT (P_c, E) of c and (P_j^i, A_j^i) of d as in Definition 12, such that the CFTs are correct w.r.t. the respective components. Then the composed CFT $(P_{c,d}, E)$ is correct w.r.t. the composition of c and d.*

Proof. The full formal proof for this theorem can be found in an accompanying technical report[1].   □

3.3   Discussion of Restrictions

In the previous sections we made several restrictions on components, their ports, allowed event types and others. Several of these restrictions were made in order to allow a compact description of our results in this paper. In the following, we lift several of these restrictions without invalidating our core compositionality result. Please note that all proofs were made such that they also hold in the less restricted case without changes.

In Sect. 3.1 we assume that connectors only connect ports with the same name. This assumption is typically not satisfied in a real model, however, it can easily be achieved with a simple renaming of ports.

We further assume that an output port is at most connected to one input port. Practically, an output port is often connected to several input ports, modeling the property that a message sent via this port is read by several other components. Again, a 1:1 relation between ports can be achieved by duplicating the output port, renaming it, and connecting one input port to one of the duplicated output ports. Similarly, multiple events on a single port are not restricted.

Concerning event types, we only considered timing and value events in Sect. 2.2. Our results hold for more complex type systems, as long as the type system defines an equivalence relation $\approx$ over messages, such that $m_1 \approx m_2$ implies that either m_1 and m_2 are irrelevant, or m_1 and m_2 are messages over the same port. For detailed examples, see [8].

For example we allow event types which state that messages may differ on the last bit, or that messages may differ on the last bit, if the first bit of the

---

[1] Greiner, S., Munk, P., and Nordmann, A.: Compositionality of Component Fault Trees - Definitions and Proofs. (2019). http://arxiv.org/pdf/1907.09920.

value is 1 (e.g., encoding a break signal), or even that a message is irrelevant iff the first bit of the value is 0 (e.g., encoding a log message).

Also in Sect. 3.1 we assume that if two ports are connected, the event types defined on the ports are equal. This assumption is made for presentational purposes. We do require that the event types defined on the ports satisfy a subtype relation. A similar, but informal, subtype definition for CFTs is provided by [21]. If p_i is the input port, and p_o is the output port with events A_i and A_o respectively, it has to be satisfied that for all messages m_1 and m_2 it holds that $m_1 \approx_{\overline{A_i}} m_2$ implies $m_1 \approx_{\overline{A_o}} m_2$. For a detailed discussion of this subtype property, the interested reader is referred to [10] and [9, Sect. 7.3].

4   Consequences

Apart from the central result of this paper, the compositionality of correctness of CFTs, our work has some fundamental consequences for safety engineering concerning fault propagation as well as security engineering. For one, compositionality allows easier re-using of components and their CFTs in different contexts since analysis results can be re-used and only have to be acquired once. Additionally, our formalization of CFTs connects the well-known security property *non-interference* with the safety method concerning CFTs. Thus the results in the respective domains can be re-used to a certain extent in the other domain.

4.1   Consequences for Safety Engineering

Limits of Compositionality. In this paper, we use equivalence relations over messages as a basis for event specifications. The main reason is that equivalence relations allow for a general and rather simple-to-use compositionality result. Other approaches from non-interference research are not that strict on the specification. In particular [4, 7] discuss specifications, where the secrecy (or criticality in our case) of some output information depends on previously communicated inputs, e.g., some information is secret if the user did not previously log in with a password. They show that in general these specifications can also be compositional. However, this result is not general, but heavily depending on internal properties of the program, in particular invariants of the program state and properties connecting those invariants to the external communication history. The proofs of these properties are specific to a concrete specification and the system, complicated, complex, time-consuming, and hence not practicable for real-world programs.

Event Types. Different work on CFTs is concerned with type systems and hierarchies for event types. Typically, this work also provides sub-type relations, often w.r.t. semantic sub types, i.e., a type is a subtype of another, if from common understanding of the expressed fault, it is more specific. Our equivalence relations in combination with their effect on compositionality (see Sect. 3.3) provide a formal condition for subtypes relations.

CFT Validation. Fault propagation descriptions are typically validated against the implementation of the system using time-consuming and inherently incomplete fault injection tests. Our formalization shows that CFTs in essence describe an information flow property, thus we can re-use validation methods originally designed for information flow analysis. Most of these methods are focused on software components.

For example, a very common method for analyzing information flow are type systems. See [12] for an overview. Here inputs and outputs of a software component are typed with security types (similar to our event types) and by automatically inferring types of statements and local variables, it can be shown that the information flow of an implementation is consistent with the specification, i.e., the CFT in our case.

Another technique is taint analysis, e.g., [3], where inputs are tainted to be secret (faulty in our case), and taints are propagated through the program. It can now be checked that public outputs (in our case outputs over critical ports) are not tainted. Taint analysis can be performed statically and dynamically.

Other techniques build on program dependency graphs (e.g., [11]), where through program slicing the flow of information (propagation of faults in our case) is analyzed. Dependency graph based analysis are in particular interesting in terms of scalability. These techniques can be useful for automatically generating information flow specifications (CFTs) from a given program.

Finally, non-interference is a well-defined property, which allows for theorem proving approaches for the verification of information flow (fault propagation). Different approaches have been developed building on different theoretical backgrounds, e.g., [27]. Since non-interference (CFT correctness) is compositional, a combination of different analyses can be relatively easily achieved by using different analyses either for different component or even different partial specifications (Clauses in our case).

4.2   Consequences for Security Analysis

While methods for the analysis of information flow properties is well-researched, it is an open problem how to gain the necessary specifications. For a non-interference specification for security-critical programs, inputs and outputs have to be marked as secret or public. Practically, those specifications do not exist for real-world programs.

Non-interference is often used for modeling confidentiality properties, i.e., properties stating that some secret information must not leak to publicly available outputs. In particular in safety-relevant systems, e.g., automotive systems, a more interesting security property is integrity, i.e. the property that an attacker is not able to influence safety-relevant outputs. Safety norms, e.g., ISO 26262 [15], recommend fault propagation analysis for those outputs in form of FTA and FMEA anyway. Thus, a CFT in essence defines an integrity specification for safety-critical outputs. This specification could generally be re-used in a threat and risk analysis in security engineering, e.g., SAE J3061 [16], to decide whether an attacker can indirectly influence a particular safety-relevant output.

5   Related Work

Extensive overviews of MBSA methods, including CFTs, are given by Aizpurua and Muxika [1], Sharvia et al. [28], and Lisagor et al. [19]. CFTs have been used in different industrial domains, such as railway [13] and automotive [22,24]. The underlying principle of all CFT approaches and implementation is to stitch together the fault tree for a given top event based on the individual CFTs and the components of the system model [17,18].

Thums and Schellhorn [31] present an FTA semantics in Computational Tree Logic (CTL). Later, Thums [30] also introduces an FTA semantics in Interval Temporal Logic (ITL) and compares it with previous formalization, e.g., in Duration Calculus (DC). However, Thums did not consider CFTs.

Bozzano et al. [5] present a trace-based formalization of hierarchical components and their contracts. Extending this formalization with contract-based fault injection, they show how fault trees can automatically be generated. While this is a very powerful approach, it requires components, their contracts, and the refinement of these contracts to be specified. As opposed to this work, we directly prove the composability of CFTs.

Mahmud et al. [20] generate Pandora temporal fault trees (TFT) based on the behavior of components defined by state machines. The approach is to generate a TFT from each state machine and combine these to a TFT of the entire system. However, the authors do not formally prove the compositionality property. To the best of our knowledge, the correctness of this composability has not been formally proven so far. Our formalization of components as Labeled Transition Systems, and formalizing the semantics of CFTs using equivalence relations is an extension of previous work in [8].

Formalizing information-flow properties with an explicit environment was pioneered by Wittbold and Jonson [32], and Rafnsson et al. [26] show that non-interference is also compositional when the presence of messages is secret.

In [8], compositionality is shown for specifications using the more general notion of equivalence relations, and the theory is extended to components which offer their functionality in the form of services. In [10], the authors show that non-interference for service components directly follows from non-interference of services, which allows a combination of analysis methods on a more fine-grained level, hence with increased precision. Bauereis et al. [4] show that compositionality of non-interference for specifications with a dependency on the history, e.g., access to information after logging in, is possible, however complicated and not generalizable.

As mentioned in Sect. 4, the analysis of information flow properties is well-known in the security domain. Several analysis methods from the security domain or the safety domain have been adopted and applied in the respective other domain [25]. One prominent example is the attack tree analysis that is conceptually based on the fault tree analysis [25]. A survey of both techniques is given by Nagaraju [23]. Fovino et al. [6] integrate attack trees and fault trees. While the authors propose a sound mathematical basis for the quantitative security risk assessment, they do not base their analysis on the system model. Steiner and Liggesmeyer [29] propose to extend CFTs with attack trees. The authors propose to leverage the data flow in the system to create new security events besides the safety events in CFTs. For cut sets that contain both, security and safety events, the rating of combined security events and the probability of combined safety events are calculated separately. Steiner and Liggesmeyer do not leverage the information flow that is already modeled in the system model and do not prove the composability of their approach.

6   Conclusion and Future Work

In this paper, we present a formalization of Component Fault Trees (CFTs) by mapping their semantics to the information-flow property non-interference for Input-Output Labeled Transition Systems. We re-use results from security research to formally prove that the correctness of CFTs for components is compositional. By bringing together a well-known safety engineering approach (CFTs) and a well-known security property (non-interference), we enable to check the validity of CFTs against their implementation, leveraging existing validation methods from security engineering such as information flow analysis using type systems, taint analysis, or program dependency graphs and program slicing. Hence, we argue that CFTs provide the integrity specification of safety-critical outputs that is required by threat and risk analysis in security engineering.

As future work, we plan to explore the mutual benefits of other combinations of safety and security engineering methods and processes.

References

1. Aizpurua, J.I., Muxika, E.: Model-based design of dependable systems: limitations and evolution of analysis and verification approaches. Int. J. Adv. Secur. 6(1 & 2), 12–31 (2013)
2. Amarnath, R., et al.: Dependability challenges in the model-driven engineering of automotive systems. In: Proceedings of ISSRE Workshops (2016). https://doi.org/10.1109/ISSREW.2016.15
3. Arzt, S., et al.: FlowDroid: precise context, flow, field, object-sensitive and lifecycle-aware taint analysis for Android apps. In: Proceedings of PLDI, pp. 259–269 (2014). https://doi.org/10.1145/2594291.2594299
4. Bauereiß, T., et al.: CoSMeDis: a distributed social media platform with formally verified confidentiality guarantees. In: Proceedings of Symposium on Security and Privacy, pp. 729–748 (2017). https://doi.org/10.1109/SP.2017.24
5. Bozzano, M., Cimatti, A., Mattarei, C., Tonetta, S.: Formal safety assessment via contract-based design. In: Cassez, F., Raskin, J.-F. (eds.) ATVA 2014. LNCS, vol. 8837, pp. 81–97. Springer, Cham (2014). https://doi.org/10.1007/978-3-319-11936-6_7
6. Fovino, I.N., Masera, M., Cian, A.D.: Integrating cyber attacks within fault trees. Reliab. Eng. Syst. Saf. 94(9), 1394–1402 (2009). https://doi.org/10.1016/j.ress.2009.02.020

7. Greiner, S., Birnstill, P., Krempel, E., Beckert, B., Beyerer, J.: Privacy preserving surveillance and the tracking-paradox. In: Proceedings of the Future Security - Security Research Conference, pp. 296–302 (2013)
8. Greiner, S., Grahl, D.: Non-interference with what-declassification in component-based systems. In: Proceedings of CSF, pp. 253–267 (2016). https://doi.org/10.1109/CSF.2016.25
9. Greiner, S.: A framework for non-interference in component-based systems. Ph.D. thesis. Karlsruher Institut für Technologie (KIT) (2018). https://doi.org/10.5445/IR/1000082042
10. Greiner, S., Mohr, M., Beckert, B.: Modular verification of information flow security in component-based systems. In: Cimatti, A., Sirjani, M. (eds.) SEFM 2017. LNCS, vol. 10469, pp. 300–315. Springer, Cham (2017). https://doi.org/10.1007/978-3-319-66197-1_19
11. Hammer, C., Snelting, G.: Flow-sensitive, context-sensitive, and object-sensitive information flow control based on program dependence graphs. Int. J. Inf. Secur. 8(6), 399–422 (2009). https://doi.org/10.1007/s10207-009-0086-1
12. Hedin, D., Sabelfeld, A.: A perspective on information-flow control. Softw. Saf. Secur. 33, 319–347 (2012). NATO Science for Peace and Security Series - D: Information and Communication Security
13. Höfig, K., et al.: Model-based reliability and safety: reducing the complexity of safety analyses using component fault trees. In: Proceedings of RAMS (2018). https://doi.org/10.1109/RAM.2018.8463058
14. International Electrotechnical Commission (IEC): IEC 61025: Fault tree analysis (FTA) (2006)
15. International Standard Organization (ISO): ISO 26262-4: Road vehicles - functional safety - Part 6: Product development at the system level (2018)
16. Society of Automotive Engineers (SAE): SAE J3061: Cybersecurity Guidebook for Cyber-Physical Vehicle Systems (2016)
17. Kaiser, B., Liggesmeyer, P., Mäckel, O.: A new component concept for fault trees. In: Proceedings of SCS, pp. 37–46 (2003)
18. Kaiser, B., et al.: Advances in component fault trees. In: Proceedings of ESREL (2018)
19. Lisagor, O., Kelly, T., Niu, R.: Model-based safety assessment: review of the discipline and its challenges. In: The Proceedings of ICRMS, pp. 625–632 (2011). https://doi.org/10.1109/ICRMS.2011.5979344
20. Mahmud, N., Walker, M., Papadopoulos, Y.: Compositional synthesis of temporal fault trees from state machines. Perform. Eval. Rev. 39(4), 79–88 (2012). https://doi.org/10.1145/2185395.2185444
21. Möhrle, F., Zeller, M., Höfig, K., Rothfelder, M.: Automating compositional safety analysis using a failure type taxonomy for component fault trees. In: Risk, Reliability and Safety: Innovating Theory and Practice (2016)
22. Munk, P., et al.: INVITED: semi-automatic safety analysis and optimization. In: Proceedings of DAC (2018)
23. Nagaraju, V., Fiondella, L., Wandji, T.: A survey of fault and attack tree modeling and analysis for cyber risk management. In: Proceedings of THS (2017). https://doi.org/10.1109/THS.2017.7943455
24. Nordmann, A., Munk, P.: Lessons learned from model-based safety assessment with SysML and component fault trees. In: Proceedings of MODELS (2018). https://doi.org/10.1145/3239372.3239373

25. Piètre-Cambacédàs, L., Bouissou, M.: Cross-fertilization between safety and security engineering. Reliab. Eng. Syst. Saf. **110**, 110–126 (2013). https://doi.org/10.1016/j.ress.2012.09.011
26. Rafnsson, W., Hedin, D., Sabelfeld, A.: Securing interactive programs. In: Proceedings of CSF, pp. 293–307 (2012)
27. Scheben, C., Greiner, S.: Information flow analysis. In: Ahrendt, W., Beckert, B., Bubel, R., Hähnle, R., Schmitt, P., Ulbrich, M. (eds.) Deductive Software Verification – The KeY Book. LNCS, vol. 10001, pp. 453–471. Springer, Cham (2016). https://doi.org/10.1007/978-3-319-49812-6_13
28. Sharvia, S., Kabir, S., Walker, M., Papadopoulos, Y.: Model-based dependability analysis: state-of-the-art, challenges, and future outlook. In: Software Quality Assurance, pp. 251–278 (2016). https://doi.org/10.1016/B978-0-12-802301-3.00012-0
29. Steiner, M., Liggesmeyer, P.: Combination of safety and security analysis - finding security problems that threaten the safety of a system. In: Proceedings of DECSSAFECOMP (2013)
30. Thums, A.: Formale Fehlerbaumanalyse. Ph.D. thesis. University of Augsburg, Germany (2004)
31. Thums, A., Schellhorn, G.: Model checking FTA. In: Araki, K., Gnesi, S., Mandrioli, D. (eds.) FME 2003. LNCS, vol. 2805, pp. 739–757. Springer, Heidelberg (2003). https://doi.org/10.1007/978-3-540-45236-2_40
32. Wittbold, J.T., Johnson, D.M.: Information flow in nondeterministic systems. In: Proceedings of RISP, pp. 144–161 (1990). https://doi.org/10.1109/RISP.1990.63846

Tiered Model-Based Safety Assessment

Kevin Delmas[✉], Christel Seguin, and Pierre Bieber

ONERA/DTIM Université de Toulouse, 2 av. E. Belin, 31055 Toulouse, France
{kevin.delmas,christel.seguin,pierre.bieber}@onera.fr

Abstract. Processes and techniques used for assessing the safety of a complex system are well-addressed by safety standards. These standards usually recommend to decompose the assessment process into different stages of analysis, so called tiered safety assessment. Each analysis stage should be performed by applying recommended assessment techniques. To provide confidence in the correctness of the whole analysis, some verification techniques, usually traceability checking, are applied between two stages. Even if the traceability provides some confidence in the correctness of the decomposition, the following problems remains How to model the system behaviours at each stage of safety assessment? How to efficiently use these stages during the design process? What is the formal relationship between these modelling stages? To tackle these problems, we propose a way to specify, formalize and implement the relations between assessment stages. The proposal and its pros & cons are illustrated on a Remotely Piloted Aircraft System (RPAS) use-case.

1 Introduction

The development of smart transport systems is classically addressed by tiered processes (for instance V cycle) where product specifications are successively refined until the final implementation phase.

The components of these systems may be subject to various kinds of faults which may result in unacceptable safety issues. The safety effects of the potential faults must therefore be carefully analysed and their acceptability assessed. Achieving such activities with a monolithic safety assessment may be tedious, error-prone, and would fail to provide confidence in the system dependability.

Standards like ARP-4754 [17] (aeronautics domain) provide a safety process used successfully in the industrial domain to perform the safety assessment of complex systems. One key of its success is the tight coupling of the development and safety processes, that is in each development tier the relevant safety assessment are processed and fed the next development steps with analyses results. A safety process therefore generates analyses made at various level of granularity and addressing various kinds of systems and components.

In addition to classical methods like fault trees or Markov chains (available in [18]), newer approaches like Model Based Safety Assessment (MBSA) can be used to perform the mentioned analyses. ALTARICA [2] is one of the most successful safety modelling and assessment language used in an industrial context [12].

© Springer Nature Switzerland AG 2019
Y. Papadopoulos et al. (Eds.): IMBSA 2019, LNCS 11842, pp. 141–156, 2019.
https://doi.org/10.1007/978-3-030-32872-6_10

Besides the modelling and assessment ease brought by these approaches, ensuring the consistency and traceability of safety analyses is still a prominent problem. We claim that, like MBSE can been used [20] to tackle traceability and consistency problems during development, the MBSA offers a suitable environment to produce consistent and traceable safety analyses for complex systems.

The contribution of this paper is twofold, first it provides a methodology to model the relations between development tiers, second it formalises these relations with ALTARICA to benefit from the automated safety assessment. The remainder of the paper is organised as follows: 1. the classical safety process and its resulting analyses are succinctly presented (Sect. 2) and the need of traceability and consistency is motivated; 2. our modelling methodology and its implementation using ALTARICA are presented (Sect. 3); 3. the benefit of our methodology (Sect. 4) is demonstrated on a simplified RPAS use-case; 4. eventually the related work on safety analysis of complex systems is detailed (Sect. 5).

2   Safety Process and MBSA

Complex systems are usually developed using a tiered process, that is some design and validation activities are performed at each stage of development and then fed the subsequent stages. Safety activities are performed throughout the design process. Designers can rely on classical formalisms (for instance listed in the ARP-4761 [16]). As identified by [14], the classical formalisms like fault-trees or Markov chains embrace an architecture-agnostic modelling. Hence, a tedious abstraction work must be achieved by the safety engineers to derive the safety models out-of the system specification. Furthermore, adapting the safety models after an evolution of the system design may be cumbersome and error-prone. Architecture-aware formalisms, like component fault trees [8], finite automata [4], mode automata [2] or hierarchic safety assessments [13] have been introduced to overcome the limitations of classical formalisms. Architecture-aware formalisms provide a way to define the dysfunctional behaviour of entities called *components* that are instantiated and connected to build the architecture of a *system*. Ultimately this interconnection of components can be analysed by automatic solvers like [3,15], this kind of analyses is the so-called Model-Based Safety Assessment.

2.1   Reminder on MBSA and Altarica

Amongst the possible formalisms, ALTARICA [2] is one of the most popular and successfully applied MBSA language in both academic and industrial fields. Since ALTARICA is a formal language, its behaviour can be simulated and automated safety assessment (like [15]) can be performed. Therefore, the underlying language used in the models presented in this paper is ALTARICA and their analysis is performed by the tool CECILIA-OCAS [5] from Dassault Aviation.

A system modelled with ALTARICA is a set of interconnected components, these connections are considered as constraints over the possibles values of the inputs and outputs of the components. These components therefore own the following elements: 1. *flow variables* the inputs and outputs that are used to interface the node with its environment; 2. *state variables* the internal variables that can encode node's functional or dysfunctional state (*e.g.* failure modes); 3. *events* the elements used to trigger the transitions amongst node's states, note that these events can be deterministic (*e.g.* reconfiguration events) or probabilistic (failure events). The node's functional and/or dysfunctional behaviour is defined by the following relations between states, flows and events: 1. *transitions* encode the possible state evolutions, each transition written $g \vdash e \rightarrow a$ informally means "when the guard g (condition over the current state and the value of the flow variables) is true when the event e is triggered then the action a is performed (assignment of state variables)"; 2. *assertions* encode the constraints between the possible values of flow and state variables. In the sequel we assume that the output flows are defined by the inputs flows and the state variables (*dataflow* restriction).

2.2 Reminder on the Safety Assessment Process

To ensure the dependability of complex systems, the safety assessment process must be tailored to the development process. The standards like ARP4754 and ISO26262 promote a safety assessment process where various safety activities are performed throughout the development process.

Generally, a safety plan can be seen as an application of the following safety assessment pattern at various levels:

Hazard Analysis (HA). Identify the conditions, in a given context, that may rise safety issues so-called *failure conditions* (FC) and allocate *safety objectives* (called SOs) to these failure conditions commensurate with the hazard's severity (or the previous safety objectives). These safety objectives are bounds over safety indicators (called SIs) such as the acceptable minimal number of root failures of a FC, the upper bound of a FC occurrence rate.

Safety Assessment (SA). Assess the proposed architecture against the objectives and derive from this assessment the safety objectives that must be met by the subsequent architectures designed during the development process.

For instance, during the aircraft specification definition an Aircraft Level, Functional Hazard Assessment (AFHA) is performed and provides the failure conditions and their severity. The *context* is specified through a set of assumptions that must be traced and ultimately confirmed to ensure the validity of the analysis.

Once the aircraft's sub-systems are known and their dependencies identified, then a Preliminary Aircraft Safety Assessment (so-called PASA) is performed. This analysis provides the appropriate safety objectives that must be fulfilled by the aircraft's systems.

The applicant must then demonstrate the fulfilment of the PASA safety objectives on each system with various assessments performed throughout the system's development process. In the sequel we will adopt the following three-stage development process (used in [7]): 1. operational: considering the system failures and their impact in its operational environment (AFHA/PASA); 2. functional: considering the safety impact of function failures on the system's environment (FHA/PSSA functional); 3. physical: considering the safety impact of implementation failures on the function or system environment (PSSA physical).

2.3   Relations Between Safety Assessments

When moving from one stage to another one, failures of the former architecture will depend on the failures of the components of the new architecture. The Fig. 1a identifies the *relations* between assessment performed during the safety activities. The explicit relations (plain arrows) are the data exchanged by the analysts to perform the safety assessments. For instance, performing the FHA of a system needed some knowledge of the system specification and the safety objectives allocated to assessed system. Some other relations are implicit (dotted line), since they fall under the expertise of the analyst to properly deriving and tracing some piece of information between stages. For instance, the analyst must identify the failure conditions (expressed over functions) that are related to a system failure mode for which a safety objective has been allocated.

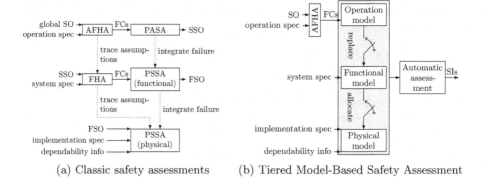

(a) Classic safety assessments   (b) Tiered Model-Based Safety Assessment

Fig. 1. Safety assessment processes

According to the Fig. 1a, we can identify two kinds of implicit relations:

Allocations express the dependencies between components of two architectures, such as the resource dependencies created by mapping functions on physical components.

Replacements link some parameters of two assessments performed at various stages, typically the environment assumptions between AFHA and FHA.

The validity of the global safety assessment relies on the identification and tracing of these relations. The prominent threats to validity are:

Traceability. If the analyst is not able to trace the dependencies or the links between assessments' parameters, the demonstration of the global safety objectives can be compromised by inconsistencies between safety assessments.

Composability. The assessments performed throughout the design process are dedicated to the identification and assessment of precise kinds of failures *e.g.* operational specification failures for PASA. The fulfilment of the global objective is achieved by a composition of the safety assessments. Some piece of information of an assessment may be considered during subsequent assessments. If the assessment framework does not provide some mechanisms to handle such dependencies between assessments, the analyst must handle them manually; that may be error-prone and time-consuming.

Maintainability. The safety assessment is more likely to be an iterative process than a linear process. The analyst needs to efficiently reflect the evolution of the design on the safety assessments. Because of the system's complexity the safety impact of a design choice may spread way beyond the considered architecture, so handling system's evolution manually is error-prone and can compromise the whole safety assessment.

To tackle these problems, we present an MBSA approach extended with a formal modelling of the relations between the safety assessments built throughout the design process, so-called Tiered Model-Based Safety Assessment.

3   Formalisation of the Tiered Safety Assessment with Altarica

We introduce the notion of Tiered Model-Based Safety Assessment providing a formal modelling of the relations between the safety assessments identified in the previous section.

3.1   Overview of the Approach

The formalisation provides a convenient way to express replacement and allocation relations between two architectures. Thanks to this modelling, the relations between safety assessments (identified in the Fig. 1a) can be greatly reduced and boils down to the ones depicted in the Fig. 1b.

The formalisation mainly addressed the relations PASA/functional PSSA and functional PSSA/physical PSSA. The former can been seen as a replacement relation where the failure modes of the systems are expressed as failure conditions over the functions of the systems. The latter is an allocation relation introducing the dependencies of functions on physical items. Thanks to MBSA, these relations can be modelled as constraints between the models of various architectures and the safety assessment can be delegated to an automatic solver. Since the relations between architectures will be formally modelled, the failure conditions contributing to the global hazards identified in the AFHA does not need to be further refined in subsequent architectures. One just enables the relations that must be considered according to the assessment level and performs its assessment (whatever the level) on the failure conditions of the operational level. Therefore the safety objective allocation phase and the adaption of system failure as function failure conditions (FHA) are not needed any more. Beyond this simplification, the proposed process provides a solution to the following threats of validity:

Traceability. By formalising the relations between the models, the analyst will need to identify and express them to perform the safety assessments. So the relations between safety assessments and the assumptions made on the impact of component failures on another architecture are natively traced.

Composability. The analyst can perform an assessment using the information dispatched over several models since the relations are formally expressed. The relations can then be activated to perform a safety assessment of the aggregation of the safety knowledge contained in the models.

Maintainability. Eventually the safety impact of any evolution of an architecture (at any level) is automatically considered during safety assessment since its impact will spread through the relations between models.

3.2   Relation Specifications

To properly integrate the notion of relation in the safety assessment models, one must provide a formal definition of such relations.

Definition 1 (Notations and Modelling assumption). *Let us consider that the behaviour of a component c is described by a set of state transitions T_c and an output function σ_c providing the output failure modes according to the inputs valuations and the current state. Let the valuation of a variable x be denoted by $V[x]$ and the Cartesian product of the valuations of a set X of variables be denoted by $V[X] = \prod_{x \in X} V[x]$. Let $V_{x \mapsto a}$ be the extension of V with $x \in X$. To introduce the definitions of the relations we assume that if a component c can fail then its possible failure modes are encoded by a unique state variable S of type FM containing the failure modes and a mode encoding the correct state denoted by ok which is the initial value of S.*

Allocation. The purpose of an allocation relation is to consider the resource dependencies of a component, in addition to its own failures. Let c be the initial component modelling the component without considering the allocation dependencies. Adding an allocation relation can be seen as a transformation of c into another component a. Let R be an input of a providing the failure mode of the component's resource, then the transitions remains unchanged, thus $T_c = T_a$ and when the resource dependencies are fulfilled ($R = ok$) then for any valuation V of I and state s we have $\sigma_a(V_{R \mapsto ok}, s) = \sigma_c(V, s)$.

Replacement. The purpose of a replacement relation is to replace the sponta-
neous occurrence of a failure mode (encoded in S) by a some function over the
component failures of another architecture. So let us consider the initial component c modelling the component without considering the replacement relation.
Replacement can be seen as a transformation of c into another component r.
Let R be an input of r providing the new failure mode then the transitions of
c involving S assignment must be no more fireable in r for any valuation of the
state and inputs. Moreover for any state s and valuation V of $I \cup R$ such that
$s = V[R]$ then $\sigma_r(V) = \sigma_c(V[I], s)$. Note that σ_r does not depends on S any
more since it is totally replaced by R.

3.3   Modelling Relations

The formalisation of the relations is founded on dependency modelling through
ALTARICA flows. These flows carry the information gathered from one architecture model to another one. The integration of the information in the targeted
architecture model is achieved by flow connection to the standard interface of
the Definition 2.

Definition 2 (Relation interface). *Let c be a component, FM be its failure
modes then the following inputs must be provided by c:*

Activation (A) *is a boolean input enabling the failure mode transitions.*
Resource (R) *is an input of type FM providing the failure mode of the underlying resources used by c.*

From the specification of the replacement and allocation relations, one can
transform any components c satisfying the assumptions of the Sect. 3.2 into a
component c' that can be used to encode the replaced and allocated version of
c. The activation of the desired relation is based on the A and R inputs of the
interface.

Definition 3 (Interface implementation). *Let c be a component, T_c be its
transition set, σ_c its output function, T_E be the set of transitions containing an
assignment of S, V be a valuation of $I \cup R$ and s be the current state. The
transition set $T_{c'}$ and output function $\sigma_{c'}$ of the adaptation c' of c implementing
the interface can be defined as follows:*

$$T_{c'} = \{g \wedge \neg A \vdash e \to a | g \vdash e \to a \in T_E\} \cup (T_c \setminus T_E)$$
$$\sigma_{c'}(V, s) = \begin{cases} \sigma_a(V, s) & \text{if } A \\ \sigma_c(V[I], V[R]) & \text{otherwise} \end{cases}$$

No Relation. If the component is not linked by a replacement nor an allocation
relation then its internal failures (S) and inputs (I) only impact its outputs,
so the activation input should be set to *true* and the resource input should be
ok. Since A is always true then in any transition of c', $g \wedge A \Rightarrow g$ so $T_{c'} = T_c$.
Moreover, for any valuation V of $I \cup R$ and state s we have $\sigma_{c'}(V, s) = \sigma_a(V, s)$, in
addition when $R = ok$ we also have $\sigma_a(V[I]_{R \mapsto ok}, s) = \sigma_c(V[I], s)$ so $\sigma_{c'}(V, s) = \sigma_c(V[I], s)$ holds.

Replacement. When a component failure modes are replaced, A must be set to *false* and R connected to the replacement function. Since $A = false$, for all transition $g \vdash e \to a \in T_{c'}$ containing an assignment of S we have $\neg A \Rightarrow \neg g$ hence the transitions encoding the failure evolution of c are not fireable. Furthermore, let $\sigma_r(V) = \sigma_c(V[I], V[R])$ then we have $\sigma_{c'}(V, s) = \sigma_r(V)$ so for any state s and valuation V of $I \cup R$ such that $s = V[R]$ we have $\sigma_{c'}(V, s) = \sigma_r(V) = \sigma_c(V[I], s)$.

Allocation. When component resource dependencies are considered A must be set to *true* and R connected to the allocation function. Since $A = true$, we have $T_c = T_{c'}$ and the output function is $\sigma_{c'}(V, s) = \sigma_a(V, s)$. By definition of σ_a for any state s, valuation V of $I \cup R$ where $V[R] = ok$ we have $\sigma_a(V, s) = \sigma_c(V[I], s)$ so $\sigma_{c'}(V, s) = \sigma_c(V[I], s)$ holds.

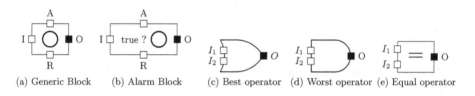

(a) Generic Block   (b) Alarm Block   (c) Best operator   (d) Worst operator   (e) Equal operator

Fig. 2. Standard components

```
1  node generic_block                      12   S := ok ;
2  flow //interface flows                  13   trans
3   I : FM : in; //input FM                14   //failures are permanent
4   O : FM : out; //output FM              15   S = ok and A ⊢ e_fm₁ → S := FM₁;
5   R : FM : in; //alloc or replace FM     16   ...
6   A : bool : in; //activate              17   S = ok and A ⊢ e_fmₙ → S := FMₙ;
7  state //component FM                     18   assert
8   S : FM;                                 19   //output FM is the worst of
9  event //one event per fm in FM           20   //R, S and I
10  e_fm₁ ,...,e_fmₙ ;                       21   O = worst(I ,worst(R,S));
11 init //initially component is ok        22  end
```

Listing 1.1: ALTARICA code of the generic Block

3.4 Standard Components

The ALTARICA models presented in the remainder of the paper are build on top of a library of generic components providing the interface of the Definition 2. The *fallible* components of the Figs. 2a and b are named *blocks* (graphically discriminated by an internal circle) and provides the relation interface. Conversely the *infallible* components of the Figs. 2c and d, named *operators*, does not provide the relation interface. The operator best of Fig. 2c (resp. worst of Fig. 2d) provides the lowest (resp. greatest) failure mode amongst I_1 and I_2 according a total order $<$ over the failure modes. A possible definition and concretisation of the generic block is provided by the Example 1.

Example 1 (Interface implementation). The generic block is generic over the set of failure modes (FM) and thus the ALTARICA code 1.1 must be concretised with a given failure mode set to obtain the ALTARICA model of this block. As requested by the Definition 2 the initial state is *ok*. To fulfil the *Transition* constraints for allocation and replacement, the transition's guards complies to the Definition 3. The function worst is used whatever the value of A *i.e.* $\sigma_{c'} = \sigma_a = \sigma_c$. Nevertheless, when A is true we have $\sigma_{c'} = \sigma_a$ and when A is false we know that $S = ok$ so $\sigma_{c'}(I, R, S) = worst(I, worst(R, ok)) = worst(I, R) = \sigma_c(I, R)$. So this implementation complies to the Definition 3.

In the sequel we will consider that blocks own the following generic failure modes: the block does not provide its intended behaviour (called *lost*); the block provides an erroneous behaviour (called *err*). A system can then be a concrete block where $FM = \{ok, err, lost\}$.

3.5 Decomposing Analyses

A safety assessment considering only the component failures of a specific architecture is obtained by deactivating all the components of the other architectures and building replacement relations. The only contributors to the high-level hazards will be the component failures of the target architecture. Through the replacement relation, the analyst will benefit from the failure propagation modelled in the higher level architectures to perform its safety assessment.

If the analyst want to consider the failure of several architecture levels simultaneously then the considered components must be activated and an allocation relation must be defined between the considered levels. For instance, such an analysis on functional and physical levels can provide the combination of function specification and physical failures that may contribute to top level hazards.

4 Safety Assessment of an RPAS System

Let us illustrate the modelling framework on a simplified remotely piloted aircraft system (RPAS)[1]. The drone's mission is to inspect an infrastructure locate in a pre-defined evolution zone. Since some populated areas located nearby, the drone should not fly, land nor crash outside the evolution zone.

If one wants to use such system, the hazards inherent to the RPAS must be identified and their likelihood demonstrated as acceptable. To do so, the hazards should be identified out-of the failure modes of the top level functions of the RPAS that are *Control Flight i.e.* stay in the evolution zone and *Abort Flight i.e.* detect the conditions where motors must be cut off.

The severity of a failure condition is classified using a severity scale derived from the ARP4754, here let us only consider *Catastrophic* as a potential ground or in-flight collision leading to one or several fatalities and *Hazardous* as a controlled crash in a predefined zone without stringent access control. The simplified AFHA of the Table 1 provides an assessment of the safety impacts.

---

[1] Available at www.onera.fr/sites/default/files/274/IMBSA2019code.zip.

In addition, the AFHA must provide the safety objectives attached to these failure conditions, in the remainder of this paper we consider that Catastrophic failure conditions must not be reached by single failures. We will not illustrate the safety assessment based on quantitative measure. Note that one can easily perform such quantitative assessment with the minimal cutsets computed for each architecture. Consequently we will assess only the failure condition *Fly away without flight abortion capability* (CAT) that could lead to collision with vehicles or other aircraft.

Table 1. Simplified AFHA of the RPAS

Function	Failure	Context	Consequences	Severity
Control flight	*err*	Cannot abort flight	Crash outside evolution zone	**Catastrophic**
		Can abort flight	Crash inside evolution zone	**Hazardous**
	lost	–	Crash inside evolution zone	
Abort flight	*lost*	Cannot control flight	Crash outside evolution zone	**Catastrophic**
		Can control flight	No safety effect	**NSE**
	err	–	Crash inside evolution zone	**Hazardous**

4.1 Operational-Level Assessment

The RPAS is constituted of a Flight Controller System (FCS) managing the flight plan and the trajectory of the drone. The Flight Termination System (FTS) monitors the FCS and can reconfigure the FCS to mitigate its failure, the ultimate action of the FTS is to trigger a controlled crash to avoid a fly-away. The identified failure conditions are encoded as observers over the FCS and FTS systems as follows: 1. a fly-away occurs when the FCS provides an erroneous control of the drone and the FTS is not able to trigger a controlled crash; 2. a crash in the zone occurs when the FCS is lost or if the FTS triggers a controlled crash. The minimal cutsets of these failure conditions has been generated automatically by Cecilia-OCAS:

$$MCS = \{\{FCS.err, FTS.lost\}\}$$

So at this stage the no single failure mode requirement for Catastrophic failure condition is fulfilled. Nevertheless the latter result holds if no common mode of failures are added during functional and physical architecture design.

4.2 Functional-Level Analysis

The functional architecture is depicted by the Fig. 3a wherein *Acquisition functions* acquire flight parameters and monitor adversary conditions; *Monitoring* acquires data are checked by independent alarms; *TrajectoryControl* functions

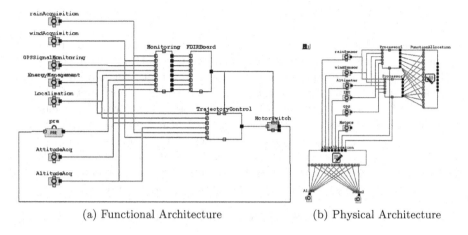

(a) Functional Architecture   (b) Physical Architecture

Fig. 3. Functional and physical architectures

controlling the drone from flight parameters and control mode; *MotorSwitch* cutting motors' power supply if the flight termination mode is selected.

The last node called **FDIRBoard** encodes the on-board safety policy that selects the control mode according to the alarm states. The selection rules are coded as an ALTARICA automaton selecting the control mode according the alarm states. More precisely, at any time flight termination is chosen when the attitude **or** trajectory are not correct, otherwise emergency landing is chosen if the rain **or** wind **or** altitude **or** energy are not correct, otherwise hovering mode is chosen in case of loss of GNSS **or** localization, otherwise the mission mode is selected.

To perform the safety assessment, the analyst must replace the operation failure modes by some failure conditions over the functional architecture. To achieve that we saw that the component must be deactivated and the new failure mode must be provided trough R. The replacement relation considered is 1. the trajectory state provides the state of the FCS; 2. when the trajectory or the attitude estimation is not correct then the flight termination must be triggered and the switch should cut the motor otherwise the FTS does not works properly.

Thanks to the replacement relation, the analyst can compute the following cutsets integrating the safety knowledge of the functional architecture. The result shows that the functional architecture does not integrate common mode of failure for the Catastrophic failure conditions. The analyst can then allocate these functions on physical resources.

$$MCS = \begin{cases} \{GPSSignalMonitoring.err, & TrajectoryControl.Pilot.err\}, \\ \{Localisation.err, & TrajectoryControl.Pilot.err\}, \\ \{MotorSwitch.lost, & AttitudeAcq.err\}, \\ \{MotorSwitch.lost, & TrajectoryControl.Pilot.err\} \end{cases}$$

4.3   Physical-Level Analysis

The physical architecture shown by the Fig. 3b is composed of two processors executing the software, sensors, motors, and two power supply channels.

Each acquisition function is allocated both on a processor and on a sensor. The monitoring, control mode selection, trajectory control and abort flight are implemented as software executed on the processors. The trajectory management additionally depends on the motor to control the drone's trajectory. Let us consider that the analyst wants to consider only one processor and power supply channel in the physical architecture. The safety assessment considering this allocation relation can be assessed by computing the new cutsets, for the sake of readability we display the cutsets containing only physical failures.

$$MCS = \{\{Alim1.err\}, \{Processor1.err\}, \{Alim1.lost, IMU.err\}\{Processor1.lost, IMU.err\}\}$$

Allocating all components on the same power supply and processor produces a common mode of failures identified by the minimal cutsets generator. The analyst must reconsider its allocation relation to avoid such a single point of failure. For instance, allocating the monitoring, FDIR and MotorSwitch on the second processor and the other software on the first one. Hence the second processor should be powered by the second power supply. The validity of the reallocation is assessed by recomputing the minimal cutsets:

$$MCS = \left\{ \begin{array}{ll} \{Alim2.err, Alim1.err\}, & \{Alim2.err, IMU.err\}, \\ \{Alim2.err, Processor1.err\}, & \{Alim2.lost, Alim1.err\}, \\ \{Alim2.lost, IMU.err\}, & \{Alim2.lost, Processor1.err\}, \\ \{Processor2.err, Alim1.err\}, & \{Processor2.err, IMU.err\} \\ \{Processor2.err, Processor1.err\}, & \{Processor2.lost, Alim1.err\}, \\ \{Processor2.lost, IMU.err\}, & \{Processor2.lost, Processor1.err\} \end{array} \right\}$$

5   Related Work

Tiered safety assessment processes propose to decompose the global task in several easiest sub-tasks to master the analysis of complex systems. Each sub-task uses a specific model for an analysis which is focussed on an abstract system view or a more detailed subpart. The issue is to ensure the maintainability, traceability and composability of all these models and analyses.

We explored in this paper the use of a unique model which can progressively integrate several models, while keeping possible the analyses of the model subparts at the relevant granularity level. We used of course the composition and hierarchy features of AltaRica. However, this is not enough. Safety models are not limited to structures: they encompass more or less sophisticated failure propagation logics. So our main contribution was to clarify the logical dependencies between the subparts of interest and to show how they can be encoded to ease the model update and its tiered analysis. A difficulty was to do it in a way which preserves the analysis tractability and the results readability for all tiers of the process.

This is rather original. Indeed, the mainstream idea of the literature is to handle the maintainability, traceability and composability of all the sub-models and analyses by characterizing the relations between analyses made at different design stages, more or less formally and outside the models.

5.1 Relation Through Refinement

The approaches propose to consider a complex system as a *layered system*. For instance in [19], a framework of safety modelling is for layered safety mechanisms is implemented using event-B [1]. The notion of layer can encompass various meaning, in [19] and [9], a layer is a model of a safety mechanism handling failures either locally, or by using dedicated safety mechanisms (sub-layers) or by invoking more general-purpose safety mechanism (up-layer). Instead of performing safety analyses for each layer of safety mechanisms and handling manually the relations between them, the authors of [9] propose to formalise the layer hierarchy with the notion of *refinement* of event-B. Using such a framework enables the designers to formalise the behaviour of fault-tolerance mechanisms and to perform a global formal analysis for some fault-tolerance properties.

Another notion of layer is exploited in [6] as a way to represent several *abstraction* stages. The proposed framework is based on component fault trees where the user can define abstract component fault trees. A notion of *concretisation* can then be used to provide a realisation of a specification. The framework assists the analyst be providing automatic consistency checks.

As shown by the presented works, providing a formal notion of refinement is a way to ensure the maintainability, the traceability and the composability of the assessment. Nevertheless, the refinement preserve logical properties and it does not offer any guaranty on the preservation of probabilities. Our approach does not pretend to solve this issue. However, the replacement and allocation enable a quick computation of cutsets and associated probabilities.

5.2 Relation Through Synchronisation

The approach of [12] addressed the safety assessment of tiered system by focusing their effort on the formalisation of the allocation between architectures produced at various design stages. The authors propose to use the MBSA to model the dysfunctional models of these architectures in a single model. The allocation is then formalised through the notion of synchronization provided by the mode automaton formalism (more information on synchronisation can be found in [14]).

Allocation through synchronisation is an efficient and light way to model the dependencies between components of various architectures. Nevertheless, an allocation dependency can be considered as an arbitrary complex function of resource failures, for instance the dependency of a function on its implementation resource can be a set of resource failure combinations. Unfortunately the synchronisation language expressivity limits the modelisable dependencies. Moreover, the synchronisation are not *oriented*, so it is not possible to encode that a failure event is caused by a combination of failure events (as a safety analyst may want to represent the resource dependency). Usual dependencies like common causes are not sufficient to cover the full spectrum of dependencies of an allocation.

5.3 Relation Through Traceability

Another kind of approaches like [11] relies on the traceability between the safety and design process. In this work the analysis and design phases are modelled as UML elements and the relations between them are explicitly modelled. The analyst is then able to link the designed architecture to the corresponding safety model. The traceability between the safety and design is used to ease the manual checking.

The approach of [7] proposes to analyse complex system using MBSA. The idea is to decompose the system's architecture at various levels straightforwardly linkable to the design phase of the system. At each level the failure conditions and the dependencies between the components of the architecture are modelled. Note that a model may embed some information from an upper level. Furthermore, the failure conditions expressed at a given level must be refined at subsequent analysis levels. The traceability and consistency between models is then manually handled. Some methods like [10] can be used to link component failures and then compare the minimal cutsets produced by the safety assessments.

Such approaches suffer from the following issues: 1. the integration of some information of an upper level architecture is tedious and can generate some inconsistencies between models if the information is not integrated properly; 2. without formal modelling of the relations the maintainability is not addressed; 3. manual handling of the traceability for complex system can be the source of inconsistencies between models and assessments. Nevertheless, our approach can be seen as an extension of the approach of [7] wherein the architectural models are formally linked through allocation and replacement relations.

6 Conclusion

Summary. The tiered safety assessment is recommended by the safety standards to master the complexity of assessment of complex systems. This recommendation is currently implemented by performing separately complementary fault tree analysis or failure mode and effect analysis and by tracing in documents the links between hypothesis or results provided by each analysis. When possible, a sub-fault tree replaces a leaf when design details are given, e.g. after allocating physical resources to a function. However, it is not easy to maintain the traceability links between all these data when the analysis of a new component is added or when hypotheses are modified. This paper identified the replacement and allocation relation used in multi-staged safety assessment. It formalises the meaning of these relations and shows how they can be implemented with ALTARICA. The practical interest of the approach is illustrated on a RPAS case study.

Limitations and Future Works. The relations considered in our approach always trace a safety knowledge to a higher architecture level. Nevertheless, the behaviour of an architecture can be needed to model the failure propagation in a lower-level architecture. This kind of relations needs to be specifically address since it can considerably enhance the accuracy of the safety assessment on complex systems. Moreover, the proposed modelling approach provides a way to build a monolithic model containing various levels of safety knowledge. Consequently, the automatic safety assessment does not benefit from this modelling paradigm, that may lead to poor assessment performance. A solution would be to develop a solver considering the modelling paradigm to enhance the efficiency of the assessment.

Acknowledgment. This work is part of the Phydias french study which is granted by the DGAC to study drone safety.

References

1. Abrial, J.-R.: Modeling in Event-B: System and Software Engineering. Cambridge University Press, Cambridge (2010)
2. Arnold, A., Point, G., Griffault, A., Rauzy, A.: The AltaRica formalism for describing concurrent systems. Fundamanta Informaticae **40**(2–3), 109–124 (1999)
3. Bittner, B., et al.: The xSAP safety analysis platform. In: Chechik, M., Raskin, J.-F. (eds.) TACAS 2016. LNCS, vol. 9636, pp. 533–539. Springer, Heidelberg (2016). https://doi.org/10.1007/978-3-662-49674-9_31
4. Bittner, B., Bozzano, M., Cimatti, A., Zampedri, G.: Automated verification and tightening of failure propagation models. In: AAAI, pp. 907–913 (2016)
5. Dassault. Cecilia OCAS framework (2014)
6. Domis, D., Höfig, K., Trapp, M.: A consistency check algorithm for component-based refinements of fault trees. In: IEEE 21st International Symposium on Software Reliability Engineering, ISSRE 2010, San Jose, CA, USA, 1–4 November 2010, pp. 171–180 (2010)
7. Farges, J.-L., et al.: Addressing safety assessment of autonomous robot operation and design with model based safety assessment. In: Lambda Mu 21 ≪Maîtrise des risques et transformation numérique: opportunités et menaces≫ (2018)
8. Kaiser, B., Liggesmeyer, P., Mäckel, O.: A new component concept for fault trees. In: Proceedings of the 8th Australian Workshop on Safety Critical Systems and Software, vol. 33, pp. 37–46. Australian Computer Society Inc. (2003)
9. Laibinis, L., Troubitsyna, E.: Fault tolerance in a layered architecture: a general specification pattern in B. In: Proceedings of the Second International Conference on Software Engineering and Formal Methods, SEFM 2004, pp. 346–355. IEEE (2004)
10. Lisagor, O., Bozzano, M., Bretschneider, M., Kelly, T.: Incremental safety assessment: enabling the comparison of safety analysis results. In: 28th International System Safety Conference (ISSC) (2010, submitted)
11. Mhenni, F., Choley, J.-Y., Nguyen, N., Frazza, C.: Flight control system modeling with sysml to support validation, qualification and certification. IFAC-PapersOnLine **49**(3), 453–458 (2016)

12. Morel, M.: Model-based safety approach for early validation of integrated and modular avionics architectures. In: Ortmeier, F., Rauzy, A. (eds.) IMBSA 2014. LNCS, vol. 8822, pp. 57–69. Springer, Cham (2014). https://doi.org/10.1007/978-3-319-12214-4_5

13. Papadopoulos, Y., McDermid, J.A.: Hierarchically performed hazard origin and propagation studies. In: Felici, M., Kanoun, K. (eds.) SAFECOMP 1999. LNCS, vol. 1698, pp. 139–152. Springer, Heidelberg (1999). https://doi.org/10.1007/3-540-48249-0_13

14. Prosvirnova, T.: AltaRica 3.0: a model-based approach for safety analyses. Ph.D. thesis. Ecole Polytechnique (2014)

15. Rauzy, A.: Mathematical foundations of minimal cutsets. IEEE Trans. Reliab. **50**(4), 389–396 (2001)

16. SAE: Aerospace Recommended Practices 4761 - guidelines and methods for conducting the safety assessment process on civil airborne systems and equipment (1996)

17. SAE: Aerospace Recommended Practices 4754a - Development of Civil Aircraft and Systems (2010)

18. Villemeur, A.: Reliability, Availability, Maintainability and Safety Assessment. Wiley, Hoboken (1992)

19. Vistbakka, I., Troubitsyna, E., Majd, A.: Multi-layered safety architecture of autonomous systems: formalising coordination perspective. In: 2019 IEEE 19th International Symposium on High Assurance Systems Engineering (HASE), pp. 58–65. IEEE (2019)

20. Zeller, M., Ratiu, D., Höfig, K.: Towards the adoption of model-based engineering for the development of safety-critical systems in industrial practice. In: Skavhaug, A., Guiochet, J., Schoitsch, E., Bitsch, F. (eds.) SAFECOMP 2016. LNCS, vol. 9923, pp. 322–333. Springer, Cham (2016). https://doi.org/10.1007/978-3-319-45480-1_26

Model Synchronization: A Formal Framework for the Management of Heterogeneous Models

Michel Batteux[1], Tatiana Prosvirnova[2,3(✉)], and Antoine Rauzy[4]

[1] IRT SystemX, Palaiseau, France
`michel.batteux@irt-systemx.fr`
[2] Laboratoire Genie Industriel, CentraleSupélec, Gif-sur-Yvette, France
[3] ONERA/DTIS, UFTMiP, Toulouse, France
`tatiana.prosvirnova@onera.fr`
[4] Norwegian University of Science and Technology, Trondheim, Norway
`antoine.rauzy@ntnu.no`

Abstract. In this article, we present the conceptual foundations and implementation principles of model synchronization, a formal framework for the management of heterogeneous models. The proposed approach relies on S2ML (System Structure Modeling Language) as a pivot language. We show, by means of a case study, that model synchronization can be used to ensure the consistency between system architecture models designed with Capella and safety models written in AltaRica 3.0.

Keywords: Heterogeneous models · Model synchronization · S2ML

1 Introduction

To face the increasing complexity of technical systems, systems engineers are designing models. These models serve different purposes: system architecture, control engineering, multi-physics simulation, safety analyses, performance assessments. They are designed at different levels of abstraction and by different teams. They may have also different levels of maturity. Ensuring that these models are consistent one another is one of today's major industrial challenges. As of today, their integration relies almost exclusively on organizational processes.

Collaborative data bases (PDM/PLM) and tools to set up traceability links between models provide a support to manage models in version and configuration, but not to ensure consistency between them. Different model transformation techniques have been proposed (e.g. [12,18]) but they often assume a master/slaves' organization of models, which is not realistic in practice. As an interesting alternative, two-sided model transformation based on triple graph grammars has been proposed see e.g. [9].

In this article, we present the conceptual foundations and implementation principles of model synchronization, a formal framework to ensure the consistency of heterogeneous models. Model synchronization relies on ideas stemmed

© Springer Nature Switzerland AG 2019
Y. Papadopoulos et al. (Eds.): IMBSA 2019, LNCS 11842, pp. 157–172, 2019.
https://doi.org/10.1007/978-3-030-32872-6_11

from Cousot's abstract interpretation [6], but its implementation is dedicated to the problem at stake. Namely, the overall approach relies on four theses:

Thesis 1. The diversity of models is irreducible. Moreover, each model has its own life-cycle. In other words, attempts to derive models for one purpose (e.g. safety analyses) from models designed for another purpose (e.g. system architecture), are essentially vain and even counter-productive.

Thesis 2. Heterogeneous models cannot be compared directly. Therefore, the synchronization process is made of three steps: first, models are abstracted in a common language; second, their abstractions are compared; third, actions are possibly taken to adjust original models according to findings of the comparison.

Thesis 3. Systems engineering models are made of two types of constructs: behavioral descriptions and structuring constructs. Behavioral descriptions are specific to each engineering domain. It is thus in general impossible to perform cross-domain comparisons. On the contrary, the structures of models reflect to some extent the structure of the system under study. Therefore, model synchronization focuses on structural comparisons.

Thesis 4. The overall objective of model synchronization is not to reach a perfect matching between (the structures of) original models. Rather, it is to agree on disagreements and to trace the possible discrepancies.

In a word, model synchronization is a pragmatic approach providing a formal framework and concrete tools to improve current processes. Its implementation relies on three basic constituents: first, one needs a pivot language in which models are abstracted. S2ML (System Structure Modeling Language) [2] is an excellent candidate for this purpose as it gathers in an organized and unified way most of the structuring constructs found in systems engineering modeling formalisms. Second, one needs tools to abstract original models into the pivot language. Ideally, the abstraction process should be fully automated. It is possible however to do this part of the work by hand or in a semi-automated way. Finally, one needs software tools to compare abstractions. The development of these tools is justified for at least two reasons: first, they depend only on the pivot language and are therefore reusable for the synchronization of any type of models; second, they ensure the soundness, the completeness and the traceability of the comparison process.

The contribution of this article is thus to present model synchronization and to discuss its conceptual foundations and its implementation into the SmartSync platform. We illustrate the discussion by applying the proposed approach on a case study – an electrical power supply system borrowed from [5]. We show how it can be used to maintain the consistency between system architecture models designed with Capella [16] and safety models written in AltaRica 3.0 [3].

The remainder of this article is organized as follows. Section 2 introduces the case study. Section 3 describes the model synchronization process. Section 4 discusses model comparison. Section 5 presents the SmartSync platform and gives some experimental results. Finally, Sect. 6 concludes this article and discusses future works.

2   Illustrative Example

2.1   Description

As an illustrative example, we shall consider a power supply system borrowed from [5] and pictured Fig. 1. We shall use this case study to illustrate the different concepts of model synchronization, i.e. to show how to ensure consistency of heterogeneous models.

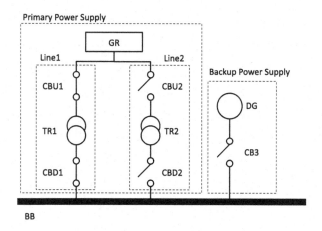

Fig. 1. A power supply system

This system is in charge of supplying electrical power to the busbar BB. It is divided into a primary power supply or a backup power supply. The primary power supply receives the power from the grid and is itself made of two redundant lines. Each of lines is made of a transformer TRi and two circuit breakers $CBUi$ and $CBDi$, $i = 1, 2$. Lines 1 and 2 are used in alternation. The passive one is in cold redundancy with the active one. The backup power supply part is made of the diesel generator DG and the circuit breaker CB3. It is in cold redundancy with the primary power supply.

2.2   Models

We consider this system from two engineering point of views: the point view of the system architect, supported by models designed in Capella [16], and the point view of the safety analyst, supported by models written in AltaRica 3.0 [3].

Figure 2 shows the functional architecture diagram of the power supply system, while Fig. 3 presents its physical architecture diagram. The latter is quite similar to the process and instrumentation diagram showed Fig. 1. Figure 4 on the left represents the life-cycle diagram of the operational architecture.

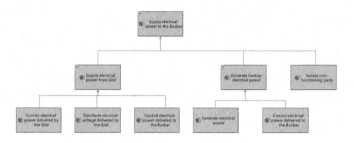

Fig. 2. Functional architecture of the power supply system represented with Capella.

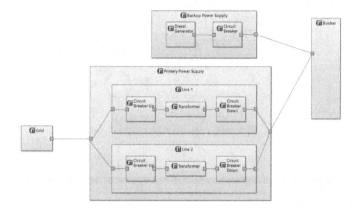

Fig. 3. Physical architecture of the power supply system represented with Capella.

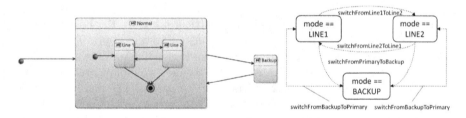

Fig. 4. Capella life-cycle diagram (operational architecture) and graphical representation of the AltaRica 3.0 controller of the power supply system.

Table 1 summarizes the allocation between functions and physical components depending on different operational phases of the system. Phase 1 corresponds to the mode *Line1* of the diagram Fig. 4, Phase 2 corresponds to the mode *Line2*, and Emergency mode – to the mode *Backup*.

Figure 5 shows an excerpt of the AltaRica code for the power supply system. There are two failure conditions of interest: loss of electrical power delivered to the busbar and loss of isolation (of non-functioning parts). They are represented by two observers in the AltaRica model. The structure of the model is inspired

Table 1. Power supply system: functions allocation table

Phase	Control electrical power delivered by the Grid	Transform electrical voltage delivered by the Grid	Control electrical power delivered to the Busbar	Generate backup electrical power	Control power delivered to Busbar	Isolate non-functioning parts
Phase 1 (Line1)	CBU1	TR1	CBD1			CBU2, CBD2, CB3
Phase 2 (Line2)	CBU2	TR2	CBD2			CBU1, CBD1, CB3
Emergency mode (Backup)				DG	CB3	CBU1, CBD1, CBU2, CBD2

by the phased-mission systems modeling pattern [4] and is close to the structure of the Capella model. The block *Controller*, which graphical representation is sketched in Fig. 4 on the right, corresponds to the life-cycle diagram given Fig. 4 on the left, the block *Functional* – to the functional architecture diagram given Fig. 2 and the block *Physical* to the physical architecture diagram given Fig. 3. The allocation of functions (see Table 1) is represented by the aggregation relation ("embeds" clause). For instance, the function *SupplyPowerByGrid* aggregates the grid, the circuit breakers and the transformer of the Line 1 of the primary power supply system in the phase 1.

System architecture and safety analyses can be seen as two faces of the same medal. System architecture focuses on how the system works, what it should do and should be. It is ruled by so-called architectural frameworks such as the CESAM framework [11]. Safety analyses focus on how the system may fail and what are the consequences of failures.

Although they consider the system at about the same level of abstraction, models designed by system architects and safety analysts are quite different. In particular, the former are pragmatic while the latter are formal [15], two characteristics that we shall define formally in the next section. Ensuring the consistency of these models is thus both extremely important and far from easy.

3   Model Synchronization

3.1   Models = Behaviors + Structures

Ensuring the consistency of two or more heterogeneous models requires to understand the nature and the role of each of these models. Models involved in systems engineering serve actually very different purposes. They can be roughly separated into two categories [15]:

```
domain MODE {LINE1, LINE2, BACKUP}
block PowerSupplySystem
  block Controller
    // body of the block Controller
  end
  block Functional
    block SupplyElectricalPowerToBusbar
      block SupplyPowerByGrid
        block Phase1
          embeds main.Physical.PrimaryPowerSupply.GR as GR;
          embeds main.Physical.PrimaryPowerSupply.Line1.CBIn as CBU1;
          embeds main.Physical.PrimaryPowerSupply.Line1.TR as TR1;
          embeds main.Physical.PrimaryPowerSupply.Line1.CBOut as CBD1;
          Boolean vfFailed (reset = true);
          assertion
            vfFailed := GR.vfFailed or TR1.vfFailed or CBU1.vfFailedToClose or
                CBD1.vfFailedToClose;
        end
        // the remainder of the block SupplyPowerByGrid
      end
      // the remainder of the block SupplyElectricalPowerToBusbar
    end
    // the remainder of the block Functional
  end
  block Physical
    block PrimaryPowerSupply
      Grid GR;
      block Line1
        embeds owner.GR as GR;
        Boolean vfInflow, vfOutflow, vfFailed (reset = false);
        CircuitBreaker CBIn, CBOut;
        Transformer TR;
        // the remainder of the block Line1
      end
      clones Line1 as Line2;
      Boolean vfOutflow (reset = false);
      assertion
        Line1.vfInflow := GR.vfOutflow;
        Line2.vfInflow := GR.vfOutflow;
        vfOutflow := Line1.vfOutflow or Line2.vfOutflow;
    end
    // the remainder of the block Physical
  end
  observer Boolean LossOfBusbarPowerSupply = if (Controller.mode==LINE1) then
      Functional.SupplyPowerByGrid.Phase1.vfFailed else if (Controller.mode==LINE2) then
      Functional.SupplyPowerByGrid.Phase2.vfFailed
      else Functional.BackupSupply.EmergencyMode.vfFailed;
  observer Boolean LossOfIsolation = if (Controller.mode==LINE1) then
      Functional.IsolateNonFunctioningParts.Phase1.vfFailed else if
      (Controller.mode==LINE2) then Functional.IsolateNonFunctioningParts.Phase2.vfFailed
      else Functional.IsolateNonFunctioningParts.EmergencyMode.vfFailed;
end
```

Fig. 5. Excerpt of the AltaRica code for the power supply system.

- Pragmatic models that are used primarily to support the communication amongst stakeholders.
- Formal models that are used primarily to calculate indicators or to perform simulations.

The latter encode eventually mathematical objects. Their syntax and their semantics must be perfectly defined. They are written in modeling languages such as Modelica [8], Matlab Simulink [10] or AltaRica [3]. On the contrary, the former can only be understood by referring to the system under study. They are often written in standardized graphical notations such as SysML [7] or Capella [16]. For this reason, they have no formal syntax and even less a formal semantics.

Note that formal languages could be used to design pragmatic models (the reverse is indeed not true). However, there is an epistemic gap between pragmatic and formal models: as the former aim primarily at supporting the communication, they keep a lot of knowledge implicit. Making this knowledge explicit would overload them uselessly. Even if we restrict our attention to formal models, their underlying mathematical frameworks can be very different, e.g. systems of ordinary differential equations for Modelica and Simulink and guarded transition systems for AltaRica. This is the reason why, comparing behaviors described by heterogeneous models is essentially meaningless: the comparison should focus on the structural part of models.

Systems engineering modeling formalisms and languages are actually made of two parts: an underlying mathematical model, that aims at describing behaviors, and a structuring paradigm that makes it possible to organize models, i.e. to design them by assembling parts into hierarchical descriptions. The structural parts of SysML and Capella are stemmed from prototype-oriented programming [13], although without clearly acknowledging it. Modelica and Simulink rely on object-orientation. AltaRica 3.0 relies on a combination of both.

3.2   Model Synchronization Principle

As already said, two models, possibly written into two different languages, cannot in general be compared directly, see [17] for an interesting survey on model comparison techniques. Therefore, the synchronization process is made of three steps: first, models are abstracted in a common language; second, their abstractions are compared; third, actions are possibly taken to adjust original models according to findings of the comparison. This third step is called concretization, according to the abstract interpretation terminology. This process is illustrated Fig. 6.

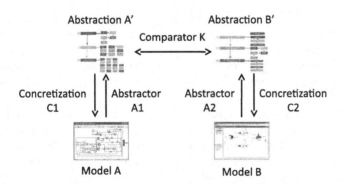

Fig. 6. Model synchronization: principle.

It is worth noticing that different abstractors and comparators can be defined. The choice of the abstractors and the comparators to apply depends on the system under study and the level of maturity of the project.

3.3   System Structure Modeling Language (S2ML)

Describing the structure of a system is fully part of the modeling process. It helps to design, to share, to maintain and eventually to synchronize models.

S2ML aims at providing a structuring paradigm of systems engineering modeling languages. It gathers and unifies concepts from object-orientation [1] and prototype-orientation [13]. Due to space limitations, we shall only sketch here S2ML ideas. The reader interested in a more detailed presentation should refer to our article [2].

As heterogeneous models can be essentially compared by their structure, S2ML is a perfect candidate as a pivot language for the abstraction.

S2ML relies on only eight constructs:

- Three types of basic objects: ports, connections and blocks.
- Three structural relations: composition, inheritance and aggregation.
- Two mechanisms making possible to reuse modeling elements: the prototype-/clone and the class/instance mechanisms.

Ports are basic objects of models, e.g. variables, events, parameters. They have a basic type such as Boolean, integer, real or some enumerated value.

Connections are used to describe relations between ports, e.g. equations, transitions, assertions.

Blocks are containers to compose ports, connections and other blocks. They are prototypes in the sense of object-oriented theory.

Attributes are pairs (name, value) used to associate information to ports, connections and blocks.

The most important and the simplest structural relation is the composition: a container (prototype or class) composes an element if this element "is part of" the container. The inheritance and the aggregation are respectively "is-a" and "uses" types of relation.

Prototypes and classes are containers. As suggested by their names, prototypes have *a priori* a unique occurrence in the model. It is however possible to clone a prototype. Classes are on-the-shelf, reusable modeling elements. Strictly speaking, they are not part of the models. Rather, they are instantiated into models. Respective advantages and drawbacks of prototypes and classes are discussed in reference [2].

The S2ML+X paradigm consists in designing domain specific modeling languages as the combination of S2ML with a given underlying mathematical framework (the X). We applied already this principle to design AltaRica 3.0, but also to design languages for constraint solving and combinatorial optimization, Boolean reliability models, hierarchical graph representations, hierarchical Markov chains and process algebras (themselves used to describe business processes).

In the S2ML+X paradigm, models are seen as scripts. S2ML provides commands to declare modeling elements. The actual model is obtained by executing these commands. This process works in two steps:

- First, the model is rewritten into a hierarchy of blocks. Each block of the hierarchy may compose ports and connections. This step is called instantiation in the S2ML jargon.
- Second, the hierarchy is removed to get a model made of only one block composing ports and connections. This step is called flattening in the S2ML jargon.

In the framework of model synchronization, the rewriting process is stopped after instantiation, as we are interested in keeping hierarchical, i.e. structural, information.

Note that the abstraction of original models into S2ML models can vary significantly from one model to the other one. It depends on the objectives of the synchronization as well as on the modeling formalism used to design the source model.

4 Model Comparison

A key step of model synchronization consists in comparing the two instantiated S2ML models.

4.1 Instantiated S2ML Models

S2ML models to be compared are instantiated, i.e. they are made of three types of objects: ports, connections and blocks. Ports and blocks are uniquely identified by their name. Connections are structured terms involving constants, ports and operators. They may also have some attributes. However, they are just considered as (anonymous) sets of ports in the comparison process. Finally, blocks can compose ports, connections and other blocks. All objects may have some attributes but we shall not consider them here. A model is just a block, possibly rooting a hierarchy of blocks.

Formally, a model is thus a quintuple $\langle P, C, B, \ltimes, r \rangle$ where:

- P and B are two disjoint finite sets of symbols called respectively ports and blocks.
- C is a multiset of connections, i.e. of subsets of P.
- $\ltimes$ is a composition relation, i.e. a subset of $B \times (P \cup C \cup B)$ verifying:
    - For each object $o \in P \cup C \cup B$, there exists at most one block $b \in B$ such that $b \ltimes o$. b is called the parent of o.
    - $r \in B$ is the unique block with no parent, moreover for all object $o \in P \cup C \cup B$, $r \ltimes^* o$, where $\ltimes^*$ denotes the transitive closure of $\ltimes$.

We denote by $\mathcal{M}$ the set of instantiated S2ML models defined as above.

4.2   Matchings

We can now define mappings from models to models. For the sake of model comparisons, we are especially interested in structure preserving mappings.

A mapping α from the model $M : \langle P_M, C_M, B_M, \ltimes_M, r_M \rangle$ to the model $N : \langle P_N, C_N, B_N, \ltimes_N, r_N \rangle$ is structure preserving if the following conditions hold.

- For any block $b \in B_M$ and any object $o \in P_M \cup C_M \cup B_M$, $b \ltimes_M o \Rightarrow \alpha(b) \ltimes_N \alpha(o)$.
- For any connection $c = \{p_1, \ldots, p_k\} \in C_M$, $\alpha(c) \supseteq \{\alpha(p_1), \ldots, \alpha(p_k)\}$, moreover for all $p \in P_M$, if $p \notin c$ then $\alpha(p) \notin \alpha(c)$.

A structure preserving mapping is injective if the following condition holds.

- For any two objects $o, o' \in P_M \cup C_M \cup B_M$, $o \neq o' \Rightarrow \alpha(o) \neq \alpha(o')$.

Injective structure preserving mappings can be seen as projections.

Now, let M, N_1 and N_2 be three models. N_1 and N_2 are matched by M if there exist two injective structure preserving mappings $\alpha_1 : M \rightarrow N_1$ and $\alpha_2 : M \rightarrow N_2$. The model M catches the commonalities between N_1 and N_2. Building such models M is the objective of the comparison process.

Note that instantiated S2ML models together with structure preserving mappings form a category, see e.g. [14] for an introduction. The notion of matching defined here is inspired from the notion of pullback in category theory.

5   Experiments

5.1   SmartSync Platform

The SmartSync platform supports model synchronization. It is based on S2ML as a pivot language for the abstraction. It works as illustrated Fig. 7. The objective is to check the consistency of two models of the same system possibly written in two different languages.

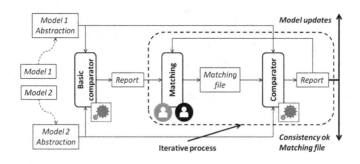

Fig. 7. Models synchronization process.

This works in three phases.

The first phase consists in abstracting original models into S2ML. As of today, this is done manually but this could be automated.

The next phase consists in comparing model abstractions. It involves designers of both models. It aims at establishing a structure preserving matching between the elements of the two abstract models This matching is concretely encoded by means of a two columns table (one per model). In a first step, elements are automatically matched by traversing down the structure of each model and according to identifiers. Elements that could not be matched are highlighted. It is then possible to match elements "by hand". It is also possible to indicate that an element should not be matched because it is specific to its model. The automatic matching process is then launch again. This process is iterated until no progress can be done anymore.

At the end of the second phase, a (possibly empty) list of inconsistencies is obtained. This list is the input for the third phase, which consists in doing some "homework" on each original model so to solve the problems.

The whole process can be itself iterated.

5.2   Case Study: A Power Supply System

We apply our model synchronization framework to the case study presented in Sect. 2. We present a collaborative design of the power supply system. The collaboration is between two teams: system architecture and safety analyses. Each team performs different activities.

The first activity is modeling which is performed independently by members of both teams using different modeling languages and tools. System architecture models designed with Capella and safety models written in AltaRica 3.0 are given in Sect. 2.2.

The second activity is model synchronization, i.e. the verification of consistency between models that ensures that both models are describing the same system. This activity is performed by the members of both teams and involves the SmartSync platform.

First, both models are abstracted, i.e. transformed into S2ML. For AltaRica 3.0 the transformation is straightforward, as the language uses S2ML as its structural paradigm. State and flow variables, events and parameters are abstracted to S2ML ports; transitions and assertions are transformed into connections; different structural constructs like inheritance, cloning, instantiation, etc. are transformed into their equivalents in S2ML.

For Capella functional and physical architecture diagrams the transformation is also quite simple: blocks are transformed into S2ML blocks, ports into S2ML ports and connections between ports are transformed into S2ML connections between corresponding S2ML ports. The allocation table (see Table 1) is transformed as follows: each functional S2ML block aggregates (via the "embeds" clause) the corresponding allocated physical S2ML blocks.

In the next step, the abstractions are compared and a report is generated. This report is analyzed by members of both teams. All the differences are listed in the matching file, which makes it possible to establish the correspondence between the two models. Table 2 shows the matching file of the first iteration. The first column is the element type (port, block, aggregated block or connection). The second column is the name of the element of the first model, the third column is the name of the corresponding element in the second model. When there is no correspondence, the keyword "forget" is used. It is possible to add a fourth column with comments to justify matching decisions. The following differences are detected:

Table 2. Power supply system architecture and safety models matching, iteration 1.

Type	Model1 (Capella)	Model2 (AltaRica 3.0)
block	SystemArchitecture	PowerSupplySystem
port	forget	LossOfBusbarPowerSupply
port	forget	LossOfIsolation
block	FunctionalPart	Functional
block	OperationalPart.StateMachine	Controller
block	PhysicalPart	Physical

– Different names of blocks (e.g. the block *FunctionalPart* in the Capella model corresponds to the block *Functional* in the AltaRica 3.0);
– Elements of the safety model not represented in the system architecture (e.g. observers *LossOfBusbarPowerSupply* and *LossOfIsolation* represent the failure conditions and do not have any equivalent in the Capella model).

The produced matching file is used to compare again the abstractions of the system architecture and safety models. In the next iteration of the comparison, new differences are detected. They are analyzed again and the matching file is populated with new matching information summarized in Table 3. Other differences are detected:

– Different names of ports (e.g. the port *Busbar.input* in the Capella model corresponds to the port *Busbar.vfInflow* in the AltaRica 3.0 model);
– Elements of system architecture model not represented in the safety model (e.g. the port *PhysicalPart.input* has no correspondence in the safety model);
– Different structural decomposition (e.g. in the Capella model the block *Grid* belongs to the block *PhysicalPart* whilst in the AltaRica 3.0 it belongs to the block *PrimaryPowerSupply*).

As we can see it is quite simple to establish the correspondence between system physical architecture *PhysicalPart* and the block *Physical* of the safety model: each Capella block has a corresponding block in the AltaRica 3.0 model, almost each port of the Capella model has a corresponding port in the AltaRica

Table 3. Power supply system architecture and safety models matching, iteration 2.

Type	Model1 (Capella)	Model2 (AltaRica 3.0)
block	SystemArchitecture	PowerSupplySystem
block	FunctionalPart	Functional
block	SupplyElectricalPowerToBusbar	SupplyElectricalPowerToBusbar
block	GenerateBackupElectricalPower	BackupSupply
block	SupplyElectricalPowerFromGrid	SupplyElectricalPowerByGrid
...	...	...
block	PhysicalPart	Physical
block	Busbar	Busbar
port	input	vfInflow
block	Grid	PrimaryPowerSupply.GR
port	input	forget
port	output	vfOutflow
block	BackupPowerSupply	BackupPowerSupply
port	output	vfOutflow
port	forget	vfFailed
block	DieselGenerator	DG
block	CB	CB
port	input	vfInflow
port	output	vfOutflow
port	forget	fail_close
...	...	...
block	PrimaryPowerSupply	PrimaryPowerSupply
block	Line1	Line1
port	input	vfInflow
port	output	vfOutflow
port	forget	vfFailed
block	CBD	CBOut
block	CBU	CBIn
...	...	...

3.0 model, there are ports in the AltaRica 3.0 model which do not have any correspondence in the Capella model (state variables, events, some flow variables representing failures). Obviously, it is possible in the abstraction step of the safety model not to consider state variables and events as they represent the internal behavior of components and are not expected to have any equivalence in the architecture model.

Concerning the operational part, it is not so obvious to establish the correspondence between the state chart diagram given Fig. 4 on the left and the AltaRica 3.0 model of the *Controller* sketched in the same figure on the right.

For the functional part, the correspondence is not so easy: the functional decomposition of the architecture model is finer than that of the safety model. However, the established correspondence is given in the following table.

Type	Model1 (Capella)	Model2 (AltaRica 3.0)
block	SystemArchitecture	PowerSupplySystem
block	FunctionalPart	Functional
block	SupplyElectricalPowerToBusbar	SupplyElectricalPowerToBusbar
block	SupplyElectricalPowerFromGrid	SupplyPowerByGrid
block	ControlElectricalPowerDeliveredByGrid. Phase1	Phase1
block	ControlElectricalPowerDeliveredToBusbar. Phase1	Phase1
block	TransformElectricalVoltageDeliveredByGrid. Phase1	Phase1
...	...	...

Models are then compared again. When no more differences are detected, the structural consistency between system architecture and safety models is verified. The matching file establishes the correspondence between the two models. In case of inconsistencies detection, the initial models need to be adjusted.

6   Conclusion

In this article, we presented model synchronization – a formal framework for management of heterogeneous models. This framework is based on S2ML (System Structure Modeling Language). We showed that this framework can be used to ensure the consistency of heterogeneous models, designed within different formalisms and different modeling environments.

To support model synchronization, we developed the SmartSync platform, which relies on S2ML as a pivot language. With SmartSync, we studied the electrical power supply system. We checked consistency between system architecture and safety models. The process of making models consistent is iterative and involves representatives of the engineering disciplines at stake. The SmartSync platform helps not only to check the consistency between models, but also to detect inconsistencies within models and to support the dialog between stakeholders.

Some questions about the comparison of heterogeneous models remain open. As future works, we plan to improve the SmartSync platform, notably by developing new comparison algorithms and abstraction methods.

References

1. Abadi, M., Cardelli, L.: A Theory of Objects. Springer, New-York (1998)
2. Batteux, M., Prosvirnova, T., Rauzy, A.: From models of structures to structures of models. In: 4th IEEE International Symposium on Systems Engineering, ISSE 2018, Rome, Italy, October 2018
3. Batteux, M., Prosvirnova, T., Rauzy, A.: Altarica 3.0 in 10 modeling patterns. Int. J. Critical Comput.-Based Syst. (IJCCBS) **9**, 133 (2019). https://doi.org/10.1504/IJCCBS.2019.10020023
4. Batteux, M.B., Prosvirnova, T., Rauzy, A., Yang, L.: Reliability assessment of phased-mission systems with AltaRica 3.0. In: 3rd International Conference on System Reliability and Safety (ICSRS 2018), Barcelona, Spain, November 2018
5. Bouissou, M., Bon, J.: A new formalism that combines advantages of fault-trees and Markov models: Boolean logic driven Markov processes. Reliab. Eng. Syst. Saf. **82**, 149–163 (2003)
6. Cousot, P., Cousot, R.: Abstract interpretation: a unified lattice model for static analysis of programs by construction of approximations of fixpoints. In: Proceedings of the 4th ACM-Sigplan Symposium on Principles of Programming Languages, POPL 1977, pp. 238–252. ACM, Los Angeles (1977). https://doi.org/10.1145/512950.512973
7. Friedenthal, S., Moore, A., Steiner, R.: A Practical Guide to SysML: The Systems Modeling Language. Morgan Kaufmann, The MK/OMG Press, San Francisco (2011)
8. Fritzson, P.: Principles of Object-Oriented Modeling and Simulation with Modelica 3.3: A Cyber-Physical Approach. Wiley-IEEE Press, Hoboken (2015)
9. Hermann, F., et al.: Model synchronization based on triple graph grammars: correctness, completeness and invertibility. Softw. Syst. Model. **14**(1), 241–269 (2015). https://doi.org/10.1007/s10270-012-0309-1
10. Klee, H., Allen, R.: Simulation of Dynamic Systems with MATLAB and Simulink. CRC Press, Boca Raton (2011)
11. Krob, D.: CESAM: CESAMES Systems Architecting Method: A Pocket Guide. CESAMES, January 2017. http://www.cesames.net
12. Mauborgne, P., Deniaud, S., Levrat, E., Bonjour, E., Micaëlli, J.P., Loise, D.: Operational and system hazard analysis in a safe systems requirement engineering process - application to automotive industry. Saf. Sci. **87**, 256–268 (2016)
13. Noble, J., Taivalsaari, A., Moore, I.: Prototype-Based Programming: Concepts. Languages and Applications. Springer, Heidelberg (1999)
14. Pierce, B.C.: Basic Category Theory of Computer Scientists. Foundations of Computing. MIT Press, Cambridge (1991)
15. Rauzy, A., Haskins, C.: Foundations for model-based systems engineering and model-based safety assessment. J. Syst. Eng. (2018). https://doi.org/10.1002/sys.21469
16. Roques, P.: MBSE with the ARCADIA method and the Capella tool. In: 8th European Congress on Embedded Real Time Software and Systems (ERTS 2016), Toulouse, France, January 2016. https://hal.archives-ouvertes.fr/hal-01258014

17. Stephan, M., Cordy, J.R.: A survey of model comparison approaches and applications. In: MODELSWARD 2013 - Proceedings of the 1st International Conference on Model-Driven Engineering and Software Development, 19–21 February 2013, Barcelona, Spain, pp. 265–277 (2013). https://doi.org/10.5220/0004311102650277
18. Yakymets, N., Julho, Y.M., Lanusse, A.: Sophia framework for model-based safety analysis. In: Actes du congrès Lambda-Mu 19 (actes électroniques). Institut pour la Maîtrise des Risques, Dijon, France, October 2014

DPN – Dependability Priority Numbers

Zhensheng Guo[✉] and Marc Zeller

Siemens AG, Corporate Technology, Otto-Hahn-Ring 6,
81739 Munich, Germany
{joe.guo,marc.zeller}@siemens.com

Abstract. This paper proposes a novel model-based approach to combine the quantitative dependability (safety, reliability, availability, maintainability and IT security) analysis and trade-off analysis. The proposed approach is called DPN (Dependability Priority Numbers) and allows the comparison of different actual dependability characteristics of a systems with its target values and evaluates them regarding trade-off analysis criteria. Therefore, the target values of system dependability characteristics are taken as requirements, while the actual value of a specific system design are provided by quantitative and qualitative dependability analysis (FHA, FMEA, FMEDA, of CFT-based FTA). The DPN approach evaluates the fulfillment of individual target requirements and perform trade-offs between analysis objectives. We present the workflow and meta-model of the DPN approach, and illustrate our approach using a case study on a brake warning contact system. Hence, we demonstrate how the model-based DPNs improve system dependability by selecting the project crucial dependable design alternatives or measures.

Keywords: Dependability analysis · Safety · Reliability · Availability · Maintainability · IT security · Trade-off analysis · Component Fault Tree (CFT) · Functional Hazard Analysis · FMEDA

1 Introduction

Reference [9] defines *dependability of a system is the ability to avoid service failures that are more frequent and more severe than is acceptable* and it contains the following properties: *safety, reliability, availability, integrity* (security), and *maintainability*. Dependability trade-off analysis is basically the analysis of dependencies and conflicts between dependability properties according to the fulfillment of targets and to make trade-offs among these properties [1, 2, 8, 11, 13]. Quantitative dependability analysis deals with quantitative analysis of safety, reliability, availability, maintainability and security properties of a system design. Examples are Failure mode Effect Diagnostic Analysis (FMEDA), Fault Tree Analysis (FTA) etc. Currently the trade-off analysis of the dependability properties assumes in many cases that the target values to be fulfilled by the design alternatives, and actual values that the design alternatives hold, are given. Based on these values, acceptable limits and evaluation criteria, trade-off analyses are performed. However, the actual quantitative values of dependability properties of design alternatives in many cases are not given and need to be obtained. The techniques to perform (model-based) quantitative dependability analysis and to perform trade-off

© Springer Nature Switzerland AG 2019
Y. Papadopoulos et al. (Eds.): IMBSA 2019, LNCS 11842, pp. 173–187, 2019.
https://doi.org/10.1007/978-3-030-32872-6_12

analysis are usually performed separately, or in other words, they are not combined sufficiently for effective quantitative dependability trade-off analysis.

In this work we describe with Dependability Priority Numbers (DPN) an approach to combine these two engineering fields and show how model-based quantitative dependability analysis techniques such as Component Fault Trees [10] can help to perform dependability trade-off analysis.

This paper is arranged in the following sections: Sect. 2 provides an overview of related work, Sect. 3 illustrates an approach, which is named Dependability Priority Number (DPN); Sect. 4 shows a case study on a brake warning contact system; Sect. 5 concludes this paper.

2 Related Work

Typically, the comparison of different design alternatives is the objective of dependability trade-off analysis. The design alternative that fulfills more dependability properties will be normally chosen as the solution. Today, there are some approaches to model the obtained dependability properties, e.g. through GSN [2], Modelica [6] etc., but the source of the quantitative value of the overall dependability is seldomly handled.

Reference [1] uses vulnerability attack graph and goal graph to determine the dependencies between the security goals and tasks. This method mentions the use of trade-off analysis parameters such as risk acceptance criteria, standards, laws, regulations, policies, stakeholder goals, budget, and time-to-market. Reference [2] utilizes DDA (Dependability Deviation Analysis) and GSN (Goal Structuring Notation) to perform trade-off analysis. This method uses GSN with acceptable limits to model the fulfillment of the design alternatives under certain scenarios. Reference [3] emphasizes the role of scenarios and upper and lower bounds of acceptable limits in the trade-off analysis that is illustrated in [2]. Reference [4] proposes a quantitative estimation method of the different dependability properties, in which expert estimations of the fulfillment of dependability properties are used. Reference [5] uses an UML extension to describes the dependability properties and uses Deterministic and Stochastic Petri Net to perform dependability modelling. Reference [6] uses Modelica and Bayesian Network simulation to identify the violence of the dependability requirements. Reference [7] presents a trade-off analysis procedure to prioritize the different dependability requirements.

References [7, 11, 12] proposed formulas to calculate the utility or value function of dependability of individual design alternatives. Reference [7] uses product of weight and values function results to calculate the evaluation result of dependability properties such as performance, security and fault tolerance. For the calculation they use the following formulas:

$$
\begin{aligned}
evaluation\ result = \ & max \tfrac{1}{n} \left[\sum_{i=1}^{n} v_i \right] with\ v_i \geq v_{min} \quad for\ without\ weight \\
& max \tfrac{1}{n} \left[\sum_{i=1}^{n} a_i v_i \right] with\ v_i \geq v_{min}\ and\ \sum a_i = 1,\ a_i > 0 \quad for\ with\ weight
\end{aligned} \tag{1}
$$

Reference [11] defines the dependability properties evaluation results as x_i and takes the sum of value function of x_i as the result of the overall dependability value. In addition, they use the sum of the products of the weights of the individual properties and their evaluation results of x_i as the dependability value. The authors argue that the sum of the weights of dependability properties shall be 1:

$$v(x_1, x_2, \ldots, x_n) = v(x_1) + v(x_2) + \ldots + v(x_n) = \sum_{i=1}^{n} v(x_i)$$
$$\text{or} \tag{2}$$
$$v = \sum_{k=1}^{n} w_i x_i \text{ with } w_i \geq 0 \text{ and } \sum w_i = 1$$

The decision-making procedure according to this work includes the following steps: identification of the subjective such as design alternatives; definition of the analysis criteria; Performance of the evaluation; selection of the value function and determination of combinable criteria. The precondition of the combining the criteria is that the criteria are mutual independent, and it is possible to determine the final equation for calculating the value of fulfillment of dependability properties. References [1, 12] proposed the following essential definitions for dependability evaluation: Preference function based on certainty (such as probability) is defined as value function, preference function based on risk (such as weights) is defined as a utility function. In [12], weights of a criteria/properties $w_{(i)}$ and value of this criteria $v_{(i)}$ are used to calculate utility of alternatives:

$$v = \sum_i w_{(i)} v_{(i)} \quad \text{or} \quad v = \sum_i p_{(i)} v_{(i)} \text{ where } p \text{ denotes probability} \tag{3}$$

Reference [8] illustrates an approach by use of GSN and its evaluation process to perform the trade-off analysis of dependability properties. The following aspects are essential to perform the trade-off analysis for this survey: goals of stakeholders; function for scenarios; related dependability properties; target value of dependability properties; traceability to the requirements; acceptance criteria; determination of compromise region. According to their work, the scenarios (consist of stimuli, responses) and target/limit are essential for performing trade-off analysis. However, in this paper, the use of the dependability analyses is not illustrated in detail. Reference [13] handles the trade-off analysis in a very thorough way. They proposed the following processes: identification of the concern of trade-analysis; definition of the deviation and failures; derivation of dependability requirements; identification of goals, target and limits; identification of alternatives; identification of trade-off argument based on GSN; evaluation of alternatives and decision making. The evaluation of the alternatives is done based on evaluation of the related criteria. The final value is produced with consideration of the weight. Matrix calculation is used for this evaluation process. The qualitative safety analysis techniques such as Hazard and Operability Analysis (HAZOP), Failure Mode and Effect Analysis (FMEA) are used for identifying the failures and further the dependability requirements. However, such analysis techniques are not reused to analyze the alternatives and the model-based quantitative safety analysis is not used in their work. [14] proposes a method to address the cost-benefit trade-off analysis. The following evaluation criteria are considered as essential: priorities; standards; laws; regulations; business goals; budget; policies. Taking a retrospective look at the related works, we can draw the conclusion that the dependability trade-off analysis were performed without integrating the model-based quantitative dependability analysis techniques.

3 Dependability Priority Numbers

In this section, we present the concept of *Dependability Priority Numbers (DPN)*. First, the result of this approach and its formula are described. Afterwards the workflow of DPN analyses is presented in detail. Moreover, the metamodel and its usage will be depicted.

By introducing a Dependability Priority Number, analysis object is extended from design alternatives to at least alternatives and the measures for mitigating hazard or risk will be analyzed. They will be analyzed qualitatively and/or quantitatively towards an overall result of the quality of the system in terms of dependability. The overall fulfillment of the dependability properties is presented by comparing the actual and expected DPN and also by comparison between the actual DPNs. The conflicts and dependencies between the dependability properties will be identified or solved during this process implicitly.

In this work, we use first the concept of weights to calculate the overall dependability value. Therefore, the utility values will be calculated according to the definition in [11]. However, the calculation of DPN can also be based on risk/probability. The result of the calculation of the utilities/values of the alternatives is named the *Dependability Priority Number (DPN)* (instead of using the rather general term, Utility or Value.). Because the result deals in deed with the prioritization of the alternatives, and this prioritization has certain similarity with the *Risk Priority Number*. Based on [7, 11, 12], the following formula is derived:

$$DPN_j = \sum_{i=1}^{n} X_{ij} * K_i \tag{4}$$

Where

n: number of the dependability properties;
X_{ij}: Evaluation result, correlates with acceptance level. If X_{ij}: 0: totally unacceptable, 1: totally acceptable. "i" for the index of dependability properties, "j" for alternatives/measures;
K_i: weight (or probability) coefficient of the individual dependability properties, according to the importance of current dependability properties. $\Sigma_i K_i$ not necessarily equals to 1.

DPN uses a slightly changed formula of (1), (2) and (3) which are presented in Sect. 2. The w_i or a_i is replaced by weight (or probability) coefficient K_i, basically they are all the weights (except that k_i can contain probability additionally). The difference of K_i and w_i or a_i is that the sum of the weight coefficients K_i used for DPN is not necessarily 1, this definition has the benefit for tracing back the causing property intuitionally in case of changing of overall DPNs. This means, that if the DPN is changed for example from 109.11 to 111.11, (assume the utilized weights are 100, 10, 1, 0.1 and 0.01 for safety, reliability, availability etc.) we know therefore in this case there is an improvement on the reliability (improvement on the second digit). The weight K_i are generally determined by the domain expert according to the importance of the dependability properties. The selection of weights follows additionally the rule of distinguishing dependability properties big enough so that the weights of properties do not counterweight in case value changes. The weights can also be derived based on results of dependability analysis such as RPN out of FMEA or failure rates out of FTA. The result of DPN as simple numbers offers an intuitive and direct way to represent the overall fulfillment of the dependability goal and to compare variants.

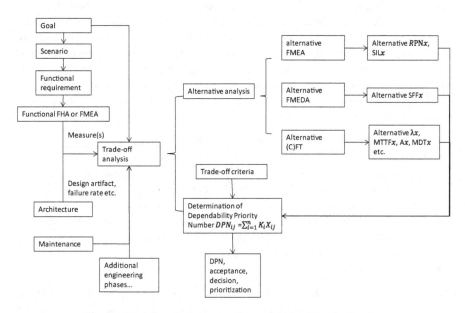

Fig. 1. Workflow to determine Dependability Priority Number

In Fig. 1 the workflow for determining Dependability Priority Numbers is illustrated. This workflow contains:

1. Elicitation of the goals of the stakeholders. Here the typical goal graph methods, such as GSN [2], i* [1] for Non-Functional Requirements etc. can be used. A coarse trade-off analysis among the identified goals can be performed, in order to identify the possible limits, dependencies and conflicts.
2. Based on the identified goals, the relevant scenarios with certain execution sequences will be determined. An example of such scenarios is robot x shall be stopped when safety bumper is engaged. Scenarios define the aims and scope of the trade-off analysis.

3. Typically, the functional requirements will be elicited based on the identified scenarios. If there are no standardized requirements and their THR, the functional requirements are to be elicited for the specific project.
4. Based on the identified functional requirements, the Functional Hazard Analysis (FHA) or function-based Failure Mode and Effect Criticality Analysis (FMECA) will be performed. The corresponding hazards, their Risk Priority Numbers (RPN), their Safety Integrity Level (SIL), and available measures will be identified. For fulfilling the predefined multiple quality goals (e.g. SIL) additional measures are to be identified. Traditionally only one measure is identified for fulfilling the predefined quality goal. By using DPN multiple measures will be identified by use of the dependability analysis repeatedly.
5. Trade-off analysis will be performed among alternative measures. If there are no further information about the system components and their failure rates, the qualitative FMEA or Functional Hazard Analysis (FHA) will be performed repeatedly, where the improvements of the quality in SIL or RPN of the alternative could be compared with the original (first) measure. The possible conflicts to other dependability properties could be identified by observing the interchanging of DPNs. In these steps of trade-off analysis, the expert estimation is required. The following trade-off analysis is to be performed based on the trade-off criteria (based on [2, 8, 11, 13, 14]):

- Determination of actual value of dependability properties v_a;
- Determination and comparison of target/expected value v_e with v_a;
- Determination and comparing of acceptable upper/lower limit with v_a;
- Evaluation of the benefit of actual better value e.g. $(v_a \geq v_e)$/drawback of actual worse value e.g. $(v_a < v_e)$;
- Determination of the cost of improvement towards expected value e.g. $(v_a < v_e)$;
- Determination of time-to-achievement of the improvement e.g. $(v_a < v_e)$;
- Determination of overall acceptance X_{ij};
- Derivation of further action.

6. The actual value in the trade-off criteria could be obtained by FHA, Risk Priority Number through FMECA qualitatively or quantitatively by the FMEDA, (Component) Fault Tree Analysis (FTA) or Fault Tree Analysis (FT) or other quantitative dependability techniques.

The results of such dependability assessments/analyses will be used for the rest of quantitative dependability trade-off analysis: Failure rate λ and SIL for the safety property, Mean Time Between/To Failure (MTBF/MTTF) for the reliability property, Availability value for the availability property, Mean Down Time for the maintainability etc. After determining measures and alternatives, they are modelled by a model-based (Component) Fault Tree. The results of these analyses are then compared between each of the system design alternatives. For Safety the calculated failure rate λ and even qualitative RPN, SIL are used as "actual value", "expected value" is typically predefined either by the authorities or by the references systems.

By using FMEDÀ for determining Safe Failure Fraction (for estimation of the Safety Integrity Level) and dangerous undetected failures, the FMEDA will be performed several times according to the number of alternatives. The calculated SFFs, failure rates and the corresponding SILs will be then be used as actual value for the trade-off analysis. In case the new measure neither leads to architecture changes, nor to a structural update in the fault tree, the changed availability can still be captured by e.g. the changed Mean Down Time. For example, if stopping the train in case of warning contact "high" (warning contact is responsible for worn out status of the brake), affects the availability too negatively (unacceptable) and the measure of "stop" has no remarkable improvement of safety, in addition "low speed drive" is sufficient (regarding safety) to handle this warning contact. The "low speed" can then be used to replace "stop" as measure in case of warning contact "high". This change will obviously improve the availability of the train, and without compromise of the safety. This change does not necessarily change the fault tree structure of the train. But down time will be then reduced. The reduced down time will affect the calculation of availability positively because of $A = \frac{MTBF}{MTBF + MDT}$ for repairable systems. Through this way the availability comparison between the original solution "stop" and new solution "low speed drive" can be done even without changing the structure of the fault tree.

In DPN the quantitative analysis techniques such as the FTA and FMEDA are reused to calculate the influence of different alternatives on the overall system. Different system failure rates could be observed, because of different architectures or even different value of the parameter. The comparison of alternatives is performed regarding trade-off criteria.

Partially according to the industrial practice, there are for instance the following categories for the subjective trade-off criteria to be used for evaluating the alternatives:

- Benefit of the actual better value: None; Better life time cause of better quality; Better reliability or availability of the system; Potential reputation benefit; Eventually better sale price.
- Drawback of the actual worse value: None; No certificate; Financial disaster; Worse availability; Damage of reputation; Postpone of the project finish time; Increased purchase cost.
- Cost for improvement towards expected value: None; Ignorable; Proportional; Quite high; Too high.
- Time for achieving the expected value: None; Ignorable; Proportional; Quite long; Too long.
- Further action: None; Redundancy; Use of higher quality component; Development of new component.
- Acceptance level: 0: totally unacceptable; 0.2: almost unacceptable; 0.4: predominantly unacceptable; 0.6: predominantly acceptable; 0.8: almost acceptable; 1: totally acceptable.

The overall acceptance (between 0 and 1) is represented by the value of X_{ij}, together with estimated value K_i. Based on these values DPNs are be calculated (according to (4)). Afterwards, the DPNs of different design alternatives are compared. The higher value means basically the better dependability. And the detailed comparison according to the single dependability properties can also be done. The comparison shall not only be done based on the subjective evaluation value, but also on the objective calculated value. Based on the such comparisons, the acceptance of the alternative can be determined. The mutual dependency, the conflicts are represented through the interchanging of evaluation (or calculated) values. For example if DPN changes from 111.10 to 110.11 directly, we know that there is a conflict between availability and security. Because increase of the security (from 0 to 1) causes decrease of the availability (from 1 to 0). DPN are calculated for instance in the following way: assume safety has the weight of 100, reliability has the weight of 10 and so on. And the X_{ij} all have value "1" for totally acceptance. The expected Dependability Priority Number would be $DPN_{expected} = 100 * 1 + 10 * 1 + \ldots = 111.11$. This expected value is then used to compare with the actual values.

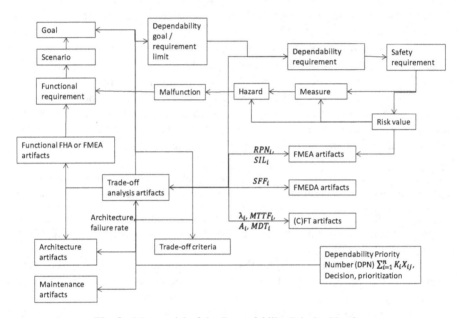

Fig. 2. Metamodel of the Dependability Priority Number

As illustrated in the Fig. 2, goal, scenario, and functional requirements are the bases of the trade-off analysis and define the subjects of the trade-off analysis. During the model-based dependability analysis, the following data are identified step by step by use of this meta model:

- Malfunction, hazards are identified by use of e.g. FHA based on the functional requirement. The limit of goals can be used as limit of underlying requirements for the further trade-off analysis;
- Based on the hazard incl. its risk value the multiple measures are identified;
- The trade-off analysis of alternative measures can be qualitative or quantitative. Qualitative trade-off analysis can be the repeated model-based FHA or FMEA analyses for determining the reduced RPN or SIL by use of different measures. Such results are represented as RPN_i and SIL_i. Where the i indicates the sequential

number representing each of the design variants. Quantitative trade-off analyses are performed through repeated FMEDA or (C)FT for calculating the λ_i, $MTTF_i/MTBF_i, A_i, MDT_i$. Through the comparison of the λ_i and λ_{i+1} the variant which is better in terms of safety or reliability can be identified. Further the comparison of aforementioned other values could contribute to an overall evaluation value of the dependability properties.

- The calculation of the expected and actual values are performed by the Eq. (4) based on the evaluation of the trade-off criteria as mentioned in the workflow section. The $DPN_{extected}$ and DPN_{actual} are then used further to determine whether the $DPN_{actual} \geq DPN_{extected}$. If this is the case, all the dependability properties are fulfilled, otherwise a or some or even all the dependability properties are possibility not fulfilled. The not fulfilled dependability properties need basically further measure until this is fulfilled. In the end all the dependability properties shall be in general fulfilled. However, there can be conflicts by fulfilling the different properties, for example the fulfillment of safety properties means in certain circumstances the harm to the availability. This happens for example if a train is stopped for certain safety reason, but this means immediately the reduction of the availability. Compromise has to be made in this case. DPN result is shown at the bottom-right corner of Fig. 1. DPN approach consists of both the process of Fig. 1 and the data set of Fig. 2.

- Not only the measures, the quality goals and the functional requirements are the possible objects of the trade-off analysis but also the design artifacts and maintenance artifacts are also potential objects. Design artifacts offer among others the design alternative. Maintenance artifacts can be for instance the size of the maintenance team, possible maintenance strategy as conditions which also play roles in determining the maintenance priority number (basically the calculable Mean Down Time). By changes of dependa. goals, the DPN process shall be repeated totally or partially, according to the result of the similarity analysis between the old and new goals.

4 Case Study – Brake Warning Contact

This section presents a case study form the railway domain based on a brake warning contact. The brake warning contact monitors the status of the brakes, if the thickness of brakes is detected less than allowed, a warning message will be sent to the dashboard, the train will be set to degraded mode. By using this example, the workflow of DPN is explained in detail:

1. Performing FMECA:
   The following functional requirement has been identified: If the warning contact is high, the warning contact sensor shall send the warning signal to the dashboard and set the train to degraded mode. Based on the identified function a FMECA is performed and multiple measures (redundancy and monitoring are identified in Table 1).

Table 1. FMECA inclusive multiple measures

Measure	New RPN	New Probab.	New Detect.	New Sever.	Further action
Measure 1: Redundant warning contact sensor	56	1	7	8	No
Measure 2: Monitoring of warning contact	16	1	2	8	

2. Performing FMEDA:

The FMEDA identifies the dangerous undetected failure rates of redundancy (5 fit, see Table 2). Moreover, the dangerous undetected failure rate of monitoring is 1, under the assumption that the monitoring detects 90% dangerous failure.

Table 2. Results of FMEDA for multiple measures

Detection and control measure	Detection coverage (DC)	Failure rate of dangerous undetected	Failure rate of dangerous detected
Redundancy	50%	5	5
Monitoring	90%	1	9

3. Performing Component Fault Tree Analyses for the following design alternatives (measures):

- **Without measure:** This fault tree contains only the components "power supply" and "brake warning contact" combined using an OR-gate.
- **With measure 1 of redundancy**: The component "brake warning contact" is doubled and because of the redundancy, the two instances are combined using an AND-gate. This subtree with the AND-gate is then combined with the "power supply" component using an OR-gate.
- **With measure 2 of monitoring (3 variants** with failure rate (FR) of 10000 fit, 10 fit, and 1 fit): As illustrated in Fig. 3, the use of the monitoring mechanism introduces additional failure possibility, because the monitoring can also fail. In this case, the brake warning contact fails if 1) the monitoring fails and the brake warning contact (9 fit) dangerous detectable fails or 2) brake warning contact dangerous undetected fails (1 fit). The failure rate of monitoring mechanism plays here a significant role. 10,000 fit, 10 fit and 1 fit are selected to perform this comparison in this case study. 8760 h (1 year) was used as mission time, 24 h were used as Mean Down Time of the basic events. Based on such data, CFT-based dependability/Reliability Availability Maintenance Safety (RAMS) properties are modelled and calculated. The modelling of the CFT is performed using ComposR, a Siemens-internal model-based safety and reliability analysis tool. The calculation is done using ZUSIM, a Siemens-internal safety and reliability calculation engines that has been used since decades.

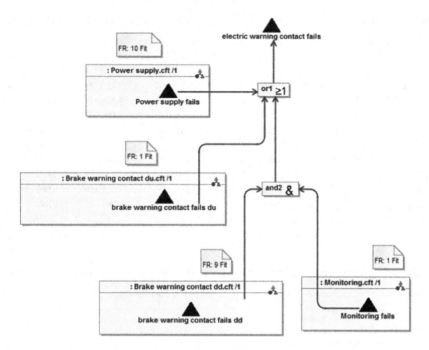

Fig. 3. Component Fault Tree of the measure monitoring

The goal of the quantitative analysis is to determine the measure which fulfills all (or more) the target values. In the CFT as depicted in Fig. 3, four components (power supply, brake warning contact dangerous undetected, brake warning contact dangerous detected, monitoring) and two gates (one AND- and one OR-gates) are modeled. The analysis results of all 5 design alternatives are summarized in Table 3. The individual analysis results (such as failure rate) are used as actual failure rate which serve as basis to be compared with the target/expected value. Other (reliability, availability etc.) actual and target values are also compared in the same way. The following formulas are used to calculate MDT by use of ZUSIM: for OR gate $MDT_{OR} = \frac{MTBF_1 * MDT_2 + MTBF_2 * MDT1_1}{MTBF_1 + MTBF_2}$ and for AND gate $MDT_{OR} = \frac{MDT_1 * MDT1_2}{MDT_1 + MDT_2}$.

Table 4 shows the comparison between the expected values and actual values of the respective dependability properties. In this case study, the acceptable limit is set to the expected value due to simplicity. Normally, the comparison is done between the acceptable limit and the actual values. This comparison describes the fulfillment of the dependability goals. The expected value of failure rate is set to 10 fit, this value is used 5 times for comparison (5 corresponds to the number of measures). Compared with this value, the acceptance value of objective failure rates of different measures is obtained (e.g. 2 fit < 10 fit in Table 4). Afterwards, the subject evaluations will be performed. Such subjective evaluation offers additional but essential acceptance criterion. For example, if reliability or availability target values cannot be totally fulfilled, it is important to know what the drawbacks of non-fulfillment are and what would be the

Table 3. Summarized dependability calculation results of the measures by use of ZUSIM

Result	Without measure	With redundancy	With monitoring FR: 10000 fit	With monitoring FR: 10 fit	With monitoring FR: 1 fit
Availability	99,999980000000%	99,99999999999%	99,999995%	99,99999%	99,999995%
Unavailability	2,40E−07	1,15E−13	4,81E−06	4,80E−06	4,80E−06
MTBF (h)	1,00E+08	1,04E+14	4,98E+08	5,00E+08	5,00E+08
Failure rate lambda (1/h)	1,00E−08	1,00E−14	2,01E−09	2,00E−09	2,00E−09
FIT	1,00E+01	9,60E−06	2,01E+00	2,00E+00	2,00E+00
MDT (h)	24	12	23.95	24	24
MTTF (h)	1,00E+08	1,00E+14	4,98E+08	5,00E+08	5,00E+08
Mission time (h)	8760	8760	8760	8760	8760

Table 4. Objective and subjective evaluation of alternatives/measures (monitoring 1 fit)

Solution	Measure monitoring 1 fit
Failure rate/Hazard rate	
Actual value (fit)	2
Expected value (fit)	10
Acceptable upper limit (fit)	10
Acceptable lower limit (fit)	
Evaluation of benefit of actual value	Better reliability of availability of the system
Evaluation of drawback of actual value	None
Cost of improvement towards expected value	None
Time-to-achievement of the improvement	
Overall acceptance	1: total acceptance

cost and time to achieve the target value. Based on the objective comparison and these subjective comparisons of the measures regarding the aforementioned acceptance criteria, the overall acceptance (e.g. 1: total acceptance in Table 4) will be subjectively determined.

Finally, the DPN is calculated based on this acceptance value and the respective weights of the properties according to $\sum_{k=i}^{n} X_{ij} * K_i$. For instance, the fifth measure of monitoring with failure rate of 1 fit fulfills the safety target value, but does not fulfill availability expected value (0,2 as shown in Table 5. and Fig. 4). Table 5 shows the results of $X_{ij} * K_i$. Therefore, the actual $DPN_{alternative1}$ $\sum_{k=i}^{n} X_{i1} * K_1 = (100 + 10 + 0.2 + 0.1 + 0.01) = 110.31$ with $K_{safety} = 100$, $K_{reliability} = 10$, $K_{availability} = 1$ et. The expected $DPN_{alternative5} = \sum_{k=i}^{n} X_{i1} * K_1 = 100 * 1 + 10 * 1 + 1 * 1 + 0.1 * 1 + 0.01 * 1 = 111.11$. These two values are visualized in Fig. 5 as the fifth points of each of the lines. The expected values of the alternatives are plotted as brown points, while the actual values the blue points. Obviously, this measure does not fulfill all the target values. In contrary, the 2nd measure, redundancy measure fulfills all the dependability

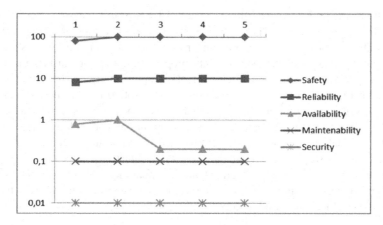

Fig. 4. Evaluation results according to the objective and subjective evaluation criteria (Color figure online)

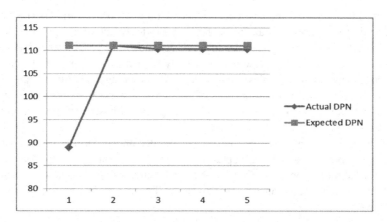

Fig. 5. Comparison of the actual DPN and expected DPN of alternatives/measures (Color figure online)

Table 5. Dependability Priority Number of measures/alternatives

Statistic	Without measure	Measure 1 (Redundancy)	Measure 2 (Monitoring: FR 1)
Safety	80	100	100
Reliability	8	10	10
Availability	0,8	1	0,2
Maintainability	0,1	0,1	0,1
Security	0,01	0,01	0,01
DPN	88.91	111.11	110.31

targets. It has the highest actual DPN. The actual DPN of this measure is on the same level as the expected DPN. The actual DPNs of other measures are lower than the expected DPNs (shown as blue points under brown points). Figure 4 also shows the comparison of changes of the dependability properties. By this for instance a conflict between safety and availability is identified. By keeping the safety on the same high value, the availability goes down by monitoring with 10000 fit (3rd measure) dramatically. However, this conflict is not handled further, because the 2nd measure was chosen as solution. Otherwise a trade-off must be found and according to the changed DPNs the optimal alternative is selected. Basically the more important property wins. Through this case study, the strength of the DPN is illustrated. Quantitative dependability analysis (CFT) is thereby integrated into dependability trade-off analysis and vice verse. This combination improves the dependability of the system and reduces the cost of ignorable conflicts between the dependability goals.

5 Conclusion

This work illustrates how the concept of Dependability Priority Numbers (DPN) supports quantitatively trade-off analyses. DPN helps to select of the optimal system design alternative or measure, in order to fulfill dependability goals. Dependencies and conflicts can be identified and resolved inherently by using this approach. DPN brings model-based dependability analysis and trade-off analysis together. An exemplary case study illustrates the concept and benefits of DPN. Our approach supports not only the quantitative trade-off analysis, but also extending model-based quantitative dependability analysis towards trade-off analysis.

DPN will be further developed both conceptually and according to tool support. More quantitative and detailed acceptance evaluation criteria, utilization of effective pre-selection algorithm in case of handling of large number of alternatives, calculation of object and subject acceptance values towards DPN in a more effective way will be investigated in the future.

Acknowledgement. This work is supported by the Framework Programme for Research and Innovation Horizon 2020 under grant agreement n. 732242 (DEIS).

References

1. Elahi, G., Yu, E.: Modeling and analysis of security trade-offs – a goal oriented approach. ftp://www.cs.toronto.edu/dist/eric/ER07-Elahi.pdf. Accessed 21 May 2019
2. Despotou, G., Kelly, T.: Design and development of dependability case architecture during system development. https://pdfs.semanticscholar.org/f8e4/6d38a451a56a4d588ca6533dbec7d52979e2.pdf. Accessed 21 May 2019
3. Despotou, G., McDermid, J., Kelly, T.: using scenarios to identify and trade-off dependability objectives in design. https://www-users.cs.york.ac.uk/tpk/issc05b.pdf. Accessed 21 May 2019

4. Trade-off examples inside software engineering and computer science. https://pdfs. semanticscholar.org/d671/e1fce79502df40d424b94790444300f0d291.pdf.   Accessed   21 July May 2019
5. Bernardi, S., Merseguer, J., Petriu, D.C.: dependability modeling and assessment in UML-based software development. http://www.sce.carleton.ca/faculty/petriu/papers/BMP11-prepub.pdf. Accessed 21 May 2019
6. Tundis, A., Buffoni, L., Fitzson, P., Garro, A.: Model-based dependability analysis of physical systems with Modelica. Hindawi Model. Simul. Eng. **2017**, 15, Article ID 1578043 (2017). https://doi.org/10.1155/2017/1578043. Accessed 21 May 2019
7. Andrews, A., Runeson, P., France, R.: requirements trade-offs during UML design. https:// ieeexplore.ieee.org/document/1316710/. Accessed 21 May 2019
8. Despotou, G., Kelly, T.: The need for flexible requirements in dependable systems. https:// www-users.cs.york.ac.uk/tpk/iwrehas06.pdf. Accessed 21 May 2019
9. Avizienis, A., Laprie, J.-C., Randell, B., Landwehr, C.: Technical research report: basic concepts and taxonomy of dependable and secure computing. https://www.nasa.gov/pdf/ 636745main_day_3-algirdas_avizienis.pdf. Accessed 21 May 2019
10. Kaiser, B., Liggesmeyer, P., Mäckel, O.: A new component concept for fault tree. https:// pdfs.semanticscholar.org/5022/6ad58579c00b7be9aacce3f1f1c704ee3f8a.pdf. Accessed 21 May 2019
11. Prasad, D.K.: Dependable systems integration using measurement theory and decision analysis. Ph.D. thesis. https://pdfs.semanticscholar.org/fcd5/fe26750c12720824ff4556c2ccc 43a64b605.pdf. Accessed 21 July May 2019
12. Keeney, R.L., Raiffa, H.: Decisions with multiple object: preferences and value tradeoffs. Wiley. http://pure.iiasa.ac.at/id/eprint/375/1/WP-75-053.pdf. Accessed 16 May 2019
13. Despotou, G.: Managing the evolution of dependability cases for systems of systems. Ph.D. thesis. https://www.researchgate.net/publication/251734596_Managing_the_Evolution_of_ Dependability_Cases_for_Systems_of_Systems. Accessed 21 May 2019
14. Houmb, S.H.: The aspect-oriented risk-driven development (AORDD) framework. https:// pdfs.semanticscholar.org/b121/6bf23456a894989be5d56d2e4d021664b1f8.pdf.   Accessed 16 May 2019

Towards Dependability and Energy Aware Asset Management Framework for Maintenance Planning in Smart Grids

Jose Ignacio Aizpurua[1]([✉]) [iD], Unai Garro[1] [iD], Eñaut Muxika[1] [iD], Mikel Mendicute[1] [iD], and Ian Paul Gilbert[2] [iD]

[1] Electronics and Computer Science Department, Signal Processing and Communications Group, Mondragon University, Goiru 2, 20500 Arrasate, Spain
{jiaizpurua,ugarro,emuxika,mmendikute}@mondragon.edu
[2] Ormazabal Corporate Technology, Parque Empresarial Boroa Parcela 3A, 48340 Amorebieta, Spain
igi@ormazabal.es

Abstract. The emergence of new electricity and energy systems opens the way to novel reliability monitoring and maintenance planning strategies. In smart grids, the increased connection between various power systems enables a resilient grid operation. Similarly, the proliferation of data sources across the grid creates opportunities for a more accurate maintenance planning with up-to-date information of degrading assets and operational information of system performance. In this context, this paper presents a dependability and energy aware asset management framework for an improved maintenance planning of power assets in smart grids through dependability, energy, prognostics and forecasting models. The benefits of the proposed approach are demonstrated with a case study inspired from smart grids.

Keywords: Prognostics & health management · Maintenance planning · Dependability · Reliability · Energy · Smart grids

1 Introduction

The smart grid is a system-of-systems with underlying power, energy, communication and digital infrastructure which adds more functionalities to the existing power grid such as resilience, self-healing and improved asset utilization [16]. Condition monitoring and maintenance planning of smart grids is a complex task due to the diverse dependencies between different systems [10]. At the same time, the increased availability of diverse data sources across the grid opens the way for up-to-date dependability and energy performance estimates, which can assist the operators in designing effective maintenance planning strategies.

This research has been funded by the Spanish Ministry of Science, Innovation and Universities - Spanish Research Agency and ERDF (RTC-2017-6349-3).

Y. Papadopoulos et al. (Eds.): IMBSA 2019, LNCS 11842, pp. 188–203, 2019.
https://doi.org/10.1007/978-3-030-32872-6_13

Dependability is an umbrella term which encompasses reliability, availability, maintenance and safety [5].

Prognostics and health management (PHM) is an expanding engineering field which focuses on diagnostics, prognostics and maintenance planning activities of systems and components [22]. PHM makes use of monitoring datasets and physics-of-failure models to estimate the remaining useful life (RUL) of systems and components. Accordingly, RUL estimates can be used to plan condition-based maintenance (CBM) strategies and initiate maintenance actions in an optimal time instant just before failure occurrence. There have been different CBM solutions for maintenance planning of power assets based on PHM results, e.g. wind turbines [17], gas turbines [15] or power transformers [2].

Most of the proposed maintenance strategies for the power grid have been focused on reliability centered maintenance (RCM) solutions, e.g. [12,19,25]. RCM strategies evaluate the system failure probability and trigger mainte-nance actions when the failure probability is above a threshold level. Intelli-gent RCM-based strategies have been also proposed connecting prognostics pre-diction results with dependability models for an up-to-date failure probability estimation and group-based maintenance planning based on the criticality of components [3].

RCM strategies define maintenance instants through the analysis of the evo-lution of the system reliability. However, decision-making based on a single parameter may not be efficient due to the complex interactions within the sys-tem. Multi-criteria maintenance planning strategies have been focused on opti-mization problems mainly centred on the trade-off between reliability and cost [6,7,14]. Although these strategies achieve an optimal solution, generally they have to limit the complexity of the problem for subsequent analytical treatment.

With the connection of diverse power systems within the smart grid such as distributed generation sources, electric vehicles or microgrids, different opera-tional datasets have been used for energy performance planning and forecasting, e.g. meteorological data or user power consumption patterns. In this context, there is room to enhance the decision-making process by combining RCM with energy estimation models and continually updating them through predictive model results. This approach obtains an enhanced view of the performance and health of the system. Accordingly, the main contribution of this paper is the proposal of a novel model-based maintenance decision-making framework which takes into account up to date dependability and energy information for mainte-nance planning.

Although there are some works that take into account the performance and reliability of power assets for an improved maintenance planning, e.g. [12,15,17,19,25], to the best of authors' knowledge, this is the first approach which combines dynamic failure probability estimates updated with prognos-tics prediction results along with energy estimation models for a more effective maintenance planning.

The rest of this paper is organised as follows. Section 2 presents the proposed approach for enhanced maintenance decision-making through dependability, prognostics and energy estimation models. Section 3 implements the approach in the smart grids case study. Finally Sect. 4 draws conclusions and identifies future work.

2   Dependability and Energy Aware Asset Management Framework

Figure 1 shows the proposed dependability and energy aware asset management framework. The first step is the specification of the system design model which defines the system components, their interactions and the functional operation [21]. Monitoring strategies control the system operation through different parameters and models [24].

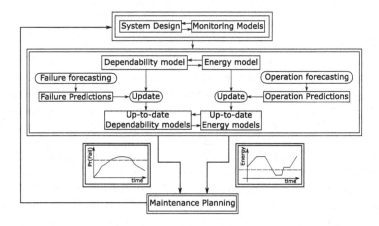

Fig. 1. Dependability and energy aware asset management framework.

In a second step, component failure causes and system failure consequences are elicited so as to evaluate the dependability of the system under study. There are different formalisms that can be used to perform the dependability analysis [4]. Given the dynamic operation of smart grids, it is necessary to model time-dependent failure conditions to obtain accurate probabilistic health indicators. This paper focuses on the use of Dynamic Fault Tree (DFT) models so as to specify the dynamic failure logic of the system [4,8]. Figure 2a shows the DFT notation and Fig. 2b shows a DFT model example where the system failure occurs if component E fails or A fails before B and both C and D fail.

Subsequently energy-related metrics are quantified. Energy estimation models are directly linked with dependability models because they influence each other, e.g. when a component fails it will not produce energy or as a component degrades the energy production will be affected.

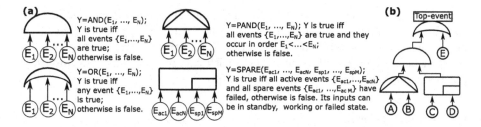

Fig. 2. (a) DFT notation; (b) DFT example.

With the increase of available data across the power grid, there are multiple possibilities to update dependability and energy models with up-to-date predictions. Component RUL predictions can be used to update dependability models [1] and performance-related parameters can be used to update energy estimation models, e.g. forecast traffic to estimate the battery consumption of an electric car or forecast weather temperature to estimate the energy production of photovoltaic or wind energy systems.

This updated view on the health and operation conditions of the power grid provides an up-to-date picture of the health and performance of the system and it helps defining an effective preventive maintenance strategy. At this stage maintenance planning decisions are based on both failure probabilities elicited from up-to-date dependability models and energy-related performance information inferred from up-to-date energy models.

3 Case Study

The case study examined in this section is inspired from smart grids with the use of photovoltaic (PV) systems and electric vehicles (EV) with dynamic charging profiles [10, 20]. Figure 3 shows the block diagram of the case study.

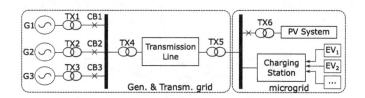

Fig. 3. Case study.

The main objective of the power grid is to avoid unexpected power outages and component failures. In this paper this problem will be limited to keep the power at the charging station at an acceptable level and the system failure probability below a threshold value. The energy generated from the generation and PV systems should be enough to supply the EV charging station. However, if the deterioration of components in the generation and transmission grid or PV components is significant, it may threaten the energy requirements. Similarly, if the failure probability of the power grid is high, but the energy requirements are met, it may be possible to extend the operation of the system. In this context, the influence of component failures along with energy levels open the way to a multi-criteria maintenance decision-making process.

3.1 Implementation

Figure 4 shows the implementation of the case study. The failure models have been specified with Stochastic Activity Network (SAN) models [23] using a DFT to SAN transformation dictionary [1]. The energy models define the energy-related operation of the smart grid using the SAN formalism.

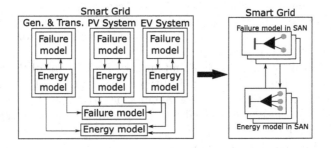

Fig. 4. Implementation of the case study in Fig. 3.

In addition to the specification of failure and performance models, SAN enables the implementation of dynamically updated transition rates which can be used to specify dynamically updated events such as component failure rates [1].

Preliminaries on SAN. SAN extends stochastic Petri Nets generalizing the stochastic relationships and adding mechanisms to construct hierarchical models [18]. Figure 5 shows SAN modelling primitives [23].

Standard Place	Extended Place	Input gate	Output gate	Instantaneous Activity	Timed Activity
●	●	◀	▶	❙	❙

Fig. 5. Notation of SAN elements.

Places represent the state of the modelled system. Each place contains tokens defining the marking of the place. A standard place contains an integer number of tokens, whereas *extended* places contain data types other than integers (e.g., floats, array). The marking function of the place x is denoted as m(x), e.g., $m(x) = 1$ means that the place x has a marking equal to 1.

There are two types of activities: instantaneous which complete in negligible amount of time, and timed whose duration has an effect on the system performance and their completion time can be a constant or a random value. The random value is ruled by a probability distribution function defining the time to fire the activity.

Activities fire based on the conditions defined over the marking of the net and their effect is to modify the marking of the places. The completion of an activity of any kind is enabled by a particular marking of a set of places. The presence of at least one token in each input place enables the firing of the activity removing the token from its input place(s) and placing them in the output place(s).

Another way to enable a certain activity consists of input gates and output gates. Input and output gates make the SAN formalism general and powerful enough to model complex real situations. They determine the marking of the net based on user-defined C++ rules.

Input Gates (IG) control the enabling of activities and define the marking changes that will occur when an activity completes. A set of places is connected to the input gate and the input gate is connected to an activity. A Boolean condition (or guard) enables the activity connected to the gate and a function determines the effect of the activity completion on the marking of the places connected to the gate. Output Gates (OG) specify the effect of activity completion on the marking of the places connected to the output gate. An output function defines the marking changes that occur when the activity completes.

The performance measurements are carried out through reward functions defined over the designed model. Reward functions are evaluated as the expected value of the reward variable and they are defined based on:

- the marking of the net (state reward function), e.g. quantification of the probability for being in a specific place;
- completion of activities (impulse reward function), e.g. count the number of times an activity triggers within a time interval.

Figure 6 shows a simple system example. In this case the SAN places are initialized to working state $<m(W), m(F)> = <1, 0>$. The token will move from W to the place F according to the cumulative distribution function (CDF) determined by the fault timed activity. The time to failure will be calculated with the parameters of the fault activity and after the time to failure has elapsed the system will move from working to the failed state $<0, 1>$.

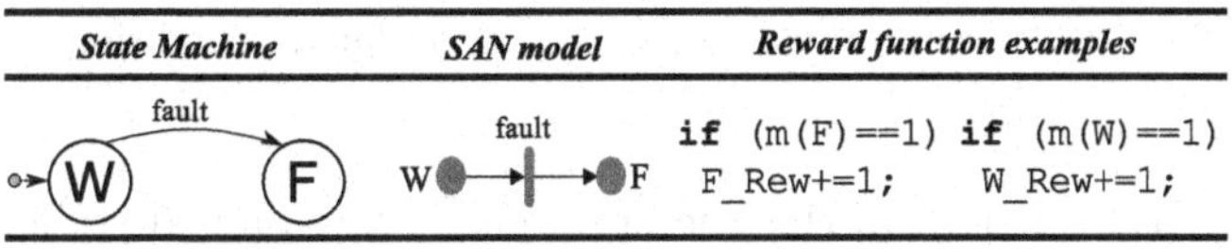

Fig. 6. Non-repairable system example in SAN.

This paper focuses on Monte Carlo simulations (MCS) for the quantification of different probabilities. Reward functions indicated in Fig. 6 with F_Rew and W_Rew reward variables can be used to evaluate the failure probability or availability. These statements are evaluated for a large number of trials and the expected value of these random variables evaluated at different time instants will give the failure probability and availability indicators. Note that the required number of iterations will depend on the required confidence level for the reward variables.

The inverse transform sampling method extracts the stochastic occurrence times of timed activities using MCS. Let r be a random variable drawn from the uniform distribution $r \sim U(0,1)$, $F(t)$ a CDF, e.g. exponential CDF $F(t) = 1 - exp(\lambda t)$, and TTF the time to fire the activity. Then, the inverse sampling method applies the relation $F^{-1}(r) = TTF$ to draw the time to fire according to the CDF [23]. SAN models have been simulated using the Möbious tool [11].

Generation and Transmission Grid. The power generated from the generation and transmitted through the transmission grid determines the incoming power for the microgrid. The generation system is comprised of a two-out-of-three generation system where there should be always two generators active and one in standby operation. As soon as one of them fails, it is reconfigured through the corresponding circuit breaker and transformer (cf. Fig. 3).

The failure condition of the generation and transmission grid is defined as follows: (i) two transformers fail after the failure of the complementary circuit breaker so that it is not possible to reconfigure the standby transformer (IE1, IE2, IE3), (ii) all transformers fail simultaneously (spare), or (iii) the transmission line or transformers Tr_4 and Tr_5 fail. Figure 7 shows the DFT model of the generation and transmission grid defining the transmission and generation grid failure condition.

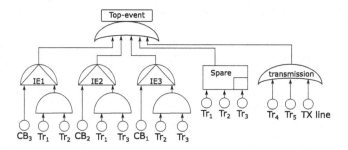

Fig. 7. Generation and transmission grid failure condition.

The power that arrives to the microgrid has been assumed stable over time only affected by the degradation of the generation and transmission grid:

$$P_{Del}(t) = P_{Gen}(t) \times R_{G\&T}(t) \tag{1}$$

where $R_{G\&T}(t)$ is the reliability of the generation and transmission system, $P_{Gen}(t)$ is the generated power and $P_{Del}(t)$ is the delivered power to the microgrid.

The DFT in Fig. 7 can be implemented through the model synthesis approach based on SAN models [3]. However, for simplicity, the DFT model in Fig. 7 has been approximated with a two-state system with working and failed states with the transition rate modelled with the conditional Weibull CDF (cf. Fig. 6):

$$F(t|T_{el}) = 1 - e^{-\left\{\left(\frac{(T_{el}+t)}{H}\right)^\beta - \frac{T_{el}}{H}^\beta\right\}} \tag{2}$$

where β and H are the shape and scale parameters of the Weibull distribution, respectively, and T_{el} is the elapsed time of operation up to the start of the new mission time at t.

The Weibull distribution can approximate different parametric distributions [8] and the conditional Weibull CDF in Eq. (2) permits the update of the CDF over time. This distribution can be used to update the component failure rates with RUL estimations performed during the system operation given the assumption $RUL \approx 1/\lambda$ [1]. That is, when $\beta = 1$, the Weibull distribution is equivalent to the exponential distribution and accordingly the scale parameter becomes the failure rate of the exponential distribution, i.e. $H = \lambda$.

Figure 8 shows the failure probability of the generation and transmission grid $F_{G\&T}(t) = 1 - R_{G\&T}(t)$. The vertical lines indicate the update instants of the CDF with the failure rate values in Table 1, where λ_0 denotes the initial failure rate, λ_1 denotes the failure rate at prediction instant 1 (assumed at 100 time units) and λ_1 denotes the failure rate at prediction instant 2 (assumed at 250 time units). It is assumed that the values in Table 1 have been obtained from prognostics prediction results of the corresponding system.

Table 1. Failure rate predictions.

System	PV system			Transm. & Distr. Grid			EV Station		
Failure rates	λ_0	λ_1	λ_2	λ_0	λ_1	λ_2	λ_0	λ_1	λ_2
Values	600	400	200	1560	1800	1200	880	750	700

Figure 9 shows the delivered power with the failure rate parameters displayed in Table 1. The degradation trend in Fig. 9 follows the degradation trend defined by $R_{G\&T}(t)$ shown in Fig. 8.

PV System. The PV system produces energy from the solar irradiation. The energy production of the PV system can be affected by the sun irradiation or degradation of its constituent components. Figure 10 shows the block diagram of the PV system [9].

The PV string module converts the sun irradiation into DC power. It is possible to have various PV strings to increase the generated DC power. The

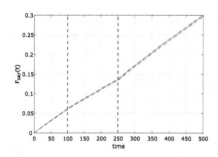
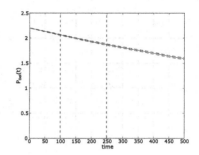

Fig. 8. Generation and transmission grid failure probability $F_{G\&T}(t)$.

Fig. 9. Delivered power to the micro-grid $P_{Del}(t)$.

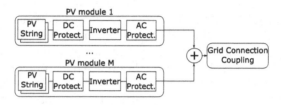

Fig. 10. PV system block diagram.

inverter converts the DC power into AC and the protection systems protect the PV module against undesired events. This configuration can be repeated for a certain amount of PV modules and these modules are connected to the grid. Accordingly, the power generated by a PV module can be defined as:

$$P_{PV}(t) = \eta(t) \times Irrad(t) \times sin(\omega(t)) \times S \tag{3}$$

where $\eta(t)$ is the efficiency of the PV module which is dependent on the degradation of the module, $Irrad(t)$ is the solar irradiation (W/m^2) and $\omega(t)$ denotes the angle of the sun with respect to the PV module and accordingly its efficiency and S denotes the surface of the PV module (m^2).

The FTA model shown in Fig. 11 defines the failure logic of the PV system comprised of M modules and N PV strings. That is, the PV system fails if all PV strings fail altogether or the DC protection fails or the AC protection fails or the inverter fails [9].

As with the generation and transmission grid, the PV FTA model in Fig. 11 has been approximated with a two state model with the conditional distribution in Eq. (2) and failure rate parameters displayed in Table 1. It has been assumed that the efficiency $\eta(t)$ in Eq. (3) is directly related with the reliability of the PV module, i.e. $R_{PV}(t) = \eta(t)$ [9]. Figure 12 shows the PV failure probability, $F_{PV}(t)$, and Fig. 13 shows the generated power, $P_{PV}(t)$.

It can be seen that periodically the PV module does not generate power due to the lack of sunlight during the night time. Additionally, it can be seen that the produced PV energy decays exponentially owing to the efficiency of the

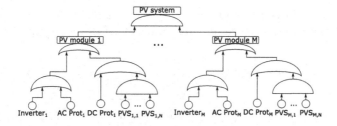

Fig. 11. FTA model of the PV system.

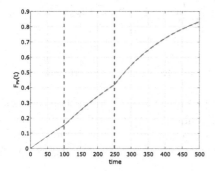

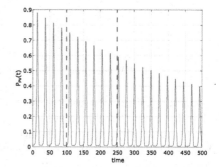

Fig. 12. PV system failure probability $F_{PV}(t)$.

Fig. 13. PV system generated energy $P_{PV}(t)$.

PV module. The predictions in Figs. 12 and 13 are constrained with the adopted assumptions, for more advance forecasting estimations dynamic reliability methods can be used which can take into account various operation conditions, e.g. see [9].

EV Charging Station. Electric vehicles pose new challenges to the power grid such as the ability to withstand dynamic load requirements according to user requests. One possibility to model user requests is to use traffic patterns along with the capacity of batteries. Equation (4) describes the state-of-charge equation of a electric car as a function of time and distance [13]:

$$SoC_k(dist) = SoC_{k-1}(dist) - F_d(dist); \quad \text{where} \quad F_d(dist) = 100 \times (dist/d_R) \quad (4)$$

where SoC_k denotes the state-of-charge at the discrete time-step k, F_d denotes the deterioration factor, defined as a function of the distance $dist$ run in one day (km) and the autonomy of the electric car d_R (assumed 100 km).

Figure 14 shows the electric vehicle (EV) and EV station operation concepts. A number of electric vehicles can be connected to the EV station at the same time at the expense of more power consumption. For each car, the designed model includes the state-of-charge Eq. (4) along with the stochastic failure model which degrades the maximum charging capacity of the car. The stochastic model has been specified with the model in Fig. 6 with the dynamic failure rate parameters specified in Table 1. See failure probability results, $F_{EV}(t)$, in Fig. 14.

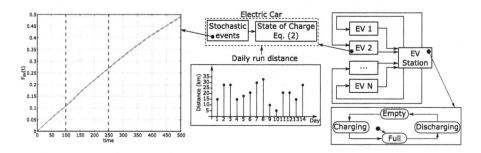

Fig. 14. EV charging station operation and electric vehicle operation.

The EV charging station operates according to the finite state machine shown in Fig. 14. Every time it passes through the charging state it will require power from the grid. It has been assumed that the charging station charges all the EV with a constant charging profile and the minimum state-of-charge level of batteries have been defined at 20%.

Every time the station is used for charging the battery, the required power is drawn from the grid. Figure 15 shows the changing state-of-charge (SoC) of the electric vehicle and the required power from the grid. It has been assumed that the car follows periodically the distance pattern shown in Fig. 14.

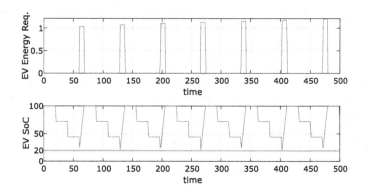

Fig. 15. (a) EV energy required; (b) EV state-of-charge.

For simplicity periodic usage and linear charging times have been assumed. Generally the car usage and charging times will vary from car to car [13].

Grid Level Analysis. The grid level analysis enables the quantification of a number of decision-making parameters including the failure probability and energy requirements. Figures 16 and 17 show the system failure logic and the system failure probability respectively. Note that the failure probability for PV and generation and transmission systems has been inferred from a two state model for simplicity, but they can be replaced with their corresponding FTA models specified in Figs. 7 and 11 respectively.

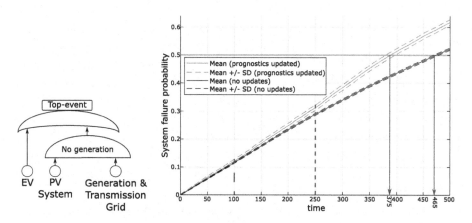

Fig. 16. FTA of the system in Fig. 3.

Fig. 17. Failure probability of the system in Fig. 3. (Color figure online)

The failure probability estimates in Fig. 17 show the results of two models. One is the system failure probability estimate without updates, i.e. using static failure rates (black line). The other is the system failure probability taking into account updated failure rates from Table 1 (blue line).

If the maintenance planning is solely based on the failure probability condition, i.e. traditional RCM strategy, the maintenance instant would be at 375 time units according to the prognostics updated approach and at 465 time units according to the model without updates.

However, if the decision-making process also takes into account the energy balance of the system, the evaluation of the maintenance action can be enhanced through energy level indicators. In this case, the balance aims to compensate for EV energy requests (Fig. 15a, $P_{EV}(t)$) with generation and transmission power (Fig. 9, $P_{Del}(t)$) and PV generation (Fig. 13, $P_{PV}(t)$). Figure 18 shows the energy balance of the power grid, i.e. $P_{Bal}(t) = P_{Del}(t) + P_{PV}(t) - P_{EV}(t)$.

It is possible to set up a threshold to identify deviations from acceptable system operation and control the time instant and the duration of when this limit is exceeded. Formally, the energy level (EL) threshold can be defined as:

$$EL = \int_0^{Tm} I_s(t)dt, \text{ where } I_s(t) = \begin{cases} 1, & \text{if } E(t) < Energy_{\text{threshold}} \\ 0, & \text{otherwise} \end{cases} \tag{5}$$

where $Energy_{threshold}$ is the cumulative energy threshold limit to trigger maintenance actions. If the energy level of the system is below $Energy_{threshold}$ it may indicate performance problems. In this context, if the engineer sets up a limit of $Energy_{threshold} \geq 20$, then the maintenance instant would be 340 time units. Figure 19 shows the energy indicator and the corresponding threshold.

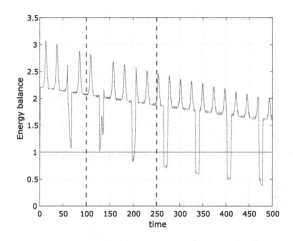

Fig. 18. Energy balance at the smart grid example in Fig. 3.

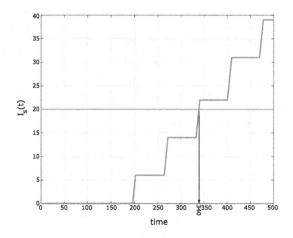

Fig. 19. Energy indicator inferred from Fig. 18 via Eq. (5).

The energy balance information generates an additional decision-making criteria which can identify early abnormal operations. This enhanced view on the health of the system provides a more complete picture of the system degradation and performance.

4   Conclusions

The connection of diverse power systems within the power grid improves the resiliency of the of the power network, but it also introduces challenges for effective monitoring and maintenance planning due to the increased dependencies and overall complexity.

This paper presents a multi-criteria maintenance decision-making framework for smart grids considering reliability and energy attributes as reference models for maintenance decision-making. Maintenance-planning solutions based on multiple attributes enable the adoption of trade-off maintenance decisions which can lead to the adoption of efficient maintenance decisions.

In addition, the proposed solution enables the dynamic update of dependability and energy estimation models from predictive model results such as failure prognostics predictions or performance forecasting results. This up-to-date view on the health and performance of the system enables the adoption of improved maintenance decisions.

Future goals may focus on the implementation of the proposed framework for an end-to-end detailed power systems case study with datasets collected from the field.

References

1. Aizpurua, J.I., Catterson, V.M., Papadopoulos, Y., Chiacchio, F., Manno, G.: Improved dynamic dependability assessment through integration with prognostics. IEEE Trans. Reliab. **66**(3), 893–913 (2017). https://doi.org/10.1109/TR.2017.2693821
2. Aizpurua, J.I., McArthur, S.D.J., Stewart, B.G., Lambert, B., Cross, J.G., Catterson, V.M.: Adaptive power transformer lifetime predictions through machine learning and uncertainty modeling in nuclear power plants. IEEE Trans. Ind. Electron. **66**(6), 4726–4737 (2019). https://doi.org/10.1109/TIE.2018.2860532
3. Aizpurua, J., Catterson, V., Papadopoulos, Y., Chiacchio, F., D'Urso, D.: Supporting group maintenance through prognostics-enhanced dynamic dependability prediction. Reliab. Eng. Syst. Saf. **168**, 171–188 (2017). https://doi.org/10.1016/j.ress.2017.04.005. maintenance Modelling
4. Aizpurua, J.I., Muxika, E.: Model based design of dependable systems: limitations and evolution of analysis and verification approaches. Int. J. Adv. Secur. **6**, 12–31 (2013)
5. Avizienis, A., Laprie, J.C., Randell, B., Landwehr, C.: Basic concepts and taxonomy of dependable and secure computing. IEEE Trans. Dependable Secure Comput. **1**(1), 11–33 (2004). https://doi.org/10.1109/TDSC.2004.2
6. Besnard, F., Patrikssont, M., Strombergt, A., Wojciechowskit, A., Bertling, L.: An optimization framework for opportunistic maintenance of offshore wind power system. In: 2009 IEEE Bucharest PowerTech, pp. 1–7, June 2009. https://doi.org/10.1109/PTC.2009.5281868
7. Cavalcante, C.A., Lopes, R.S.: Multi-criteria model to support the definition of opportunistic maintenance policy: a study in a cogeneration system. Energy **80**, 32–40 (2015). https://doi.org/10.1016/j.energy.2014.11.039

8. Chiacchio, F., Cacioppo, M., D'Urso, D., Manno, G., Trapani, N., Compagno, L.: A weibull-based compositional approach for hierarchical dynamic fault trees. Reliab. Eng. Syst. Saf. **109**, 45–52 (2013)

9. Chiacchio, F., D'Urso, D., Famoso, F., Brusca, S., Aizpurua, J.I., Catterson, V.M.: On the use of dynamic reliability for an accurate modelling of renewable power plants. Energy **151**, 605–621 (2018). https://doi.org/10.1016/j.energy.2018.03.101

10. Colak, I., Kabalci, E., Fulli, G., Lazarou, S.: A survey on the contributions of power electronics to smart grid systems. Renew. Sustain. Energy Rev. **47**, 562–579 (2015). https://doi.org/10.1016/j.rser.2015.03.031

11. Deavours, D.D., et al.: The mobius framework and its implementation. IEEE Trans. Softw. Eng. **28**(10), 956–969 (2002). https://doi.org/10.1109/TSE.2002.1041052

12. Ge, H., Asgarpoor, S.: Reliability and maintainability improvement of substations with aging infrastructure. IEEE Trans. Power Delivery **27**(4), 1868–1876 (2012). https://doi.org/10.1109/TPWRD.2012.2198672

13. Godina, R., Rodrigues, E.M., Matias, J.C., Catalao, J.P.: Smart electric vehicle charging scheduler for overloading prevention of an industry client power distribution transformer. Appl. Energy **178**, 29–42 (2016). https://doi.org/10.1016/j.apenergy.2016.06.019

14. Kralj, B., Rajaković, N.: Multiobjective programming in power system optimization: new approach to generator maintenance scheduling. Int. J. Electr. Power Energy Syst. **16**(4), 211–220 (1994). https://doi.org/10.1016/0142-0615(94)90012-4

15. Li, Y., Nilkitsaranont, P.: Gas turbine performance prognostic for condition-based maintenance. Appl. Energy **86**(10), 2152–2161 (2009). https://doi.org/10.1016/j.apenergy.2009.02.011

16. Liu, C.C., McArthur, S., Lee, S.J. (eds.): Smart Grid Handbook. Wiley, Hoboken (2016)

17. Marquez, F.P.G., Tobias, A.M., Perez, J.M.P., Papaelias, M.: Condition monitoring of wind turbines: techniques and methods. Renewable Energy **46**, 169–178 (2012). https://doi.org/10.1016/j.renene.2012.03.003

18. Meyer, J.F., Movaghar, A., Sanders, W.H.: Stochastic activity networks: structure, behavior, and application. In: International Workshop on Timed Petri Nets, pp. 106–115. IEEE Computer Society, Washington (1985)

19. Mkandawire, B.O., Ijumba, N., Saha, A.: Transformer risk modelling by stochastic augmentation of reliability-centred maintenance. Electric Power Syst. Res. **119**, 471–477 (2015). https://doi.org/10.1016/j.epsr.2014.11.005

20. Mwasilu, F., Justo, J.J., Kim, E.K., Do, T.D., Jung, J.W.: Electric vehicles and smart grid interaction: a review on vehicle to grid and renewable energy sources integration. Renew. Sustain. Energy Rev. **34**, 501–516 (2014). https://doi.org/10.1016/j.rser.2014.03.031

21. Papadopoulos, Y., et al.: Engineering failure analysis and design optimisation with hip-hops. Eng. Failure Anal. **18**(2), 590–608 (2011)

22. Pecht, M.: Prognostics and Health Management of Electronics. Wiley, Hoboken (2008)

23. Sanders, W.H., Meyer, J.F.: Stochastic activity networks: formal definitions and concepts*. In: Brinksma, E., Hermanns, H., Katoen, J.-P. (eds.) EEF School 2000. LNCS, vol. 2090, pp. 315–343. Springer, Heidelberg (2001). https://doi.org/10.1007/3-540-44667-2_9

24. Yin, S., Ding, S.X., Xie, X., Luo, H.: A review on basic data-driven approaches for industrial process monitoring. IEEE Trans. Ind. Electron. **61**(11), 6418–6428 (2014)
25. Yssaad, B., Khiat, M., Chaker, A.: Reliability centered maintenance optimization for power distribution systems. Int. J. Electr. Power Energy Syst. **55**, 108–115 (2014). https://doi.org/10.1016/j.ijepes.2013.08.025

Formal Verification of Network Interlocking Control by Distributed Signal Boxes

Stylianos Basagiannis[1] and Panagiotis Katsaros[2(✉)]

[1] United Technologies Research Center, Cork, Ireland
BasagiS@utrc.utc.com
[2] School of Informatics, Aristotle University of Thessaloniki,
54124 Thessaloniki, Greece
katsaros@csd.auth.gr

Abstract. Interlocking control prevents certain operations from occurring, unless preceded by specific events. It is used in traffic network control systems (e.g. railway interlocking control), piping and tunneling control systems and in other applications like for example communication network control. Interlocking systems have to comply with certain safety properties and this fact elevates formal modeling as the most important concern in their design. This paper introduces an interlocking control algorithm based on the use of what we call Distributed Signal Boxes (DSBs). Distributed control eliminates the intrinsic complexity of centralized interlocking control solutions, which are mainly developed in the field of railway traffic control. Our algorithm uses types of network control units, which do not store state information. Control units are combined according to a limited number of patterns that in all cases yield safe network topologies. Verification of safety takes place by model checking a network that includes all possible interconnections between neighbor nodes. Obtained results can be used to generalize correctness by compositional reasoning for networks of arbitrary complexity that are formed according to the verified interconnection cases.

1 Introduction

In the past, interlocking control was mainly developed and studied in the context of railway signaling, where its task is to prevent trains from colliding and derailing, while at the same time allowing their movements. Our view is that interlocking control is a mean for synchronizing exclusive access to distributed network resources (network segments) and its application extends beyond this of railway signaling. Interlocking control is also used in piping and tunneling control systems and may be involved in other applications like for example network management systems [2].

In this work, we introduce a distributed control algorithm with network control units that do not store information related to the algorithm's state. This

© Springer Nature Switzerland AG 2019
Y. Papadopoulos et al. (Eds.): IMBSA 2019, LNCS 11842, pp. 204–221, 2019.
https://doi.org/10.1007/978-3-030-32872-6_14

option eliminates the intrinsic complexity of other solutions that are mainly centralized and the complexity of the few distributed approaches with control units that maintain state. More precisely, as shown in [19], algorithmic verification of interlocking safety properties is an extremely complex task, due to the state space explosion involved. Typically, the internal state of the analyzed system has 2^n possible configurations, where n is the number of components such as interlocking points, signals, etc. with which the system is built. Our contribution is summarized in the following:

- The Distributed Signal Boxes (DSBs) algorithm is verified within the SPIN model checker [14]. Interlocking safety is verified in a network formed by combining all possible interconnections between neighbor nodes. The control units of our algorithm can be composed only in the ways tested in this small network.
- Interlocking logic of the control units is decoupled from the network topology and this eliminates the need to locally store information related to the algorithm's state. Although network routing is not within the scope of our algorithm, we assume non-deterministic routing as an abstract modeling approach for verifying all routing possibilities in a network node [16]. Interlocking safety is provided as a network service, irrespective of the operation control commands.

For more complex networks, one can use the compositional verification technique for synchronous message passing [18] that decomposes the verification problem into correctness properties for smaller networks. Thus, we avoid the risk of interlocking schemes that cannot be fully analyzed, due to their large state space.

A preliminary version of the algorithm was presented in [3], where it was applied to a simple railway-interlocking problem, which did not include all the cases of node interconnections that are covered in present article. Section 2 presents the considered network interconnection cases and their corresponding DSBs connectivity. Section 3 introduces the algorithm and the obtained SPIN model-checking results. Finally, in Sect. 4 we review the related works and we compare them with the proposed approach. We conclude with comments on the potential impact of the presented work.

2   Network Interlocking Nodes and Distributed Signal Boxes

The messages for the control of a single node that connects multiple network segments depend on the node's interconnection with neighbor nodes. In this section, we establish the terminology used to describe a general interlocking problem and we introduce the different cases of nodes' interconnection and the corresponding DSBs topologies.

Definition 1. *Nodes define the ends of interconnected network segments, which are distributed network resources. They cannot communicate with each other. A node – depending on the number of interconnected segments – controls access to at least one resource, i.e. access to the resource(s) is only possible through the controlling node.*

Figure 1 illustrates a simple network consisting of interconnected nodes X, A, B, C, D and Y. Node A controls access to resource $R(AB)$, but direct communication with node B is not possible.

Definition 2. *Each node is connected with a DSB and communicates with it through a synchronous signal channel. The DSBs corresponding to a pair of connected nodes communicate with each other. Since nodes cannot directly contact, they manage the controlled resources only by messages to their corresponding DSBs.*

In Fig. 1, node A and *DSBoxA* are connected by the signal channel *NodeAtoDSBoxA*. As a consequence of Definition 2, *DSBoxA* exchanges messages with *DSBoxB*.

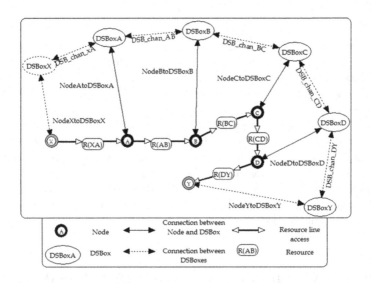

Fig. 1. One-to-one node interconnection and the DSBs topology

Definition 3. *When a moving entity requests access to a network resource, it can be granted only by the controlling node of this resource. All entities that request access move in a given direction.*

Definition 4. *Interlocking control synchronizes requests generated by entities, for exclusive access to the controlled resource(s).*

Nodes are represented by *control processes* that accept as input an entity arrival, exchange messages with their corresponding *DSBs* and subsequently release the moving entity, when possible, thus granting access to the requested resource. Entity arrivals trigger a message dispatch to the node's *DSB* and upon receipt of the reply the entity is released. Thus, control processes do not need to store information for the algorithm's state, since this state is communicated to the network instantly. Within the SPIN model-checker, we assume synchronous communication, which is modeled by rendezvous communication channels [15]. This specification assumption keeps our model computationally tractable, since we avoid asynchronous communication that would increase interleaving between the modeled processes. Applicable implementation alternatives include all modern time-triggered communication options, with safety critical features (e.g. the TTP/C and the FlexRay protocols) that are often used in distributed embedded systems. However, we do not address issues related to implementation details like for example how to guarantee atomic message dispatch, since we are only interested to verify the correctness of our algorithm.

We have identified three types of resource interconnection namely, the *one-to-one link*, the *one-to-many split link* and the *many-to-one join link*. One-to-many and many-to-one links require synchronization between the *DSBs* of the nodes in the many side. Figure 1 introduced an example with one-to-one resource interconnections, where for some entity that occupies resource $R(XA)$ node A grants access to resource $R(AB)$, if it is not occupied by another entity. The figure shows the implied *DSBs* topology and represents a part of Athen's underground metro network, which was used in [3] for introducing a first version of our algorithm.

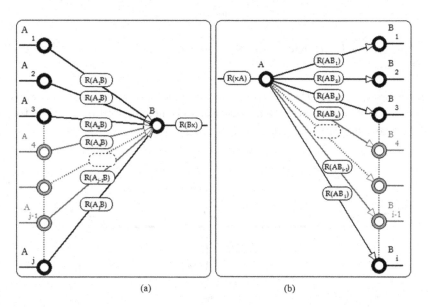

(a)   (b)

Fig. 2. (a) Many-to-one join node interconnection and (b) one-to-many split node interconnection

Figure 2a presents the many-to-one join node interconnection, where a number of network resources, say $R(A_1B), R(A_2B), ..., R(A_jB)$ is connected through some node B to a single resource shown as $R(Bx)$. Access to the controlled network resource $R(Bx)$ is performed by the synchronous exchange of control messages transmitted between: (i) nodes $A_1, A_2, ..., A_j$ and their corresponding $DSBs$, (ii) neighbor $DSBs$ (e.g. the $DSBs$ of nodes A_1 and B), (iii) node B and its corresponding DSB and (iv) for synchronizing the $DSBs$ of nodes $A_1, A_2, ..., A_j$ in the many side.

Figure 2b shows the one-to-many split node interconnection, where some network resource, say $R(xA)$ is connected to i network resources denoted by $R(AB_1), R(AB_2), ..., R(AB_i)$. We already pointed out that for verifying all routing possibilities for a passing entity, we include all possible entity routing decisions, i.e. a non-deterministic selection of the requested controlled resource (symmetrically, in Fig. 2a we assume non-deterministic selection between the entities waiting in the many side). Access to the requested resource is regulated by the synchronous exchange of control messages transmitted between: (i) nodes $B_1, B_2, ..., B_i$ and their corresponding $DSBs$, (ii) neighbor $DSBs$ (e.g. the $DSBs$ of nodes A and B_1), (iii) node A and its corresponding DSB and (iv) for synchronizing the $DSBs$ of nodes $B_1, B_2, ..., B_i$.

For a two-to-two resource interconnection by a single node, a suitable solution can be developed by decomposing the problem into two distinct two-to-one interconnection cases and by intermixing the algorithm's logic accordingly. This means that a synchronization message non-deterministically selects, which destination resource from the two-to-one interconnection cases will be occupied. A many-to-many resource interconnection is implemented as a complex with a many-to-one join link attached to a one-to-many split link.

3   Network Interlocking Nodes and Distributed Signal Boxes

Figure 3 shows the $DSBs$ topology for a typical one-to-one resource interconnection, as well as the exchanged messages guaranteeing exclusive access to the controlled resources. Our algorithm encompasses:

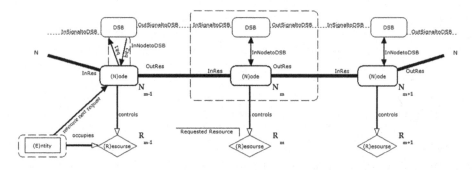

Fig. 3. DSBs and message communications for an one-to-one resource interconnection

– the control processes for the shown interlocking nodes (N),
– the resources (R), with each of them being controlled by some node (N),
– the DSBs control processes, where each DSB corresponds to some node (N),
– the moving entities (E) that request access to the available resources (R) and
– the messages between nodes and $DSBs$, and those exchanged between $DSBs$.

Resource allocation is established by using two message types, namely $bit1$ and $bit2$. These messages do not carry any information; they block or release processes, but none is dedicated to a specific role throughout the whole algorithm logic.

```
1 proctype Node(chan inRes,
2                    outRes,
3                    inNodetoDSB)
4 {
5 byte entity;
6      do
7      :: inRes?entity;
8         inNodetoDSB!bit1;
9         inNodetoDSB?bit2;
10        outRes!entity;
11     od
12 }
```

Fig. 4. The Node control process of the DSBs algorithm

The algorithm is introduced in PROMELA, the input language of SPIN. In Fig. 3, let us assume that an entity E occupies R_{m-1} and requests access to R_m, which is controlled by N_m (line 7 of *proctype Node* in Fig. 4 is enabled for N_m). N_m then sends $bit1$ to its corresponding DSB (line 8) through the signal channel $inNodetoDSB$ that synchronizes the two processes. We distinguish two different possibilities:

– Resource R_m is available, which means that the DSB of node N_m has already sent message $bit2$ to its corresponding node (line 18 of *proctype DSBox* in Fig. 5 for the node N_m). Message $bit2$ is received by node N_m that subsequently provides access to resource R_m (lines 9, 10 of *proctype Node* for N_m). The DSB of node N_m is then blocked waiting for message $bit1$ in the communication channel $outSignaltoDSB$ that synchronizes it with the DSB of node N_{m+1} (line 19 of *proctype DSBox* for the node N_m).
– Resource R_m is currently occupied by another entity. In this case, there is no message $bit2$ in the $inNodetoDSB$ signal channel for node N_m and this blocks the requesting entity from accessing R_m (line 9 of *proctype Node* for N_m). The DSB of N_m also waits for message $bit1$ (line 19 of *proctype DSBox* for N_m). The expected message will be received when the DSB of node N_{m+1} controlling the requested resource R_{m+1} will send $bit1$ (line 21 of *proctype DSBox* for N_{m+1}) thus indicating that R_{m+1} can be used by the entity that currently occupies R_m. Upon receipt of $bit1$ by the DSB of N_m (line 19 of *proctype DSBox*) the message $bit1$ in the signal channel $inNodetoDSB$ is

consumed (line 20 of *proctype DSBox*) and subsequently a *bit*1 message is dispatched to the *DSB* of node N_{m-1} (line 21 of *proctype DSBox* for N_m). Then, the *DSB* of node N_m sends *bit*2 to the signal channel *inNodetoDSB* that synchronizes it with its corresponding node (line 18 of *proctype DSBox* for N_m) and this message releases the requested resource R_m (lines 9, 10 of *proctype Node* for N_m).

```
13 proctype DSBox(chan inSignaltoDSB,
14                     outSignaltoDSB,
15                     inNodetoDSB)
16 {
17      do
18      :: inNodetoDSB!bit2;
19         outSignaltoDSB?bit1;
20      :: inNodetoDSB?bit1;
21         inSignaltoDSB!bit1;
22      od
23 }
```

Fig. 5. The DSBox control process of the DSBs algorithm

Figure 6 shows the message communications for a network with a two-to-one join node connected to a node one-to-two. The control processes for these two nodes differ from the control process of a simple node (Fig. 3) in the use of *one more synchronous message exchange for every pair of adjacent resources in the many side*. This additional message is necessary, in order to synchronize concurrent requests for access to the same resource coming from the many side of the nodes.

The PROMELA code in Fig. 7 introduces the control process for the shown two-to-one join node that connects the network resources specified by the *inRes*1 and *inRes*2 parameters to the network resource specified by the *outRes* parameter. For a single pair of adjacent resources in the many side, we need only one synchronization channel named here *synchronizerA* and one additional message that we call *bit*3*i*. Besides the use of the synchronizer, the algorithm's logic is essentially the same with the logic shown in Fig. 4, apart from the fact that we use now two signal channels named *inNode1toDSB* and *inNode2toDSB* that synchronize the two-to-one join node with its corresponding DSB. Finally, the process logic for the two-to-one join node addresses the requirement for non-deterministic selection between concurrent requests of controlled resources. Figure 8 provides the process logic for the symmetric case of the one-to-two node shown in Fig. 6.

The complete PROMELA code for the small network of Fig. 9 includes all types of possible interconnections and at the same time gives us the opportunity to verify safety and to study existing possibilities for deadlock, livelock or other violations of progress. Resource $Rsrc34$ is connected to resource $Rsrc41$. $Node(1)$ represents a one-to-two split link to the resources $Rsrc12$ and $Rsrc13$ and $Node(3)$ is a two-to-one join link to the resource $Rsrc34$.

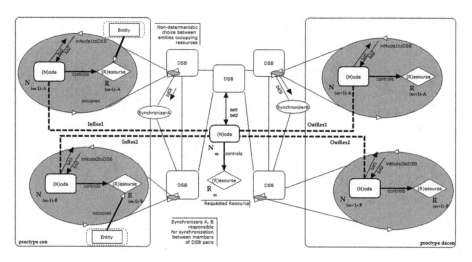

Fig. 6. DSBs and message exchanges for a two-to-one join node connected to a one-to-two node

```
24 proctype con ( chan inRes1,
25                     inRes2,
26                     inNode1toDSB,
27                     inNode2toDSB,
28                     outRes)
29 {
30     byte entity;
31     do
32     :: inRes1?entity;
33        inNode1toDSB!bit1;
34        inNode1toDSB?bit2;
35        synchronizerA?bit3i;
36        outRes!entity;
37        synchronizerA!bit3i;
38        inRes2?entity;
39        inNode2toDSB!bit1;
40        inNode2toDSB?bit2;
41         outRes!entity;
42     :: inRes2?entity;
43        inNode2toDSB!bit1;
44        inNode2toDSB?bit2;
45        synchronizerA?bit3i;
46        outRes!entity;
47        synchronizerA!bit3i;
48        inRes1?entity;
49        inNode1toDSB!bit1;
50        inNode1toDSB?bit2;
51        outRes!entity;
52     od
53 }
```

```
54 proctype decon (chan inRes,
55                      inNode1toDSB,
56                      inNode2toDSB,
57                      outRes1,
58                      outRes2)
59 {
60     byte entity;
61     do
62     :: inRes?entity;
63        inNode1toDSB!bit1;
64        inNode1toDSB?bit2;
65        synchronizerB?bit3i;
66        outRes1!entity;
67        synchronizerB!bit3i;
68        inRes?entity;
69        inNode2toDSB!bit1;
70        inNode2toDSB?bit2;
71         outRes2!entity;
72     :: inRes?entity;
73        inNode2toDSB!bit1;
74        inNode2toDSB?bit2;
75        synchronizerB?bit3i;
76        outRes2!entity;
77        synchronizerB!bit3i;
78        inRes?entity;
79        inNode1toDSB!bit1;
80        inNode1toDSB?bit2;
81        outRes1!entity;
82     od
83 }
```

Fig. 7. Algorithm's logic for two-to-one resource interconnection

Fig. 8. Algorithm's logic for one-to-two resource interconnection

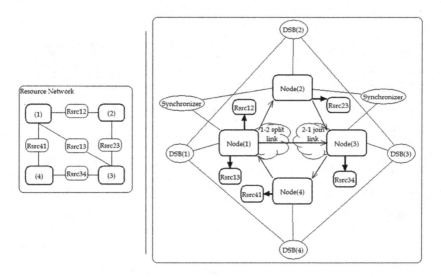

Fig. 9. A network of resources and the associated DSBs topology

3.1   Safety Verification

The basic safety property for the DSBs interlocking control is expressed by the monitor assertion of Fig. 10, which is used to check that *"in all reachable states, at most one entity occupies any resource"*. We utilize the predefined boolean function

$$nfull(q) = (len(q) < QSZ)$$

for testing that a network resource represented by channel q is occupied by a number of entities ($len(q)$) less than the number QSZ that represents violation of safety.

In order to detect violation of exclusive access to any resource, we set $QSZ = 2$. If it is possible to reach a state where for some resource, say $Rsrc$, holds $len(Rsrc) = QSZ$, then the model checking output reports an error (assertion violation).

For the network shown in Fig. 9, the initial conditions guaranteeing constant protection involve the notion of what we call *network section*. A network section is defined based on some basic graph-theoretic terms: the undirected graph representing the resource network at hand is *connected*, if every pair of distinct nodes in the graph can be connected through some path. A *node cut set* (also known as vertex cut) of a connected network is a set of nodes, whose removal renders the network disconnected.

Definition 5. *A network section is defined over a node cut set with one-to-many and/or many-to-one nodes. It is represented by a biconnected subnetwork, whose nodes are given as the superset of the node cut set, i.e. a subnetwork that is not* *broken into disconnected networks by deleting any single node and its incident resources.*

Definition 6. *A closed chain of occupied resources is given as a cycle of occupied resources where all entities request some resource that is already occupied by another entity in the same cycle. Such a chain may be extended into multiple network sections. Every single network section is characterized by the* **minimum required number of entities for a closed chain of occupied resources** *in the overall resource network.*

```
proctype Mntr_assertion()
{
        do
        :: assert(nfull(Rsrc12)
                && nfull(Rsrc23)
                && nfull(Rsrc34)
                && nfull(Rsrc41)
                && nfull(Rsrc13))
        od

}
```

Fig. 10. Safety assertion for the DSBs interlocking control of the network of Fig. 9

Predicate 1. *Under the following initial conditions, we verified that DSBs interlocking control guarantees non-blocking execution and safety in all reachable states:*

- *At least one entity occupies a resource that is not in a separated network section.*
- *For all possible cycles, there is at least one network section, where the initial number of entities is less than the minimum required number of entities for a closed chain of occupied resources.*

If for example the network of Fig. 9 is initialized with two entities occupying both $Rsrc34$ and $Rsrc41$ and another entity occupying some resource in the network section that is highlighted in Fig. 11, then the second condition of *Predicate 1* implies that the *DSBs* algorithm cannot guarantee non-blocking execution. This configuration opens a possibility for a closed chain of occupied resources.

However, in networks where moving entities represent traffic (e.g. in railway) the initial conditions of *Predicate 1* represent a marginal restriction. Usually, the number of moving entities within the individual network sections is very small compared to the minimum required number of entities for a closed chain of occupied resources.

In our case, non-blocking execution and safety with three entities is guaranteed only when at most one of the resources $Rsrc34$, $Rsrc41$ is initially occupied. In total, we model checked 4 valid initial configurations with three entities in the resource network of Fig. 9 and 7 valid initial configurations with two entities. When having four entities in the network, the initial conditions of *Predicate 1* are not fulfilled.

Figure 12 provides representative model checking results for one of the valid initial configurations with three entities. The model checking output reports no assertion violation or invalid end states - deadlock - (errors: 0) in all reachable states (1697 stored states, when applying partial order reduction for state space pruning).

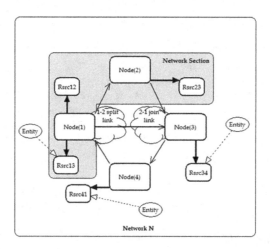

Fig. 11. Initial configuration that implies a closed chain of occupied resources

DSBs interlocking control is a compositional control algorithm. Control processes for the interconnected nodes can be composed as shown in the discussed resource network, such that the resulting communication by synchronous message passing provides the safety guarantees of interest. Model checking of large-scale networks with other topologies and node combinations fails to scale up well, since the state space that has to be explored can grow exponentially in the number of the implied control processes.

Compositional reasoning shifts the burden of verification from the network level to the subnetwork level, so that a global safety property for the network is established by composing together independently verified subnetwork properties like the one proved in the examined network. The closest compositional reasoning approach in the related bibliography is the *assumption– commitment* (A-C) method that was first proposed by [17] and that was subsequently developed in [18] into a sound and semantically complete proof method. This method integrates the use of inductive assertions and the proof method of [1] for verifying synchronous distributed message passing systems.

An A-C correctness formula has the form:

$$< A, C >: \{\phi\}P\{\psi\}$$

where P denotes a (PROMELA) program and A, ϕ, ψ, C represent predicates. We require that A and C predicates involve values that do not depend on the values of any program variables. A valid $A-C$ formula has the following meaning: If ϕ holds in the initial state, in which P starts its execution, then

- C holds initially, and C holds after every communication provided A holds after all preceding communications, and
- if P terminates and A holds after all communications then ψ holds in final state.

3.2   Model Checking Resource Occupancy and Availability

Under the conditions of *Predicate 1* for the network of Fig. 9 and for infinitely many requests for any network resource, we verified that there is always some entity that temporarily acquires and subsequently releases this resource.

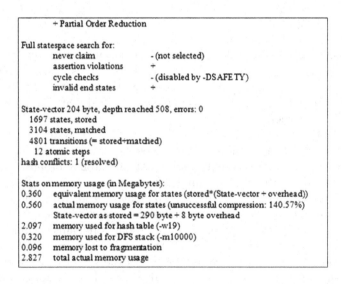

Fig. 12. Model checking DSBs interlocking control safety for the network of Fig. 9

The aforementioned progress property guarantees availability of the network's resources for infinitely many uses and excludes the possibility for an entity to hold the occupied resource forever. For model checking this property we developed an appropriate formulation in the Linear Propositional Temporal Logic (LTL) of the SPIN model checker. The LTL operators used are the following:

$$<> x \qquad \text{eventually}$$
$$[]x = \neg <> \neg x \quad \text{always}$$
$$\rightarrow \qquad \text{logical implication}$$

The recurrence formula $[](<> p)$ asserts that in an infinite sequence of states the proposition p occurs infinitely many times [15]. For any network resource $Rsrcij$ we consider the propositions

$$\#defineR\_f(len(Rsrcij) == 0)$$
$$\#defineR\_o(len(Rsrcij) == 1)$$

corresponding to states of free or occupied resources. The checked correctness property is then expressed as

$$[](<> R\_f)- > (<> R\_o)- > (<> R\_f)$$

where $\rightarrow$ is left associative with higher precedence than $[]$. Thus, the formula is interpreted as $[](((<> R\_f)- > (<> R\_o))- > (<> R\_f))$ and expresses the property:

"In an infinite sequence of system states a temporarily occupied resource becomes free infinitely often".

For the network of Fig. 9 the discussed LTL formula was model checked in the 4 valid initial configurations with 3 entities, as well as in the 7 valid initial configurations with 2 entities. In these cases, SPIN generated the never claim (automaton in Fig. 13) of the above formula and verified that the property holds in all possible executions.

In SPIN, never claims specify either finite or infinite system behavior that should never occur. When a never claim is generated from an LTL formula, all its transitions are condition statements, formalizing atomic propositions on the global system state. SPIN checks infinite executions for the specified behavior. Execution of the claim starts at labeled statement $T0\_init$, where the conditions trigger transitions to the accept states, when the resource is occupied. Violation is detected as an acceptance cycle, i.e. if the resource remains occupied forever. If the resource is not occupied forever we do not have an acceptance cycle. Figure 14 reports representative results for one of the valid initial configurations with three entities, where we observe that SPIN performed a state space search for acceptance cycles. The shown output reports no errors (errors: 0).

```
/*
     * Formula As Typed: [] (<> R_f) -> (<> R_o) -> (<> R_f)
     * The Never Claim Below Corresponds
     * To The Negated Formula !([] <> R_f -> <> R_o -> <> R_f)
     * (formalizing violations of the original)
     */

never {   /* !([] <> R_f -> <> R_o -> <> R_f) */
T0_init:
          if
          :: (! ((R_f))) -> goto accept_S4
          :: (! ((R_f))) -> goto accept_S7
          fi;
accept_S4:
          if
          :: (! ((R_f))) -> goto accept_S4
          fi;
accept_S7:
          if
          :: (! ((R_f))) -> goto accept_S4
          :: (! ((R_f))) -> goto T0_init
          fi;
}
```

Fig. 13. Never claim of LTL formula to model check that no entity occupies some resource forever

```
+ Partial Order Reduction

Full statespace search for:
          never claim            +
          assertion violations   + (if within scope of claim)
          acceptance  cycles     + (fairness disabled)
          invalid end states     - (disabled by never claim)

State-vector 204 byte, depth reached 508, errors: 0
    1697 states, stored
    3104 states, matched
    4801 transitions (= stored+matched)
      12 atomic steps
hash conflicts: 1 (resolved)

Stats on memory usage (in Megabytes):
    0.360   equivalent memory usage for states (stored*(State-vector + overhead))
    0.813   actual memory usage for states (unsuccessful compression: 225.93%)
            State-vector as stored = 471 byte + 8 byte overhead
    2.097   memory used for hash table (-w19)
    0.320   memory used for DFS stack (-m10000)
    0.198   memory lost to fragmentation
    3.032   total actual memory usage
```

Fig. 14. Model checking resource occupancy and availability for the network of Fig. 9

4 Related Work

Research on interlocking control has been mainly advanced in the area of railway interlocking systems. Since the introduction of mechanical interlockings in late 1800's the control has been progressively centralized with fewer control centers, individually responsible for larger portions of networks. This trend continued with the advent of computer controlled signaling to the railway networks. In related works, the most widely studied railway signaling system is the Solid State Interlocking (SSI) [6]. Many railway operators have adopted such geographic-data-driven solid-state control units in their interlockings. In [9], the author proposes an approach to formalize the principles and the concepts of interlocking systems in VDM.

The work reported in [20] introduces a model for the interlocking of the network used by a local Australian railway operator. Interlocking control is encoded in control tables and the described analysis aims to find erroneous or incomplete entries in these tables. Modeling and safety checking is performed with the NuSMV model checker, but in earlier works the same group used a Communicating Sequential Processes (CSP) approach and the Failure Divergence Refinement (FDR) model checker.

The work in [13] reports the safety checking of the Line Block interlocking system that also adopts a centralized approach. The control strategy runs on a Central Control Unit that communicates with Peripheral Control Units (PCUs). PCUs are expected to drive particular interlocking system components and detect external events.

In [10], the authors focus on a computer interlocking system, for the control of railway stations. The system's architecture is based on redundancy and is composed of a central nucleus connected to peripheral posts for the control of physical devices. A formal model of the system's safety logic was developed in Verus [4], a tool that combines symbolic model checking and quantitative timing analysis. In [8], the authors present a model of the same system and validate safety in the presence of Byzantine system components or of some hardware temporary faults. The safety logic of the same system was also modeled in [5], where the authors used the SPIN model checker to analyze all system's functions that may be requested by an external operator.

We already noted the fundamental differences of our algorithm compared to the mentioned approaches. First, in DSBs interlocking control, safety is decoupled from entity routing and is an integrated network service that works independently from operation control and geographic data for the network topology. Second, we adopt a communication-based network control approach that makes our solution similar to the following distributed interlocking control proposals found in the related bibliography.

In [11], the authors note that *today's centralized interlocking systems are far too expensive for small or possibly private networks*. They propose to distribute the tasks of train control, train protection and interlocking over a network of cooperating components, using the standard communication facilities offered by mobile telephone providers. Their approach uses the so-called switch boxes, which locally control the point where they are allocated. Train engines are carriers of train control computers, which collect the local state information from switch boxes along the track to derive the decision whether the train may enter the next track segment. However, mobile communication requires security and reliability provisions that in a large-scale network increase the cost, when compared to solutions that transmit signals over wires.

EURIS [7] is a modular specification method used to formulate distributed interlocking logics for railway yards. The EURIS architecture consists of a collection of generic blocks representing control units that communicate by means of data structures called telegrams. EURIS uses the notion of routes, i.e. sets of network segments for which a train is granted exclusive access to all of them atomically. The building blocks maintain a state and can also exchange telegrams with the logistic layer that incorporates the logic behind operation control. Safety guarantees can be analyzed only through the available interactive simulation facilities. Compared to EURIS, our approach intentionally avoids application-domain-dependent concepts and system requirements, since we aim in the development of a generic interlocking algorithm. In our case, control decisions are taken on the basis of exchanged messages between the control units that, as opposed to the EURIS building blocks, do not store state related to the algorithm's logic. Moreover, our solution is fully verified with respect to the required safety guarantees.

5   Conclusions and Future Work

In the last years, with the ever-increasing computing power of small and inexpensive computing devices, distributed interlocking control is a promising alternative towards reducing the complexity involved in the systems' design, and towards reducing the costs for installation and maintenance of the needed equipment. Most current interlocking control approaches are centralized and they are defined on the basis of geographic data and commands of the networks' operation control. Usually, interlocking safety of centralized solutions cannot be fully verified, due to the state space explosion involved.

In response to these concerns, we introduced a distributed interlocking control algorithm, where control logic for guaranteeing safety is decoupled from the network topology data and the used control units do not store information related to the algorithm's state. The basic control function is based on what we call Distributed Signal Boxes that are attached to the network's interlocking nodes. The algorithm works on the basis of point-to-point communication between control processes. We described the message communications between nodes and DSBs and the message communications between neighbor DSBs, for a series of node interconnection cases. The initial conditions of the verified properties guarantee safety and progress for the considered network that included all described network interconnection cases.

Future research includes adaptation of appropriate architectural solutions (e.g. [12]) for control processing redundancy and communication redundancy towards implementing fail-safe DSBs control architectures. An important concern is to demonstrate the applicability of the compositional verification technique of [18] for synchronous distributed message passing systems. This will enable the verification of large-scale networks by decomposing the verification problem into the model checking of properties for smaller networks, which will be independently verified.

References

1. Apt, K.R., Francez, N., de Roever, W.P.: A proof system for communicating sequential processes. ACM Trans. Program. Lang. Syst. **2**(3), 359–385 (1980)
2. Arozarena, P., et al.: Madeira: A peer-to-peer approach to network management. In: Proceedings of the Wireless World Research Forum (2006)
3. Basagiannis, S., Katsaros, P., Pombortsis, A.: Interlocking control by distributed signal boxes: Design and verification with the spin model checker. In: Parallel and Distributed Processing and Applications, pp. 317–328 (2006)
4. Campos, S., Clarke, E., Minea, M.: The verus tool: a quantitative approach to the formal verification of real-time systems. In: Grumberg, O. (ed.) CAV 1997. LNCS, vol. 1254, pp. 452–455. Springer, Heidelberg (1997). https://doi.org/10.1007/3-540-63166-6_46
5. Cimatti, A., Giunchiglia, F., Mongardi, G., Romano, D., Torielli, F., Traverso, P.: Formal verification of a railway interlocking system using model checking. Formal Aspects of Comput. **10**(4), 361–380 (1998)
6. Cribbens, A.: Microprocessors in railway signalling: the solid-state interlocking. Microprocess. Microsyst. **11**(5), 264–272 (1987)
7. van Dijk, F., Fokkink, W., Kolk, G., van de Ven, P., van Vlijmen, B.: EURIS, a specification method for distributed interlockings. In: Ehrenberger, W. (ed.) SAFECOMP 1998. LNCS, vol. 1516, pp. 296–305. Springer, Heidelberg (1998). https://doi.org/10.1007/3-540-49646-7_23
8. Gnesi, S., Latella, D., Lenzini, G., Abbaneo, C., Amendola, A., Marmo, P.: A formal specification and validation of a critical system in presence of byzantine errors. In: Graf, S., Schwartzbach, M. (eds.) TACAS 2000. LNCS, vol. 1785, pp. 535–549. Springer, Heidelberg (2000). https://doi.org/10.1007/3-540-46419-0_36
9. Hansen, K.M.: Formalizing railway interlocking systems. In: Proceedings of FME Rail Workshop #2. FME: Formal Methods Europe (1998)
10. Hartonas-Garmhausen, V., Campos, S., Cimatti, A., Clarke, E., Giunchiglia, F.: Verification of a safety-critical railway interlocking system with real-time constraints. Sci. Comput. Programm. **36**(1), 53–64 (2000)
11. Haxthausen, A.E., Peleska, J.: Formal development and verification of a distributed railway control system. IEEE Trans. Soft. Eng. **26**(8), 687–701 (2000)
12. Hecht, M., Agron, J., Hecht, H., Kim, K.H.: A distributed fault tolerant architecture for nuclear reactor and other critical process control applications. In: [1991] Digest of Papers. The 21st International Symposium of Fault-Tolerant Computing, pp. 462–498, June 1991
13. Hlavaty, T., Preucil, L., Stepan, P., Klapka, S.: Formal methods in development and testing of safety-critical systems : railway interlocking system. In: Conference on Intelligent Methods for Quality Improvement in Industrial Practice, pp. 14–25 (2002)
14. Holzmann, G.J.: The model checker spin. IEEE Trans. Softw. Eng. **23**(5), 279–295 (1997)
15. Holzmann, G.: The SPIN Model Checker: Primer and Reference Manual, 1st edn. Addison-Wesley Professional, Boston (2011)
16. Jain, A., Nelson, K., Bryant, R.E.: Verifying nondeterministic implementations of deterministic systems. In: Srivas, M., Camilleri, A. (eds.) FMCAD 1996. LNCS, vol. 1166, pp. 109–125. Springer, Heidelberg (1996). https://doi.org/10.1007/BFb0031803

17. Misra, J., Chandy, K.M.: Proofs of networks of processes. IEEE Trans. Softw. Eng. SE **7**(4), 417–426 (1981)
18. Roever, W.P., et al.: Concurrency Verification: Introduction to Compositional and Noncompositional Methods. Cambridge University Press, New York (2001)
19. Simpson, A.: Model checking for interlocking safety. In: Proceedings of FME Rail Workshop #2. FME: Formal Methods Europe (1998)
20. Winter, K., Robinson, N.J.: Modelling large railway interlockings and model checking small ones. In: Proceedings of 26th Australasian Computer Science Conference, ACSC 2003, vol. 16, pp. 309–316 (2003)

SQUADfps: Integrated Model-Based Machine Safety and Product Quality for Flexible Production Systems

Chee Hung Koo[1]([✉]), Stefan Rothbauer[2], Marian Vorderer[1], Kai Höfig[2,3], and Marc Zeller[2]

[1] Corporate Sector Research and Advance Engineering, Robert Bosch GmbH, 71272 Renningen, Germany
{CheeHung.Koo,marian.vorderer}@de.bosch.com
[2] Siemens AG, Corporate Technology, Otto-Hahn-Ring 6, 81739 Munich, Germany
{stefan.rothbauer,kai.hoefig,marc.zeller}@siemens.com
[3] University of Applied Science Rosenheim, Hochschulstrasse 1, 83024 Rosenheim, Germany
kai.hoefig@fh-rosenheim.de

Abstract. Growing individualization of products up to lot-size-1 and high volatility of product mixes lead to new challenges in the manufacturing domain, including the need for frequent reconfiguration of the system and reacting to changing orders. Thus, apart from functional aspects, safety aspects of the production system as well as product quality assurance aspects must be addressed for flexible and reconfigurable manufacturing systems at runtime. To cope with the mentioned challenges, we present an integrated model-based approach SQUADfps (machine *S*afety and product *QUA*lity for *f*lexible *proD*uction *s*ystems) to support the automatic conduct of the risk assessment of flexible production scenarios in terms of safety as well as the process-FMEA to ensure that the requirements w.r.t. the quality of the production process and the resulting product are met. Our approach is based on a meta-model which captures all information needed to conduct both risk assessment and process-FMEA dynamically during the runtime, and thus enables flexible manufacturing scenarios with frequent changes of the production system and orders up to a lot-size of one while guaranteeing safety and product quality requirements. The automatically generated results will assist human in making further decisions. To demonstrate the feasibility of our approach, we apply it to a case study.

Keywords: Safety assessment · Flexible production · Model-based safety · Process-FMEA · Risk analysis

1 Introduction

Major trends in the manufacturing sector are the growing individualization of products and volatility of product mixes. If taken to extremes, this scenario

© Springer Nature Switzerland AG 2019
Y. Papadopoulos et al. (Eds.): IMBSA 2019, LNCS 11842, pp. 222–236, 2019.
https://doi.org/10.1007/978-3-030-32872-6_15

also counts for products being produced only one time (lot-size-1) or only on demand. In order to reach this goal, the concept of *Flexible Manufacturing Systems (FMS)*, which can change their software during runtime [29], and *Reconfigurable Manufacturing Systems (RMS)*, which can adapt their software as well as their hardware [20], play a vital role. Moreover, standalone systems from different manufacturers are interconnected to accomplish a common production goal and the production processes can be orchestrated automatically in so-called *Plug-and-Produce* scenarios [2].

Due to frequent changes of the products being manufactured, the rapid adjustment of a factory is a major challenge to implement application scenarios of flexible production systems (often called Industry 4.0 or Cyber-Physical Production Systems) successfully. Although the high flexibility of future flexible production scenarios promises a faster market adaptation and responsiveness, it raises at the same time dependability-related concerns due to unknown configurations at runtime. Thus, apart from functional aspect (i.e. the check if a factory is able to manufacture a specific product), safety aspects as well as product quality assurance aspects must be addressed.

Safety standards, such as ISO 13849 [17] or IEC 62061 [16] in context of industrial production systems, provide guidelines to keep the residual risks in machine operation within tolerable limits. For every production system, a comprehensive risk assessment is performed, which includes risk reduction measures if required (e.g. by introducing specific risk protective measures such as fences). The resulting safety documentation describes the assessment principles and the resulting measures that are implemented to minimize hazards. This documentation lays the foundation for the safe operation of a machine and it proves the compliance with the Machinery Directive 2006/42/EC of the European Commission [10]. In flexible production scenarios, risk assessment must be conducted after each reconfiguration of the production system. Since this is a prerequisite for operating the factory in the new configuration, a manual approach can no longer effectively fulfill the objectives for assuring the safety in highly flexible manufacturing scenarios. Hence, the acquisition of safety-related information from each individual production step and the analysis of possible emergent hazards must be conducted in an automated way to quickly assess a new configuration of a manufacturing plant.

To evaluate the quality of a product considering the production process, a *Process Failure Mode and Effects Analysis* (process-FMEA) is typically performed. During production, every process step can negatively influence the quality of the product depending on the negative outcome of the process step. This is captured in a process-FMEA with the concept of failure modes of a process step as well as the respective severity. It also defines measures to detect and deal with unwanted effects on product quality. Such an analysis is important to document the applied quality measures and to find out where drawbacks in the production process are and how they can be addressed. Since the factory's configuration as well as its products constantly change in adaptable and flexible factory scenarios, a process-FMEA must be performed dynamically during the production of each product based on the configuration used. This is necessary to ensure that the products requirements w.r.t. quality will be met by the provided production process.

In this paper, we present an approach for the model-based assessment of flexible and reconfigurable manufacturing systems based on a meta-model. This integrated approach SQUADfps (machine *S*afety and product *QUA*lity for *f*lexible *proD*uction *s*ystems) captures all information needed to conduct both risk assessment and process-FMEA dynamically during the runtime of the manufacturing system in an automated way. In this way, the approach enables flexible manufacturing scenarios with frequent changes of the production system up to a lot-size of one. In order to provide a better understanding for our proposed approach, we assume that the considered production systems are already installed as intended and focus only on the reconfigurability in terms of equipment and process changes.

The rest of the paper is organized as follows: In Sect. 2, an overview of related work is given. Section 3 introduces a meta-model (Sect. 3.1) that enables an automated hazard and risk assessment for the factory (Sect. 3.2) and a process-FMEA for a product to be produced in a factory to ensure that the its quality is on track (Sect. 3.3). Section 4 presents a case study to show how the model can be applied. Section 5 summarizes the main results and provides an outlook for further research topics.

2   Related Work

The usage of model-based approach to carry out safety analyses or safety assessment aims to achieve compositional, reusable safety assessment and to improve traceability of information provided from the system design phase [21]. The collective term *model-based safety assessment* includes a wide range of techniques proposed in the academia [18,21] that have already been applied extensively nowadays in varying domains such as the automotive industry [23], IT security [1,15], aviation sector [4], train protection system [28] and industrial automation e.g. collaborative robots application [3]. In most of these applications, the safety requirements of the designed systems are assessed based on the functional system models created. Different tools and modeling techniques have also been developed since then to facilitate and maintain model-based safety engineering and safety analysis [5,13,24]. However, most of the mentioned publications deal with model-based applications during design and development phases instead of *runtime* applications, which is one of the most important aspects for highly flexible manufacturing scenarios. To facilitate flexible and reconfigurable manufacturing systems in a practical way, as safety analyses nowadays are an inherently manual tasks in which only very few steps are automated, it is necessary to support these manual processes with automation as far as possible. Frequent system changes needed for lot-size-1 scenarios require runtime safety assessment to be done in an economically feasible manner [19]. In this paper, we propose a method to carry out safety assessment automatically at runtime using a proposed meta-model, which can facilitate human during the decision-making to approve new system configuration.

Failure mode and effects analysis (FMEA) has its origins in military applications [9] and was used in the same decade to analyze the influence of failures in production processes [12]. Since it is an effective but costly analysis technique, automating it has a long history in functional safety [6–8,22,27] and also for analyzing machinery. In [26], it is mentioned that process-FMEA is part of an integrated approach for safe products, but that classic process-FMEA does not consider the manufacturability of a product influenced by quality problems. In [14], the authors use FMEA among other techniques to assess the manufacturability and estimating the cost of a conceptual design in early product design phases. They introduce an approach to estimate costs of failures during manufacturing using an extended FMEA approach introduced in [25]. This is a manual task that is used to prioritize different manufacturing options. Their work can be used in combination with the approach presented here to include costs of potential failures during manufacturing. In [11], product process resource-based approach is presented that uses an ontology to model the manufacturing capabilities and the required process steps to produce a product. Similar to the approach presented here, the authors use a standardized language set in an ontology to (semi-)automate the process of mapping production steps for a product to machinery. Nevertheless, they do neither aim for quality aspects of the output nor for rejected items in the mapping process.

3   Model-Based Safety and Quality Assessment of Flexible, Adaptable Production Systems

3.1   Meta-model

Figure 1 shows the proposed meta-model of SQUADfps for a flexible and reconfigurable production system. The meta-model is divided into four categories, considering both machine safety and product quality aspects:

- **Process Definition**: In the product category, the elements address the order and steps related to *what* has to be done to produce a product. This category also addresses the required safety approval process before the production is allowed to commence.
- **Abstract Services**: The model elements of the category abstract services collect common specification of services and service parameters across all factories. These elements enable the specification of a product independently from a concrete production equipment. Besides, this category provides abstract service to carry out safety assessment for any concrete production equipment.
- **Production Equipment**: The elements of this category model a concrete factory or production system along with its machinery equipment, describing what it can do, what quality measures are available and what safety functions are implemented.

– **Process Implementation**: In the process implementation category, the elements address the concrete process used to produce a product. Here, the process steps address concrete ordered actions that are executed to produce a product. These steps provide a solution on *how* a product is produced. Besides, concrete hazards associated to the process are identified.

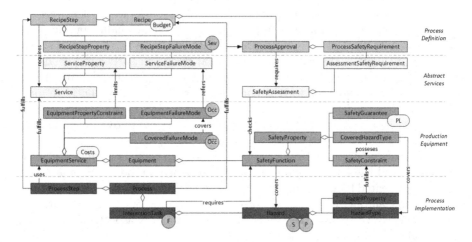

Fig. 1. SQUADfps meta-model for process-FMEA and safety assessment supporting automation

These categories allow users to map different activities, use cases and roles in the domain of dynamic reconfigurable production scenarios to automatically generate a process-FMEA (quality of the product) and a risk assessment result (safety of the production system) for the production system under consideration.

In the *process definition* category, the product owner specifies *which* steps are needed and in which order they need to be executed to produce a product (recipe). The product owner addresses abstract services that can satisfy steps of its recipe. Those abstract services provide a global library of all available services. Each service declaration can have constraints and parameters that can be set for a recipe step (service property). For example, the abstract service *drill* requires the rotation speed of the drill and the size of the drill hole as parameters. When the abstract service is instantiated in a recipe step, these parameters need to be set.

Different failure modes can be stored (failure mode declarations) during the abstract service declaration. Independent from the concrete equipment or machinery (equipment), failure modes are known and defined in general. For example, the service *drill* has the potential failure mode *skew drill hole* for all concrete machinery implementing this service.

For each addressed service declaration in a recipe step, the failure mode declarations are known to the product owner that defined the recipe. He now can specify how severe the different failure modes (using recipe step failure modes) are for his product. Thus, the first step for the quality assessment using a process-FMEA can be performed without knowledge of the concrete equipment that later produces the product. This can be done for the combination of recipe steps and failure modes rated with a severity value.

Independent from this specification scenario of a recipe, the owner of a factory can model the equipment (*production equipment*) with equipment services and safety functions. Equipment services address the abstract service declarations available in the global library. Equipment property constraints are used to specify the possible operating parameters and limitations of service property declarations, while equipment failure modes address the service failure modes of the abstract service.

During declaration of *production equipment*, the factory owner can specify the available machinery and the equipment service along with its parameter limitations, which can be provided for a specific recipe. With this, the factory owner gets a list of possible abstract failure modes and can specify how often the abstract failure mode occurs for the concrete service (equipment failure mode). This can be known either by previously collected data or data provided by the manufacturer of the machinery. In this case, the factory owner can provide information about the occurrence value of concrete failure modes while using the equipment during the production.

In order to consider the safety of the production, the process will require safety approval before operation (process approval) during *process definition*. Process safety requirements specify the minimal safety requirements to be achieved. For instance, the product owner can specify that only safety functions with a certain minimal safety guarantee are allowed due to safety criticality of the product or enforced safety guidelines. This process approval addresses the relevant abstract service (safety assessment), which checks whether all expected hazards are covered by the available safety functions considering the risk level.

Beside modeling the failure model for process-FMEA, the factory owner can also model the safety functions provided by an equipment. For instance, an equipment protective measure such as light curtain that is installed can protect the personnel during interaction with the equipment, which provides safety guarantee in term of *performance level* to describe the reliability of the safety device. A safety function covers certain hazard types, which can be described through predefined semantics. A light curtain can protect personnel against mechanical hazards (crushing, shearing etc.), as long as the hazard source lies within the allowed working area and occurs during certain interaction tasks (safety constraint).

During *process implementation*, the factory owner will get a list of possible hazards in relation to the interaction tasks, in which the frequency of the task can be defined. The risk parameter frequency describes the interaction of personnel with the production system. For a lot-size-1 scenario, the frequency can still be defined as high if the responsible personnel needs to carry out manual tasks for a foreseeable high amount of time. In combination with the concrete risk parameters (severity and possibility for avoidance) provided by the equipment, an identified hazard with its evaluated risk level (hazard property) can be checked against the safety function to ensure the production safety. Further examples for hazard properties include runtime location of hazard source, moving speed of its equipment, relevant interaction tasks etc.

3.2   Model-Based Risk Assessment

As mentioned before, a production process might include some human interaction tasks in different life cycle phases, such as setup of equipment, interactions during the production or maintenance activities. These interactions are specific to the concrete process and independent from the recipe, which describes the product to be manufactured. Each interaction task can include one or more hazards for the personnel involved, which have a certain level of severity. Each hazard also possesses a possibility of avoidance, which determine how possible a person can avoid the hazard during its occurrence. According to the risk graph in the standard ISO 13849 [17], the risk level of a particular hazard can be evaluated using the severity of associated hazard (S), the frequency of tasks (F) and the possibility of avoidance (P). This leads to a risk level described in term of *required performance level* (PLr).

Safety functions are typically installed to protect humans against a certain hazard and have a *performance level* (PL) value, which describes the overall reliability of the safety device considering the components used. Having this information provided by the machine vendors, the required performance level gained from risk assessment (PLr) can be evaluated against the provided safety function performance level (PL). In a conservative manner, the production process can only be approved manually by the factory owner when all the identified risks are covered successfully by the available safety functions considering PL value.

3.3   Dynamic Process-FMEA

Since equipment is not only able to execute production steps in a recipe, but is also able to execute quality measures, an equipment service can therefore cover certain failure modes. These measures can be originating from the same service, from a different service of the same equipment or from a service of a different equipment. For example, a robot arm that can be used to perform pick and place can also supervise its own actions using a camera. In this case, the failure mode *misplacement* of the service *pick and place* can be covered by the service *camera supervision* from the same equipment. Using this methodology, the factory owner can specify which machinery can be used to increase the quality of the production. Since quality measures decrease the occurrence of certain failure modes, each covered failure mode stores a decreased occurrence value.

Using the severity of a failure mode from the product specification (recipe failure mode) multiplied by the occurrence value of the equipment failure mode or with the decreased occurrence value of a quality measure, a process-FMEA can be conducted for a product produced by a certain process on a concrete set of equipment.

This model-based approach ensures a structured and systematic analysis for all known failure modes that are captured within the model. This is valuable, as systematic and complete analysis is a requirement e.g. required by safety or quality standards. If experience from production about failures that actually were observed but not yet captured in the model is included, over time the analysis should become complete with regard to present knowledge. During the first applications in real production there might be a need to at least verify completeness by a manual inspection. A manual inspection and possibly extension of a pre-generated pFMEA is much less effort than starting from scratch, so even at the introductory phase there is already a reduction in effort to be expected.

4   Case Study

In this small case study, we want to demonstrate how to use the meta-model as described in Sect. 3. The product that we investigate here is a small roll that consist of a roll body, an axle and two metal discs as depicted in Figs. 2 and 3. The entire material is delivered on a tray, see Fig. 4, and is set together by a robot arm that also greases the contact area of the parts. After that, a visual inspection detects insufficient products. To rate failure modes, we use an risk priority number (RPN) based approach for the parameters *severity (sev)*, *occurrence (occ)* and *detection (det)* with a range from one to five whereas one represents the lowest severity, a negligible occurrence rate and a sure detection and five represents a high severity, a high occurrence rate and an nearly impossible detection. For the assessment of machine safety for the setup production system, performance level (PL) is used in accordance with ISO 13849-1 [17]. Risk level of the identified hazards can be described through *required* performance level (PLr), with the risk parameters *severity*, *frequency* and *possibility of avoidance*, whereas *PL a* represents the lowest tolerable risk and *PL e* represents the highest risk.

Fig. 2. Roll with axle

Fig. 3. Disc to be mounted and greased

Fig. 4. Tray with products

Dynamic Process-FMEA

The recipe steps for production are depicted on the left side in Table 1 for recipe $R = r_1, \ldots, r_6$. For the first process $P = p_1, \ldots, p_{6a}$, the tray is delivered using an abstract service *convey* which is implemented by the equipment *belt conveyor*. The failure modes of this service are *misplacement* and *shock* rated by the design team with a severity value of four and five respectively. The production equipment produces failures with a occurrence of two and one. A visual inspection can safely detect both failure modes (detection value *Det* is 1).

Table 1. Example product recipe and two processes using abstract services.

Recipe R		Failure Mode	Sev	Service	Occ	Process P		Det	RPN	Occ'	Process P'		Det'	RPN'
r_1	Deliver tray	Misplacement	4	Convey	2	p_1	Belt conveyer	1	8	2	p'_1	Belt conveyer	1	8
		Shock	5		1			1	5	1			1	5
r_2	Mount axle	Misplacement	4	Pick&place	2	p_2	Robot Arm	1	8	2	p'_2	Robot Arm 2	1	8
		Crimping	2		4			5	40	2			2	8
r_3	Circular grease roll	Too little	5	Apply liquid	4	p_3	Robot Arm	1	20	4	p'_3	Robot Arm 2	1	20
		Too much	2		4			1	8	4			1	8
r_4	Mount 1st disc	Misplacement	4	Pick&place	2	p_4	Robot Arm	1	8	2	p'_4	Robot Arm 2	1	8
		Crimping	3		4			5	60	2			2	12
r_5	Circular grease 2nd disc	Too little	5	Apply liquid	4	p_5	Robot Arm	1	20	4	p'_5	Robot Arm 2	1	20
		Too much	2		4			1	8	4			1	8
r_6	Mount roll on 2nd disc	Misplacement	4	Pick&place	2	p_6	Robot Arm	1	8	2	p'_6	Robot Arm 2	1	8
		Crimping	5		2			5	100	2			2	20
				Visual Inspection		p_{6a}	Worker				p'_{6a}	Laserscanner		

The next step is to mount the axle inside the roll. This step is fulfilled by the service *pick and place* which is implemented by a robot arm. This service can fail in two ways, the object can be misplaced but can also be crimped by the clutch. Crimping is not very severe to the axle since it is made from solid metal. This cannot be detected by a visual inspection (detection value Det is 5). Both discs need to be greased and there can be too much and too little grease. Having too little grease is quite severe, and the worker can detect it. Having too much grease is just a minor failure. Since the roll itself is made from plastic material, crimping is severe since the roll can be damaged. This failure mode can hardly be detected by the worker, since he is not doing a stress test (detection value Det is 5). The elements of properties and constraints are not depicted in the table for the reason of space limitations. Service properties of *pick and place* would include, for example, start- and endpoint, trajectory and weight, whereas an equipment implementing this service provides limitations of those parameters and recipe steps requesting the service would provide the required information to fulfill the step.

With the failure mode information provided by the service definition, the design team can specify *what* failure mode is severe (requirement) and the vendor can specify *how* often the failure mode appears on its machinery and *how* the effect of the failure mode can be prevented in later products (implementation). The process P generally is capable to implement the recipe R since the equipment fulfills the required service of each recipe step and the relative order of the process steps matches the order of the recipe steps with an additional step at the end of the process: p_{6a}.

Also depicted in Table 1 is an additional process $P' = p'_1, \ldots, p'_{6a}$ that also fulfills recipe R but with different equipment. A different robot arm is used, that has a lower probability of crimping. Additionally, the visual inspection is implemented by a more precise laser scanner that better detects crimping. With these two adoptions in place, the highest risk priority number is lowered from 100 to 20.

This approach in its basic implementation is of a qualitative nature. It therefore enables comparing different production alternatives and facilitates the selection of a appropriate schedule selection for the production of a concrete product. In a specific domain the quality criteria might be specified in a quantitative manner, failure probabilities replacing occurence values and actual costs at risk replacing severity values. If this is possible for a certain domain or use case then for products and production quantitative goals can be specified and the selection or ranking of different schedules with regard to fulfilling quality requirements of a product can be done. A manual selection will probably still be necessary to balance e.g. quality goals with other goals not captured within this model.

Model-Based Risk Assessment

Using the same production process described above, an example for the conduct of safety assessment using an abstract service, as depicted in Fig. 1, can also be shown. In this production process, the operator is required to load the product parts (roll body with axle) in a frequent manner onto the belt conveyor. Besides, the robot's handling tool needs to be adjusted and maintained occasionally to ensure its high precision. Hence, the task frequency of these two interaction tasks can be described as F2 (high frequent) and F1 (low frequent) respectively. As the frequency is defined in relation to the overall process duration required, its definition is hence independent from the product lot sizes.

The initial production system with *Belt conveyor* and *Robot Arm* in Table 2 introduces three different hazards for the described interaction tasks. During the loading of production parts, the movement of robot arm can cause shearing points with high severity (S2), which can hardly be avoided due to its high movement speed (P2). On the other hand, the moving belt conveyor introduces possible squeezing points to the operator with the risk parameters S1 and P1 thanks to its relatively well-considered inherent design. During the maintenance of robot arm, the operator might still be bruised by the arm movement (S2) although the movement speed is monitored by its safety control function (P1). Here, only a light curtain is provided as a safety function with the performance level PL d.

As shown in Table 2, the current setup does not fulfill all the safety requirements. Hazard h_1 with a high level of risk PL e does not receive a suitable safety function that fulfill the required performance level. In addition, there is no available safety function that can counter the hazard h_3. Based on this result, the responsible individual can decide whether to reduce the risks, to eliminate the risks or to provide extra protective devices to the system. This involves creative decision-making process and is not being considered in the proposed meta-model. The generated risk assessment result can then provide instant updated information after every system modification to assist the decision-making process.

It is assumed that the financial situation allows the factory owner to acquire new equipment. In order to improve the safety of the production system, a different robot arm (*Robot Arm 2*) that provides the same services is now used, as depicted in Table 3. This robot arm is equipped with an integrated sensor skin (*safety sensitive cover*) that can detect human approaches and turn off the robot once the operator violates the safety distance. This sensor skin provides a safety assurance of PL e. With this new robot arm, all previously unfulfilled safety requirements are now satisfied by the provided safety functions. The abstract service now confirms the results and awaits safety engineer to make the final approval.

Table 2. Exemplary risk assessment for the provided product recipe using abstract services (safety requirements are not completely fulfilled).

Process P	Interaction task T	F	Hazard H		S	P	PL_r	Safety function	PL
Robot Arm	Loading of roll body wilh axle	F2 (high)	h_1	Shearing due to robot movement	S2 (high)	P2 (high)	PL e	Light curtain	PL d
Bell conveyor	Loading of roll body wilh axle	F2 (high)	h_2	Squeezing due to bell's capturing	SI (low)	P1(low)	PL b	Light curtain	PL d
Robot Arm	Maintenance of robot's handling tool	F1 (low)	h_3	Bruising due to robot movement	S2 (high)	P1 (low)	PL c	none	none

Table 3. Risk assessment after implementing counter measures using a different robot arm (safety requirements are now fulfilled).

Process P′	Interaction task T	F	Hazard H	S′	P′	PL′r	Safety function	PL
Robot Arm 2	Loading of roll body wilh axle	F2 (high)	h₁ Shearing due to robot movement	S2 (high)	P2 (high)	PL e	Safety sensitive cover	PL e
Bell conveyor	Loading of roll body wilh axle	F2 (high)	h₂ Squeezing due to bell's capturing	SI (low)	P1(low)	PL b	Light curtain	PL d
Robot Arm 2	Maintenance of robot's handling tool	F1 (low)	h₃ Bruising due to robot movement	SI (low)	P1 (low)	PL a	Safety sensitive cover	PL e

This example shows how the usage of an abstract service allows the definition of an abstract production recipe without addressing concrete production equipment. The product design team uses abstract service declarations and properties to formulate production requirements. It can be decided (semi-)automatically if the production equipment can manufacture a product defined by a recipe. By providing information about the severity of certain failure modes, those requirements are extended by quality requirements. In a second step, a factory can map its production equipment to this abstract language and evaluate if it can produce the recipe. By providing information about the occurrence of failure modes of the existing production equipment, it can be evaluated using RPNs if the required quality can be met or if additional quality measures need to be implemented to increase the quality. By having a budget for a recipe, the vendor of a product can evaluate the economic efficiency of its possible production scenarios and decide to produce a product or to decline an offer. By comparing the RPNs of prospective processes and their economic deficiencies, an optimal process can be selected.

The same applies to the risk assessment procedure. By using abstract service definitions, the integrated production equipment can be checked automatically during runtime to guarantee the safety of operators while interacting with the production system. The known interaction tasks are firstly associated with information regarding possible involved hazards, whereas the severity and possibility of avoidance are then described concretely by the integrated production equipment. The frequency of interaction tasks can also be predefined in order to evaluate the required risk level using performance level PLr along with the other risk parameters. Considering the available safety functions along with its constraints at runtime, the production system can be assessed against the identified hazards, emphasizing hence the critical points that require further safety considerations and safety measures. This ensures a higher efficiency, quality and completeness of the risk assessment result, which is usually done manually nowadays.

5   Conclusion and Future Work

In this publication, we presented an integrated model-based approach SQUADfps that enables both the automated conduct of risk assessment and the dynamic creation of a process-FMEA for a flexible, adaptable or reconfigurable production system. Our proposed meta-model provides the foundation to enable flexible production scenarios in which individual and customer-specific productions can be manufactured up to lot-size-1. The proposed model-based risk assessment can ensure the safe operation of a new, previously unknown configuration of the manufacturing system by conducting the required risk assessment in an automated way based on the information available in the meta-model. Moreover, the evaluation on whether a specific product can be manufactured while meeting the customer's quality requirements by a specific configuration of the plant (as well as a cost-efficient use of quality assurance mechanisms within the manufacturing process) can be conducted by generating a process-FMEA in an automated manner. By applying the proposed model-based approach, all information required to perform these assessments can be provided automatically during runtime. The currently manual and time-consuming tasks to conduct assessments can be automated. This assists the decision-making process of human and thus, enables the fast reconfiguration of production systems in flexible production scenarios. In the future, this integrated model-based approach will be applied to further use cases to improve the completeness and significance of the generated results.

Acknowledgement. The work leading to this paper was funded by the German Federal Ministry of Education and Research under grant number 01IS16043Q and 01IS16043O (CrESt).

References

1. Aagedal, J.O., den Braber, F., Dimitrakos, T., Gran, B.A., Raptis, D., Stolen, K.: Model-based risk assessment to improve enterprise security. In: Proceedings. Sixth International Enterprise Distributed Object Computing, pp. 51–62 (2002)
2. Arai, T., Aiyama, Y., Maeda, Y., Sugi, M., Ota, J.: Agile assembly system by "plug and produce". CIRP Ann. **49**(1), 1–4 (2000)
3. Awad, R., Fechter, M., van Heerden, J.: Integrated risk assessment and safety consideration during design of hrc workplaces. In: 2017 22nd IEEE International Conference on Emerging Technologies and Factory Automation (ETFA), pp. 1–10, September 2017
4. Bernard, R., Aubert, J.J., Bieber, P., Merlini, C., Metge, S.: Experiments in model based safety analysis: flight controls. IFAC Proc. Vol. **40**(6), 43–48 (2007)
5. Cancila, D., et al.: Sophia: a modeling language for model-based safety engineering. In: 2nd International Workshop on Model Based Architecting and Construction of Embedded Systems, CEUR. Denver, Colorado, pp. 11–26 (2009)
6. Cichocki, T., Górski, J.: Failure mode and effect analysis for safety-critical systems with software components. In: Koornneef, F., van der Meulen, M. (eds.) SAFECOMP 2000. LNCS, vol. 1943, pp. 382–394. Springer, Heidelberg (2000). https://doi.org/10.1007/3-540-40891-6_33
7. Cichocki, T., Górski, J.: Formal support for fault modelling and analysis. In: Voges, U. (ed.) SAFECOMP 2001. LNCS, vol. 2187, pp. 190–199. Springer, Heidelberg (2001). https://doi.org/10.1007/3-540-45416-0_19

8. David, P., Idasiak, V., Kratz, F.: Towards a better interaction between design and dependability analysis: FMEA derived from UML/SysML models. In: Safety, Reliability and Risk Analysis: Theory, Methods and Applications, pp. 2259–2266 (2008)
9. Department of Defence: MIL-STD-1629A, Procedures for Performing a Failure Mode. Effects and Criticality Analysis, Washington (1980)
10. European Commission: Machinery Directive 2006/42/EC (2006)
11. Ferrer, B.R., Ahmad, B., Lobov, A., Vera, D.A., Lastra, J.L.M., Harrison, R.: An approach for knowledge-driven product, process and resource mappings for assembly automation. In: 2015 IEEE International Conference on Automation Science and Engineering (CASE), pp. 1104–1109. IEEE (2015)
12. Ford Motor Company: Potential Failure Mode and Effects Analysis - Instruction Manual (1988)
13. Grigoleit, F., et al.: The qSafe project-developing a model-based tool for current practice in functional safety analysis (2016)
14. Hassan, A., Siadat, A., Dantan, J.Y., Martin, P.: Conceptual process planning - an improvement approach using GFD, FMEA, and ABC methods. Robot. Comput.-Integr. Manuf. **26**, 392–401 (2010). https://doi.org/10.1016/j.rcim.2009.12.002
15. Houmb, S.H., Den Braber, F., Lund, M.S., Stølen, K.: Towards a UML profile for model-based risk assessment. In: Critical Systems Development with UML-Proceedings of the UML 2002 Workshop, pp. 79–91 (2002)
16. International Electrotechnical Commission (IEC): IEC 62061: Safety of machinery - Functional safety of electrical, electronic and programmable electronic control systems (2005)
17. International Organization for Standardization (ISO): ISO 13849–1 Safety of machinery - Safety-related parts of control systems - Part 1: General principles for design (2006)
18. Joshi, A., Whalen, M., Heimdahl, M.: Model-based safety analysis final report. NASA Techreport (2005)
19. Koo, C., Vorderer, M., Junker, S., Schröck, S., Verl, A.: Challenges and requirements for the safety compliant operation of reconfigurable manufacturing systems. Proc. CIRP **72**, 1100–1105 (2018)
20. Koren, Y., et al.: Reconfigurable manufacturing systems. CIRP Ann. **48**(2), 527–540 (1999)
21. Lisagor, O., Kelly, T., Niu, R.: Model-based safety assessment: review of the discipline and its challenges. In: The Proceedings of 2011 9th International Conference on Reliability, Maintainability and Safety, pp. 625–632. IEEE (2011)
22. Papadopoulos, Y., Parker, D., Grante, C.: Automating the failure modes and effects analysis of safety critical systems. In: International Symposium on High Assurance Systems Engineering (HASE 2004), pp. 310–311 (2004)
23. Papadopoulos, Y., Grante, C.: Evolving car designs using model-based automated safety analysis and optimisation techniques. J. Syst. Softw. **76**(1), 77–89 (2005). computer Software and Applications
24. Prosvirnova, T., et al.: The altarica 3.0 project for model-based safety assessment. IFAC Proc. Vol. **46**(22), 127–132 (2013)
25. Tarum, C.D.: Fmera-failure modes, effects, and (financial) risk analysis. Technical report, SAE Technical Paper (2001)
26. Teng, S.G., Ho, S.M.: Failure mode and effects analysis: an integrated approach for product design and process control. Int. J. Qual. Reliab. Manage. **13**(5), 8–26 (1996)

27. Walker, M., Papadopoulos, Y., Parker, D., Lönn, H., et al.: Semi - automatic FMEA supporting complex systems with combinations and sequences of failures. SAE Int. J. Passeng. Cars - Mech. Syst. **2**(1), 791–802 (2009)
28. Wang, H., Liu, S., Gao, C.: Study on model-based safety verification of automatic train protection system. In: 2009 Asia-Pacific Conference on Computational Intelligence and Industrial Applications (PACIIA), vol. 1, pp. 467–470. IEEE (2009)
29. Yilmaz, O., Davis, R.P.: Flexible manufacturing systems: characteristics and assessment. Eng. Manage. Int. **4**(3), 209–212 (1987)

Security Assessment

A Serverless Architecture for Wireless Body Area Network Applications

Pangkaj Chandra Paul[✉], John Loane, Fergal McCaffery,
and Gilbert Regan

Regulated Software Research Centre, Dundalk Institute of Technology, Dundalk,
Co. Louth, Ireland
paulp@dkit.ie

Abstract. Wireless body area networks (WBANs) have become popular for providing real-time healthcare monitoring services. WBANs are an important subset of Cyber-physical systems (CPS). As the amount of sensing devices in such healthcare applications is growing rapidly, security, scalability, availability and privacy are a real challenge. Adoption of cloud computing is growing in the healthcare sector because it can provide high scalability while ensuring availability and affordable healthcare monitoring services. Serverless computing brings a new era to the design and deployment of event-driven applications in cloud computing. Serverless computing also helps the developer to build a large application using Function as a Service without thinking about the management and scalability of the infrastructure. The goal of this paper is to propose a dependable serverless architecture for WBAN applications. This architecture will improve the dependability of WBAN applications through ensuring scalability, availability, security and privacy by design, in addition to being cost-effective. This paper presents a detailed price comparison between two leading cloud service providers. Additionally, this paper reports on the findings from a case study which evaluated security, scalability and availability of the proposed architecture. This evaluation was conducted by load testing and rule-based intrusion detection.

Keywords: Wireless body area network · Cloud computing · Serverless architecture

1 Introduction

With the rapid growth of wireless communication and sensor technology, Wireless body area network (WBAN) applications are an increasingly important technology in providing healthcare services. WBAN applications can provide an affordable healthcare service with real-time monitoring [1]. A WBAN application can provide long-term health monitoring of a patient's physiological states including body temperature, blood pressure and heart rate without constraining their normal activities. These sensor-based applications can be used to monitor patients with different chronic diseases such as diabetes, hypertension, and cardiovascular disease [2]. In [3], the authors proposed a solar-powered sensor-based smartphone healthcare application to display data from

© Springer Nature Switzerland AG 2019
Y. Papadopoulos et al. (Eds.): IMBSA 2019, LNCS 11842, pp. 239–254, 2019.
https://doi.org/10.1007/978-3-030-32872-6_16

multiple sensor nodes. Sensors and smartphones can be combined with cloud computing to provide smart and affordable healthcare systems.

Cloud computing is a model which provides on-demand self-service for provisioning resources and rapid elasticity with minimal management effort and service provider interaction [4]. Software as a Service (SaaS), Platform as a Service (PaaS) and Infrastructure as a Service (IaaS) are three types of service model available in cloud computing. Currently, Amazon web services (AWS), Microsoft Azure, Google and IBM are the leading cloud service providers. According to the Gartner magic quadrant 2018 report, AWS and Azure are recognised as leaders in IaaS.

In [5], the authors propose a remote healthcare application developed using a combination of Android apps and cloud computing to provide medical services for older adults. In a healthcare application, it is necessary to ensure minimal latency while exchanging information between sensor devices and servers. This minimal latency will increase the availability of patient health record for providing real-time healthcare service. In [6], the authors presented a cloud-based smart healthcare monitoring system using a docker container-based virtual environment to reduce latency and bandwidth.

As WBANs have limited memory, energy and computing power, a scalable high-performance computing and storage infrastructure is required to provide real-time data processing and storage. Serverless computing started a new era in the cloud computing industry, allowing minimum maintenance and providing cost-effective infrastructure for application development. Serverless computing is a cloud computing execution model where a cloud provider will run the server and dynamically manage the resource allocation. Serverless computing only charges for execution time, which helps in developing a cost-effective service. The goal of this paper is to present a serverless architecture for developing a dependable cloud-assisted WBAN application. By dependable we mean the application will be secure, available, scalable and ensure privacy.

The rest of the research paper is organised as follows; Sect. 2 briefly describes current trends in cloud computing in WBAN. Section 3 details the proposed serverless architecture, while Sect. 4 presents the implementation of the proposed architecture. Load testing results and attack mitigations for the proposed architecture are presented in Sect. 5. Finally, Sect. 6 concludes the paper by detailing future work.

2   Cloud Computing in WBAN

A fundamental issue in a WBAN healthcare application is the effective and efficient management of a large amount of data generated from sensor nodes. Cloud infrastructure can provide scalability of data storage, perform data analysis and give access to the user's health records [7]. In [8], the authors proposed a SaaS approach called BodyCloud. This SaaS approach supports the storage and management of sensor data streams for sensor-based healthcare applications. It also provides offline and online processing of stored data by using Google PaaS infrastructure, which allows for rapid prototyping of applications, easy customisation of architectural components, and scalability. In [9], the authors present cloudlet-based efficient WBAN healthcare applications which provide reliable large-scale sensor data to the end user. The proposed prototype consists of a virtual machine which provides scalable data storage and processing infrastructure for large-scale WBAN systems. Sensor nodes used in a WBAN application can have different data transmission rates which require optimal resources for computing to avoid performance degradation or data loss. In [10], the authors proposed a cloud-based experimental framework named Cloud-WBAN, which will automatically adjust computing resources based on data volume and application type.

In [11], the authors proposed a green cloud-assisted WBAN based health monitoring service by adjusting the sleep time of sensor nodes for energy saving. The authors proposed to use the cloud-based MapReduce algorithm to analyse sensing frequency of decentralised data transmission between cloud and sensor nodes. In [12], the authors proposed a virtual hospital architecture by integrating WBAN and software-defined networking (SDN) in cloud computing to provide a better quality of service. As cloud computing provides scalability, elasticity and cost efficiency, the SDN will add further dimensions by providing adaptability and high bandwidth capability.

As sensor nodes of a WBAN application generate large amounts of data, cloud computing can provide a scalable storage option in addition to assisting with processing data in real-time. Cloud computing can also help with quick prototyping and deployment of the application. Furthermore, easy customisation of cloud infrastructure will help with feature enhancement of WBAN applications.

3 Proposed Serverless Architecture

Serverless computing is getting popular as a new and compelling paradigm for the development of cloud-based applications, largely due to the recent migration of enterprise applications to containers and microservices [13]. In the traditional cloud computing scenario, the healthcare application provider will pay a fixed and recurring cost, whether the application is used or not. In serverless computing, the user will only pay per-execution, not for the idle time. Serverless computing helps the developer to build a larger application using Function-as-a-Service (FaaS) platforms where each component of the application can scale separately. It also gives the flexibility to develop an application without thinking about managing infrastructure.

To develop system architecture, we first need to gather requirements and define the use cases. In this research paper, we choose a fitness tracking application designed by a mid-size enterprise, Company A, located in Ireland. This fitness tracking application consists of a wearable device which sends sensor data to a mobile application. This mobile application then transmits the data received from the sensors to a cloud-based backend application for further analysis. The user can access previously uploaded sensor data through the mobile application. Additionally, a user management process needs to be in place to manage sign in, sign up, and profile updates. This section presents an overview of the services required to develop the fitness tracking application, along with the cost structure of providing these required services from two leading cloud providers, that is AWS and Azure.

3.1   Domain Name System Service

Amazon Route 53 is a highly available, scalable and cost-effective Domain Name System (DNS) service for translating a domain name to an IP address. It can be used to manage user traffic globally through a variety of routing types, including latency-based routing or Geo DNS [14]. Additionally, it can also connect user requests to other AWS services such as Elastic load balancer, Amazon S3, CloudFront and API Gateway. The Azure DNS service also provides a similar service by using the Microsoft global network of name servers along with anycast networking. To provide high availability and faster performance, each DNS query is resolved by the closest available DNS server [15]. AWS Route 53 and Azure DNS have a similar monthly charge which is based on the number of hosted zones. AWS Route 53 ensures availability and traffic management using latency-based and geoproximity based routing protocols.

3.2   User Management and Authentication Service

Amazon Cognito is an authentication, authorisation and user management service for web and mobile applications. The user can sign up and sign in using their user name and password, without building and managing a backend solution or any infrastructure to handle identity management [16]. The Cognito service can save authentication information locally inside the device, which will allow applications to work offline. In the Azure cloud environment, Azure Active Directory (Azure AD) B2C is a business-to-consumer identity management service [17]. This service helps to customise and control how the user will communicate with the application. Azure AD B2C was developed using OpenID connect and OAuth2.0 protocols to provide security tokens and secure access to resources. This authentication and authorisation service will ensure privacy by preventing unauthorised access of personally identifiable information.

AWS Cognito charges are based on the number of monthly active users, while Azure AD B2C charges for each authentication. Both services have additional charges for enabling a multi-factor authentication service.

3.3   Content Delivery Service

A content delivery web service is used to deliver content to end users with low latency, high data transfer speeds, and no minimum usage commitments. When a user places a request for content, it will be automatically routed to the nearest edge location, so content is delivered with the best possible performance. Both cloud providers have content delivery services named AWS CloudFront and Azure CDN. Azure CDN serves the content from 30 point of presence (PoP) server locations worldwide [18], while AWS CloudFront serves content from 79 PoP server locations across 49 countries [19]. CloudFront supports dedicated custom SSL certificates and field level encryption.

AWS CloudFront provides content delivery from more PoP server locations compared to Azure CDN. Both service providers have a different pricing model based on the origin of the request, but in CloudFront there is no charge for the first 2,000,000 HTTP/HTTPS requests and 50 GB data transfer out per month for the first year.

3.4   Serverless Computing Service

Developing applications using serverless architectures requires event-driven or micro computing services to virtually run code for any application or backend service without the need to provision or manage servers. This service also needs to provide high scalability and availability with zero hardware and system administration.

AWS Lambda is an event-driven computing service which helps to build a serverless backend system to handle requests from the web and mobile applications using API Gateway [20]. The Lambda service helps to run and trigger code in parallel processes and scales with the size of the workload. By integrating Cognito services, Lambda can authenticate each request by using access tokens. Lambda supports several programming languages, including Java, Go, PowerShell, Node.js, C#, Python, and Ruby.

Azure Functions or Azure Service Fabric can be used to develop a serverless application using event-driven or micro computing services [21]. Azure Functions can directly integrate with mobile or web applications without attaching an application gateway. Azure Functions support C#, JavaScript, F# and Python in preview mode which is only available on request. Preview mode is excluded from the Microsoft service level agreement and might not be brought forward into general release.

Azure Functions provide different pricing models such as per execution, resource consumption and premium plan, whereas AWS Lambda only has a pay-as-you-go pricing model. However, AWS Lambda supports more programming languages than Azure Functions, which allows more flexibility during development of the application.

3.5   API Management Service

An API management service is required to publish APIs to integrate web or mobile applications with serverless backend services. The Amazon API Gateway and Azure API Management services are fully managed services which makes it easier for developers to create, publish, maintain, monitor, and secure RESTful application programming interfaces (APIs) at any scale and to expose backend and frontend HTTPs endpoints [22]. The Amazon API Gateway uses the Amazon CloudFront edge location service and can therefore provide lower latency responses when compared to Azure. The Azure API management service has three different pricing plans whereas the AWS API Gateway charges per request [23]. Additionally, the AWS API gateway supports multiple stages for API development, which provides better API lifecycle management when compared to Azure.

3.6   Database Service

In a serverless application, it is better to have a database with low latency that requires zero maintenance. Amazon DynamoDB is a fully managed fast and flexible cloud NoSQL database service. It is suitable for all applications which require single-digit millisecond latency at any scale [24]. This database supports both document and key-value data models. In DynamoDB, the user only needs to create a database table and set throughput. The rest of the database management tasks such as hardware or software provisioning, autoscaling, and automatic partitioning will be handled by AWS. The Azure Cosmos DB is a fully managed, globally distributed, multi-model database service with high scalability and single-digit read-write latency with multiple NoSQL supports such as document, graph database and key-value data models [25].

In DynamoDB the user is charged per read and write request, whereas Cosmos DB charges for provisioned throughput and consumed storage by the hour. Furthermore, the databases are distinguished by their backup processes, as Cosmos DB provides automatic backup whereas it is a manual process with DynamoDB.

3.7   Web Application Firewall

Finally, a firewall service will be required to protect web and mobile applications from common web exploits which could affect application availability, compromise security, or consume excess resources. The AWS Web Application Firewall (WAF) provides control over which traffic to allow or block to the web application by defining customisable web security rules. WAF charges per rule [26]. By creating a custom rule, the WAF can block common attack patterns, such as distributed denial-of-service (DDoS) attack, SQL injection or cross-site scripting. The WAF can integrate with other services such as CloudFront, Elastic load balancer and the API gateway. A lambda function can be used to analyse the CloudFront access log and automatically update security rules in the WAF.

In the Azure cloud platform, the WAF service can be enabled as part of the Application Gateway [27]. This Application Gateway WAF service is based on the Core Rule Set 3.0 provided by the Open Web Application Security Project (OWASP). This WAF service does not provide any protection against DDoS attacks. To protect the application from DDoS attacks in the Azure cloud platform, a separate service named Azure DDoS Protection needs to be enabled. It comes with a fixed monthly charge, whereas AWS WAF charges are based on the number of rules created.

3.8   SSL/TLS Certificate

SSL/TLS certificates are used to secure communication between two entities in the system. AWS certificate manager (ACM) provides easy provisioning, management and deployment of public or private SSL/TLS certificates. ACM also provides easy certificate integration with other AWS services such as elastic load balancer, CloudFront and API Gateway. Azure only provides a public certificate for the Azure CDN and App services. Both service providers provide public certificates free of charge. There is an additional charge for private certificates.

3.9   Cost Comparison Between Azure and AWS

In this section, a cost comparison between the selected AWS and Azure services is presented. This comparison is based on different parameters such as the number of users, database size and read and write requests per second. During the cost calculation, a pricing calculator provided by the respective cloud providers for the Ireland region was used. As AWS and Azure use different pricing models, in some cases, an adjustment will be required for the selected parameters. For example, the AWS API management charge is based on the number of requests per second, whereas the Azure API management has four tiers including developer, basic, standard and platinum. The basic tier was selected for Azure API management. AWS Cognito charges for the number of active users in a month, whereas Azure AD B2C charges for the number of authentication requests. Based on Company A's business goal to have 50,000 monthly active users with an average of five authentication requests per user, 50,000 monthly active users for AWS Cognito and 250,000 authentication requests for Azure are considered in the calculation. Additionally, one Web access control list (WEB ACL) and 15 custom rules for AWS WAF, 10 TB data transfer for content delivery and a database size of 50 GB was selected for the calculation. Table 1 outlines the cost for individual services of Azure and AWS.

Table 1. Azure and AWS monthly cost comparison

Service name	Azure	AWS
Domain name system service	$6.50	$6.50
User management and authentication service	$560.00	$0
Content delivery service	$828	$870
Serverless computing service	$96.80	$2.30
API management service	$250.62	$5.00
Database service	$70.90	$56.89
Web application firewall	$3456	$26.00
SSI/TLS certificate (public)	$0	$0
Support plan	$100	$100
Total	$5368.82	$1,066.69

During the cost analysis, we notice a large difference in the API management and WAF services. For API management, Azure requires the combination of Application gateway and API management services which results in higher costs compared to AWS API Gateway. AWS API Gateway charges are based on the number of requests, whereas Azure charges are based on the tier subscription and the number of instances. For WAF, Azure provide a package that secures web and infrastructure for a fixed monthly price. For AWS, the user needs to configure web security rules which cost $1 per rule. To secure the infrastructure with AWS, the user can rely on AWS with zero cost. For user management and authentication services, AWS Cognito charges are based on monthly active users and no charge will be required with free tier support, but Azure B2C will charge $560 for 250,000 authentications.

3.10   Summary of Comparison Between AWS and Azure

After reviewing the services from AWS and Azure, we notice some key differences in terms of cost and features. AWS will provide more availability in terms of content delivery due to having more PoP than Azure. AWS Lambda supports more programming language options than Azure Functions service. A summary of the comparisons between AWS and Azure is presented in Table **2**.

3.11 System Architecture

After reviewing the available features and cost comparison the AWS cloud platform was selected to develop the serverless architecture as it will provide larger programing language support, lower latency for content delivery, easy management of WAF, costs less and the developer was more familiar with AWS. To develop the fitness tracking application, the design of the core backend application system started by adding AWS Cognito. Lambda and DynamoDB were selected to process user requests and store data. To connect the backend application with mobile applications API gateway was deployed and attached with CloudFront to ensure wider availability. Additionally, the integration of Lambda functions allows for the analysis of CloudFront access logs Finally, Route 53 with an SSL certificate issued from the Certificate manager will be connected with CloudFront. The serverless architecture is illustrated in Fig. 1.

4 Implementation of the Proposed Architecture

This section describes the configuration process for the different AWS services contained within the proposed architecture.

4.1 Configuration of AWS Services

An AWS Cognito user pool is created to manage all user accounts and configured to handle end user sign in and sign up requests. The sign up process requires an email address and username, along with other attributes related to the application such as name, address, birthdate, gender and phone number. When a user successfully signs in, Cognito will provide a JWT token with a one-hour expiration time limit. Therefore, the mobile app will be configured to request a token refresh operation before the token expiration time. Each table in DynamoDB is created by assigning a name and primary key with partition and sort keys for better scalability and availability. To minimise the database cost, each table was provisioned with a capacity of five reads and writes per second. To ensure scalability, based on DynamoDB best practice guidelines, auto-scaling was configured with a target utilisation of 70%. Finally, encryption at rest is set up by assigning a key from the AWS Key Management Service (KMS).

The AWS Lambda platform supports several programming languages such as . NET, Go, Java, Python, Node.js and Ruby to create functions. During this implementation, all functions were developed using Node.js 8.10. Based on application benchmarking, functions to process and retrieve data were configured with 256 MB memory and 10 s timeout. The rest of the functions related to other use cases such as user profile creation, getting and updating endpoints and used a minimum of 128 MB memory with a 5 s timeout. Each function is designed to be invoked by requests coming from the API gateway. Additionally, a domain name is registered in AWS

Table 2. Comparison summary between AWS and Azure

Service name	AWS	Azure
DNS service	AWS Route53: • Latency-based and geoproximity based routing protocols • Pricing model: cost per hosted zone and number of requests	Azure DNS: • DNS query resolved by the closest available DNS server • Pricing model: cost per hosted zone and number of requests
User management and authentication	AWS Cognito: • Offline and online authentication support • Pricing model: charge based on monthly active users	Azure AD B2C: • Only support online authentication • Pricing model: charge per authentication
Content delivery service	AWS CloudFront: • 79 PoP server locations • Pricing model: charge based on the origin of the request and data transfer rate with free-tier support for first year	Azure CDN: • 30 PoP servers worldwide • Pricing model: charge based on the origin of the request and data transfer rate with no free-tier support
Serverless compute service	AWS Lambda: • More supported languages and all generally available for use • Pricing model: pay per execution and memory consumption	Azure function: • Less supported language with preview mode • Pricing model: pay per execution and memory consumption or premium plan
API management service	AWS API gateway: • Multiple API lifecycle stages support • Better response time and lower latency with CloudFront • Pricing model: pay per request	Azure API management: • No lifecycle stage support for API • Pricing model: three different pricing plans: developer, standard and premium
Database service	AWS DynamoDB: • Document and key-value data models • Manual backup • Pricing model: pay per read and write request	Azure Cosmos DB: • Document, graph database and key-value data models • Automatic backup • Pricing model: pay per provisioned throughput and consumed storage
Web application firewall	AWS WAF: • Customisable web security rules • Standalone service can be integrated with other AWS services • Implement DDoS protection by analysing CloudFront log • Pricing model: pay per web security rule	Azure WAF: • Web security rules not customizable and managed by the service provider • Only available with the Application gateway • For DDoS protection require Azure DDoS Protection service • Pricing model: a fixed monthly charge

(*continued*)

Table 2. (*continued*)

Service name	AWS	Azure
SSL/TLS Certificate	AWS ACM: • Central certificate management for other AWS services • Pricing model: no charge for the public certificate. Additional charge for a private certificate	• Certificates are managed separately for Azure CDN and App service • Pricing model: no charge for the public certificate. Additional charge for a private certificate

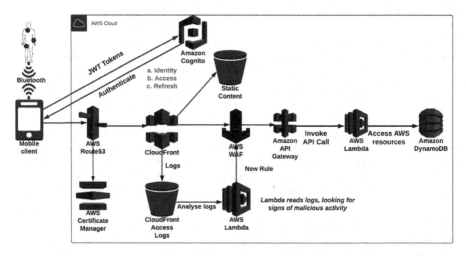

Fig. 1. Proposed serverless architecture for WBAN applications

Route 53 to route end-user requests using CloudFront. To enable HTTPS, a public certificate was assigned from the ACM.

4.2   Deploy RESTful API Using API Gateway

The API gateway exposes the AWS Lambda functions as a RESTful API. A new REST API is created by assigning a name with edge optimised endpoint option to serve from the end user's nearest location. As the WAF service is not fully integrated with the API gateway, the CloudFront access log will be used with the WAF service for intrusion detection. To fulfil each end user request, the following steps are necessary to create a RESTful API using the API gateway:

1. Create the API gateway resource with POST method and attach to associated Lambda function;
2. Configure the API gateway to use Cognito user pool as an authoriser to validate user requests using JWT tokens before invoking any Lambda function;
3. Deploy API gateway resources with a stage name called "Prod" and collect the URL;

4. Create a CloudFront web distribution with HTTPS;
   a. Add alternate domain name and respective SSL certificate from the ACM list;
   b. Create a root origin entry with default behaviours using the step 3 URL;
   c. Assign an S3 bucket to store the access log and create distribution;
5. Finally, configure Route 53 entry with respective CloudFront distribution.

This proposed architecture uses the OWASP top 10 recommendations for intrusion detection and prevention. An AWS CloudFormation template was used to deploy the WEB ACL, condition types and rules. Additionally, a lambda function was used to analyse the CloudFront access log to identify the source of DDoS attacks and automatically update the security rules in the WAF.

5   Performance Analysis of Proposed Architecture

Performance of the proposed architecture was evaluated by load testing and carrying out a vulnerability assessment. Load testing will evaluate the scalability and availability of the system. A vulnerability assessment will help to identify the weaknesses, potential areas of intrusion, and configuration issues in the system. It will also help to implement proper countermeasures for identified vulnerabilities to ensure the availability and security of the proposed architecture. To evaluate the system, load testing and vulnerability assessments were conducted in two phases: (1) In-house and (2) Penetration testing service provider (PTSP). Due to having limited resources for creating real-world scenarios for load testing and limited knowledge for conducting a vulnerability assessment in-house, we consulted with several PTSPs. A PTSP was selected based on budget and experience.

In the following sections, we first provide the load test results and then describe how the proposed architecture is affected by common web exploits such as distributed denial-of-service (DDoS) and SQL injection attacks.

5.1   Load Testing Results

A load test is used to evaluate how the application or REST API backend will perform with hundreds or thousands of concurrent users requests, and respective data volumes in a real-life scenario. Load testing was performed for two scenarios: (1) users will first download the mobile app and sign up for an account; (2) a user signs in to the mobile app and starts sending sensor data along with other profile metadata. Table 3 presents the list of REST API endpoints used during the load test.

Table 3. List of rest API endpoints for load testing

Scenario 1 (Sign Up)	Scenario 2 (Sensor data transmission)
• Cognito: SignUp endpoint	• Cognito: Sign In
• Cognito: InitiateAuth endpoint	• Cognito: InitiateAuth
• API:/user/registration	• API:/user/profile
• API:/user/profile	• API:/sensordata/upload
	• API:/sensordata/get
	• API:/user/profile/update

In-House Load Testing: It is recommended to use a modern, powerful and easy to use tool for load testing. A custom bash script with the help of AWS SDK (Command line version) was designed to test the sign up and sign in processes. Additionally, the ab benchmarking tool (Apache HTTP server benchmarking tool) was used to generate adequate traffic for testing API endpoints. During the test process, 100 sample users were created with randomly generated emails and passwords using a bash script. All users were successfully created in the AWS Cognito User pool. No exceptions or time-outs were noticed during this test. To assess the scalability and availability of the API, the ab benchmarking tool was used with ten concurrent users, each generating 200 API requests. The authentication tokens were used to verify each API request. During testing, 15% of the requests for one of the API endpoints timed-out due to throughput issues with the DynamoDB tables. Therefore, target utilisation was reduced to 60% for DynamoDB tables related to this endpoint. After the reconfiguration of DynamoDB the same test was run again and no timeout issues were noticed.

PTSP: To perform the load test, the PTSP used the Artillery tool with different combinations of arrival rates and durations. Artillery is a modern, powerful and easy-to-use distributed load testing toolkit. Distributed load testing will help to create real-world scenarios by generating traffic from different locations worldwide. The arrival rate is the number of incoming users per second. Generally, this is ramped up evenly from a start point to an endpoint throughout the test period. During the load test three rounds of tests were conducted with (1) arrival rate starting with 1 and ending with 5 for 300 s (henceforth known as Arrival rate A) (2) arrival rate starting with 5 and ending with 10 for 900 s (henceforth known as Arrival rate B) (3) arrival rate starting with 5 and ending with 10 for 1800 s (henceforth known as Arrival rate C). Table 4 illustrates the load test results for both scenarios for different arrival rates.

Table 4. Load test results for two scenarios by the PTSP

	Scenario 1 (Sign Up)	Scenario 2 (Sensor data transmission)
Arrival rate A: Start: 01 End: 05 Duration: 300 s	No timed-out requests Latency: <0.5 s	No timed-out requests Latency: <1.0 s
Arrival rate B: Start: 05 End: 10 Duration: 900 s	No timed-out requests Latency: <0.5 s	∼10% requests timed-out Latency: >5.0 s (for ∼10% requests) Test result after DynamoDB reconfiguration: No Timed-out requests Latency: <1.0 s
Arrival rate C: Start: 05 End: 10 Duration: 1800 s	No timed-out requests Latency: <0.5 s	∼25% requests timed-out Latency: >20.0 s (for ∼25% requests) Test result after DynamoDB reconfiguration: No timed-out requests Latency: <1.0 s

For scenario 1, a significant load was created with over 10,000 users signing up over 30 min. No issues were encountered with either timed-out requests (HTTP 504) or high latency. For scenario 2, no issues were encountered with either timed-out requests or high latency for Arrival rate A, however, for Arrival rate B, 10 percent of requests encountered a latency greater than 5 s and thus timed-out. For Arrival rate C more than 25% of requests encountered a latency greater than 20 s and thus timed-out. The key finding is that the DynamoDB takes a little time to scale, and the sudden high-traffic spikes caused the time-outs and throughput problems. To mitigate this issue, an adjustment was made in DynamoDB. Using the auto-scaling configuration feature, the minimum read and write capacity per second was increased to 10, and the target utilisation was reduced to 55% for Arrival rate B. For Arrival rate C the minimum read and write capacity per second was increased to 20 and the target utilisation was reduced to 45%. After making these configuration changes a similar test was run again for scenario 2 for both Arrival rates B and C, resulting in latency being reduced to <1.0 s and no requests timed-out.

5.2   Vulnerability Assessment

In-House Assessment: A denial-of-service scenario was created using the ab bench-marking tool which generated 400 requests from 30 concurrent users. Additionally, an IP address-based security rule was configured in the AWS WAF to prevent more than 100 requests per minute from an address. Results indicate that the lambda function automatically identified the IP address which generated more than 100 requests per minute. Finally, this lambda function also updated the source IP address in the WAF block list. The result shows that the proposed architecture assists to ensuring the availability of the system by preventing more than 100 requests from the same source over a short period.

Assessment by PTSP: The PTSP uses manual and automated methods to assess and perform vulnerability testing to attempt to gain access or compromise the service. The tools and methods used for exploitation during penetration testing are the same as those commonly used by people trying to compromise systems with malicious intent. Before testing begins, clear ground rules were established for stop points of the testing process, which will help to prevent unexpected damage to systems. For instance, when testing an API which contains an SQL injection flaw, it is enough to identify the compromise without attempting to obtain further access to the database servers. Network requests are relayed through several tools for manual and automated inspection, to allow listening and watching what the platform was doing. These data dumps are then taken into different tools and tested for any injection points and manual investigation. Table 5 presents the list of tools used during the vulnerability assessment process:
Additionally, manual and scripted testing was used to examine the results found during automated testing. Below are some of the major vulnerabilities found during the assessment process along with possible solutions.

Potential Denial of Service Points: During testing, there were several potential DDoS points found. These are requests that timeout within 10 s due to malformed data inside

Table 5. List of tools used for vulnerability assessments

Name	Description
OWASP ZAP	The open web application security project - Zed Attack Proxy (ZAP) is a penetration testing tool for finding vulnerabilities in applications
BURP SUITE	Burp Suite is a platform for performing security testing of applications
NMAP	Nmap (Network mapper) is a free and open source utility for network exploration or security auditing
SSLSCAN	SSLScan tests for different SSL exploits, such as heartbleed and the POODLE vulnerability, it also tests the cipher suites and key exchanges
HYDRA brute force	Hydra is a rapid dictionary attacker which can be configured against over 50 different protocols. It is most commonly used for brute forcing user accounts to test for weak passwords
KALI LINUX	Kali is a Debian-derived Linux distribution designed for digital forensics and penetration testing installed with hundreds of different tools

the payload. These can be run multiple times in multiple threads, driving up the usage and putting stress and strain on the service.

Solution: Action was taken in the API endpoints backend lambda code to handle potential malformed data gracefully by assessing each field from the payload. Additionally, a proper HTTP response was added to allows the user to retry a request later.

Security Misconfiguration – Stack Traces Enabled :During testing, it was discovered that stack traces were enabled for some API endpoints.

Solution: Stack traces were turned off in the lambda code base, and logging was copied to an encrypted AWS S3 bucket for future analysis from AWS CloudWatch.

After making the necessary changes in the lambda code and infrastructure to address the issues found during the assessment process, we informed the PTSP. A re-test of the updated system was unable to reproduce the vulnerabilities.

In summary, load testing and vulnerability assessments are required to evaluate system availability, scalability and security. In-house testing helped to identify issues and implement countermeasures in the early stages of the development lifecycle. The DynamoDB throughput bottleneck issue was identified by both in-house and PTSP. This issue required reconfiguration of the DynamoDB. Additionally, the PTSP identified other issues which required code changes in the Lambda functions.

6 Conclusion

Cloud computing is becoming a popular way to develop WBAN based healthcare applications which provide real-time monitoring. The recent introduction of serverless computing in the cloud paradigm helps developers to build more dependable applications which are highly scalable, available and cost-effective. In this paper, we presented a serverless architecture using AWS serverless computing to develop a dependable WBAN based healthcare application which is secure, highly scalable and available. Serverless computing applications can be developed without thinking about the maintenance of the infrastructure. Furthermore, as the cost model for serverless computing is based on execution time, the cost of the core backend services will be minimised. We also performed load testing and vulnerability assessment by in-house and PTSP to test the security, scalability and availability of the proposed architecture. Load tests indicated some initial latency and time-out problems which were resolved by the reconfiguration of DynamoDB. Additionally, the mitigation of DDoS attacks using the WAF was tested to verify the availability of the application. Future work will involve extending the architecture by integrating AWS CloudTrail for privacy governance, AWS Kinesis Data Analytics and the AWS EMR service to perform big data analysis.

Acknowledgement. This work was supported with the financial support of the Science Foundation Ireland grant 13/RC/2094 and co-funded under the European Regional Development Fund through the Southern and Eastern Regional Operational Programme to Lero - the Irish Software Research Centre (www.lero.ie). Additionally, this work was partly funded by the DEIS H2020 project (Grant Agreement 732242).

References

1. Bouazizi, A., Zaibi, G., Samet, M., Kachouri, A.: Wireless body area network for e-health applications: overview. In: International Conference on Smart, Monitored and Control Cities (2017)
2. Taha, M.S., Rahim, M.S.M., Hashim, M.M., Johi, F.A.: Wireless body area network revisited. Int. J. Eng. Technol. **7**, 3494–3504 (2018)
3. Shaji, J.E., Varghese, B., Varghese, R.: A health care monitoring system with wireless body area network using IoT. Int. J. Recent Trends Eng. Res. **3**, 112–117 (2017)
4. Mell, P., Grance, T.: The NIST definition of cloud computing (2011)
5. Luarasi, T., Durresi, M., Durresi, A.: Healthcare based on cloud computing. In: Proceedings - 16th International Conference on Network-Based Information Systems. NBiS 2013, pp. 113–118 (2013)
6. Kavita, J., Srichandan, S., Ashok, K.T., Sahoo, L.B., Bhabendu, K.M., Debasish, J.: An IoT-cloud based smart healthcare monitoring system using container based virtual environment in Edge device. In: ICETIETR, pp. 1–7 (2018)
7. Fortino, G., Di Fatta, G., Pathan, M., Vasilakos, A.V.: Cloud-assisted body area networks: state-of-the-art and future challenges. Wireless Netw. **20**, 1925–1938 (2014). https://doi.org/10.1007/s11276-014-0714-1
8. Fortino, G., Parisi, D., Pirrone, V., Di Fatta, G.: BodyCloud: a SaaS approach for community body sensor networks. Future Gener. Comput. Syst. **35**, 62–79 (2014)
9. Quwaider, M., Jararweh, Y.: Cloudlet-based efficient data collection in wireless body area networks. Simul. Model. Pract. Theory **50**, 57–71 (2015)
10. Bhardwaj, T., Sharma, S.C.: Cloud-WBAN: an experimental framework for cloud-enabled wireless body area network with efficient virtual resource utilization. Sustain. Comput. Inform. Syst. **20**, 14–33 (2018)
11. Chiang, H.P., Lai, C.F., Huang, Y.M.: A green cloud-assisted health monitoring service on wireless body area networks. Inform. Sci. (Ny) **284**, 118–129 (2014)

12. Al Shayokh, M., Kim, J.W., Shin, S.Y.: Cloud based software defined wireless body area networks architecture for virtual hospital. In: 10th EAI International Conference on Body Area Networks, pp. 4–7 (2015)
13. Baldini, I., et al.: Serverless computing: current trends and open problems. In: Chaudhary, S., Somani, G., Buyya, R. (eds.) Research Advances in Cloud Computing, pp. 1–20. Springer, Singapore (2017). https://doi.org/10.1007/978-981-10-5026-8_1
14. AWS: AWS Route53. https://aws.amazon.com/route53/
15. Azure: Azure DNS. https://azure.microsoft.com/en-in/services/dns/
16. AWS: AWS Cognito. https://aws.amazon.com/cognito/
17. Azure: AD B2C. https://azure.microsoft.com/en-us/services/active-directory-b2c/
18. Azure: Azure CDN. https://azure.microsoft.com/en-gb/services/cdn/
19. AWS: AWS CloudFront. https://aws.amazon.com/cloudfront/
20. AWS: AWS Lambda – Serverless Compute. https://aws.amazon.com/lambda/
21. Azure: Azure Functions. https://azure.microsoft.com/en-gb/services/functions/
22. AWS: Amazon API Gateway. https://aws.amazon.com/api-gateway/
23. Azure: API Management. https://azure.microsoft.com/en-us/services/api-management/
24. AWS: Amazon DynamoDB. https://aws.amazon.com/dynamodb/
25. Azure: Azure Cosmos DB. https://azure.microsoft.com/en-us/services/cosmos-db/
26. AWS: AWS WAF - Web Application Firewall. https://aws.amazon.com/waf/
27. Azure: WAF. https://docs.microsoft.com/azure/application-gateway/waf-overview/

Automated Model-Based Attack Tree Analysis Using HiP-HOPS

Declan Whiting[1]([envelope]), Ioannis Sorokos[1], Yiannis Papadopoulos[1],
Gilbert Regan[2], and Eoin O'Carroll[3]

[1] Faculty of Computer Science and Engineering, University of Hull,
Cottingham Road, Hull HU6 7RX, UK
`{D.Whiting-2018,I.Sorokos,Y.I.Papadopoulos}@hull.ac.uk`
[2] Dundalk Institute of Technology, Dublin Road, Dundalk A91 K584, Ireland
`gilbert.regan@dkit.ie`
[3] Portable Medical Technology, 41/42 High Street, Killarney V93 T8K7, Ireland
`eoin@portablemedicaltechnology.com`

Abstract. As Cyber-Physical Systems (CPS) grow increasingly complex and interact with external CPS, system security remains a nontrivial challenge that continues to scale accordingly, with potentially devastating consequences if left unchecked. While there is a significant body of work on system security found in industry practice, manual diagnosis of security vulnerabilities is still widely applied. Such approaches are typically resource-intensive, scale poorly and introduce additional risk due to human error. In this paper, a model-based approach for Security Attack Tree (SAT) analysis using the HiP-HOPS dependability analysis tool is presented. The approach is demonstrated within the context of a simple web-based medical application to automatically generate attack trees, encapsulated as Digital Dependability Identities (DDIs), for offline security analysis. The paper goes on to present how the produced DDIs can be used to approach security maintenance, identifying security capabilities and controls to counter diagnosed vulnerabilities.

Keywords: Attack trees · Digital dependability identities · HiP-HOPS

1 Introduction

Cyber-Physical Systems (CPS) enhance traditional physical engineering systems with computational, often networked, control. CPS applications of particular importance are those found in domains of critical societal impact such as healthcare, transportation, energy, manufacturing and infrastructure control. Such applications offer considerable benefits in terms of enabling new capabilities, such as distributed control in traditionally centralized systems, e.g. power grids. Another potential benefit is improved efficiency, as semi-automatic, automatic and autonomous control can reduce human input and error and identify resource-optimal system behavior. In this respect, examples include autonomous

Y. Papadopoulos et al. (Eds.): IMBSA 2019, LNCS 11842, pp. 255–269, 2019.
https://doi.org/10.1007/978-3-030-32872-6_17

control of vehicles and smart structures. The European Commission's Smart CPS programme, part of the Horizon 2020, is indicative of their importance[1]. A more in-depth discussion of CPS considerations, requirements and potential solutions can be found in [14,19].

In the aforementioned domains, safety is a key concern, as the implication of CPS failures could be catastrophic to the well-being of affected societies and the environment. As CPS combine both physical and digital aspects, they inherit the traditional concerns of reliability of their physical components impacting safety due to mechanical and/or development failure. However, with the introduction of digital control and network communication, CPS operation is also subject to security risks. Such risks are not necessarily in themselves novel, as they originate from digital technologies and infrastructure subject to extensive use and research. However, the complexity and novel internal and external interactions of CPS, coupled with the typical safety concerns mentioned previously, aggravates the impact of potential security attacks and necessitates rigorous treatment to mitigate the associated risks [6,18].

Security concerns are addressed in highly variable methods in practice, depending on the application domain. Methods of systematic analysis, validation and verification can be employed to produce guarantees of system robustness against security attacks [4,7,20].

Tackling nominal system development alongside safety, reliability, security and, more generally, dependability concerns requires alignment of requirements elicitation and allocation, design and implementation activities with dependability assessment and assurance activities. When the above activities are not properly synchronized and dependent information is shared inaccurately or with delay, the associated discrepancy can cause further modification of the developed system later in the development life cycle, introducing much higher costs or even failure to appropriately identify and address critical system risks. Model-based dependability analysis is a paradigm that evolved from model-based design, centralizing both nominal and dependability-related development activities around a common, shared system model. The common model enables efficient and frequent synchronization across both tracks of development. As the models involved are also typically digital, tool support can provide additional benefits to efficiency, correctness and knowledge reuse, to name a few benefits [10].

As part of the Dependability Engineering Innovation for cyber-physical Systems (DEIS) research project[2], the concept of the Digital Dependability Identity (DDI) is being investigated [21]. DDIs are modular, composable and executable dependability information models associated with a CPS or its constituent subsystems or components. DDIs can be used as a medium for model-based security assessment and assurance, offering commensurate benefits to the development of security-critical CPS. The approach presented here will be employed in the context of a DDI.

---

[1] https://ec.europa.eu/programmes/horizon2020/en/h2020-section/smart-cyber-physical-systems.

[2] http://www.deis-project.eu.

In the following sections, a novel, model-based approach of systematically analyzing systemic security risks, identifying both high and low-level vulnerabilities and assigning appropriate requirements and measures will be presented. The approach will be demonstrated within the context of a CPS system for the healthcare domain. In Sect. 2, previous work on security risk analysis will be reviewed. In Sect. 3, our novel approach will be presented. Section 4 will describe the use case the approach is evaluated upon. Section 5 concludes by presenting the results, alongside further discussion of implications and future work.

2 Background

2.1 Security Threat and Risk Analysis

Due to the diverse applications for cyber-physical systems various industry-specific standards or best practices are applied. Each standard approaches risk differently depending on the factors deemed relevant to risk for the operating context. For example within the medical domain there is the IEC/TR 80001-2-1:2012, this is a technical report and guide on the application of risk management of medical IT networks it describes a 10 step process that system creators and maintainers can use in order to adhere to IEC 80001-1:2010 throughout a systems life-cycle.

Confidentiality is often a key requirement of any software system especially when dealing with sensitive personal data such as medical histories. In many countries personal data is covered by law, such as General Data Protection Regulation (GDPR) in European countries. Infringing on GDPR within the European Union can result in large fines of 4% of international annual turnover or € 20 million depending on which is the greater (GDPR, Article 83).

The growing need to ensure privacy of data and the ever increasing capabilities and complexity of CPS has driven the development of frameworks and methodologies for privacy risk assessments and analysis's such as PRIAM (Privacy RIsk Analysis Methodology) which within the context of risk assessment breaks a system into 7 components: the system itself including its logical boundaries, stake-holders, data, risk sources, privacy weaknesses, feared events and privacy harm [8]. Each component is comprised of categories and attributes. Categories describe the type of data of attribute for example this could be health data, financial data, location data etc and categories can be linked to other components. Attributes are used to identify the aspects of a component which contribute to privacy risk. They can be qualitative (low, medium, high) or quantitative such as "costs less than € 5000". The application of PRIAM is divided into two stages the information gathering stage where information on the components, categories and attributes is collated, and the risk assessment phase where risk levels (severity and likelihood) are calculated for each privacy item.

2.2   Security Attack Trees Analysis

Fault Tree Analysis (FTA) is an established practice in the domain of safety-critical applications. [3] showed that FTA can be applied in the domain of security-critical applications. SATs are similar to Fault Trees but specialised for the security domain. SATs provide a formal, hierarchical, model-based description of a system's security under a tree structure.

At the root of an SAT are outcomes which represent security-critical negative events. Examples include maliciously gaining access to confidential information or obtaining administrator privileges for a safety-critical system. From the root node, intermediate nodes and logical gates link towards its leaf nodes. Intermediate nodes represent combined events that causally lead from their children to the root node. Logical gates usually represent Boolean logic operators such as AND and OR. A node's children linked via an AND gate describe that all of the events described in the children nodes are required for the parent node's event to occur. Accordingly, any event in a child's node is sufficient to trigger a parent node linked via an OR gate. Leaf nodes represent events which are out of scope or cannot be further analysed within the given SAT. In the context of SATs, base events typically include direct, singular actions that form part of an attack.

An example of an SAT can be seen in Fig. 1, where a simplistic attack to gain administrator privileges on an abstract system is described. To achieve their goal, the attacker must either trick the system into executing privileged commands without authenticating as an administrator or successfully authenticate as an administrator (and then presumably execute any commands they wish). Each of these options are analyzed further; to execute commands without administrator authentication, the attacker can use a vulnerable user command and attach commands as the payload of a buffer overflow attack. Alternatively, to authenticate as an administrator, the attacker can use a brute force technique to discover the credentials or use a 'phishing' attack i.e. trick the administrator into disclosing them.

Each component of a system often has its own SAT, these are combined to create the overall SAT for a system. In this way, it is possible to reason about a complex system's security vulnerabilities in a modular fashion. This modularity is useful when dealing with system boundaries at different levels of abstraction.

Binary properties are often assigned to each node of an SAT, such as Possible/Impossible, Expensive/Not Expensive, 'Special Equipment Required'/'No Special Equipment Required'. Numeric properties such as financial cost are also possible. Such properties can extend the SAT, enabling quantitative systems security analysis. For example using the SAT shown in Fig. 2, system creators can refine the SAT by using the following query "attacks with an accumulative value of less than £5,000". This means the only attack that meets this criteria is threatening the legitimate administrator.

Such additional attributes can be described as 'resistance' attributes [22]. The example SAT modified with such resistances can be seen in Fig. 2, where financial costs have been assigned to each leaf node. The semantics of the resistance attributes decide how they are combined as they move upwards through logic

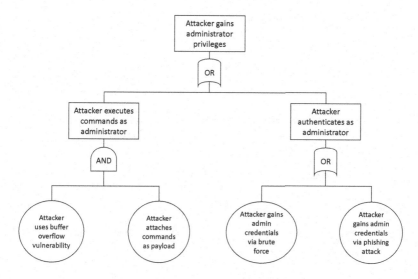

Fig. 1. Security attack tree example

gates. In the example, the AND gate combines financial costs, as both actions must be undertaken, whereas the OR gate provides the attacker choice over the options; under the assumption that all the options are known and available, the attacker is also assumed to choose the most economic one available.

Buldas et al. presented a Multi-Parameter Attack Tree, in this type of SAT the assumption that an adversary will act within rationally and will not persevere with an attack if the cost outweighs the potential benefits [5]. This type of SAT also means the relationship between attributes can be considered such as the overall effort involved and the competency of the adversary.

In fact an entire family of closely related AND-OR tree structures exists, which have been developed since SATs were first introduced, including, Attack-Defence Trees [13] and Ordered Weighted Average (OWA) Trees [23].

2.3 Security Capabilities and Controls

Security Capabilities and Controls are designed to protect systems against attacks on the confidentiality, integrity, and/or availability of a system's information. The USA's National Institute of Standards and Technology (NIST), defines a security control as 'a safeguard or countermeasure prescribed for an information system or an organization designed to protect the confidentiality, integrity, and availability of its information and to meet a set of defined security requirements'. Additionally, NIST defines a Security Capability as 'a combination of mutually-reinforcing security controls (i.e., safeguards and countermeasures) implemented by technical means (i.e., functionality in hardware, software, and firmware), physical means (i.e., physical devices and protective measures), and procedural means (i.e., procedures performed by individuals)' [9].

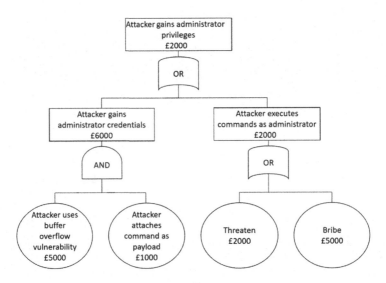

Fig. 2. Attack tree with a cost resistance

There are a number of international standards and frameworks which promote good security practice in part by defining security capabilities and controls. The key considerations in choosing a framework include: understanding what an organisation needs to comply with from a contractual, statutory, and regulatory perspective; the comprehensiveness of the framework. Two of the most well-known frameworks include NIST SP 800-53 and the ISO 27000 series of standards which provide a framework for security management. While the fundamentals of both frameworks are largely the same, they differ in content and layout. Figure 3 visualises the relationship between these two frameworks and indicates that ISO 27002 is a subset of NIST 800-53, as ISO 27002 has 14 security control categories which are encompassed by the 18 categories within NIST 800-53. Examples of such categories include: Incident Response; Access Control; and Audit and Accountability. NIST 800-53 is considered best practice within the US and vendors to the US government must meet its requirements. Outside the US, the ISO 27002 is the de-facto security framework and is considered less complex and easier to implement.

Another framework gaining in popularity is the NIST Cybersecurity Framework. It is more high level and concise than other frameworks and references NIST 800-53 and ISO 27002 for detail on how to implement specific controls and processes. As the NIST Cybersecurity Framework is more lightweight than the other existing frameworks, it may be more suitable for smaller organisations and more readable for executives who do not have a technical background.

More specific to the healthcare domain, which is the domain of the Use Case described in Sect. 4 of this paper, are the Health Information Trust Alliance (HITRUST) Common Security Framework (CSF) and the IEC 80001 series of technical reports. The HITRUST framework incorporates healthcare-specific

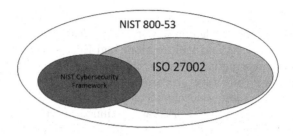

Fig. 3. Relationship between NIST 800-53 and ISO 27002

security, privacy and other regulatory requirements from existing standards such as ISO 27002 and is divided into 19 different domains or capabilities. The IEC 80001 series of technical reports provides guidance on the application of risk management for IT-networks incorporating medical devices. IEC TR 80001-2-8 provides guidance for the establishment of each of the security capabilities presented in IEC TR 80001-2-2 by identifying security controls from key security standards which aim to provide guidance to a responsible organisation when adapting the framework outlined in IEC TR 80001-2-2. IEC TR 80001-2-2 contains 19 security capabilities, with each capability having numerous security controls extracted from the following standards: NIST SP-800-53, ISO 27002, ISO/IEC 15408-2, ISO/IEC 15408-3, IEC 62443-3-3, ISO 27799. From these standards ISO 27002 and ISO 27799 are fully aligned. ISO IEC 27002 specifies a set of detailed controls for managing information security while ISO 27799 specifies additional guidance specifically for health information security and provides health information security best practice guidelines.

In Table 1, a small sample of security capability to controls mapping can be seen. Also included, are references to appropriate security standards, from where guidance on the controls can be referenced in detail.

Table 1. Sample of security capability-control mapping

Security capability	Security control	Reference
Transmission integrity	Access control for transmission medium	SP 800-53
	Network controls	ISO IEC 27002
	...	...

2.4   HiP-HOPS

Hierarchically Performed Hazard Origin and Propagation Studies (HiP-HOPS) is a well established method and tool in the field of dependability analysis [16].

HiP-HOPS has been successfully commercialised and adopted in industry[3]. It originally stems from the amalgamation of several classical dependability analysis techniques such as FTA and Failure Mode and Effects Analysis (FMEA). Its core function is the automation of such techniques with a view to increasing the quality (less mistakes) and the turn around time (efficiency) of dependability analysis of a system across its development lifecycle.

Over the past two decades, work has continued on HiP-HOPS and it has proven itself as a valuable lever for extending the corpus of research within dependable systems. For example, recently Papadopoulos et al. showed that dependable systems design and analysis does not have to rely solely on advances in formal logic by using less conventional bio-inspired evolutionary techniques by extending HiP-HOPS to include meta-heuristics [17] and Kabir et al. demonstrated that HiP-HOPS can be extended to create and analyse temporal fault trees using a systems architectural models [11] which can be used for constructing safety arguments.

Although HiP-HOPS has contributed to a steady stream of research and publications across the field of dependable systems analysis and design, the chief focus has been safety as an attribute of dependability. In terms of dependability it can be said the method presented here focuses on availability, confidentially and integrity, which are the composite properties that define security as an attribute of dependability [2].

Although alternative tooling for modelling SATs exists, such as SecurITree[4] and AttackTree[5], they do not provide the required functionality and integration to automatically generate Digital Dependability Identities. This concept is explained in Sect. 2.5.

2.5 Digital Dependability Identity

The Digital Dependability Identity (DDI) [21] is a modular, composable and executable dependability model that links system structure with dependability information. The DDI offers numerous benefits. It enables convenient translation and exchange of heterogeneous dependability models across different tools and techniques. It supports execution of model-agnostic evaluation on its models, which in turn enables automation of assessment and assurance activities during design and monitoring and supervision during operation. As security is an aspect of dependability, the DDI also aims to capture security risk, threats, requirements, measures and other associated models. The Open Dependability Exchange (ODE) metamodel[6] is the DDI's metamodel and includes specific provisions for modeling security-related concepts. In particular, the ODE includes a TARA package, whose definition can be seen in Fig. 4.

---

[3] http://hip-hops.eu/.

[4] https://www.amenaza.com/.

[5] https://www.isograph.com/software/attacktree/.

[6] https://github.com/DEIS-Project-EU/DDI-Scripting-Tools/tree/master/ODE_Metamodel.

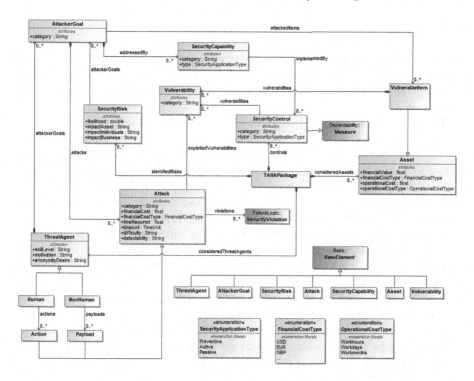

Fig. 4. ODE metamodel's TARA package definition

The package was defined drawing inspiration from the work in [15], as well as experience and deliberation across the DEIS project partners. The TARAPackage is the central containment unit, collecting security risks, measures, assets and 'Threat Agents' i.e. attackers under it. Risks are associated with the success of attacker goals, which are pursued via attacks, singular actions or payload executions. Attacks often exploit specific vulnerabilities that lie within the system's elements. Security capabilities and controls aim to address said vulnerabilities and safeguard the assets of a system.

Besides security aspects, the DDI can also encapsulate failure logic and reproduce fault trees, using an appropriate metamodel package. Analysis of DDI-embedded fault trees and failure logic is supported by HiP-HOPS. More details can be found via the DEIS project's public deliverable D4.2[7].

3   Approach

We base our approach on a top-down life cycle development process, wherein system concept informs functionality. Dependability requirements (including security) are identified and allocated to functions. The above pattern repeats as

---

[7] http://www.deis-project.eu/fileadmin/user_upload/DEIS_D4.2_Engineering_Tools_for_DDIs_V1_PU.pdf.

functions decompose into more refined systems until low-level software/hardware components are specified. Following this lifecycle process, security capabilities are initially mapped to high-level security requirements. As requirements mirror the decomposition of systems to subsystems and components, low-level security requirements are addressed by the selection and, eventually, implementation of security controls.

To guide the choice of security capability and control selection, the TARA or equivalent risk analysis process can be applied to evaluate sources of security risk against the system. Threat agents, potential vulnerabilities, vulnerable system elements and other factors can be accounted for as part of the TARA. However, a TARA initially only addresses risk at a relatively high-level; further detail necessary to address the inner workings and complex relationships within the system architecture requires more refined techniques applicable both vertically (from systems to components) as well as horizontally (across the entire architecture). As per Sect. 2.2, SATs are one such technique.

Following the TARA adopted by our approach, to launch a specific security attack, a threat agent must undertake a combination of actions or execution of payloads. The strategy of the attack is that security vulnerabilities in constituent system elements are exploited. The immediate effect of an action or payload execution can be viewed as a low-level event impacting security, referred to as a 'security violation'. Two examples of such a violation would be a malicious administrator introducing via portable storage and launching a malicious executable within an internal network. The attack in the example consists of an action - introduction of the executable by the malicious administrator - and a payload execution, each representing a security violation. Each security violation of the example can itself propagate and trigger further events. If security measures fail to address the chain of events, the attack is successful and the attacker's goal will eventually be reached, compromising one of the key assets that should have been protected.

Using SATs, the propagation logic that forms cause-effect chains of security violations to successful attacks can be described efficiently, with tool support providing all the benefits of model-based dependability analysis. What is required of the users is an appropriate annotation of the system architecture with local (i.e. per relevant system element) security violation propagation logic. Effectively, for each element that can contribute or is affected by the propagation of security violations, the user should assign appropriate Boolean logic linking combinations of incoming or generated to outgoing security violations. Once this process is complete, automated security attack tree analysis tools, such as HiP-HOPS, can be used to perform qualitative analysis. The result of such an analysis is the identification of the necessary and sufficient combinations of security violations that can lead to attacks successfully compromising system assets.

Once the analysis results are available, the mapping provided in Sect. 2.3 can be used to plan appropriate security controls. For the scope of the work presented here, the mapping process will be limited to a simple look-up and selection from the list of available controls. In general, numerous criteria can be included in the decision process e.g. functional, design and financial constraints. The decision process itself can apply optimization strategies, both manual and semi-automatic, for further improvement.

4   ONCOAssist Use Case

ONCOAssist[8] is a mobile platform (available on IOS, Android and in a web format) for oncology professionals. It gives them a number of clinical tools and validated medical information that helps clinicians make a more informed decision when treating patients with cancer. As a use case, a clinician uses ONCOassist to calculate the body surface area and the drug dosage to be administered to the patient. It has been created by Portable Medical Technology Ltd (PMT), which are located in Ireland.

ONCOAssist interacts with private patient data and the users' account data as well. Since PMT is based in Ireland, they are subject to the GDPR as set out by the EU. Failure to comply with GDPR could result in the penalties mentioned in Sect. 2.1. The penalties of violating GDPR regulation due to ineffective security assessment, along with the expected security requirements healthcare establishments would likely set on their own before using ONCOAssist, necessitates that rigorous security assurances are provided.

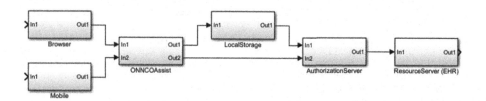

Fig. 5. ONCOAssist authentication system model

For brevity, authentication will be the focus of the case study, as the process can be illustrated using a relativity small system model. Before a user can perform any Create, Read, Update or Delete (CRUD) operations on the patient data stored in an Electronic Health Register (EHR), they must authenticate. Various open standards exist to be used as protocols for authentication. ONCOAssist uses OAuth2[9] with OpenID[10]. Using open standards such as these is often considered a good practice, as they have maximum exposure to public, third-party scrutiny [1].

1. *Establish a system model.* Following discussions with and using activity diagrams provided by PMT we were able to produce a simplified abstract system

---
[8] https://oncoassist.com/about/.
[9] https://oauth.net/2/.
[10] https://openid.net/.

model of ONCOAssist's authentication process using MATLAB, shown in Fig. 5. As seen in the figure, ONCOAssist can be accessed via a web application, with access to local device storage, authenticates with an authentication server, by requirement of the OAuth2 protocol, and finally retrieves patient data from a resource server, which is an EHR.

2. *Establish a suitable TARA.* Once we have established the system model, we can define feared events relevant to the system. In the case of ONCOAssist the feared events are data that becomes totally or partially compromised i.e. patient data that has been accessed to any extent by an unauthorised person.

3. *Apply the TARA to the system model using HiP-HOPS.* At this stage in the process, the system model is annotated with information gathered during the TARA using HiP-HOPS in conjunction with MATLAB's Simulink.

4. *Conduct qualitative analysis on the SAT produced by HiP-HOPS.* Once the model is annotated, HiP-HOPS can be used to produce the SATs shown in Fig. 6.

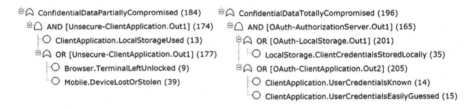

Fig. 6. ONCOAssist SATs generated by HiP-HOPS

5. *Refine the system model as necessary and repeat 1–4.* If necessary, further refinement can take place, depending on application, design and further considerations. For brevity, we limit our illustration to one iteration.

6. *Capture the TARA, SAT, HiP-HOPS results and system models within a DDI using the ODE.* As mentioned in Sect. 2.5, HiP-HOPS models can be exported as DDIs. Available tools developed by DEIS can convert embedded HiP-HOPS annotations into structures meaningful for DDIs such as the TARA and FailureLogic metamodel packages. Development of these tools is ongoing; an open-source version is available[11].

7. *Use the Security Capability-Control mapping to validate requirements and identify controls for the DDI.* Once the above information has been captured in a DDI, further tool support can be used to help requirements validation and appropriate control selection. Tool support developed by DEIS in this direction is provided in the form of executable scripts written in the Epsilon language[12]. Through Epsilon scripts, semi-automatic functionality

---

[11] https://github.com/DEIS-Project-EU/DDI-Scripting-Tools/tree/master/ODE_Tooladapter.

[12] https://www.eclipse.org/epsilon/.

can be designed and executed for DDIs generically. For instance, the process in Algorithm 1 described in pseudocode can be implemented in the Epsilon Object Language (EOL) [12] for validating security capabilities and proposing controls.

```
foreach AttackerGoal g in subjectDDI do
    if g.addressedBy.size() = 0 then g is not addressed
    else
        foreach SecurityCapability sc in g.addressedBy do
            if sc.category != g.category then sc inappropriate for g
            else
                if sc.implementedBy.size() = 0 then sc is not implemented
                else
                    foreach SecurityControl c in sc.implementedBy do
                        if c.category != sc.category then c inappropriate for sc
                        else c implements sc
                    end
                end
            end
        end
    end
end
```

Algorithm 1. Security Capability Validation Diagnostic Example

5   Discussion and Future Work

Security analysis and development can be an expensive process; for example, the development of the ONCOAssist authentication system discussed in Sect. 4 represents approximately 6 weeks of work-hours for their development team, per PMT's account. However, failure to complete adequate security analysis can have catastrophic consequences. Therefore, efforts towards minimising this cost without compromising the quality of analysis are worthwhile. Digital management of SATs streamlines the process of security analysis by enabling automation (Security measures/controls and cost/benefit analysis can be derived semi-automatically) and by reducing the risk of human error.

Our proposed approach does have some notable limitations. Using HiP-HOPS for security analysis requires that system owners create and maintain an appropriately annotated system model. Thus, errors introduced in the model may critically compromise the subsequent analysis. For instance, such errors may occur due to lack of synchronization between the model and the implemented software, obscuring potential vulnerabilities present in the implementation. A further limitation of the process we have described is the lack of support for run time preventative security actions to be taken.

In summary, security and threat analysis is a complex process, often governed by regulation and frameworks have emerged to deal with this complexity. SATs are a valuable tool for security analysis and have been extended to deal with a wide variety of use cases. HiP-HOPS was originally created as a tool for traditional safety analysis but can be used for security analysis as well. DDIs are used to model a system's dependability, encompassing security concerns such as availability, confidentially and integrity. The approach described in Sect. 3 and demonstrated in Sect. 4 can be used for semi-automated security analysis. Considering future work, we are focusing on addressing run time security concerns. Specifically, appropriate methods for reasoning, negotiating and executing dependability-critical services using DDIs are the subject of ongoing research, as part of DEIS.

Acknowledgements. This work was supported by the DEIS H2020 Project under Grant 732242.

References

1. Adam Freeman, A.J.: Programming .Net Security, 1 edn. O'Reilly Media, Sebastopol (2003)
2. Avizienis, A., Laprie, J.C., Randell, B., Landwehr, C.: Basic concepts and taxonomy of dependable and secure computing. IEEE Trans. Dependable Secur. Comput. **1**(1), 11–33 (2004)
3. Brooke, P.J., Paige, R.F.: Fault trees for security system design and analysis. Comput. Secur. **22**(3), 256–264 (2003)
4. Bugliesi, M., Calzavara, S., Focardi, R.: Formal methods for web security. J. Logical Algebraic Methods Program. **87**, 110–126 (2017)
5. Buldas, A., Laud, P., Priisalu, J., Saarepera, M., Willemson, J.: Rational choice of security measures via multi-parameter attack trees. In: Lopez, J. (ed.) CRITIS 2006. LNCS, vol. 4347, pp. 235–248. Springer, Heidelberg (2006). https://doi.org/10.1007/11962977_19
6. Cardenas, A.A., Amin, S., Sastry, S.: Secure control: towards survivable cyber-physical systems. In: 2008 The 28th International Conference on Distributed Computing Systems Workshops, pp. 495–500. IEEE (2008)
7. Chong, S., et al.: Report on the NSF workshop on formal methods for security. arXiv preprint arXiv:1608.00678 (2016)
8. De, S.J., Le Métayer, D.: PRIAM: a privacy risk analysis methodology. In: Livraga, G., Torra, V., Aldini, A., Martinelli, F., Suri, N. (eds.) DPM/QASA -2016. LNCS, vol. 9963, pp. 221–229. Springer, Cham (2016). https://doi.org/10.1007/978-3-319-47072-6_15
9. Joint Task Force Transformation Initiative: Security and privacy controls for federal information systems and organizations. Technical report NIST SP 800–53r4, National Institute of Standards and Technology (2013). https://doi.org/10.6028/NIST.SP.800-53r4, https://nvlpubs.nist.gov/nistpubs/SpecialPublications/NIST.SP.800-53r4.pdf
10. Joshi, A., Miller, S., Whalen, M., Heimdahl, M.: A proposal for model-based safety analysis. In: 24th Digital Avionics Systems Conference. IEEE (2005). https://doi.org/10.1109/dasc.2005.1563469

11. Kabir, S., et al.: A model-based extension to HiP-HOPS for dynamic fault propagation studies. In: Bozzano, M., Papadopoulos, Y. (eds.) IMBSA 2017. LNCS, vol. 10437, pp. 163–178. Springer, Cham (2017). https://doi.org/10.1007/978-3-319-64119-5_11

12. Kolovos, D.S., Paige, R.F., Polack, F.A.C.: The epsilon object language (EOL). In: Rensink, A., Warmer, J. (eds.) ECMDA-FA 2006. LNCS, vol. 4066, pp. 128–142. Springer, Heidelberg (2006). https://doi.org/10.1007/11787044_11

13. Kordy, B., Mauw, S., Radomirović, S., Schweitzer, P.: Foundations of attack-defense trees. In: Degano, P., Etalle, S., Guttman, J. (eds.) FAST 2010. LNCS, vol. 6561, pp. 80–95. Springer, Heidelberg (2011). https://doi.org/10.1007/978-3-642-19751-2_6

14. Lee, E.A.: Cyber physical systems: design challenges. In: 2008 11th IEEE International Symposium on Object and Component-Oriented Real-Time Distributed Computing (ISORC), pp. 363–369. IEEE (2008)

15. Oates, R., Thom, F., Herries, G.: Security-aware, model-based systems engineering with SysML. In: Proceedings of the 1st International Symposium on ICS & SCADA Cyber Security Research, pp. 78–87. BCS (2013)

16. Papadopoulos, Y., McDermid, J.A.: Hierarchically performed hazard origin and propagation studies. In: Felici, M., Kanoun, K. (eds.) SAFECOMP 1999. LNCS, vol. 1698, pp. 139–152. Springer, Heidelberg (1999). https://doi.org/10.1007/3-540-48249-0_13

17. Papadopoulos, Y., et al.: A synthesis of logic and bio-inspired techniques in the design of dependable systems. Ann. Rev. Control 41, 170–182 (2016)

18. Pasqualetti, F., Dörfler, F., Bullo, F.: Attack detection and identification in cyber-physical systems. IEEE Trans. Autom. Control 58(11), 2715–2729 (2013)

19. Rajkumar, R., Lee, I., Sha, L., Stankovic, J.: Cyber-physical systems: the next computing revolution. In: Design Automation Conference, pp. 731–736. IEEE (2010)

20. Rivera, J.: Cyber security via formal methods: a framework for implementing formal methods. In: 2017 International Conference on Cyber Conflict (CyCon US), pp. 76–81. IEEE (2017)

21. Schneider, D., Trapp, M., Papadopoulos, Y., Armengaud, E., Zeller, M., Höfig, K.: Wap: digital dependability identities. In: 2015 IEEE 26th International Symposium on Software Reliability Engineering (ISSRE), pp. 324–329. IEEE (2015)

22. Whitley, J.N., Phan, R.C.W., Wang, J., Parish, D.J.: Attribution of attack trees. Comput. Electr. Eng. 37(4), 624–628 (2011)

23. Yager, R.R.: Owa trees and their role in security modeling using attack trees. Inf. Sci. 176(20), 2933–2959 (2006). https://doi.org/10.1016/j.ins.2005.08.004, http://www.sciencedirect.com/science/article/pii/S0020025505002598

What Today's Serious Cyber Attacks on Cars Tell Us: Consequences for Automotive Security and Dependability

Markus Zoppelt$^{(\boxtimes)}$ and Ramin Tavakoli Kolagari

Nuremberg Institute of Technology, Hohfederstr. 40, 90489 Nuremberg, Germany
{markus.zoppelt,ramin.tavakolikolagari}@th-nuernberg.de

Abstract. Highly connected with the environment via various interfaces, cars have been the focus of malicious cyber attacks for years. These attacks are becoming an increasing burden for a society with growing vehicle autonomization: they are the sword of Damocles of future mobility. Therefore, research is particularly active in the area of vehicle IT security, and in part also in the area of dependability, in order to develop effective countermeasures and to maintain a minimum of one step ahead of hackers. This paper examines the known state-of-the-art security and dependability measures based on a detailed and systematic analysis of published cyber attacks on automotive software systems. The sobering result of the analysis of the cyber attacks with the model-based technique SAM (Security Abstraction Model) and a categorization of the examined attacks in relation to the known security and dependability measures is that most countermeasures against cyber attacks are hardly effective. They either are not applicable to the underlying problem or take effect too late; the intruder has already gained access to a substantial part of the vehicle when the countermeasures apply. The paper is thus contributing to an understanding of the gaps that exist today in the area of vehicle security and dependability and concludes concrete research challenges.

Keywords: Automotive security · Automotive system architecture · Dependability · Model-driven engineering methodologies

1 Introduction

The development of automobiles has ever been a subject to constant change. None of these changes, however, were as striking as the incorporation of software. Since the turn of the millennium, scientific contributions on software security of cars have been published [5,13,37]. Earlier publications are practically non-existent due to the scarcity of software in vehicles back then. One of the first systematic analyses of attacks on automotive (software) security [38, p. 6f] describes the prevailing attacks in the automotive sector as either theft or modification of critical components: for example, an attacker would like to achieve

© Springer Nature Switzerland AG 2019
Y. Papadopoulos et al. (Eds.): IMBSA 2019, LNCS 11842, pp. 270–285, 2019.
https://doi.org/10.1007/978-3-030-32872-6_18

financial gain by stealing the car or valuable components. Modification refers to the car owner that would like to change components (tuning), for example in order to increase the value of the car (reduced mileage) or decrease it for taxation reasons (increased mileage). The analysis also mentions that attackers want to steal competitors' expertise and intellectual property. The cyber attacks against vehicles presented in this paper show that the attack potential has increased considerably in the last decade due to the interconnectivity and architecture of modern vehicles. The described attack motivations and attacks from the early days of the rise of software in vehicles make up only a small fraction of today's hackers' motivations and attacks. In comparison to those of the past, attacks on modern vehicles are particularly worrying because attackers can take control of the entire vehicle. This often requires no or only short physical access. Our society, which is on the threshold of autonomous mobility, takes this challenge seriously. Therefore, research is very active in the field of vehicle IT security and partly also in the field of functional safety (dependability) in order to develop effective countermeasures. Cyber attack protection does not initially imply dependability; this paper will argue, though, that at the interface between dependability and security research, innovative protection mechanisms emerge just as capable of providing protection against malicious attacks as established security measures. The countermeasures published so far are manifold adaptations of classical IT security approaches in the area of automotive security, for example [3, 4, 7, 15, 18, 19, 23, 26, 30].

The remainder of this paper is structured as follows: Sect. 2 reviews the most effective attacks on automotive software systems. In Sect. 3 we describe typical automotive security and dependability mechanisms and analyse their protection potential with respect to the published attacks described earlier. Section 4 gives an overview of related work in this field. In our conclusion in Sect. 5, we provide indications for future research challenges in the area of automotive security and dependability.

2 Attacks on Automotive Software Systems

In this section we first present the Security Abstraction Model (SAM) [40] and the Common Vulnerability Scoring System (CVSS) [20] for evaluating and analysing attack vectors on automotive software systems. Afterwards, we give an overview of today's serious attacks on modern, highly connected vehicles.

2.1 SAM and CVSS

In an earlier publication, we introduced SAM, a Security Abstraction Model for automotive software systems. SAM allows for a security analysis of automotive attack vectors. Systematic security analyses can be used to quantify the required effort for a potential attack. The approach tightly couples security management and model-based systems engineering by an abstract description of automotive security modeling principles. The resulting SAM language specification is based on security requirements elicited from common industrial scenarios. It is a suitable solution for representing attack vectors on vehicles and provides a thorough security modeling for the automotive industry. SAM has a close connection to the architecture description via the coupling of *Item* from the architecture model. SAM attack models express all important criteria of attack vectors—from an adversary's motivation up until a breach—to allow for system's modeling in an early software engineering phase. Besides attack motivations, SAM also describes all intrinsic and temporal properties of an attack, e.g., impact on security goals (confidentiality, availability, integrity, etc.), attack complexity, affected item and the attackable property. SAM can be used with generic security scoring systems for attack rating like, e.g., the Common Vulnerability Scoring System (CVSS). The CVSS is an acclaimed industry standard for rating vulnerabilities in computer systems and proposes three different metric groups for calculating the vulnerability scores. The Base Metric Group reflects the intrinsic properties of an attack: from SAM's automotive-oriented perspective, this group therefore indicates the characteristics that result when the attack in question is aimed at the automotive domain in general. The Temporal Metric Group allows for adjustment of the score after more information of the exploited vulnerability is available. The CVSS provides an online calculator [1] where specific vulnerabilities can be referenced with a unique CVSS vector string. We will provide those vector strings below every SAM model of the respective attack. Readers who are interested in the attack properties of specific attacks are able to check them on the online calculator. The additional benefit of having SAM models compared to directly giving the properties and a vulnerability score is that not only the CVSS (or scoring systems in general) is used, but also the possibility to construct attack trees via sub-attacks and follow-up attacks. SAM is also a method for hierarchical processing of attack vectors. In terms of substance, this goes beyond the classic attack rating. SAM makes the scoring system available to the software architect or in other words: SAM's strength lies in its ability to integrate with existing automotive architectures. What is brought together are architectural considerations with pure security considerations as regards the attack itself (attack vectors that can be derived from it, motivations, target areas) and all scoring systems that are known, which can derive all necessary information from the properties.

2.2 Overview of the Attacks

Scientific contributions on software security in cars publish a large number of attacks on automotive software systems. Table 1 gives an overview of the most serious of the published attacks on modern, highly connected vehicles. The selection of the attacks was made strictly according to the following attack characteristics: The selected attacks (1) are aiming at a broad range of security goals, ideally all security goals, and (2) have high severity levels (CVSS Temporal Score greater than 4.0). The CVSS Vector String is omitted in the table, but is shown below each of the figures of the attack models later in this paper. For the purposes of this study, we differentiate between *gateway attacks* and *follow-up attacks*. Gateway attacks usually change the extent of a vulnerability and typically serve as door openers, enabling the adversary to launch one or more follow-up attacks. A typical follow-up attack would be to reverse Controller Area Network (CAN) bus messages to learn how the vehicle's Electrical Control Units (ECUs) communicate and injecting malicious messages into the system. Some follow-up attacks are just as trivial as starting Denial-of-Service (DoS) attacks. Many follow-up attacks are fairly high-level though, e.g., remotely driving/steering the car, disturbing functions of the vehicle or disabling driver-assisting systems.

Table 1. The most serious attacks, sorted by CVSS [20] Temporal Score

Attack	AttackableProperty	Item	Score
Tesla Remote Control	Webkit Browser	Autopilot ECU	8.0/7.2
SecurityAccess via UDS	Substandard ciphers	Body Control Module	7.1/6.7
CAN Message Injection	(Multiple)	Pow. Steer. Contr. Mod	7.0/6.5
BMW Remote Diagnostics	NBT Backdoor	Infotainment Domain	7.1/6.4
Control via OBD Injection	Clear CAN traffic	Diagnostics	7.7/6.3
Telematics Attack	SSH, SMS	Telematics Control Unit	6.4/6.1
Remote Keyless Entry	Rolling Code	Remote Keyless Entry	5.7/5.4
CAN DoS Attack	CAN Protocol	Any CAN bus	4.6/4.5

2.3 Tesla Remote Control Attack

One of the most serious attacks is the Tesla Remote Control Attack [24,25,35]. This gateway attack enables an adversary to break into the AutoPilot ECU (APE) via the Webkit Browser of the infotainment unit. The researchers of Tencent Keen Security Lab [35] have demonstrated how to remotely control and steer the vehicle, disturbing the autowipers by confusing the machine learning (ML) component with a technique called adversarial examples [11,29] and eliminating the lane detection of the vehicle. The following is a brief explanation of the entities shown in Fig. 1: The adversary in this scenario is a remote attacker with the attack motivation to harm car occupants by crashing the vehicle. The attack is possible when the mode of the vehicle is "Slow or Standing". The exploited vehicle feature is Tesla's Autopilot, specifically the item AutoPilot ECU (APE). The exploited vulnerability is the Webkit browser framework of the infotainment unit which offers the JSArray function. This function is the attackable property the adversary is looking for, i.e., his anchor of the attack. After analysing with the attack properties via the CVSS metrics, one can calculate the base score and temporal score of the attack and derive the requirement: code signing protection for over-the-air (OTA) updates.

For the remaining attacks in this paper, further textual explanation of the models is omitted. Readers might refer to the explanation of the entities of this attack or look at SAM/CVSS references.

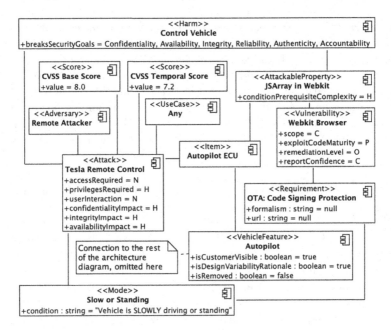

Fig. 1. SAM model of Tesla Remote Control Attack—CVSS v3.0 Vector String: CVSS:3.0/AV:N/AC:H/PR:H/UI:N/S:C/C:H/I:H/A:H/E:P/RL:O/RC:C

2.4   Security Access via UDS Attack

Many security-sensitive preferences or functions of a vehicle are secured via the Unified Diagnostic Service (UDS). Getting advanced security access to an ECU makes it possible for an adversary to fully reprogram the respective ECU or get confidential information out of the ECU's secure memory, what makes this attack a gateway attack. In contrast to the Tesla Remote Control attack, the attack motivation is product modification. The Security Access via UDS Attack as shown by den Herrewegen [12] is illustrated in the SAM model in Fig. 2.

2.5   CAN Message Injection Attack

Miller and Valasek's [36] attack on an unaltered passenger vehicle [21] was widely discussed in research and press. A CAN Message Injection Attack [22] is one of the logical consequences after a successful gateway attack. After an adversary has gained access to the powertrain, he can reverse engineer the messages communicated via the bus and inject his own malicious messages of choice. Once an adversary has the ability to send arbitrary network messages (e.g., via CAN) he is able to control the braking system, engine behaviours or the air vents, (un-)lock the doors, etc. Therefore, there is a strong need to secure the vehicle before the adversary can even gain access to the bus as then it is already too late. Figure 3 illustrates the CAN message injection attack in SAM.

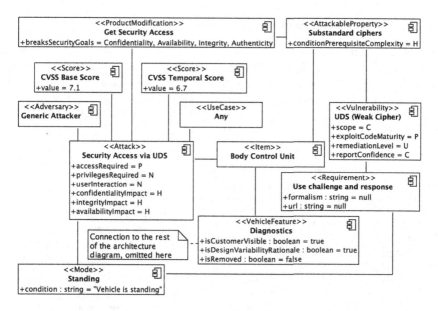

Fig. 2. SAM model of Security Access via UDS Attack—CVSS v3.0 Vector String: CVSS:3.0/AV:P/AC:H/PR:N/UI:N/S:C/C:H/I:H/A:H/E:P/RL:U/RC:C

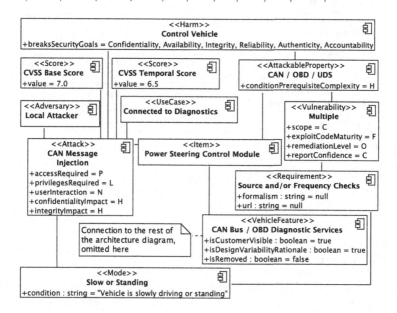

Fig. 3. SAM model of CAN Message Injection Attack—CVSS v3.0 Vector String: CVSS:3.0/AV:P/AC:H/PR:L/UI:N/S:C/C:H/I:H/A:H/E:F/RL:O/RC:C

2.6 BMW Remote Diagnostics Attack

The BMW Remote Diagnostics Attack [34] is the second attack by Tencent Keen Security Lab on our list. It is a hybrid of the Tesla Remote Control attack and the UDS Security Access attack. The researchers were able to control a BMW after exploiting a back door in the in-vehicle infotainment system (also known as NBT Head Unit). This was possible because UDS was not locked at high speed. This gateway attack is shown as a SAM model in Fig. 4.

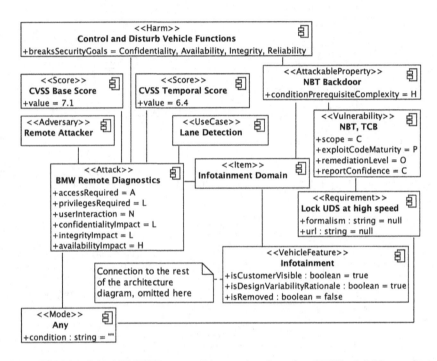

Fig. 4. SAM model of BMW Remote Diagnostics Attack—CVSS v3.0 Vector String: CVSS:3.0/AV:A/AC:H/PR:L/UI:N/S:C/C:L/I:L/A:H/E:P/RL:O/RC:C

2.7 OBD Injection Attack

On-board diagnostics (OBD) is a vehicle's self-diagnostic and reporting capability for vehicles. Over the OBD port, which is easily accessible inside the vehicle, many simple attack vectors are possible, especially in older car models, where OBD injection attacks [39] are astoundingly easy to perform gateway attacks. The SAM model of such an attack is omitted here. CVSS v3.0 Vector String: CVSS:3.0/AV:L/AC:L/PR:N/UI:N/S:U/C:H/I:N/A:H/E:U/RL:W/RC:U

2.8   Telematics Attack

A large part of the remote attack surface of a modern vehicle is determined by telematics units. A potential adversary might use software defined radios or similar tools for remote exploitation of said telematics to obtain access to a device connected to the CAN bus or similar powertrain as a gateway attack. Foster [8] describes an example telematics attack. The SAM model is omitted here. CVSS v3.0 Vector String: CVSS:3.0/AV:N/AC:H/PR:L/UI:N/S:U/C:H/I:L/A:L/E:P/RL:U

2.9   Remote Keyless Entry Attack

Almost every modern vehicle has the ability for "keyless entry" or "keyless start engine". Those convenience features raise security risks as they provoke a gateway attack as shown by Garcia et al. [9]. With common hardware and low-level software skills, potential adversaries are able to unlock, open or start foreign vehicles after capturing and decoding radio signals for a Remote Keyless Entry Attack. The SAM model for this attack is omitted here as this particular attack is extensively described in various literature. CVSS v3.0 Vector String: CVSS:3.0/AV:A/AC:L/PR:N/UI:R/S:U/C:H/I:N/A:N/E:H/RL:W/RC:R

2.10   CAN DoS Attack

One of the simplest but highly safety-critical follow-up attack is a CAN DoS Attack as described by Palanca et al. [28]. Due to the CAN protocol definition, CAN bus messages are arbitrated by ID. Lower IDs, i.e., with more starting zeros, have higher priority than higher IDs. In a simple sense, spamming the bus with messages that have a lower ID leads to network constipation and is the equivalent to a classic denial-of-service attack. The SAM model for this attack is omitted here as well, as its vulnerability and attackable property are widely known. CVSS v3.0 Vector String: CVSS:3.0/AV:P/AC:L/PR:N/UI:N/S:U/C:N/I:N/A:H/E:H/RL:W/RC:C

3   Countermeasures and Analysis

In this section we describe typical automotive security and dependability mechanisms and analyse their protection potential with respect to the published attacks described in Sect. 2. The result of the analysis of the relationship between attacks on vehicle security and the protection potential of countermeasures is presented in Table 2. It shows that message cryptography, as a popular representative of software security, is only effective for a small part of the attacks as a protection measure. Lesser known representatives can partially compensate, but overall, it can be stated that there are no adequate security protection mechanisms for some serious and well-known attacks on automotive software.

3.1   Message Cryptography (MC)

Message cryptography entails encryption, authentication and verification of messages communicated over the vehicle's bus, e.g., CAN, LIN, Flexray, Automotive Ethernet, etc. Message cryptography is an immensely large field of research and a big amount of apparent solutions does exist [3,4,19,23,26,30]. Unfortunately, reliable and adaptive key distribution in heterogeneous automotive bus networks is a difficult challenge. Keys need to be distributed, updated and revoked in case of some soft- or hardware-updates. For some attacks, even properly implemented cryptography would offer just a partial protection, e.g., authenticity for CAN messages but no confidentiality due to the network topology. If an attacker gains access to an ECU, she might also retrieve the cryptographic keys. Cryptographically verifying messages would pose an obstacle for connecting rogue devices to the bus but would not mitigate remote attack scenarios.

3.2   ID Hopping (IDH)

ID Hopping is a technique to obfuscate network bindings or messages by changing ("hopping") between arbitration IDs without changing the actual arbitration. Order preserving encryption (OPE) is also considered as ID Hopping. This technique is also widely explored in the research field of automotive network security [15,18,19] and hinders adversaries to easily reverse engineer network messages.

3.3   Challenge and Response (CR)

Challenge and response is a common technique used widely in the security and network domain, though it is disturbingly unpopular in the automotive domain. Physical car keys (keyfobs) mostly still use a rolling code system when transmitting, enabling adversaries with mediocre skills and a software defined radio to perform replay or relay attacks. Those could easily be mitigated by using a challenge and response mechanism. Unfortunately, keyfobs are not equipped with the necessary hardware components due to financial reasons in the automotive industry.

3.4   ECU Hardening (ECUH)

ECU Hardening stops the adversary to change the state of the flashed software in any way. A popular application of ECU hardening is "Autonomous Security" and "Karamba Carwall" by Karamba Security [7] which hardens ECUs based on factory settings, eliminating the risks of false positives, detection delays, and performance drag issues. ECU hardening relies heavily on static analysis of the factory settings and firmware. It seems that this security mechanism is not really inquired by researchers but popular in the industry, as it is easy to implement and does not require increased effort.

3.5 Run Time Correctness (RTC)

Synergies between safety and security are exploited in the area of fault tolerance and software protection by tamper-tolerant software [16]. Shared approaches are developed to get programs run-time error free [10, p. 9ff]. While dependability aims at protection against systematic errors and random errors caused by malfunction or unintended interference, security additionally wants to protect against targeted, intended and possibly malicious manipulation. According to Kriha [17, p. 13f], security attacks are input or output related. This can be made verifiable by, e.g., validation frameworks. It must be stated, though, that the availability of complete frameworks for validation is generally rather deficient. Today's security vulnerabilities rarely lie in cryptographic algorithms or protocols but are almost always implementation-related, e.g., wrongly chosen (weak) ciphers or keys, memory safety, the inability to update software over-the-air, wrongly configured network interfaces, and more. Lists like the "Recent Vulnerability Notes" [2] demonstrate that vividly. Techniques like Voting could mitigate attacks that happen at random or are bound by probability, e.g., botnet attacks.

3.6 Integrity Protection (IP)

Dependability measures insist on maintaining integrity through redundancy checks, i.e., repeatedly or concurrently sending messages on the bus, checking ECU state, double computing, etc. Integrity checks for data through redundancy requires an adversary to compromise more individual pinpoints in order to break the security goal integrity.

3.7 Virtualisation (V)

Virtualisation as a dependability and security measure, e.g., running applications of different automotive safety integrity levels (ASIL) on different virtual computers can be used to virtually draw a line between applications and networks to seal off applications who are safety-critical from functionally unrelated applications. Glas et al. [10, p. 12f] show that virtualisation may serve as a measure for both dependability and security. Rosenstatter [32, p.4] and Othmane [27] also describe virtualisation and Virtual Local Area Networks (VLANs) as a possible solution for access control. The biggest benefit of virtualisation is, that it limits the scope of a vulnerability to U (unchanged), as it is isolated in the virtualised sandbox. The scope of a vulnerability is changed, if an attack impacts more than the vulnerable component. That means, that if the scope is unchanged, an attacker is not able to start a successful follow-up attack. Furthermore, lean use of virtualisation could obliterate lacking CAN authenticity, as standard CAN messages alone have no assignable source identifier.

3.8   Analysis and Mapping of Countermeasures on Attacks

The analysis of the respectively selected attacks (cf. Sect. 2.2) does not have to be very detailed in order to reveal the obvious mismatch between largely proposed countermeasures and their effective protection in practice. In this section we describe this mentioned mismatch by mapping effective countermeasures proposed by academic research to the selected attacks. This mapping shows that the most researched countermeasure (MC) is only effective in less than half of the attacks. The first discussed attack (Tesla Remote Control Attack) is analyzed both in text and in an illustrating figure. Due to the strict space limits, illustrations for the other attacks are omitted, but the analyses are always textually described.

The essential element of the Tesla Remote Attack is the access to the APE via exploiting Webkit, which must be capable of being updated from offboard. MC cannot help here, because it is about the exchange of an entire component. ECUH could completely prevent this attack, but does not offer any flexibility with regard to updates. V could at least limit the scope of the vulnerability from an unacceptable C to a U (see CVSS), requiring much more attack effort.

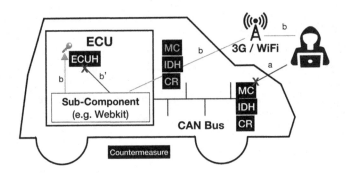

Fig. 5. Adversary attacking an ECU by-passing countermeasures (a) via an unprotected communication channel (b). ECUH (b') would have prevented the attack

Although, some countermeasures prevent adversaries from accessing or successfully attacking a system, some attacks, engineer the attack vector around the countermeasure applied by targeting a sub-component of a system via unprotected communication channels and systematically traverse the system from the inside out. For example, in the Tesla remote attack, the adversaries could not directly access the secret key embedded in the ECU via network (a) so they first compromised the unprotected and vulnerable webkit framework (b) and got access to the key by-passing other countermeasures. In the (b) scenario, MC is used but does not stop the attacker because it is used as intended. IDH cannot be used because the channel is not a bus. CR cannot be applied either. If ECUH was in place for the (b) scenario then it would have prevented the attack (illustrated as (b') in Fig. 5). The dependability measures are not depicted because they are too complex to be captured in an illustrating figure.

The SecurityAccess via UDS attack is possible because a weak cipher for the security challenge was chosen. A strong cipher in the UDS protocol would mitigate such an attack. In addition, IP could at least determine, that an ECU has been tampered with as integrity checks fail.

CAN message injection is one of the most researched attacks because the topology of the CAN bus allows rogue participants of the network to send arbitrary messages to the bus. Unfortunately, MC quickly reaches its limits due to the complex network topology and then can only if at all be used for partial encryption or authentication. V, however, could virtually separate critical applications, thereby mitigating cross-ECU message injection, maybe even offering some authenticity on top of the CAN protocol. V can also help in the case of the BMW Remote Diagnostics Attack for the same reason. Plus, ECUH would prevent attackers from tampering with the ECU firmware through diagnostic protocols. RTC can be used to limit the ability to corrupt software functions over diagnostic protocols.

The Control via OBD Injection attack shows many parallels to the CAN Message Injection attack, though it is in this case possible to prevent the attack with IDH or IP. IDH makes it harder for the attacker to reverse-engineer and send valid messages to the car, while IP would recognize that some injected messages are outliers.

Telematics attacks are very similar to CAN Message Injection attacks, except that their gateway attack vector, i.e., the actual telematics unit, can be secured better with MC, because their protocols are not entirely automotive specific. The Remote Keyless Entry attack is actually already a solved problem, using CR. Unfortunately, industry (hardware) pricing policies prevent this solution from being used. Coming up with a software-only solution is a much sought-after research challenge.

CAN DoS attacks are possible because of CAN's arbitration characteristic. They cannot be stopped with MC or other security countermeasures. It is possible, though, to use RTC techniques, e.g., watchdogs to prevent such attacks.

Table 2 shows that MC—where the majority of research is conducted—does not mitigate all of the top attacks. The attacks and countermeasures discussed in up-to-date research papers are—while being interesting in academia—not feasible in industrial automotive software. The attacks most successful in practice are usually not prevented by typical published security research results. Fortunately, dependability measures (RTC, IP, V) would offer some remarkable protections against the majority of our investigated attacks.

4   Related Work

Rosenstatter and Olovsson [32] provide a mapping between automotive security mechanisms and security levels in great detail. Auernhammer et al. [6] use a systematic mapping of published attacks on ML components on the security goals violated in autonomous vehicles. Their research shows that accountability (for ML) is not covered by literature as there have not yet been any attacks

Table 2. Analysis of automotive security and dependability countermeasures with respect to attacks against automotive software systems. We distinguish between security (left) and dependability (right) countermeasures. The X indicates a feasible protection; (X) indicates a partial protection

Attack	MC	IDH	CR	ECUH	RTC	IP	V
Tesla Remote Control [24,25,35]				X	X	X	X
SecurityAccess via UDS [12]	X					(X)	
CAN Message Injection [21,22,36]	(X)						X
BMW Remote Diagnostics [34]				X	X		X
Control via OBD Injection [39]	X	X				X	X
Telematics Attack [8]	X						X
Remote Keyless Entry [9]			X				
CAN DoS Attack [28]					X		

published, because accountability for ML is difficult to attack and the security goal is, therefore, not compulsory. Moreover, the work of Ray [31] lists practice and challenges in automotive security, discussing the need for extensibility and the constraints and considerations involved in achieving it. Huber's survey [14] shows how organizations from the automotive industry in the Euroregion tackle the challenge of integrating dependability and security aspects during system development. Their conclusion is that the utilization of a conceptual model unifying relevant documentation artifacts from requirements engineering, system modeling, risk assessment and evidence documentation could address these issues. We addressed this by using SAM as a modeling technique. Finally, the six-step model for integrating autonomous vehicle safety and security analysis by Sabaliauskaite [33] achieves and maintains integration and alignment among safety and security artefacts throughout the entire AV life-cycle.

5   Conclusion

In this paper, we analyzed today's serious attacks with the model-based technique SAM and ranked them with the CVSS. The result of our study shows a revealing spectrum that research can actively take up and investigate. It is interesting that the majority of today's automotive security research is focused on (message) cryptography, which does not mitigate an essential part of the top attacks, although many other countermeasures offer advantages that should not be neglected. A highly topical research challenge is flexible extensibility, which at the same time provides protection against arbitrary manipulation (like ECUH) and would generally be a helpful approach for OTA updates. Moreover, it turned out that virtualisation is a promising countermeasure against attacks. A possible research challenge is a lean system for (embedded) virtualisation, as it limits the scope of the vulnerability and can obliterate some of the weaknesses in automotive security, e.g., CAN authenticity. Future research challenges should also focus on a combination of security and dependability countermeasures to provide adequate and flexible protection against cyber attacks on cars, e.g., mixing ECUH with extensibility or updatability enabled via cryptography. Autonomous vehicles in the future will probably be more susceptible to attacks than today's cars already are. Our work aims to offer the necessary insights and fundamentals to continue conducting relevant research in this domain.

Acknowledgment. This work is funded by the Bavarian State Ministry of Science and the Arts in the framework of the Centre Digitisation.Bavaria (ZD.B).

M.Z. was supported by the BayWISS Consortium Digitization.

References

1. Common Vulnerability Scoring System Version 3.0 Calculator. https://www.first.org/cvss/calculator/3.0. Accessed 14 May 2019
2. Vulnerability Notes Database. http://www.kb.cert.org/vuls/. Accessed 29 Oct 2014
3. Nürnberger, S., Rossow, C.: vatiCAN: vetted, authenticated CAN bus. In: Gierlichs, B., Poschmann, A.Y. (eds.) CHES 2016. LNCS, vol. 9813, pp. 106–124. Springer, Heidelberg (2016). https://doi.org/10.1007/978-3-662-53140-2_6
4. Agrawal, M., Huang, T., Zhou, J., Chang, D.: CAN-FD-Sec: improving security of CAN-FD protocol. In: Hamid, B., Gallina, B., Shabtai, A., Elovici, Y., Garcia-Alfaro, J. (eds.) CSITS 2018, ISSA 2018. LNCS, vol. 11552, pp. 77–93. Springer, Cham (2019). https://doi.org/10.1007/978-3-030-16874-2_6
5. Amendola, S.: Improving automotive security by evaluation-from security health check to common criteria. White paper, Security Research & Consulting GmbH 176 (2004)
6. Auernhammer, K., Tavakoli Kolagari, R., Zoppelt, M.: Attacks on machine learning: lurking danger for accountability. In: Proceedings of the AAAI Workshop on Artificial Intelligence Safety 2019 co-located with the Thirty-Third AAAI Conference on Artificial Intelligence 2019 (AAAI 2019), Honolulu, Hawaii, p. 9 (2019)
7. Barzilai, D.: Autonomous Security, pp. 1–14 (2018)
8. Foster, I., Prudhomme, A., Koscher, K., Savage, S.: Fast and vulnerable: a story of telematic failures. In: 9th USENIX Workshop on Offensive Technologies (WOOT 15) (2015)
9. Garcia, F.D., Oswald, D., Kasper, T., Pavlidès, P.: Lock it and still lose it–on the (in)security of automotive remote keyless entry systems. In: Proceedings of the 25th USENIX Security Symposium, pp. 929–944 (2016)
10. Glas, B., et al.: Automotive safety and security integration challenges. In: Automotive-Safety & Security 2014 (2015)
11. Hayes, J., Danezis, G.: Machine Learning as an Adversarial Service: Learning Black-Box Adversarial Examples **2** (2017)
12. Van den Herrewegen, J., Garcia, F.D.: Beneath the bonnet: a breakdown of diagnostic security. In: Lopez, J., Zhou, J., Soriano, M. (eds.) ESORICS 2018. LNCS, vol. 11098, pp. 305–324. Springer, Cham (2018). https://doi.org/10.1007/978-3-319-99073-6_15
13. Hubaux, J.P., Capkun, S., Luo, J.: The security and privacy of smart vehicles. IEEE Secur. Privacy **3**, 49–55 (2004)

14. Huber, M., Brunner, M., Sauerwein, C., Carlan, C., Breu, R.: Roadblocks on the highway to secure cars: an exploratory survey on the current safety and security practice of the automotive industry. In: Gallina, B., Skavhaug, A., Bitsch, F. (eds.) SAFECOMP 2018. LNCS, vol. 11093, pp. 157–171. Springer International Publishing, Cham (2018). https://doi.org/10.1007/978-3-319-99130-6_11

15. Humayed, A., Luo, B.: Using ID-hopping to defend against targeted DoS on CAN. In: Proceedings of the 1st International Workshop on Safe Control of Connected and Autonomous Vehicles - SCAV 2017, pp. 19–26 (2017)

16. Jakubowski, M.H., Saw, C.W.N., Venkatesan, R.: Tamper-tolerant software: modeling and implementation. In: Takagi, T., Mambo, M. (eds.) IWSEC 2009. LNCS, vol. 5824, pp. 125–139. Springer, Heidelberg (2009). https://doi.org/10.1007/978-3-642-04846-3_9

17. Kriha, W., Schmitz, R.: Sichere Systeme: Konzepte, Architekturen und Frameworks. Springer, Heidelberg (2009). https://doi.org/10.1007/978-3-540-78959-8

18. Lukasiewycz, M., Mundhenk, P., Steinhorst, S.: Security-aware obfuscated priority assignment for automotive CAN platforms. ACM Trans. Des. Autom. Electron. Syst. 21(2), 1–27 (2016)

19. Madl, T., Brückmann, J., Hof, H.J.: CAN Obfuscation by Randomization (CANORa) A technology to prevent large-scale malware attacks on driverless autonomous vehicles (September), 1–7 (2018)

20. Mell, P., Scarfone, K., Romanosky, S.: Common vulnerability scoring system. IEEE Secur. Privacy 4(6), 85–89 (2006)

21. Miller, C., Valasek, C.: Remote exploitation of an unaltered passenger vehicle. In: Defcon 23 2015, pp. 1–91 (2015). http://illmatics.com/Remote%20Car%20Hacking.pdf

22. Miller, C., Valasek, C.: CAN message injection, pp. 1–29 (2016). http://illmatics.com/canmessageinjection.pdf

23. Mundhenk, P., et al.: Security in automotive networks: lightweight authentication and authorization (2017)

24. Nie, S., Liu, L., Du, Y.: Free-fall: hacking tesla from wireless to CAN bus. In: Defcon, pp. 1–16 (2017)

25. Nie, S., Liu, L., Du, Y., Zhang, W.: Over-the-air: how we remotely compromised the gateway, BCM, and autopilot ECUs of tesla cars. In: Defcon 1 (2018)

26. Nowdehi, N., Lautenbach, A., Olovsson, T.: In-vehicle CAN message authentication: an evaluation based on industrial criteria. In: 2017 IEEE 86th Vehicular Technology Conference (VTC-Fall), pp. 1–7. IEEE (2017)

27. Othmane, L.B., Weffers, H., Mohamad, M.M., Wolf, M.: A survey of security and privacy in connected vehicles. In: Benhaddou, D., Al-Fuqaha, A. (eds.) Wireless Sensor and Mobile Ad-Hoc Networks, pp. 217–247. Springer, New York (2015). https://doi.org/10.1007/978-1-4939-2468-4_10

28. Palanca, A., Evenchick, E., Maggi, F., Zanero, S.: A stealth, selective, link-layer denial-of-service attack against automotive networks. In: Polychronakis, M., Meier, M. (eds.) DIMVA 2017. LNCS, vol. 10327, pp. 185–206. Springer, Cham (2017). https://doi.org/10.1007/978-3-319-60876-1_9

29. Papernot, N., McDaniel, P., Goodfellow, I.: Transferability in Machine Learning: From Phenomena to Black-Box Attacks Using Adversarial Samples (2016)

30. Radu, A.-I., Garcia, F.D.: LeiA: a lightweight authentication protocol for CAN. In: Askoxylakis, I., Ioannidis, S., Katsikas, S., Meadows, C. (eds.) ESORICS 2016. LNCS, vol. 9879, pp. 283–300. Springer, Cham (2016). https://doi.org/10.1007/978-3-319-45741-3_15

31. Ray, S., Chen, W., Bhadra, J., Al Faruque, M.A.: Extensibility in automotive security: current practice and challenges. In: 2017 54th ACM/EDAC/IEEE Design Automation Conference (DAC), pp. 1–6, June 2017

32. Rosenstatter, T., Olovsson, T.: Towards a standardized mapping from automotive security levels to security mechanisms. In: IEEE Conference on Intelligent Transportation Systems, Proceedings, ITSC 2018-November, pp. 1501–1507 (2018)

33. Sabaliauskaite, G., Liew, L.S., Cui, J.: Integrating autonomous vehicle safety and security analysis using STPA method and the six-step model. Int. J. Adv. Secur. 11(1&2), 160–169 (2018)

34. Tencent Keen Security Lab: Experimental Security Assessment of BMW Cars: A Summary Report (2018)

35. Tencent Keen Security Lab: Experimental Security Research of Tesla Autopilot, p. 38 (2019)

36. Valasek, C., Miller, C.: Adventures in automotive networks and control units. Technical White Paper 21, 99 (2013)

37. Wolf, M., Weimerskirch, A., Paar, C.: Security in automotive bus systems. In: Workshop on Embedded Security in Cars (2004)

38. Wolf, M., Weimerskirch, A., Wollinger, T.: State of the art: embedding security in vehicles. EURASIP J. Embedded Syst. 2007(1), 74706 (2007)

39. Zhang, Y., Ge, B., Li, X., Shi, B., Li, B.: Controlling a car through OBD injection. In: Proceedings - 3rd IEEE International Conference on Cyber Security and Cloud Computing, CSCloud 2016 and 2nd IEEE International Conference of Scalable and Smart Cloud, SSC 2016, pp. 26–29 (2016)

40. Zoppelt, M., Tavakoli Kolagari, R.: SAM: a security abstraction model for automotive software systems. In: Hamid, B., Gallina, B., Shabtai, A., Elovici, Y., Garcia-Alfaro, J. (eds.) CSITS/ISSA -2018. LNCS, vol. 11552, pp. 59–74. Springer, Cham (2019). https://doi.org/10.1007/978-3-030-16874-2_5

Safety and Security Aspects of Fail-Operational Urban Surround perceptION (FUSION)

Georg Macher[1]([✉])([iD]), Norbert Druml[2], Omar Veledar[3], and Jakob Reckenzaun[4]

[1] Graz University of Technology, Graz, Austria
`georg.macher@tugraz.at`
[2] Infineon Austria, Graz, Austria
`norbert.druml@infineon.com`
[3] AVL GmbH, Graz, Austria
`omar.veledar@avl.com`
[4] Virtual Vehicle Competence Center, Graz, Austria
`jakob.reckenzaun@v2c2.at`

Abstract. Among the strong trends that are impacting society, autonomous driving stands out clearly as one of the prime candidates to cause disruptive changes in automotive industry. Fully automated driving is identified as a major enabler for mastering the grand societal challenges of safe, clean, and efficient mobility. A major probation for highly automated driving is the step change from partial to conditional automation and above. At these high levels of automation, the driver is unable to intervene in a timely and appropriate manner. Consequently, the automation must be capable of independently handling safety-critical situations. Fail-operational behavior is essential at all layers of automated driving. These layers include sensing, computation and vehicle architecture. The PRYSTINE project targets realization of Fail-operational Urban Surround perceptION (FUSION), based on robust Radar and LiDAR sensor fusion, and control functions enabling safe automated driving. PRYSTINE addresses development and validation of new fail operational platforms, as well as high performing and dependable sensor fusion on different levels. In this paper, an overview of fail-operational approaches on different layers (vehicle and sensor level) is provided, together with a description of the interplay between safety and security aspects. It is further enhanced with description of a fail-operational sensor-fusion framework on component and system level.

Keywords: Safety · Security · Fail-operational · Sensor-fusion · Autonomous driving

1 Introduction

The automotive industry has been a synonym for innovative solutions and concepts from its beginnings through to the present day. The European automotive

© Springer Nature Switzerland AG 2019
Y. Papadopoulos et al. (Eds.): IMBSA 2019, LNCS 11842, pp. 286–300, 2019.
https://doi.org/10.1007/978-3-030-32872-6_19

sector currently secures 12.2 million jobs and is provides significant efforts and finances for R&D activities [10]. Among all current development trends that will affect society radically in the coming years, autonomous driving stands out as having the potential to disruptively change the automotive industry as we know it. Fully automated driving is identified as a major enabler for mastering the grand societal challenges of safe, clean, and efficient mobility. This implies that the automotive domain is undergoing dramatic changes, where complex tasks that were traditionally performed by the human driver are gradually being automated. In order to provide fault-free operation and to deal with rapidly revolutionizing and unforeseen tasks and environments, these automation systems need to continuously adapt, learn, and improve.

For user acceptance, the human users demand trustworthy, safe, and secure – or for short: dependable – autonomous vehicles, one of the major challenges for highly automated driving. At high levels of automation, the driver is unable to intervene in a timely and appropriate manner. Consequently, the automation must be capable of independently handling safety-critical situations. Fail-operational behavior is essential at all layers of automated driving.

State of the art autonomous driving functions sense their immediate environment and rely entirely on built-in sensors. These technologies lay the foundation to enable the deployment of more advanced control strategies and are expected to be the next evolutionary step to obtain a large scale view of the traffic situation. However, the common approaches for dependable system development now need to be adjusted to consider additional constraints coming from highly automated and connected vehicle functionality. Understanding the design, structure and integration of the necessary infrastructure and road user, information must become an integral part of developing modern vehicles. Unfortunately, there is a lack of available inter-domain experts and best practices which are geared specifically for those novel concepts. The PRYSTINE project targets realization of Fail-operational Urban Surround perceptION (FUSION), based on robust Radar and LiDAR sensor fusion, and control functions enabling safe automated driving. PRYSTINE addresses the development and validation of new fail operational platforms, as well as high performing and dependable sensor fusion on different levels. In this paper, an overview of fail-operational FUSION approaches on different layers (vehicle, controller and sensor level) is provided, together with a description of the interplay between safety and security aspects on the individual levels.

2   FUSION on Vehicle Level

Through development of high-performance fail-operational systems, PRYSTINE is committed to increasing technological maturity at different levels of the automotive supply chain. Such fail-operational systems, which are based on sensor fusion, are also targeting deeper involvement of semiconductor manufacturing. The project contribution to innovations in automotive and semiconductor fields is demonstrated through use cases contributing to the development of autonomous driving in unstructured urban environments. Taking the diminishing role of drivers in such an application into consideration, a rationally hyped demand for high safety is requiring development of sophisticated fail-operational systems. Hence, the proposed solutions must comply with the challenging demands for an uninterrupted functional correctness even in the presence of component failures. Potential answers are seen in redundancy and technological diversity. Additional constraints for sensor fusion structures are possible run-time reconfiguration in the events of failure, as proposed in [12]. We are proposing a generic fail-operational E/E system capable of managing such events. The system development is supported by an integration platform, which serves as the basis for enhancing and adapting architectures. It also supports functionality and control strategies. The overall aim is to enable an efficient integration of various FUSION technologies with a strong focus on dependability, testing and validation.

2.1   Fail-Operational E/E Architecture

The high-performance control units are a response to the increasing need for integration of centralized adaptive control automotive systems. The localized processing is also minimizing the security risks and potential negative impact of latency related to cloud communication, but it must also eliminate safety risks.

The available heterogeneous solutions and the lack of standardization, are also pushing towards usage of generic, technology agnostic platforms. Unique solutions limit portability and are predestined for use by a small range of vehicles only. The proposed concept of a generic fail-operational E/E architecture (see Fig. 1) is offering a basis for integration of optimized sensors, electronic components, embedded safety controllers, processing systems with dependable vehicular electrical/electronic infrastructure and communication systems. The architecture relies on semi-redundant control which enables fail-operational monitoring, control and collection of vehicle data close to the physical world. In the event of a computing failure, the module which normally monitors the operation, takes over the command of the architecture and has an option to continue standard operation and issue a warning to the vehicle user.

An alternative option is to continue operation of safety-relevant functions of the vehicle, but with reduced non-safety-relevant performance until adequate technical attention is given to the system. This centralized high-performance in-car computing unavoidably contributes towards distribution of intelligence which in turn endorses reliable and robust operation.

It is the parallelism of the high-performance CPUs within the control unit that solidifies the fail-operational performance. The safety approved controller is also there to monitor the two high performance CPUs, but also to perform safety relevant activities that require less computational power.

As efficient vehicle development calls for teamwork, the proposed E/E architecture enables integration of generic hardware components that satisfy a predefined interfacing convention. Hence, it is possible for teams from different disciplines to bring together their independently developed hardware solutions in a modular fashion and to create a complex system of systems, such as a vehicle.

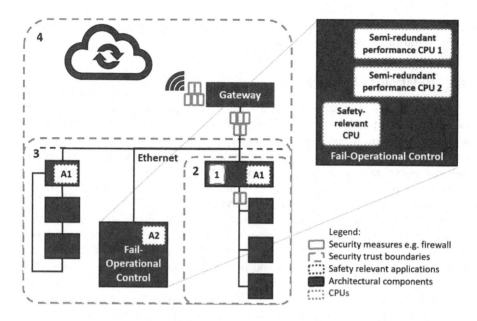

Fig. 1. Conceptual E/E architecture

Ideally, the hardware contributions should allow technology agnostic usage, to ensure that common portability issues are avoided.

As the existing devices that provide vehicle connectivity offer limited possibilities in terms of data exchange, there is an unsatisfied demand by a growing number of services in terms of data throughput.

The high-computational nature of the presented solution and the need for its safe operation are calling for new generations of sensors and integrated circuits. The architecture offers a testing ground needed for definition of new requirements for semiconductor manufacturing.

2.2 FUSION at E/E Architecture Level

Sensor fusion at low-level is a well known concept of turning a combination of sensors to act as one unit. The potential benefits of fusion at E/E architecture level, however, offer additional redundancy and resilience to the E/E architecture. Each high level functionality integrated into autonomous vehicle relies on multiple different sensor types and is executed on a specific control unit. However, in fail conditions, the redundancy of sensor signals can support resilience; when considering fusion on E/E architecture level also the migration of complex intelligent algorithms demanded by autonomous functions to other systems of the E/E architecture is enabled. Such approaches of the E/E architecture can exploit robust (high-level) fusion to retain a certain functionality level upon critical faults, sensor failures or cyber-attacks. The higher level sensor overview from the E/E architecture also can contribute to potential self-calibration or run time reconfiguration as and when required.

2.3 Relation to Safety

The main challenge of autonomous driving applications related to standardization activities is the current lack of consolidation in terms of autonomous driving and especially run-time adaptations from the safety perspective. However, the evolution of related technologies and maturing of the available solutions are providing a more fertile environment for contributions. The available gap in this field is leaving a possibility for active involvements and greater impact for dynamic applications and re-configurable or adaptive systems.

ISO 26262 [13] addresses possible hazards that originate from malfunctioning behaviour of E/E safety-related systems, including their interactions. But neither the functional safety standard ISO 26262 nor Automotive SPICE [21] are designed for dynamic applications and re-configurable or adaptive systems. The current safety approaches provide means for risk identification and classification and give guidance on how to reduce the risk involved to an acceptable level at development time. These practices require the entire system and all system contexts to be defined and known at design time.

Novel so-called Systems of Systems (SoS) approaches [7] are integrations of heterogeneous systems delivering capabilities and services without exact knowledge of the internals of an involved subsystem. A promising method for definition of SoS architectures lies in interface specification and a quasi contract-based development, as proposed, among others, by [7,17]. Thus novel safety engineering approaches are required for such systems. Promising approaches to tackle these issues rely on a set of contracts to describe component attributes and evaluate the robustness of the configuration at run-time.

Service-oriented Architecture (SOA) is known as one popular method for creating dynamically changing, distributed applications. It basically consists of encapsulating all functionalities into so-called services that can be reached via a well-defined interface from anywhere in the network. Each service holds a contract that describes the ways of accessing this functionality, and the different services are composed by an orchestration algorithm. In [4] a combination of this composable contract approach with an ontology-based run-time reconfiguration (ORR) is proposed for the use in automotive applications. VerSaI (Vertical Safety Interfaces) [24] is a contract-based modeling approach created to assist the integrator of an integrated architecture in checking whether the application software components are able to run safely on the execution platforms of the system. VerSaI checks the safety compatibility between the application and the platform through demands and guarantees (contract-based approach).

2.4   Relation to Security

In the security context, the work of Iber et al. [11] presents a concept for modeling contracts and a vision of a generic modeling language for specifying contracts for extra-functional properties, such as safety and cyber-security.

Many cyber-security related approaches are concerned with investigation and techniques that deal with non-intrusive runtime logging and event tracing of a specific system. Importance is predominantly placed upon distributed mission critical functions, which are shadowed by runtime models. The models aid detection of dependability incidences e.g. security attacks or safety relevant issues. Such recognition is achieved through detection of misalignment between modelled functionality and the sensed physical data. The detection calls for reaction and adaptation at runtime. By this means the system can detect intentional manipulations, based on misalignment between the anticipated and actual signals (cyber-security attack). This also facilitates the provision of adequate information and algorithms for predictive maintenance.

SAE J3061 [23] and ISO 21434 [15] state cybersecurity engineering requirements and lifecycle processes, which shall ensure security-by-design approaches, analogous to the process framework described in ISO 26262.

Apart from that, other standards, such as the IEC 62443 [1] or the ISO 27000 series [2] are not directly aimed at automotive systems. Nevertheless, they are relevant for the production and backend systems of the automotive domain. The aeronautics domain ARP4754 [19] provides guidance for system level development and defines steps for the adequate refinement and implementation of requirements. Security concerns in aeronautics industry are tackled by the Common Criteria [14,20] specification. An analysis done by SoQrates Security AK[1] indicates that the available standards are frequently fragmented or incomplete, and typically assume that their open issues are covered by other guidelines or standards.

3   FUSION on System Level

PRYSTINE also aids development of FUSION on system level, where the main objective is a highly efficient and safe modular autonomous driving platform. The main research and development activities include design, development, and demonstration of computing infrastructure, supporting fully/partially functionality in case of faults or impairing of environment perception. The targeted fail-operational behaviour is tackled through essential implementation of redundancies and diversity within the control and computational components. FUSION, as a key feature on this level is ensuring fail-operational functionality. Only by achieving fail-operational hardware/software architectures, can automated driving functions be continuously provided (with a reduced set of capabilities) even if a fault is detected or environment perception is impaired. Therefore, redundancy and diversity within the control elements of the architecture are essential for guaranteeing fail-operational behavior.

---

[1] http://soqrates.eurospi.net/.

The AUTOSAR Adaptive Platform [6] implements a run-time environment for Adaptive Applications (ARA). The platform follows a Service-oriented Architecture (SOA) approach for future use of automated driving functionalities (ADF) and advanced driver assistance systems (ADAS). In comparison the AUTOSAR run-time environment (RTE) for the Adaptive Platform [5] dynamically links services and clients during run-time.

The works of [3, 4, 11] focus on a safety certification solution for safety-critical, open, and adaptive multi-core systems. This approach consists of modular and composable contracts created during development time as part of a sound and mostly traditional safety argumentation. The focus is set on ensuring safety through the system lifecycle, even if parts of the system are replaced or updated as part of maintenance or upgrades.

3.1   Software Architecture for FUSION on System Level

For highly automated or autonomous vehicles the on-board sensors, which are implemented in the vehicle itself are the approaches predominantly relied on. However, there is a tendency to work towards integration of environmental data and off-board information. The detected surrounding objects are incorporated into an environmental model, capturing all collected information about the physical environment and the vehicles motion and location. These values are obtained from vehicle sensors and measurement units. Using this variety of information, the environment model is able to perform situation analysis and the decision-making algorithms are used to predict driving maneuvers in advance. The situation analysis algorithm exploits the environment model to identify the free road space and hence forecast the most likely behaviour of other traffic participants. Consequently, it is able to identify vehicle's safe movement paths. As the multitude of tasks and algorithms used in an automated vehicle have specific hardware requirements, there is a necessity for a wide range of computing platforms. These vary in computational power, electrical interfaces and safety concepts to ensure fail-operational behaviour. The software components, which are mostly developed in modular App manner, provide necessary functionalities for autonomous driving at the expense of being distributed over multiple computation platforms. The applications that are executed on a single computation platform, control non-related vehicle functions. An implication is that the system platform needs to provide basic separation and fail-operational concepts as depicted in Fig. 2.

A vital novelty within PRYSTINE is the development of new sensor fusion algorithms. These are of two types: established classic control algorithms and the ones that are based on AI. AI algorithms are currently deemed to be one of the most promising contributors for development of highly automated driving, as they have a strong potential to be trained for detecting objects in various situations and also for learning from previous events. They require data structures representing objects and the object attributes (relative speed, trajectory, type etc) as input. An unfortunate consequence for these systems is that such inputs expose vulnerabilities to cyber-security attacks. On the other hand, provision of

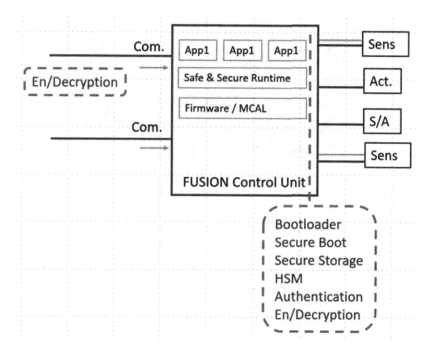

Fig. 2. FUSION System xCU Concept

a holistic AI algorithm that replaces the entire human decision making process is unlikely in the near future, due to the need to ensure critical safety and due to a lack of standardised certification methods. The dependability of highly automated driving functions (vehicle intelligence) is still considered as inadequate. Their operation is thus monitored by a safety envelope concept (as depicted in Fig. 3).

This conceptual approach is required due to the product liability requirements, which state that products be brought to the market must provide reasonable and expected safety and they must have been developed in accordance with the state-of-the-art. The state-of-the-art requirements are roughly defined by the common methodologies employed at the time and are defined in national and international standards, maintained by standardization bodies, such as the International Standardization Organization (ISO) and/or national standardization agencies. The main goal of this work is to provide comparable and uniform means for analysis of results independently performed in different partner organizations. The international standards ISO 26262 [13], ISO PAS 21448 [16] and ISO CD 21434 [15] are placed into a focal point when considering the development of automated driving functions on a system level.

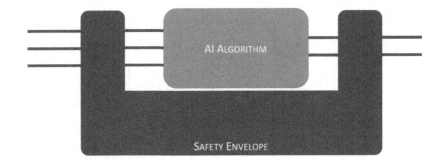

Fig. 3. Depiction of the Safety Envelope Concept

3.2   Relation to Safety

The functional safety activities are supported by two international standards. A safety study based on the latest ISO 26262(2018) is to be conducted for the FUSION approaches. The second edition of the ISO 26262 was released in December 2018 and it provides improvements in the clarity of the standards as well as an awaited extension of its scope to trucks, buses and motorcycles. One of the main goals behind the standardization related activities and work products is to ensure that no fault within the system can cause a hazardous situation and potentially harm individuals. The standard is thus geared, from the PRYSTINE perspective, towards the development of systems that ensure detection of software and hardware malfunctions and mitigation of their effects, so that vehicle is continually operational in safe state.

ISO PAS 21448 [16] deals with safety of the intended functionality (SotIF) and technical shortcomings if the system works according to its specification. SotIF is gaining importance with increasing vehicle automation levels, because such systems do not have the option of falling-back on the driver who could take over the vehicle controls in an emergency. Safety measures for non-automated driving and assisted only driving usually ensure fail-silent operation, which guarantees that the driver can control the vehicle until a defined safe state is reached. However, fail-silent operation, which is a necessity for highly automated driving, is only achievable by using fail-operational systems. The development of fail-silent systems is already established and is covered by the ISO 26262, where faults within the system are analyzed and corresponding mitigation strategies are defined. However, additional technical shortcomings, which are in the scope of the ISO PAS 21448, must be addressed by the ISO 26262; especially for upcoming fail-operational systems, The main challenge in the SotIF activities is, that not all technical deficiencies are known during development stages, but in the worst case scenario they have a potential to be revealed during operation, after the vehicle has been brought onto the market. For this reason, the ISO PAS 21448 – SotIF is complementary to the ISO 26262 and focuses on the prevention of hazardous situations caused by technical shortcomings or misuse of the system. The ISO PAS 21448 standard assumes that the system behaves as specified and no fault is present. Nevertheless, due to technological weaknesses, certain effects (e.g. strong light source in the field of view of a camera, metal objects in front of a RADAR sensor, or an optical illusion) might incorrectly be identified as obstacles and could cause a hazardous situation. SotIF minimizes and mitigates risks by describing the process of dealing with such scenarios that include road conditions, surrounding landscape, object texture, weather.

Systems must be exposed to rigorous verification and testing to ensure that known technical inadequacies do not result with potentially hazardous situations. Consequently, a correct system verification procedure should mandate that all known critical scenarios are tested under varying environment conditions to avoid unknown unsafe scenarios during development (as depicted in Fig. 4).

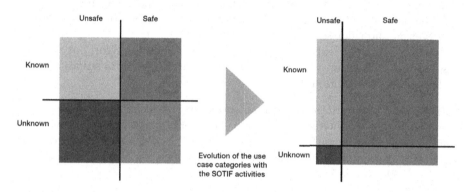

Fig. 4. SotIF approach to minimize the number of unknown and unsafe scenarios [22].

3.3   Relation to Security

Automotive security standardization activities are comparable to the safety standardization that was initiated a decade ago. The CD draft ISO 21343 [15] has been released recently and is based on SAE 3061(2016) [23]. This standard, in combination with the guidebook mentioned, defines a security development process for the complete product lifecycle. The described process starts with a system analysis and its potential threats, as well as vulnerabilities that could potentially allow the execution of the threats. The different and partly mutual exclusive requirements for developing a safe and secure system requires a novel co-engineering approach, where the differences and synergies are precisely understood, and the applied analysis methods are most effectively used. Such a co-engineering approach (described also in [18]) must consider all the relevant standards and shall be reflected in the organization's internal development processes to increase efficiency and minimize development cost.

4   Fail Operational on Sensor Level

Fail-operational sensor components represent the fundamental building blocks that contribute to an overall robust and fail-operational environment perception system. The PRYSTINE project focuses on novel fail-operational concepts for LiDAR and Radar sensors. These sensors, together with cameras, will be used in virtually any perception system in the future.

PRYSTINE's component-level safety concepts for sensors focus on two main abstraction levels. On high abstraction level, each sensor type (LiDAR, Radar and camera) carries inherent and very distinct benefits and drawbacks, such as:

- LiDAR sensors possess sound characteristics in terms of resolution (range, angle, etc.), but are very poor in sensing colors or measuring speed.
- Radar is a speed measuring instrument, but has poor ability in terms of resolution and color sensing.
- Cameras commonly exhibit good properties when sensing color, but are poor speed measuring sensors and also have poor characteristics in situations with changing light conditions.

It is the fusing (either on raw-data, point-cloud, or object-list level) of these three sensor types that eliminates the negative effects of individual sensor drawbacks. Simultaneously, the fusion aids a crucial creation of a robust and safe perception system that is capable on drawing from strengths of each individual sensor type.

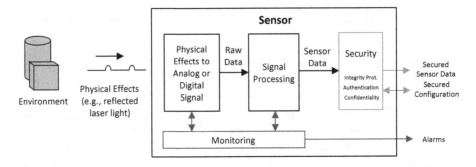

Fig. 5. Fundamental automotive sensor architecture. While monitoring circuits regard safe operation, security circuits regard integrity, authentication, and confidentiality.

4.1   Relation to Safety

On low abstraction level, each sensor implements in principle the same concept as depicted in Fig. 5, which commences with a physical effect being sensed and translated into an electrical signal. Signal processing is involved in manipulation of digitized information (e.g., distance between sensor and object), which is then provided to a higher-level ECU (such as a dedicated sensor fusion ECU). On this low, ASIC semiconductor-level, functional safety is achieved by monitoring the integrated functions up to a certain coverage according to the ISO 26262 [13] standard. These monitors continuously observe the operation of the sensor ASIC and trigger an alarm or, depending on the severity of the fault, even a reset, in case a fault was detected that impairs the sensor's functionality. Such an alarm or reset alerts the sensor fusion ECU to initiate appropriate countermeasure. As depicted in Fig. 6, PRYSTINE drives innovation way beyond state-of-the-art by introducing novel concepts that enable fail-operational environment sensing. These concepts enable degraded sensing also in the case of detected faults. As an example, Infineon's LiDAR vision (cf. [9]) is based on an automotive qualified oscillating 1D MEMS mirror that is controlled by a MEMS Driver ASIC. Both MEMS mirror and MEMS Driver ASIC form the most crucial part of the LiDAR system. The fundamental functional safety concept of the MEMS Driver ASIC, which is based on a redundant and diverse sense and control strategy, clusters faults of the MEMS mirror and the MEMS Driver ASIC into three severity classes:

- Warnings are triggered in the case of faults that do not degrade the LiDAR's functionality in the short run, such as a detected over-voltage of the supply.
- Alarms are triggered in case of faults that impair the LiDAR functionality but still allow a degraded operation, such as damaged mirror comp-drivers that result in a reduced mechanical field-of-view.
- A Reset of the MEMS Driver ASIC is initiated in cases when the severity of the detected fault prohibits a degraded operation at all, such as a detected under-voltage of the supply that leads to a malfunction of the digital core.

Once the sensor fusion ECU recognizes a warning, alarm, or reset event, it may read out further status information and then has a possibility to decide whether, or not, a degraded operation can be accepted given the current application context.

4.2   Relation to Security

While monitoring the function of the sensor ASIC's is of paramount importance in terms of achieving safe environment perception, the security aspect may not be disregarded. The more complex the sensor function (such as support for firmware updates or re-configurability during operation), the higher is the functional safety impact in the event of a malicious security breach. As an example, a short-range LiDAR may be configured for a 120° field-of-view. Due to a given security breach, this field-of-view is then maliciously re-configured to 60°. On the one hand, without security measures, the LiDAR sensor assumes that the sensor fusion ECU initiated a valid and trustworthy re-configuration. On the other hand, the sensor fusion ECU still assumes a 120° field-of-view and is not aware of the actual reduced sensing area, which may result in a fatal accident due to undetected obstacles. Therefore, on lowest sensor ASIC abstraction layer,

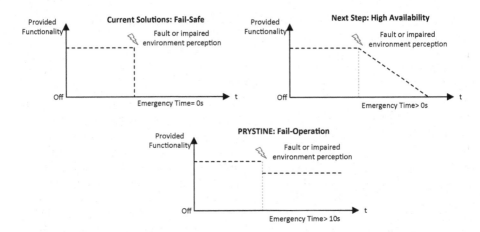

Fig. 6. PRYSTINE: from fail-safe to fail-operational, obtained with changes from [8].

the following security measures must be considered in order to support safe operation:

- The sensor shall check the integrity and authenticity of configuration data including firmware updates. As a consequence, malicious configuration of the sensor is prohibited.
- The sensor's output data stream shall be protected by means of integrity and authenticity. As a consequence, the sensor fusion ECU can trust the sensor data.
- In case no other entity is to be able to either read or interpret any kind of data transaction, data communication shall be protected via state-of-the-art encryption methods.
- The authenticity of the whole sensor box shall be verifiable in order to prevent counterfeiting of spare parts.

In summary, semiconductor companies must take full account of both functional safety according to the ISO 26262 [13] and security according to the ISO 21434 [15], in order to achieve a safe and robust sensor system that is used in the context of highly-automated driving and connected cars.

5   Conclusion

Connected and automated vehicles belong to the main research trends of the radically changing automotive industry. Autonomous cars are characterized by a high level of dynamics at multiple layers: learning and adapting systems that continuously evolve and do so to such an extent that guarantees about their dependability are extremely difficult to provide. At the same time, the customer demands for dependability (trustworthiness, reliability, safety, and security) within these highly dynamic systems is and will be intrinsic. Ensuring the dependability of these complex systems is thus a precondition for lowering the resistance against their acceptance in general and consequently for the public to be trusting and accepting towards them.

To that aim, we provided a brief overview of state-of-the-art safety and security standards that need to be considered for a Fail-operational Urban Surround perceptION (FUSION) approach. The realization of this FUSION approach is targeted by the PRYSTINE project on different layers of the vehicle architecture (E/E architecture, control system, and sensor level).

Acknowledgment. This project has received funding from the Electronic Component Systems for European Leadership Joint Undertaking (ECSEL-JU) under grant agreement No 783190 (PRYSTINE Project).

References

1. IEC 62443: Industrial communication networks – network and system security
2. ISO 27000 series, information technology - security techniques
3. Amorim, T., Ruiz, A., Dropmann, C., Schneider, D.: Multidirectional modular conditional safety certificates. In: Koornneef, F., van Gulijk, C. (eds.) SAFECOMP 2015. LNCS, vol. 9338, pp. 357–368. Springer, Cham (2015). https://doi.org/10.1007/978-3-319-24249-1_31
4. Amorim, T., et al.: Runtime safety assurance for adaptive cyber-physical systems - ConSerts M and ontology-based runtime reconfiguration applied to an automotive case study. In: Druml, N., Genser, A., Krieg, A., Menghin, M., Hoeller, A. (eds.) Handbook of Research on Solutions for Cyber-Physical Systems Ubiquity, pp. 137–168. IGI Global (2018)
5. AUTOSAR development cooperation: AUTOSAR AUTomotive Open System ARchitecture (2009). www.autosar.org
6. AUTOSAR Development Cooperation: Adaptive Platform Release Overview (2017). https://www.autosar.org/fileadmin/files/standards/adaptive/17-03/AUTOSAR_TR_AdaptivePlatformReleaseOverview.pdf
7. Bryans, J., Payne, R., Holt, J., Perry, S.: Semi-formal and formal interface specification for system of systems architecture. In: 2013 IEEE International Systems Conference (SysCon), pp. 612–619, April 2013. https://doi.org/10.1109/SysCon.2013.6549946
8. Druml, N., et al.: PRYSTINE-PRogrammable sYSTems for INtelligence in automobilEs. In: 2018 21st Euromicro Conference on Digital System Design (DSD), pp. 618–626 (2018)
9. Druml, N., Maksymova, I., Thurner, T., van Lierop, D., Hennecke, M., Foroutan, A.: 1D MEMS micro-scanning LiDAR. In: International Conference on Sensor Device Technologies and Applications (SENSORDEVICES) (2018)
10. European Automobile Manufacturers Association: The Automobile Industry Pocket Guide 2016–2017. Technical report, European Automobile Manufacturers Association (2016). www.acea.be
11. Iber, J., Hoeller, A., Rauter, T., Kreiner, C.: Towards a generic modeling language for contract-based design. In: 2nd International Workshop on Model-Driven Engineering for Component-Based Software Systems (ModComp) 2015 Workshop Proceedings, p. 24 (2015)

12. Iber, J., Rauter, T., Krisper, M., Kreiner, C.: The potential of self-adaptive software systems in industrial control systems. In: Stolfa, J., Stolfa, S., O'Connor, R.V., Messnarz, R. (eds.) EuroSPI 2017. CCIS, vol. 748, pp. 150–161. Springer, Cham (2017). https://doi.org/10.1007/978-3-319-64218-5_12

13. ISO - International Organization for Standardization: ISO 26262 Road vehicles Functional Safety Part 1–10 (2011)

14. ISO - International Organization for Standardization: ISO/IEC 15408. In: van Tilborg, H.C.A., Jajodia, S. (eds.) Encyclopedia of Cryptography and Security, 2nd edn. Springer (2011)

15. ISO - International Organization for Standardization: ISO/SAE CD 21434 Road Vehicles - Cybersecurity engineering (under development)

16. ISO - International Organization for Standardization: ISO/WD PAS 21448 Road vehicles - Safety of the intended functionality (work-in-progress)

17. Macher, G., Armengaud, E., Schneider, D., Brenner, E., Kreiner, C.: Towards dependability engineering of cooperative automotive cyber-physical systems. In: Stolfa, J., Stolfa, S., O'Connor, R.V., Messnarz, R. (eds.) EuroSPI 2017. CCIS, vol. 748, pp. 205–215. Springer, Cham (2017). https://doi.org/10.1007/978-3-319-64218-5_16

18. Macher, G., Messnarz, R., Armengaud, E., Riel, A., Brenner, E., Kreiner, C.: Integrated safety and security development in the automotive domain. In: SAE Technical Paper. SAE International (2017). http://papers.sae.org/2017-01-1661/

19. SAE International: Guidelines for Development of Civil Aircraft and Systems (2010). http://standards.sae.org/arp4754a/

20. The Common Criteria Recognition Agreement Members: Common Criteria for Information Technology Security Evaluation (2014). http://www.commoncriteriaportal.org/

21. The SPICE User Group: Automotive SPICE Process Assessment/Reference Model V3.0, July 2015. http://www.automotivespice.com/fileadmin/software-download/Automotive_SPICE_PAM_30.pdf

22. Doms, T., Rauch, B., Schrammel, B., Schwald, C., Spahovic, E., Schwarzl, C.: Highly automated driving- the new challenges for functional safety and cyber Security (2018). https://www.v2c2.at/wp-content/uploads/2018/11/tuv-austria-white-paper-iv-highly-automated-driving_web.pdf

23. Vehicle Electrical System Security Committee: SAE J3061 Cybersecurity Guidebook for Cyber-Physical Automotive Systems. http://standards.sae.org/wip/j3061/

24. Zimmer, B., Bürklen, S., Knoop, M., Höfflinger, J., Trapp, M.: Vertical safety interfaces – improving the efficiency of modular certification. In: Flammini, F., Bologna, S., Vittorini, V. (eds.) SAFECOMP 2011. LNCS, vol. 6894, pp. 29–42. Springer, Heidelberg (2011). https://doi.org/10.1007/978-3-642-24270-0_3

Safety Assessment in Automotive Industry

An Approach for Validating Safety of Perception Software in Autonomous Driving Systems

Deepak Rao[1,2] ⓘ, Plato Pathrose[1(✉)], Felix Huening[2] ⓘ,
and Jithin Sid[1]

[1] Visteon Electronics Germany GmbH, Amalienbadstraße 41a,
76227 Karlsruhe, Germany
{deepak.rao,ppathros,sjithin}@visteon.com
[2] University of Applied Sciences Aachen, Eupener Straße 70,
52066 Aachen, Germany
deepak.rao@alumni.fh-aachen.de, huening@fh-aachen.de

Abstract. The increasing complexity of Advanced Driver Assistance Systems (ADAS) presents a challenging task to validate safe and reliable performance of these systems under varied conditions. The test and validation of ADAS/AD with real test drives, although important, involves huge costs and time. Simulation tools provide an alternative with the added advantage of reproducibility but often use ideal sensors, which do not reflect real sensor output accurately. This paper presents a new validation methodology using fault injection, as recommended by the ISO 26262 standard, to test software and system robustness. In our work, we investigated and developed a tool capable of inserting faults at different software and system levels to verify its robustness. The scope of this paper is to cover the fault injection test for the Visteon's DriveCore™ system, a centralized domain controller for Autonomous driving which is sensor agnostic and SoC agnostic. With this new approach, the validation of safety monitoring functionality and its behavior can be tested using real-world data instead of synthetic data from simulation tools resulting in having better confidence in system performance before proceeding with in-vehicle testing.

Keywords: Advanced driver assistance systems (ADAS/AD) · ISO 26262 · Safety-critical systems validation · Safety of the intended functionality (SOTIF)

1 Introduction

The advancement of technology in the field of driver assist systems and automated driving features are becoming a norm. These systems provide safety and comfort features to the driver and passengers but their reliability and safety are still questionable. Testing and validation of such systems involves significant effort and demands new approaches to cover a multitude of test scenarios. Conventional software-in-the-loop (SIL), hardware-in-the-loop (HIL) as well as vehicle-in-the-loop (VIL) test methods are used extensively but covering edge cases and testing for the safety functionalities to gain confidence before series deployment still needs research. Many

© Springer Nature Switzerland AG 2019
Y. Papadopoulos et al. (Eds.): IMBSA 2019, LNCS 11842, pp. 303–316, 2019.
https://doi.org/10.1007/978-3-030-32872-6_20

studies have aimed at developing validation strategies to test new sensor setups used in ADAS/AD for evaluating the dependability. In our study, we have attempted to develop another validation approach, which aims at testing the components of an ADAS/AD system at various levels and validate the robustness of an autonomous software stack at system level.

This paper is organized as follows: Sect. 2 presents an overview of related work and relevant background. Section 3 describes the adopted methodology. Section 4 discusses the evaluation of our approach with the use case of an object detection algorithm and the results obtained are described. Finally, Sect. 5 presents conclusions with a short overview of possible future work.

2 Related Work and Background

The first subsection presents related work with respect to the application of fault injection methods in the field of automotive systems verification and validation. The second subsection lists challenges about the validation of advanced driver assistance systems.

2.1 Fault Injection – State of the Art in ADAS/AD

Since many years, conventional in-the-loop techniques such as software-in-the-loop (SIL) as well as hardware-in-the-loop (HIL) have been used for testing the functionalities of an automotive Electronic Control Unit (ECU). The number of ECU's in a modern day car has multiplied in recent years. The onset of infotainment systems as well as driver assistance systems has increased the complexity of ECU validation at the functional and system level. Fault injection methods, as described in [1], have been commonly employed in automotive testing for the past few decades. However, these methods prove to be insufficient with the advancement of automotive electronics resulting in complex ECUs depending on multiple new sensors such as cameras, radars LIDAR, as well as the increasing complexity of the vehicle network.

Many studies have been conducted using fault injection for testing of ADAS/AD systems. In [2], the authors presented a test method for vision-based algorithms of an ADAS/AD considering an automotive camera-in-the-loop. The method used a real camera in front of a monitor screen to feed synthetic data of various scenarios to observe the impact on the performance of vision algorithms. This is a commonly used approach for testing input from mono cameras.

In another study [3], a safety assessment of automated vehicle functions was conducted and the authors focused on determining critical parameters of fault detection interval for permanent faults. As per ISO 26262 standards [4], fault injection is highly recommended as one of the methods to derive the Automotive Safety Integrity Level (ASIL) of an ECU component. In [5], the authors presented the application of fault injection as per ISO 26262 with the use case of an Electronic Steering Control Lock (ESLC) system.

2.2   Challenges of ADAS/AD Validation

Modern day cars equipped with ADAS/AD have a suite of sensors, which have given rise to complex system architectures. With every passing day, functionalities being offered as part of ADAS/AD or partially automated driving solutions are increasing. The sheer complexity of such systems makes testing and validating such systems before deployment in series vehicles challenging. Of the many common problems faced, one of the most important is the verification and validation of ADAS/AD.

Unlike traditional methods, validating an ADAS/AD/AD system requires extensive test coverage to prove safe and dependable operation. Vehicle testing needs evidence from millions of kilometers, which is costly and not feasible. ADAS/AD relies on technologies such as machine learning that is difficult and expensive to test. Therefore employing simulation tools is useful to test corner cases as well as have reproducible cases. With simulation, the scenarios can be varied for different environmental conditions, but the degree of reality from these tools is limited. Recorded data from vehicle tests can be utilized to bridge the gap of simulation tools. However, it is critical to test these systems at multiple levels of abstraction such as software, software integrated with hardware and at the system level.

Fault injection can play a useful role as part of a validation strategy that also includes traditional testing and non-test-based validation [6]. This is especially true if fault injection is applied at multiple levels of abstraction rather than just at the level of stuck-at electrical connectors [6].

Most of the research in this field has positively contributed in defining new ways to adapt with the evolving systems in automotive domain to handle the testing and validation of ADAS/AD ECU's. However, a majority of studies focus on functional validation or sensor specific validation. As outlined in the challenges of ADAS/AD, achieving the desired ratings to certify an ECU for a specific ASIL level still needs to investigate new methods to validate functional as well as safety modules. This paper focuses on investigating a validation approach, which can handle the validation of these systems at multiple different levels.

3   Methodology

In our approach, we aimed at developing a tool which can aid in creating validation data sets from recorded vehicle data. The tool is aimed at testing ADAS/AD functions or the entire system using fault injection methods. As the recorded data from vehicle consists of raw sensor data involving the vehicle network data as well, this can be helpful in having more reliability in terms of richness of information in comparison with scenario-based testing using simulation tools.

Figure 1 shows a simplified block diagram of the framework under development. Our motivation stems from the fact that it is necessary to find out vulnerabilities at different levels of automated systems. As shown in the figure, we are developing a flexible framework which can inject faults at each level such as sensing layer, perception layer, decision layer or control layer. These faults can be inserted and system behavior can be observed inside SIL as well as HIL environments.

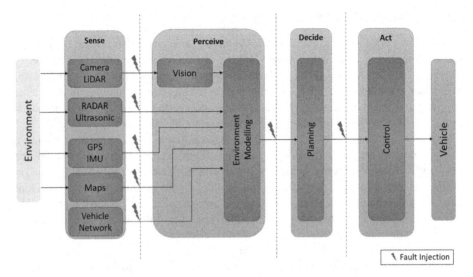

Fig. 1. Simplified block diagram of the fault injection framework with different layers of an autonomous system stack.

The architecture of an ADAS/AD/AD ECU consists of multiple domains. The functions offered by an ADAS/AD system can be broadly classified into safety functions and comfort functions. The functionalities are split between Quality Management (QM) domain and ASIL domains. Based on the safety criticality of the functions either of the domains is responsible for its functioning. Safety functions such as an Autonomous Emergency Braking System (AEBS) have strict requirements and fall under the ASIL domain. These functions have stringent timing requirements and failure of function or delayed response can lead to severe hazards. In case of failure to react to danger in the stipulated time, there must be redundancies or safety monitoring functionalities (SMF), which should take action and act in a safe manner to have the least damage in case of danger. In normal conditions, these redundancies or SMF are not checked and fault injection is used to check these.

With the developed tool as shown in Fig. 2, one of the primary objectives is to inject faults in the sensor as well as communication lines to verify the behavior of SMF. This is for the Visteon's DriveCore™ system which is taking input from 13 cameras, 8 radars, 4 Lidars and 12 ultrasonic sensors As per recommendations of ISO 26262 and SOTIF [7], we have focused on injecting timing based faults, sensor data corruption, and signal level faults. In case of timing faults, we play the sensor data ahead of the original timestamp or delay the message. As sensor fusion algorithms fuse data from multiple sensors to check the integrity of information for further decisions, timing faults can expose the system and can help in checking the system reaction in the presence of such faults.

With sensor corruption, there are multiple failures possible for each sensor such as camera, LiDAR, and radar. When the sensor information is noisy or corrupt, then the information cannot be trusted for further control actions. These faults can be inserted and check whether the safety monitoring functions take action or still the normal operating software output is utilized for decision making even though the confidence level is low. This can be dangerous and not safe for the driver as well as for the passengers. In the given example, we focused on setting up the pipeline using one camera sensor and implemented sensor impurity faults. After inserting the fault, the output can be checked at the output of individual algorithms, at the end of the perception stack or at the end of the control layer. This flexibility can help check fault penetration and the impact at each level in SIL and HIL environments. In the following section, we have elaborated the types of faults for a camera that can be injected to test software and system robustness.

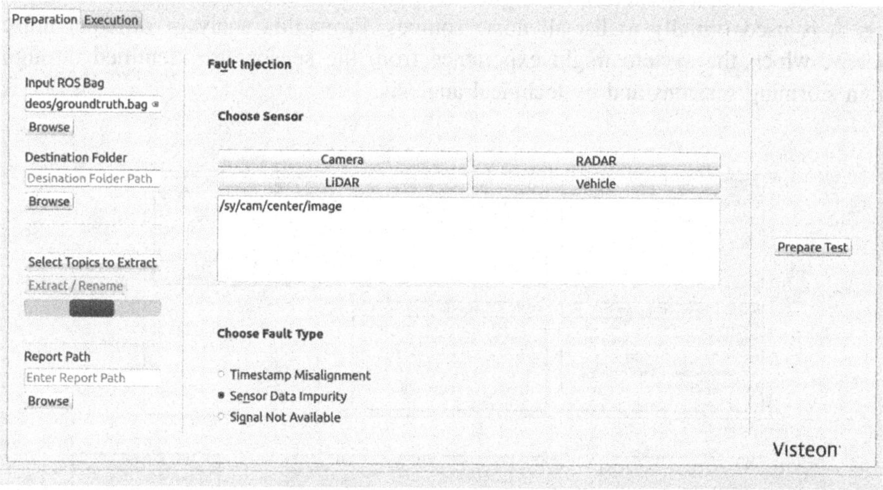

Fig. 2. Screenshot of the graphical user interface of the fault injection tool

Fault Injection in Cameras. Many perception tasks such as object detection, lane detection, traffic sign and light recognition rely on input from cameras. The camera amongst other ADAS/AD sensors provides rich information about the environment but is prone to degraded output due to several reasons such as poor illumination, adverse weather conditions, sensor faults, etc. Corrupt or poor camera output can have a drastic impact on the output of vision algorithms. Although data augmentation techniques [8] are being used to improve the reliability of a neural network output, they still cannot assure robust performance from a validation point of view.

In our approach, we used fault injection methods for camera sensors as recommended by ISO/PAS 21448:2019 [7]. The types of faults that can be injected using our tool are summarized in Table 1.

DriveCore™ Compute is the autonomous driving platform of Visteon, which is sensor and SoC (System on a chip) agnostic. The input received from the sensors are important as the platform relies mostly on sensor output fed into the hardware. As a

Table 1. Camera fault types

Sensor	Timing faults	Sensor impurity
Camera	Play messages in advance than the original timestamp Play messages delayed than the original timestamp	Salt & pepper noise Gaussian noise Bright image Dark image Translated image Rotated image Flipped image

part of the system engineering activity of identifying all the possible inputs, outputs and other influencing parameters, a P-Diagram (Parameter Diagram) approach, as shown in Fig. 3, is used initially to list all noise sources. From this analysis, different noise factors, which the system might experience from the sensor, are identified through brain storming sessions and by technical analysis.

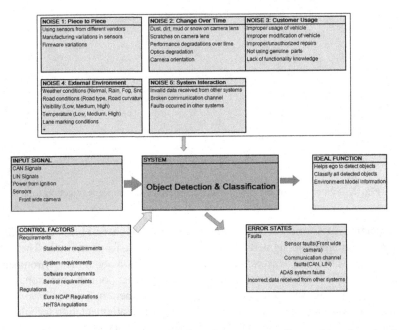

Fig. 3. Parameter Diagram describing the influencing parameters for an object detection feature

A tree diagram approach was used, as shown in Fig. 4, for decomposing the feature to its sub sections and the influencing parameters in terms of environment, other systems etc. were identified.

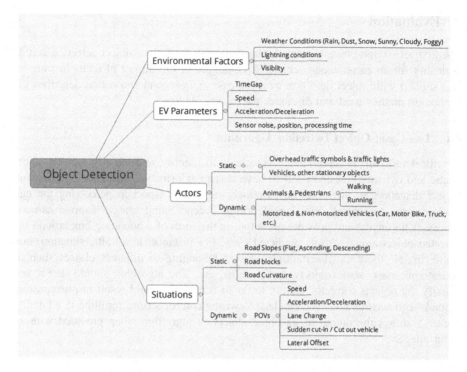

Fig. 4. Classification tree diagram for factors affecting object detection

After identifying the influencing parameters and the possible noise factors, a prioritization was created based on the analysis of impact of each parameter for a particular ADAS/AD feature under test. In the case of object detection feature, the risk associated with the noise factor over the communication channel (Salt and Pepper Noise) was found to be having higher precedence and weightage over other noise factors. This was decided considering frequency of occurrence, detectability and severity of the influencing factor for a particular ADAS/AD feature based on the FMEA (Failure Mode and Effect Analysis) done.

Amongst the faults described in Table 1, salt and pepper noise as sensor data impurity was studied in particular to evaluate the developed framework. Salt and pepper noise refers to a wide variety of processes that result in the same basic image degradation: only a few pixels are noisy, but they are very noisy. The effect is similar to sprinkling white and black dots—salt and pepper—on the image [9]. The cause of this fault type can be due to camera sensor, software failure or hardware failure during imaging capturing or transmission. In the evaluation section, the application of this fault type on a video stream is discussed and the observed results have been presented.

4   Evaluation

The first subsection presents a small introduction to the task of object detection and its criticality for an autonomous vehicle. An example of the impact of faults in cameras was studied with object detection as a use case. The second subsection describes the evaluation metrics used and discusses the results obtained.

4.1   Use Case: Object Detection Algorithm

A critical task for an autonomous vehicle is to identify and classify various actors (static and dynamic) around itself to have correct information about its environment. Object detection is, therefore, an extremely important aspect in perceiving the ego environment. An object detection algorithm accepts input images from a camera, processes the image and provides an output in the form of a bounding box around the detected object along with its predicted class. For instance, in a traffic situation, in a single image, there can be multiple objects belonging to different classes such as pedestrians, cars, static objects, traffic signs, etc. The algorithm should detect and classify the objects correctly; failure to do so accurately might result in misrepresentation of ego surroundings and can lead to wrong control actions resulting in a fatality. Figure 5 shows the output of an object detection algorithm when provided with an input image.

Fig. 5. Original input image (left), output of object detection algorithm with a marked bounding box along with the probability of prediction (right)

In our approach, we use real recorded vehicle data in the form of Robot Operating System (ROS) bags and introduce the faults in these ROS bag files. We added salt and pepper noise to the input image stream for an initial evaluation. Pepper noise, salt noise, and a combination of salt and pepper noise together were added to the original image. Figure 6 shows the result of adding variations of salt and pepper noise to the original image.

Fig. 6. Images added with noise – Original image (top left), pepper noise 5% (top right), salt noise 5% (bottom left), salt and pepper noise 5% (bottom right)

4.2 Evaluation Metrics and Results

There are several methods available to evaluate the object detection task. In our work, we used the evaluation protocol developed by the KITTI vision benchmark suite [10] The performance of a classification model often uses evaluation metrics such as precision, recall and mean-average-precision (mAP). The calculation of precision and recall values are done based on a confusion matrix [11]. Figure 7 shows a confusion matrix, which summarizes the conditions for these values.

		Ground Truth	
		Actual Condition Positive	Actual Condition Negative
Prediction	Predicted Condition Positive	True Positive	False Positive
	Predicted Condition Negative	False Negative	True Negative

Fig. 7. Confusion matrix

From the confusion matrix, precision is defined as the ratio of true positives to the total predicted positive values as stated in Eq. 1.

$$Precision = \frac{True\ Positive}{True\ Positive + False\ Positive} \tag{1}$$

From the confusion matrix, recall is defined as the ratio of true positives to the actual positive values as stated in Eq. 2.

$$Recall = \frac{True\ Positive}{True\ Positive + False\ Negative} \tag{2}$$

Intersection over Union (IOU), also known as the Jaccard coefficient, is a measure of the percentage of overlap between sets defined as [12]:

$$IoU = \frac{|A \cap B|}{|A \cup B|} \tag{3}$$

where A and B are the sets of predicted data and ground truth data respectively.

The IOU can be a value between 0 and 1, with 0 indicating no overlap and 1 complete overlap between the sets [12]. An observation is classified as true positive when the IOU value is above a certain threshold else it is classified as false positive. In the KITTI benchmark suite, the evaluation of the object detection performance is done using the PASCAL criteria [10]. For cars, an IOU of 70% is required, while for pedestrians and cyclists an IOU of 50% is required. The average precision is computed as the area under the Precision-Recall (PR) curve. The average precision (AP) score of the PR curve is used to indicate the overall performance, i.e., the larger AP score indicates the better performance of the object detection algorithm [13].

Figure 8 shows a block diagram of the above approach used to evaluate the impact of noise addition to an image on the output of the object detection algorithm.

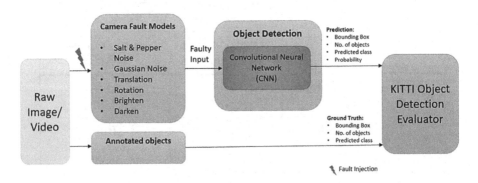

Fig. 8. Block diagram of the evaluation method of the object detection

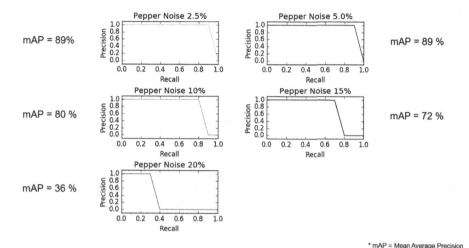

* mAP = Mean Average Precision

Fig. 9. Precision-Recall curves for different amounts of pepper noise on input images

The images from a camera stream of recorded ROS bag were extracted and the objects present in the images were marked with bounding boxes and the associated class. The ground truth data was generated and stored in a text file format as required by the KITTI evaluation script. The corrupted images after adding salt and pepper noise were provided as an input to the object detection algorithm. The algorithm detected and classified objects giving the output in the form of bounding box dimensions and a confidence value (probability) for the predicted class.

The input images were added with salt and pepper noise individually and in combination. The evaluation was carried out for different percentages of noise and the PR curves were plotted for each of the variations. Figure 9 shows the impact of adding pepper noise to the input image stream. From the plots, it can be seen that the system is robust enough to handle noisy images with up to 10% pepper noise with a drop in mean AP score from 89 to 80%. The performance drops sharply after adding 20% pepper noise which is not reliable anymore.

Figure 10 shows the impact of adding salt noise to the input image stream. From the plots, it can be seen that the system is vulnerable to salt noise as the mean AP score drops to 36% at 2.5% noise. With an increase in the noise percent, the performance gets worse and mean AP drops to zero at 10% noise. The performance drop is drastic in contrast with the same amount of pepper noise, hence the system output cannot be considered reliable in the presence of salt noise.

Figure 11 shows the impact of adding a 50:50 combination of salt and pepper noise to the input image stream. In comparison with salt noise alone at 2.5%, the system performance is still acceptable with a mean AP score of 80%.

From these PR curves it can be seen that object recognition suffers drastically in the presence of granular noise in the image source. In particular, salt noise has a greater impact than pepper noise.

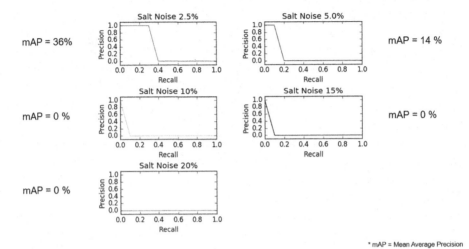

Fig. 10. Precision-Recall curves for different amounts of salt noise on input images

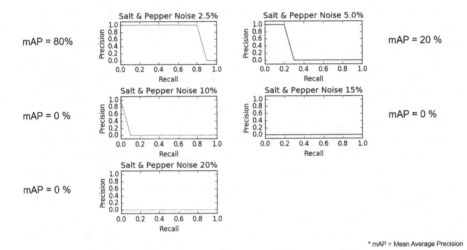

Fig. 11. Precision-Recall curves for different amounts of salt and pepper noise on images

This could be primarily due to how the object detection algorithms are designed. These algorithms use CNNs to detect and classify the objects in an image. The training of a neural network is done on a large dataset of images containing different objects and the neural network learns feature extraction to identify the class of an object. The performance of a neural network largely depends on the dataset used to train them.

The neural network used in this evaluation was trained on an image dataset without noise. This is one of the reasons why the performance suffers in presence of noise. Another reason of this behavior is because the color images are converted to grayscale before being processed for detection and classification. As salt and pepper noise are randomly distributed white and black pixels spread on the image, they can introduce discontinuities in the feature of an object which can make it difficult for the network to identify the object. If pepper noise is added, as they are black pixels they can be assumed as parts of the road surface by the network and therefore in case of pepper noise the performance drop was not drastic. On the other hand, salt noise which are white pixels can break the feature patterns of the object thus making it difficult for the networks to detect and classify.

5 Conclusion and Future Work

The deployment of partially automated cars or cars with advanced driver assistance systems functioning safely without harm can only be achieved by exhaustive testing of such systems in all possible conditions to prove their safe behavior. The need for robust and dependable performance of such systems is vital for safe co-existence of such cars along with human drivers. The currently developed tool can help in expanding the existing validation toolchain alongside traditional verification and testing methods. Along with conventional SIL and HIL testing using simulated environments, we advocate that the use of fault injection using real data can prove to be a valuable validation approach resulting in having better confidence in system performance and realize the system boundaries effectively. With this approach, we were able to introduce various faults as recommended by the automotive safety standards and determine the impact of such faults on the performance of a component of an autonomous system. As expected, we observed that the performance drops in the presence of faulty sensor data and were able to quantify the drop so that the system robustness can be estimated.

This was the initial step of this work, and it can still be improved to accommodate faults for other sensor inputs for an ADAS/AD/AD platform. Along with sensor faults, in the future, the tool can be extended to introduce communication faults as well, which can assist in simulating network related errors too. In multi-domain controllers, as in the case of an ADAS/AD/AD electronic control unit, the behavior of safety monitoring functionality can also be realized.

References

1. Ziade, H., Ayoubi, R., Velazco, R.: A survey on fault injection techniques. Int. Arab J. Inf. Technol. 1, 171–186 (2004)
2. Reway, F., Huber, W., Ribeiro, E.P.: Test methodology for vision-based ADAS/AD algorithms with an automotive camera-in-the-loop. In: International Conference on Vehicular Electronics and Safety (ICVES), pp. 1–7. IEEE, Madrid (2018)
3. Uriagereka, G.J., Lattarulo, R., Rastelli, J.P., Calonge, E.A., Ruiz Lopez, A., Espinoza Ortiz, H.: Fault injection method for safety and controllability evaluation of automated driving. In: Intelligent Vehicles Symposium (IV), pp. 1867–1872. IEEE, Los Angeles (2017)
4. ISO website for automotive ISO 26262 standard. https://www.iso.org/standard/68383.html. Accessed 02 Apr 2019

5. Pintard, L., Fabre, J.-C., Kanoun, K., Leeman, M., Roy, M.: Fault injection in the automotive standard ISO 26262: an initial approach. In: Vieira, M., Cunha, J.C. (eds.) EWDC 2013. LNCS, vol. 7869, pp. 126–133. Springer, Heidelberg (2013). https://doi.org/10.1007/978-3-642-38789-0_11

6. Koopman, P., Wagner, M.: Challenges in autonomous vehicle testing and validation. SAE Int. J. Transp. Saf. **4**, 15–24 (2016)

7. ISO website for SOTIF standard. https://www.iso.org/standard/70939.html. Accessed 02 Apr 2019

8. Mikołajczyk, A., Grochowski, M.: Data augmentation for improving deep learning in image classification problem. In: International Interdisciplinary Ph.D. Workshop (IIPhDW), Swinoujście, pp. 117–122 (2018)

9. Boncelet, C.: The Essential Guide to Image Processing. Academic Press, Inc., Orlando (2009)

10. Geiger, A., Lenz, P., Urtasun, R.: Are we ready for Autonomous Driving? In: The KITTI Vision Benchmark Suite. Conference on Computer Vision and Pattern Recognition (CVPR) (2012)

11. Fawcett, T.: Introduction to ROC analysis. Pattern Recogn. Lett. **27**, 861–874 (2006). https://doi.org/10.1016/j.patrec.2005.10.010

12. Article for Jaccard Index, Science Direct. https://www.sciencedirect.com/topics/computer-science/jaccard-coefficient. Accessed 17 May 2019

13. Wen, L.: UA-DETRAC: new benchmark and protocol for multi-object detection and tracking. arXiv CoRR, abs/1511.04136 (2015)

Stochastic Modelling of Autonomous Vehicles Driving Scenarios Using PEPA

Wei Chen[1,2][✉] and Leïla Kloul[1]

[1] Laboratory DAVID, Versailles Saint-Quentin-en-Yvelines University,
45, avenue des États-Unis, 78000 Versailles, France
`wei.chen@ens.uvsq.fr, leila.kloul@uvsq.fr`
[2] Institute of Technological Research SystemX, 8, Avenue de la Vauve,
91120 Palaiseau, France

Abstract. Autonomous vehicles perceive the environment with different kinds of sensors (camera, radar, lidar...). They must evolve in an unpredictable environment and a wide context of dynamic execution, with strong interactions. Therefore, ensuring the functionality and safety of the autonomous driving system has become one of the focuses of research in the field. In order to guarantee the safety of the autonomous vehicle, its occupants and the others road users, it is necessary to validate the decisions of the algorithms for all the situations that will be met by the vehicle. These situations are described and generated as different scenarios. The main objective of this work is to generate all these scenarios and find out the critical ones. Therefore, we use a scenario-generation methodology which uses the Performance Evaluation Process Algebra (PEPA) for modelling the transitions between the driving scenes. To apply our approach, we consider a running example about a riding autonomous vehicle in the context of a three-lane highway.

Keywords: Autonomous vehicle · Critical scenarios · Formal method · PEPA

1 Introduction

Autonomous vehicles combine a variety of sensors to perceive their surroundings, such as cameras, radars and lidars. Based on the data provided by the sensors, perception algorithms provide observations on the environmental elements, while decision algorithms generate the actions to be implemented by these vehicles. Therefore, it is necessary to specify, validate and secure the dependability of the architecture and the behavioural logic of the Advanced Driver-Assistance Systems (ADAS) running on the vehicle for all the situations that will be met by the vehicle to guarantee the safety of the autonomous vehicle.

These situations are described and generated as different test cases of autonomous vehicles. Our objective is modelling these test cases for testing

Supported by IRT SystemX.

Y. Papadopoulos et al. (Eds.): IMBSA 2019, LNCS 11842, pp. 317–331, 2019.
https://doi.org/10.1007/978-3-030-32872-6_21

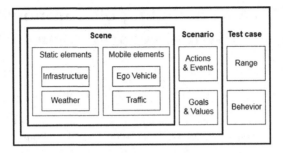

Fig. 1. Scene, Scenario and Test Case.

ADAS. We should first define the terms of *test case* and what it includes. We define the *test case* as the description of one or several scenarios applied to some ranges and behaviours to simulate the ADAS (Fig. 1) (Chen and Kloul 2019). A *scenario* describes the temporal development between several scenes in a sequence of scenes (Fig. 2) (Chen and Kloul 2018). These scenes are developed by the actions made by autonomous vehicle *Ego* or the events occurring due to the actions made by other vehicles, and this from the point of view of *Ego*. A *scene* is described as a snapshot of the vehicle environment including the static and mobile elements, and the relationships among those elements.

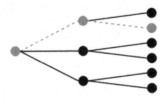

Fig. 2. A scenario (dashed line) made by actions/events (edges) and scenes (nodes)

We have presented an ADAS test cases generation methodology based on highway traffic situation description ontologies in (Chen and Kloul 2018). We focused on highway infrastructure because compared to other types of roads, there are uniform specifications (Ministère de l'écologie 1988; Ministère de l'équipement 2000) for highways. We built three ontologies for the conceptualization and characterization of the components of test cases: a highway ontology and a weather ontology to specify the environment in which evolves the autonomous vehicle, and a vehicle ontology which consists of the vehicle devices and the control actions. Relationships and rules, such as traffic regulation, are expressed using a first-order logic. Our methodology is composed of a hierarchy of three layers: basic layer, interaction layer and generation layer (Fig. 3). A scene can be defined using the concepts in the basic layer and the relationships in the interaction layer. But these scenes are static like snapshots, not enough to be the test cases for the simulation and validation of ADAS. Thus we are interested in the PEPA modelling technique to generate the scenarios according to the state-change elements of the system. In (Chen and Kloul 2019), we model a sample scenario using Performance Evaluation Process Algebra (PEPA) (Hillston 1994).

In this paper, we also focus on the generation layer for modelling the dynamic transitions between the driving scenes to generate scenarios. We consider a more general situation *"Riding autonomous vehicle in the context of a three-lane highway"* as an example to describe more specifically how to build the corresponding PEPA model, and how to generate all scenarios, specially the critical ones.

Structure of the paper: Sect. 2 is dedicated to Related Works. An overview of our methodology of test cases generation is presented in Sect. 3. An introduction of the stochastic formal modelling language PEPA is given in Sect. 4. We use a case study in Sect. 5 to show the construction of corresponding PEPA model, the generation of all scenarios, specially the critical ones. Finally, we conclude our work in Sect. 6.

2   Related Works

Several researchers have used ontologies for the conceptualization of the ADAS or the control of the autonomous vehicle.

An ontology of recognition for ADAS system is presented in (Armand et al. 2014). The authors define an ontology composed of concepts and their instances. This ontology includes contextual concepts and context parameters. It is able to process human-like reasoning on global road contexts. Another ontology is proposed by Pollard et al. (2013) for situation assessment for automated ground vehicles. It includes the sensors/actuators state, environmental conditions and driver's state. However, as the classes of both ontologies are highly generalized, they are not enough to describe test cases allowing to simulate and validate ADAS.

To build a knowledge base for smart vehicles and implement different types of ADAS, (Zhao et al. 2015) proposed three ontologies: map ontology, control ontology and car ontology. They focus on algorithms for rapid decision making for autonomous vehicle systems. They provide an ontology-based knowledge base and decision-making system that can make safe decisions about uncontrolled intersections and narrow roads. However, the authors did not consider the equipment of the road infrastructure in their map ontology, for example the traffic signs which are an important part for test cases construction.

Morignot and Nashashibi (2012) propose an ontology to relax traffic regulation in unusual but practical situations, in order to assist drivers. Their ontology represents the vehicles, the infrastructure and the traffic regulation for the general road. It is based on the experience of the members of the lab with driving license, not based on a texts corpus. That may be useful for modelling the concepts involved in traffic regulation relaxation, but we need more rigorous ontologies for modelling the concepts involved in general situations.

In (Bagschik et al. 2017), the authors propose, using ontology, to create scenarios for development of automated driving functions. They propose a process for an ontology based scene creation and a model for knowledge representation with 5 layers: road-level, traffic infrastructure, temporary manipulation of the first two levels, objects and environment. A scene is created from first layer to fifth layer. This ontology has modelled German motorways with 284 classes, 762 logical axioms and 75 semantic web rules. A number of scenes could be automatically generated in natural language. However, the natural language is not a machine-understandable knowledge and the transformation of natural language based scenes to simulation data formats with such a huge ontology is a tremendous work.

In (Hülsen et al. 2011) and in (Hummel et al. 2008) the authors use a description logic to describe the scenes. The first work provides a generic description of road intersections using the concepts *Car*, *Crossing*, *RoadConnection* and *SignAtCrossing*. They use description logic to reason about the relations between cars and describe how a traffic intersection situation is set up in this ontology and define its semantics. The results are presented for an intersection with 5 roads, 11 lanes and 6 cars driving towards the intersection. Hummel et al. (2008) also propose an ontology to understand road infrastructures at intersections. This methodology focuses on the geometrical details related to the multi-level topological information. It presents scene comprehension frameworks based on the description logic, which can identify unreasonable sensor data by checking for consistency. All these ontologies are limited to the situation of intersection which is not enough to simulate an environment and validate the ADAS.

In (Furda and Vlacic 2009, 2011), the authors deal with the high-level vehicle control tasks and address the topic of real-time decision making for autonomous vehicles. There is a large number of factors to be considered in the decision making unit for the selection of feasible driving manoeuvres. Petri nets are used to model this decision stage.

The authors of (Lee et al. 2009) introduced a complete parking mechanism for autonomous car-like vehicles to solve the parallel parking problem. The Petri net is used to recognize suitable parking regions and plan alternative parking routes especially in global space. This method provides an effective parking path and strategy, it also extends the case of single parking space to the case of multiple parking spaces.

A process algebra based on basic operators of classical process algebras (CCS, CSP, ACP) is used in (Varricchio et al. 2014) as a formal specification language to express complex tasks for autonomous electric vehicles in a mobility-on-demand scenario. The authors proposed an algorithm whose solution converges to the optimal continuous-time trajectory that satisfies the task specification.

A formalisation of the Comhordú model has been achieved in (Bhandal et al. 2011). Comhordú is a coordination model for reasoning about some of autonomous mobile systems that communicate over a wireless network. This model incorporates a collection of entities some of which are mobile vehicles. Every entity has a type which determines the behaviour of an entity. The state of an entity contains its location and activity information. A mode is an abstraction of a state. This model is formalised by the language TCBS' which is based on the Timed Calculus of Broadcasting Systems (TCBS) (Prasad 1996). This formalism eliminates the ambiguity and provides a basis for future verification work.

In the context of formal modelling techniques for concurrent systems, the authors in (Cerone and Zhao 2013) use the Markovian process algebra PEPA (Hillston 1994) to describe quantitative aspects of driver behaviour to understand the relation between driver behaviour and transport systems. A three-way junction consisting of a two-way main road with a diverging one-way road is used as an example to illustrate their approach. They are interested in the probability of possible collisions, the average waiting time in a queue from arrival at the junction to finally passing the junction and the average number of cars waiting in a queue. They have modelled the effects of driver's experience in terms of state transitions associated with a finite number of pre-defined probability factors. The results show a trade-off between junction performance (reflected in number of cars in a queue and waiting time) and safety (reflected in probability of possible collision) under certain conditions on driver behaviour.

In this paper, we use the PEPA for modelling the transitions between the driving scenes.

3   Overview of the Methodology

In order to generate scenarios, we have defined a three-layers methodology (Fig. 3). Our methodology is based on ontologies we have defined in (Chen and Kloul 2018). We define three ontologies: highway ontology and weather ontology to specify the environment in which evolves the autonomous vehicle, and the vehicle ontology which consists of the vehicle devices and control actions. Our methodology consists of the following three layers: basic layer, interaction layer and generation layer.

Basic Layer. It includes all static and mobile elements for the scenarios. We represent them with ontologies as a structural framework. Ontology is often conceived as a set of concepts with their definitions and relationships (Uschold and Gruninger 1996). This layer includes the static concepts and the mobile concepts of the highway, the weather and the vehicle ontologies (Chen and Kloul 2018).

The highway infrastructure ontology consists of the physical components of highway system providing facilities essential to allow the vehicle driving on the highway. We have defined fifty-four (54) concepts for highway ontology. The weather ontology describes the state of the atmosphere at a particular place and time. Some phenomena influence the visibility of captors on the autonomous vehicle. We have defined twelve (12) concepts for the weather ontology. Vehicle ontology describes the performance of a vehicle with nine (9) properties. We have defined twenty-six (26) concepts for vehicle ontology (see (Chen and Kloul 2019) for more details).

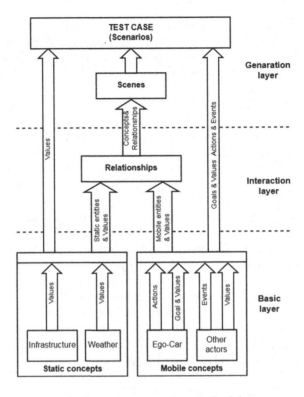

Fig. 3. Scenarios generation methodology.

Interaction Layer. This layer describes the interaction relationships between, on the one hand, the static entities, and on the other hands the mobile entities. Moreover this layer describes the relationships between static and mobile entities.

In order to represent the complex and intricate relationships between the entities, we consider three kinds of relationships (Fig. 4): the relationships between the highway entities, the relationships between the vehicle entities, and the relationships between the entities of highway and vehicle. Moreover, the traffic regulation and the interactions between the concepts are written as rules to simulate

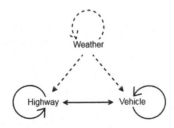

Fig. 4. Relationships (solid lines) and effects (dashed lines).

the environment of autonomous vehicle. We use first-order logic to represent these relationships and rules.

Generation Layer. The task of the generation layer is to build test cases which include one or several scenarios. The scenario is defined as a sequence of scenes, assailed with goals, values and actions of Ego, values and events from the other actors, and values of the static concepts. A scene can be defined using the concepts in the basic layer and the relationships in the interaction layer (Fig. 3). In the following sections, we focus on this layer for modelling the dynamic transitions between the driving scenes to generate scenarios using Performance Evaluation Process Algebra (PEPA).

4 Performance Evaluation Process Algebra (PEPA)

Performance Evaluation Process Algebra (PEPA) is a stochastic process algebra designed for modelling computer and communication systems and introduced by Jane Hillston in the 1990s (Hillston 1994). PEPA is a simple language with a small set of operators. It is easy to reason about the language as it provides a great deal of flexibility to the modeller (Hillston 1994).

A PEPA model is constructed by identifying components performing activities. The operators and their syntax are defined as follows:

$$S \stackrel{\text{def}}{=} (\alpha, r).P \mid P + Q \mid P \underset{L}{\bowtie} Q \mid P/L \mid A$$

Prefix: $S \stackrel{\text{def}}{=} (\alpha, r).P$, component S carries out activity (α, r) which has action type α and a duration which is exponentially distributed with parameter r before behaving as P

Choice: $S \stackrel{\text{def}}{=} P + Q$, S may behave either as component P or as component Q

Cooperation: $S \stackrel{\text{def}}{=} P \underset{L}{\bowtie} Q$, S is the result of the cooperation or synchronisation between components P and Q. Shared activities in the cooperation set L determine the interaction between components P and Q, replacing the individual activities of the individual components P and Q with a rate reflecting the rate of the slower participant.

Hiding: $S \stackrel{\text{def}}{=} P/L$,   the system behaves as component P except that any activity of a type within the set L is hidden. Its type is not witnessed upon completion. It appears as the unknown type τ and can be regarded as an internal delay by the component

Constant: $S \stackrel{\text{def}}{=} A$ it assigns S the behaviour of component A. In general, it assigns names to components

PEPA abstracts activities performed by components into a continuous-time Markov process. The generation of this underlying Markov process is based on the derivation graph of the model. The derivation graph is a directed multigraph whose nodes are the reachable states of model and whose arcs represent the possible transitions between them. These edges are labelled only by the rates of activities which become the corresponding entries in the infinitesimal generator matrix (Kloul 2006).

5 Case Study

We consider the situation *"Riding autonomous vehicle in the context of a three-lane highway"* as an example to show how to build the corresponding PEPA model, and how to generate all scenarios, specially the critical ones.

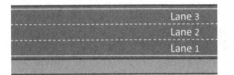

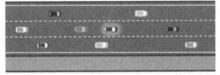

Fig. 5. Scenography of the example

Fig. 6. The initial scene. (Color figure online)

The highway is separated into two carriageways by median. In the scenography of this running example (Fig. 5), a portion of one carriageway is selected. This carriageway has three main lanes: the right lane–$Lane_1$, the center lane–$Lane_2$ and the left lane–$Lane_3$. The left hard shoulder is located on the immediate outside of the median. The edge of the left hard shoulder is marked by two single solid white lines and the right soft shoulder is located on the immediate outside of the right hard shoulder. The dashed lines are of type T1 which definition is provided in the official French document for road symbols (Ministère de l'écologie 1988).

We consider the example of the scene in Fig. 6, where the autonomous vehicle *Ego* (blue vehicle) rolls on the center lane of a separated lane road. On this lane, one (1) vehicle rolls in front of *Ego* and two (2) vehicles behind *Ego*. There are two (2) vehicles rolling on the left lane and three (3) vehicles rolling on the right lane.

Fig. 7. Critical zone of example scene.

Depending on the speed of *Ego* and the speed of the vehicle following *Ego*, we can define a critical zone in the center lane considering the minimum safety distance that must separate *Ego* from other vehicles (Fig. 7). Therefore, we separate the portion of carriageway into six (6) zones as shown in Fig. 8.

Fig. 8. Zones of the scene.   **Fig. 9.** Zones' numbers in the scene.

We number these zones from one to six (Fig. 9). Zone 1 indicates the left lane. Zone 2 and Zone 5 indicate the uncritical zones in front and behind *Ego*. Zone 3 indicates the critical zone in front of *Ego* while Zone 4 indicates the critical one behind it. Zone 6 indicates the right lane. Both Zone 1 and Zone 6 are uncritical zones for *Ego*.

In our PEPA model, there are 3 components: *Ego*, VA_1 and $Scene_1$. These model the behaviour of the *Ego* car, any vehicle, say VA, in the scene and the scene itself, respectively. Suppose *Ego* is always in the center lane with no lane change actions. The PEPA equation of the sequential component *Ego* is the following:

$$Ego = (runEgo, e_1).Ego + (accelerateEgo, e_2).Ego + (decelerateEgo, e_3).Ego;$$

The action *runEgo* means that *Ego* rolls on the lane without changing its direction or its speed. The actions *accelerateEgo* and *decelerateEgo*, respectively, indicate that *Ego* accelerates and decelerates. *Ego* always stays in the initial state after these actions. e_1, e_2 and e_3 are the rates of the corresponding actions.

Now consider that a car VA is rolling on a portion of carriageway and its initial state, noted VA_1, is on the left lane. The PEPA equations of the sequential component VA_1 are the following:

$$
\begin{aligned}
VA_1 = {}& (accelerateVA_1, a_1).VA_1 + (decelerateVA_1, a_2).VA_1 + (goRightVA_1, p_1 * a_3).VA_2 \\
& + (goRightVA_1, p_2 * a_3).VA_3 + (goRightVA_1, p_3 * a_3).VA_4 \\
& + (goRightVA_1, (1 - p_1 - p_2 - p_3) * a_3).VA_5; \\
VA_2 = {}& (goLeftVA_2, a_6).VA_1 + (goRightVA_2, a_7).VA_6 + (accelerateVA_2, a_4).VA_2 \\
& + (decelerateVA_2, p_4 * a_5).VA_2 + (decelerateVA_2, (1 - p_4) * a_5).VA_3; \\
VA_3 = {}& (goLeftVA_2, a_6).VA_1 + (goRightVA_2, a_7).VA_6 + (accelerateVA_2, (1 - p_5) * a_4).VA_2 \\
& + (accelerateVA_2, p_5 * a_5).VA_3 + (decelerateVA_2, a_5).VA_3; \\
VA_4 = {}& (goLeftVA_2, a_6).VA_1 + (goRightVA_2, a_7).VA_6 + (accelerateVA_2, a_4).VA_4 \\
& + (decelerateVA_2, p_4 * a_5).VA_4 + (decelerateVA_2, (1 - p_6) * a_5).VA_5;
\end{aligned}
$$

$$VA_5 = (goLeftVA_2, a_6).VA_1 + (goRightVA_2, a_7).VA_6 + (accelerateVA_2, (1 - p_7) * a_4).VA_4$$
$$+ (accelerateVA_2, p_7 * a_5).VA_5 + (decelerateVA_2, a_5).VA5;$$
$$VA_6 = (accelerateVA_3, a_8).VA_6 + (decelerateVA_3, a_9).VA_6 + (goLeftVA_3, p_8 * a_{10}).VA_2$$
$$+ (goLeftVA_3, p_9 * a_{10}).VA_3 + (goLeftVA_3, p_{10} * a_{10}).VA_4$$
$$+ (goLeftVA_3, (1 - p_8 - p_9 - p_{10}) * a_{10}).VA_5;$$

In state VA_1, $goRightVA_1$ is the action modelling the displacement of VA from its current lane to the right immediate lane. This action may lead to 4 different cases. VA may arrive at Zone 2 (state VA_2), Zone 3 (state VA_3), Zone 4 (state VA_4) or Zone 5 (state VA_5). State VA_2 models the behaviour of the car when being in Zone 2. In this case, action $decelerateVA_2$ may lead to 2 different cases: VA stays in state VA_2 when it slowly decelerates and it will go to state VA_3 if it drastically decelerates. State VA_3 models the behaviour of the car when being in Zone 3. In this case, action $accelerateVA_2$ may lead to 2 different cases: VA stays in state VA_3 when it slowly accelerates and it will go to state VA_2 when it drastically accelerates. State VA_4 models the behaviour of the car when being in Zone 4. In this case, action $decelerateVA_2$ may lead to 2 different cases: VA stays in state VA_4 when it slowly decelerates and it will go to state VA_5 when it drastically decelerates. State VA_5 models the behaviour of the car when being in Zone 5. In this case, action $accelerateVA_2$ may lead to 2 different cases: VA stays in VA_5 when it slowly accelerates and it will go to state VA_4 when it drastically accelerates. In state VA_6, $goLeftVA_3$ is the action modelling the displacement of VA from its current lane to the left immediate lane. This action may lead to 4 different cases: VA may arrive at Zone 2 (state VA_2), Zone 3 (state VA_3), Zone 4 (state VA_4) or Zone 5 (state VA_5).

a_i, $1 \leq i \leq 10$ are the rates of the corresponding actions and p_i, $1 \leq i \leq 10$, in the equations is the probability of the corresponding action occurrence. For example, when VA rolls on Zone 1 and it does action $goRightVA_1$, it may arrive at Zone 2, Zone 3, Zone 4 or Zone 5. The corresponding probabilities are p_1, p_2, p_3 and $(1 - p_1 - p_2 - p_3)$ respectively.

The initial scene $Scene_1$ indicates that Ego is rolling on the center lane and vehicle VA on the left lane. The PEPA equations of the sequential component $Scene_1$ are:

$$Scene_1 = (accelerateVA_1, \top).Scene_1 + (decelerateVA_1, \top).Scene_1 + (goRightVA_1, \top).Scene_2$$
$$+ (goRightVA1, \top).Scene_3 + (goRightVA_1, \top).Scene_4 + (goRightVA_1, \top).Scene_5;$$
$$Scene_2 = (acceleraeVA_2, \top).Scene_2 + (decelerateVA_2, \top).Scene_2 + (decelerateVA_2, \top).Scene_3$$
$$+ (goLeftVA_2, \top).Scene_1 + (goRightVA_2, \top).Scene_6;$$
$$Scene_3 = (accelerateVA_2, \top).Scene_2 + (accelerateVA_2, \top).Scene_3 + (decelerateVA_2, \top).Scene_3$$
$$+ (goLeftVA_2, \top).Scene_1 + (goRightVA_2, \top).Scene_6;$$
$$Scene_4 = (accelerateVA_2, \top).Scene_4 + (decelerateVA_2, \top).Scene_4 + (decelerateVA_2, \top).Scene_5$$
$$+ (goLeftVA_2, \top).Scene_1 + (goRightVA_2, \top).Scene_6;$$

$Scene_5 = (accelerateV A_2, \top).Scene_4 + (accelerateV A_2, \top).Scene_5 + (decelerateV A_2, \top).Scene_5$
$\quad + (goLeftV A_2, \top).Scene_1 + (goRightV A_2, \top).Scene_6;$
$Scene_6 = (accelerateV A_3, \top).Scene_6 + (decelerateV A_3, \top).Scene_6 + (goLeftV A_3, \top).Scene_2$
$\quad + (goLeftV A_3, \top).Scene_3 + (goLeftV A_3, \top).Scene_4 + (goLeftV A_3, \top).Scene_5;$

In each state of scene $Scene_i$, there is an action which leads to the transition to another state. Zone 3 and Zone 4 being the critical zones, states $Scene_3$ and $Scene_4$ indicate the critical scenes when $V A$ rolls on Zone 3 and Zone 4, respectively. All the scenarios which include state $Scene_3$ or $Scene_4$ are critical scenarios which may lead to accidents.

The complete PEPA model equation is as the following:

$$Scenario \overset{def}{=} (V A_1 \underset{L}{\bowtie} Scene_1) \parallel Ego$$

where L is the actions set on which components $V A_1$ and $Scene_1$ must synchronise. It is defined as:

$$L = \{accelerateV A_1, decelerateV A_1, goRightV A_1, accelerateV A_2, decelerateV A_2,$$
$$goLeftV A_2, goRightV A_2, accelerateV A_3, decelerateV A_3, goLeftV A_3\}.$$

5.1   The Model Parameters

In order to test our model, we define a set of values for the rates of actions and their probabilities. At present, we can calculate the rates of some actions such as *accelerate* and *decelerate*.

For example, the rates of action $accelerateV A_2$ can be calculated using $V A$'s initial speed v_1, final speed v_2 and the distance d between the initial state and the final state of $V A$. The initial speed, is the speed of $V A$ before the action $accelerateV A_2$, which is 100 km/h. The final speed, is the speed of $V A$ after the action $accelerateV A_2$, which is 110 km/h and the distance is 0.1 km. We can get the rate a_4 of this action using standard kinetic:

$$a_4 = \frac{v_2^2 - v_1^2}{2d\Delta v} = \frac{110^2 - 100^2}{2 \times 0.1 \times 10} = 1050$$

Unlike the values of actions *accelerate* and *decelerate* rate, the values of the other actions rates are set arbitrary. Tables 1 and 2 present the values parameters for the activities of components Ego and $V A_1$, respectively.

Table 1. Activites of Ego

Action		Rate
$runEgo$	e_1	500
$accelerateEgo$	e_2	950
$decelerateEgo$	e_2	1900

Table 2. Activites of VA

Action		Rate	Action		Rate
$accelerateVA_1$	a_1	850	$goLeftVA_2$	a_6	600
$decelerateVA_1$	a_2	1700	$goRightVA_2$	a_7	600
$goRightVA_1$	a_3	500	$accelerateVA_3$	a_8	950
$accelerateVA_2$	a_4	1050	$decelerateVA_3$	a_9	1900
$decelerateVA_2$	a_5	2100	$goLeftVA_3$	a_{10}	500

The values of the probabilities for this example are given randomly and they are shown in Table 3.

Table 3. Probabilities of rates

	Probability		Probability
p_1	0.3	p_6	0.5
p_2	0.2	p_7	0.6
p_3	0.1	p_8	0.1
p_4	0.7	p_9	0.2
p_5	0.2	p_{10}	0.3

5.2 Numerical Results

PEPA abstracts the activities performed by components into a continuous-time Markov process. We can get the steady-state probability distribution (see Table 4) using Eclipse PEPA (Hillston and Gilmore 2014). This PEPA model has 18 states, and the probability of being in each state is provided. We find that there are high possibilities to pass the state 1 and the state 18, whose probabilities are nearly one-third. state 1 and 18 represent the states where VA is in Zone 1 and Zone 6, respectively. VA rolls on the center lane in all other states which share the remaining probabilities.

Table 4. State space of model PEPA

State	VA	Scene	Ego	Probability	State	VA	Scene	Ego	Probability
1	VA_1	$Scene_1$	Ego	0.352941176470588	10	VA_4	$Scene_2$	Ego	0.0151257114470111
2	VA_2	$Scene_2$	Ego	0.015952714555464	11	VA_4	$Scene_3$	Ego	0.0119727683943635
3	VA_2	$Scene_3$	Ego	0.0157723350149253	12	VA_4	**$Scene_4$**	Ego	0.0151257114470111
4	VA_2	$Scene_4$	Ego	0.0159527145554646	13	VA_4	$Scene_5$	Ego	0.0119727683943635
5	VA_2	$Scene_5$	Ego	0.0157723350149253	14	VA_5	$Scene_2$	Ego	0.024773123985088
6	VA_3	$Scene_2$	Ego	0.0085948014167240	15	VA_5	$Scene_3$	Ego	0.0363636902911840
7	VA_3	$Scene_3$	Ego	0.018503678424650	16	VA_5	$Scene_4$	Ego	0.0247731239850882
8	VA_3	$Scene_4$	Ego	0.0085948014167240	17	VA_5	$Scene_5$	Ego	0.0363636902911840
9	VA_3	$Scene_5$	Ego	0.0185036784246506	18	VA_6	$Scene_6$	Ego	0.352941176470588

We can generate all possible scenarios and identify critical scenarios from the transition graph of the whole model. One scenario includes one or several states in transition graph which are connected. Each state of the system is a node of transition graph, and the activities are the labels on the transitions between the initial states and final states. The scenarios are considered as the paths in the transition graph which include at least one state. Critical scenarios are those which include critical states. In this example, critical states are those referring to critical scenes $Scene_3$ and $Scene_4$ (Table 4).

We choose a path with four (4) states to form an example of critical scenario to show how the method works. These states are state 1, state 2, state 7 and state 18. In Fig. 10, the red vehicle rolls on left lane ($Lane_3$) represents the initial state (state 1). The action $goRightVA$ is performed by VA in state VA_1 with the rate $p_1 \times a_3$ and it goes to state 2. Then, VA in the state VA_2 does the action $decelerateVA_2$ with a rate $(1 - p_4) \times a_5$ and it goes to state 7. Next, VA in the state VA_3 continue to change lane using action $goRightVA_3$ with a rate a_7 and it goes to state state 18. In this path, state 7 is the critical state as it includes the state $Scene_3$ (Table 4). Therefore, this scenario, which includes state 7, is a critical scenario.

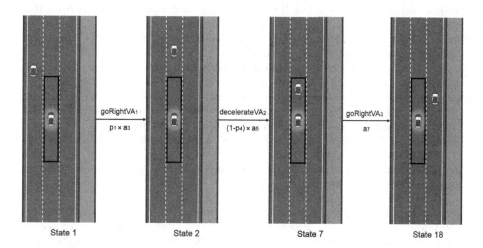

| State 1 | State 2 | State 7 | State 18 |

Fig. 10. Critical scenario include critical state (red word). (Color figure online)

We can calculate the probability of a scenario occurrence by multiplying the probabilities of all passed states. The probability of the occurrence of this scenario is:

$$P_{Scenario} = P_1 \times P_2 \times P_7 \times P_{18}$$
$$= 0.35294117647058826 \times 0.01595271455546461$$
$$\times 0.01850367842465067 \times 0.3529411764705882$$
$$= 0.00003677031$$

where P_i is the probability to be in state i, $i = 1, 2, 7, 18$.

6   Conclusions

In this article, we showed how to use the stochastic formal modelling language PEPA to model the dynamic transitions between the driving scenes to generate scenarios. This formal modelling method is an important part of our ADAS test cases generation methodology which is composed of a hierarchy of three layers: basic layer, interaction layer and generation layer. In the future, we plan to extend our work to include the highway infrastructure and weather impact.

Acknowledgements. This research work has been carried out in the framework of IRT SystemX, Paris-Saclay, France, and therefore granted with public funds within the scope of the French Program "Investissements d'Avenir".

References

Armand, A., Filliat, D., Guzman, J.I.: Ontology-based context awareness for driving assistance systems. In: 2014 IEEE Intelligent Vehicles Symposium Proceedings, Dearborn, MI, USA, 8–11 June 2014, pp. 227–233 (2014)

Bagschik, G., Menzel, T., Maurer, M.: Ontology based scene creation for the development of automated vehicles. CoRR Computing Research Repository, abs/1704.01006 (2017)

Bhandal, C., Bouroche, M., Hughes, A.: A process algebraic description of a temporal wireless network protocol. ECEASST **45** (2011)

Cerone, A., Zhao, Y.: Stochastic modelling and analysis of driver behaviour. ECEASST **69** (2013)

Chen, W., Kloul, L.: An ontology-based approach to generate the advanced driver assistance use cases of highway traffic. In: Proceedings of the 10th International Joint Conference on Knowledge Discovery, Knowledge Engineering and Knowledge Management, IC3K 2018, vol. 2: KEOD, Seville, Spain, 18–20 September 2018, pp. 73–81 (2018)

Chen, W., Kloul, L.: An advanced driver assistance test cases generation methodology based on highway traffic situation description ontologies. In: Communications in Computer and Information Science. Springer (2019, to appear)

Furda, A., Vlacic, L.B.: Towards increased road safety: real-time decision making for driverless city vehicles. In: Proceedings of the IEEE International Conference on Systems, Man and Cybernetics, San Antonio, TX, USA, 11–14 October 2009, pp. 2421–2426 (2009)

Furda, A., Vlacic, L.B.: Enabling safe autonomous driving in real-world city traffic using multiple criteria decision making. IEEE Intell. Transport. Syst. Mag. **3**(1), 4–17 (2011)

Hillston, J.: A compositional approach to performance modelling. Ph.D. thesis, University of Edinburgh, UK (1994)

Hillston, J., Gilmore, S.: Pepa tools (2014). http://www.dcs.ed.ac.uk/pepa/tools/

Hülsen, M., Zöllner, J.M., Weiss, C.: Traffic intersection situation description ontology for advanced driver assistance. In: IEEE Intelligent Vehicles Symposium (IV), Baden-Baden, Germany, 5–9 June 2011, pp. 993–999 (2011)

Hummel, B., Thiemann, W., Lulcheva, I.: Scene understanding of urban road intersections with description logic. In: Logic and Probability for Scene Interpretation (2008)

Kloul, L.: From performance analysis to performance engineering: some ideas and experiments. Ph.D. thesis (2006)

Lee, C., Lin, C., Shiu, B.: Autonomous vehicle parking using hybrid artificial intelligent approach. J. Intell. Rob. Syst. **56**(3), 319–343 (2009)

Ministère de l'écologie, Equipements des routes et des rues: Arrêté du 16 février 1988 relatif à l'approbation de modifications de l'instruction interministérielle sur la signalisation routiere, instruction interministerielle sur la signalisation routiere. Journal officiel du 12 mars 1988 (1988)

Ministère de l'équipement, des Transports, du Logement, du Tourisme et de la Mer: Décret n° 2000-1355 du 30/12/2000 paru au JORF n° 0303 du 31 décembre 2000 (2000)

Morignot, P., Nashashibi, F.: An ontology-based approach to relax traffic regulation for autonomous vehicle assistance. CoRR Computing Research Repository, abs/1212.0768 (2012)

Pollard, E., Morignot, P., Nashashibi, F.: An ontology-based model to determine the automation level of an automated vehicle for co-driving. In: Proceedings of the 16th International Conference on Information Fusion, FUSION 2013, Istanbul, Turkey, 9–12 July 2013, pp. 596–603 (2013)

Prasad, K.V.S.: Broadcasting in time. In: Ciancarini, P., Hankin, C. (eds.) COORDINATION 1996. LNCS, vol. 1061, pp. 321–338. Springer, Heidelberg (1996). https://doi.org/10.1007/3-540-61052-9_54

Uschold, M., Gruninger, M.: Ontologies: principles, methods and applications. Knowledge Eng. Rev. **11**(2), 93–155 (1996)

Varricchio, V., Chaudhari, P., Frazzoli, E.: Sampling-based algorithms for optimal motion planning using process algebra specifications. In: 2014 IEEE International Conference on Robotics and Automation, ICRA 2014, Hong Kong, China, 31 May–7 June 2014, pp. 5326–5332 (2014)

Zhao, L., Ichise, R., Mita, S., Sasaki, Y.: Core ontologies for safe autonomous driving. In: Proceedings of the ISWC 2015 Posters & Demonstrations Track co-located with the 14th International Semantic Web Conference (ISWC-2015), Bethlehem, PA, USA, 11 October 2015 (2015)

A Runtime Safety Analysis Concept for Open Adaptive Systems

Sohag Kabir[1(✉)], Ioannis Sorokos[1], Koorosh Aslansefat[1],
Yiannis Papadopoulos[1], Youcef Gheraibia[1], Jan Reich[2], Merve Saimler[3],
and Ran Wei[4]

[1] Department of Computer Science and Technology, University of Hull, Hull, UK
{s.kabir,i.sorokos,k.aslansefat-2018,y.i.papadopoulos,
y.gheraibia,}@hull.ac.uk
[2] Fraunhofer Institute for Experimental Software Engineering (IESE),
Kaiserslautern, Germany
jan.reich@iese.fraunhofer.de
[3] AVL/TR, Istanbul, Turkey
merve.saimler@avl.com
[4] Department of Computer Science, University of York, York, UK
ran.wei@york.ac.uk

Abstract. In the automotive industry, modern cyber-physical systems feature cooperation and autonomy. Such systems share information to enable collaborative functions, allowing dynamic component integration and architecture reconfiguration. Given the safety-critical nature of the applications involved, an approach for addressing safety in the context of reconfiguration impacting functional and non-functional properties at runtime is needed. In this paper, we introduce a concept for runtime safety analysis and decision input for open adaptive systems. We combine static safety analysis and evidence collected during operation to analyse, reason and provide online recommendations to minimize deviation from a system's safe states. We illustrate our concept via an abstract vehicle platooning system use case.

Keywords: Platooning · Bayesian networks · Model-based
dependability analysis · Runtime assurance

1 Introduction

Autonomous driving has gained significant financial and public interest in recent years. The idea of reducing or even removing the human control factor from driving is inherently quite exciting and promises many direct benefits to drivers, such as increased safety, comfort, improved fuel efficiency and flexible parking in cities [7]. With regards to financial potential, a widely cited market forecast for the UK's government's Centre for Connected and Autonomous Vehicles (CAVs) estimates the market for CAVs to be worth "£28bn in 2035, capturing

© Springer Nature Switzerland AG 2019
Y. Papadopoulos et al. (Eds.): IMBSA 2019, LNCS 11842, pp. 332–346, 2019.
https://doi.org/10.1007/978-3-030-32872-6_22

3% of the £907bn global market" [4, pg. 3]. The topic also presents a significant research challenge, incorporating multi-disciplinary issues from domains such as artificial intelligence, cyber-security, sensor fusion, safety and more. A defining characteristic of autonomous driving are the highly dynamic and rapidly changing conditions experienced by CAVs during operation. CAVs must continuously adapt to varying road layouts, infrastructure, neighbouring vehicle composition and driving behaviors. These considerations compound existing dynamics experienced in non-autonomous vehicles such as variable weather conditions and road conditions. In particular, the issue of safety presents a significant concern. Traditional safety assurance is defined as activities performed during development to support the overall claim that the system will be safe to operate. These activities are typically bound to the development, not the runtime phase of the system life-cycle. In safety standards like ISO26262 [10] and IEC 61508 [9], safety analysis activities are expected to only be performed during design and not during operation. However, the dynamism that CAVs feature, renders traditional, exhaustive approaches of safety assurance intractable against the potentially infinite combinations of factors and scenarios to consider. To reap the full potential offered by CAVs, assurance must adapt to their open and collaborative nature. Previous work in [14] investigated the use of their proposed Dynamic Safety Contracts (DSCs) and earlier Conditional Safety Certificates (ConSerts) [19] to address the issue of safety assurance for CAVs. The authors describe how evidence collected at runtime from various sources can be processed by predefined DCSs and Con-Serts to provide runtime safety guarantees, enabling collaborative services to be negotiated dynamically. However, we note some limitations with regards to this previous work; both DSCs and ConSerts rely on the use of binary conditional variables to evaluate guarantees.

In this paper, we expand upon previous contract-oriented approaches in the following ways:

- We introduce the use of Bayesian Networks (BNs) as an alternate inference mechanism for probabilistic reasoning of guarantees. BNs provide means of expressing uncertainty and accounting for uncertainty in the assurance process.
- Beyond inference, our expanded framework also proposes recommended actions to be applied to minimize system risk during operation; these actions are predefined and linked to a state machine. This element allows the system to address partially unanticipated scenarios by re-evaluating previous assumptions about the state of the system and responding appropriately.

To illustrate our methodology, we apply it towards an abstract vehicle platooning system use case. Notably, we believe the approach is flexible and could be transferred to other domains. The use case discussed is largely based on the ongoing research contributed by AVL/TR[1] and earlier research by Fraunhofer IESE[2], partners of the Dependability Engineering Innovation for cyber-physical

---

[1] https://www.avl.com/-/avl-turkey.

[2] https://www.iese.fraunhofer.de/en.html.

Systems (DEIS) research project[3]. The remainder of the paper is structured as follows; in Sect. 2, an overview of previous research and associated literature is reviewed. In Sect. 3, our proposed framework is presented in detail. Section 4 discusses the application of the framework on the vehicle platoon case study mentioned earlier.

2   Brief Background and Literature

2.1   Runtime Assurance for Vehicle Platooning

Integration of automated control in vehicles is not a recently proposed idea; for instance, the PATH project[4], as early as 1986, begun pursuing the topic of Intelligent Transportation Systems (ITS). As vehicles are safety-critical systems, providing equal or even more robust guarantees for safety, security and other dependability characteristics is paramount for the successful adoption of ITS. Vehicle platooning systems are an application of ITS also explored in PATH, and in other research projects such as KONVOI, SARTRE and more [2,23], [17, p. 19].

Vehicle platooning also falls under the definition of self-adaptive systems. In [5], an overview of the topic of assurance using models at runtime for self-adaptive software systems (SASSs) is provided. Platoons are SASSs in the sense that they are formed, modified and dissolved dynamically at runtime. The authors view SASSs as compositions of steady-state programs, managed by controllers or autonomic managers. SASSs require assurance to be performed at runtime as well, as part of their functionality is conditional on their adaptation. Thus, dependability-critical properties of SASSs must be assured before, during and on completion of each adaptation over the course of operation.

Earlier, in [18], the idea of using monitoring for adaptive system runtime verification is explored. The author notes that adaptive systems may feature unanticipated interactions at runtime. Rushby proposes a framework based on assurance cases and monitors generated from runtime verification languages to oversee whether assumptions and other safety properties of the case are not violated during operation. In cases where violations are detected, fault diagnosis can be applied, to trace indirect violations back to their source and identify appropriate options for recovering from failure or mitigating risk e.g. switching to backup systems or degrading services.

In [14], the issue of safety assurance for emergent collaboration of open distributed systems is explored. The authors note, like others have e.g. [18, p. 1–2, 5–6], [5, p. 1], [17, p. 2], that established practice restricts validation and verification processes to be performed exclusively during development. System behavior is decided and assured before operation, severely restricting the potential of runtime collaborative operations. The established view is rejected by the authors, who claim that available information on the operational context can

---

[3] http://www.deis-project.eu/.

[4] https://path.berkeley.edu/home.

be exploited to inform and assure collaborative functions at runtime. Their proposed approach is to predefine certain collaboration options during development. As the options are predefined, a priori analysis can determine what should be the appropriate reaction be to specific conditions during operation. The reaction would ideally reduce or eliminate the risk of collaborative services during operation, such that it is acceptable for the services to be performed. The decision of the appropriate reaction during operation relies on the systems' capacity to monitor the condition of dependability properties. A notable concept that support this view are Conditional Safety Certificates (ConSerts) [19]. ConSerts extend the notion of a modular assurance case with conditional dependability guarantees. Guarantees are provided using user-defined Boolean logic gates (AND, OR) to combine demands imposed on further ConSerts or runtime evidence that will be collected during operation. Further ConSerts satisfy imposed demands by evaluating their own guarantees and so on. The authors of [14] note that their proposed scheme can be expanded to identify potential collaborative services at runtime and negotiate their assurance via ConSerts.

In their current state, ConSerts use binary variables to provide/request guarantees/demands. ConSerts Trees (CSTs) are formed to represent connectivity and hierarchical relationships between multiple ConSerts. To evaluate CSTs during operation, each CST is converted to a Binary Decision Diagram (BDD) [19, p. 13]. In [15], the authors note that ConSerts does not address uncertainty and propose an additional safety manager to be added to the AUTOSAR standard. The introduced manager actively manages policy, not only monitoring safety rules, but also enforcing them via the existing AUTOSAR mode manager. The proposed manager addresses uncertainty by monitoring the data quality and integrity of safety-critical information stored in safety contracts, the latter being a comparable concept to ConSerts. Alternative approaches for addressing uncertainty in CAV platoons include using formal methods [6], Hidden Markov Models [21] and a requirements language [24].

2.2 State Machines and Bayesian Networks

State machines (SMs) are a high-level modelling formalism used to explicitly express the behaviour of systems. In its basic form, a SM could be defined as:

$$SM = (S, \Sigma, \delta, s_0) \qquad (1)$$

where S is the set of all possible states in the SM, Σ is the set of all possible events, δ is the transition function $\delta : S \times \Sigma \to S$ and s_0 is the initial state. From a system behaviour modelling point of view, at the beginning of operational time, the system is in state s_0. When an event occurs, a state transition defined by the transition function can happen to take the system to another state. As SMs can readily model the effects of different events on different states of a system, they are well-suited for capturing the effects of failure and faults on the behaviour of a system. As a result, SMs have been utilised in a number of model-based safety analysis paradigms such as AADL [8], Altarica [1], xSAP [3], HiP-HOPS [12,16], etc.

Bayesian networks (BNs) as a probabilistic graphical model have flexible architecture, which can make decisions under uncertainty and can provide a global assessment about different dependability properties such as reliability and availability by combining local level information from different sources. Graphically, BNs represent the relationships between a set of random variables in the form of a directed acyclic graph. These relationships can be interpreted as parent-child relations. In a BN, if an arc originates from a node X and terminates at another node Y, then X is the parent node and Y is the child node. A parent has direct effect on its child nodes. Such effects can be either be deterministic (in the sense they are guaranteed to occur) or probabilistic [13]. The probability distribution of a node X_i conditioned on its parents can be expressed as $Pr\{X_i|Parents(X_i)\}$. A node without a parent and one without children are known as root and leaf nodes, respectively. Using the BNs, the joint probability distribution of a set of random variables $\{V_1, V_2, V_3, \ldots V_{n-1}, V_n\}$ can be obtained by a chain rule as:

$$Pr\{V_1, V_2, V_3, \ldots V_{n-1}, V_n\} = \prod_{i=1}^{n} Pr\{V_i|\ Parent(V_i)\} \qquad (2)$$

where $Pr\{x\}$ is the probability of x and $Pr\{x|y\}$ is the conditional probability of x given y.

In recent years, BNs have gained popularity in the dependability engineering area and an overview of widespread applications of BNs in safety and reliablity analysis can be found in [11].

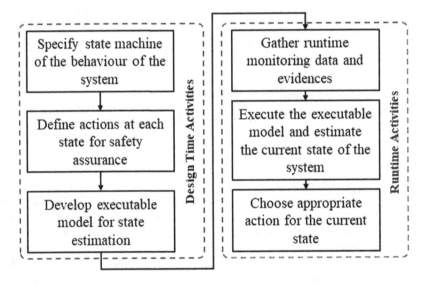

Fig. 1. Framework of the proposed approach

3   Proposed Framework

Our proposed framework relies on certain assumptions, described here. As mentioned earlier, during operation, self-adaptive systems can react to different unexpected and/or expected events and reconfigure themselves to continue providing services. That means such systems can operate in different mode of operations and each mode can be considered as a distinct system state. In this paper, we assume that during design stage, it is possible to foresee all the different possible states a system can be in during operation. The only a priori unknown is the actual state of the system at a given point during operation.

Figure 1 shows the proposed framework for runtime safety assurance of self-adaptive systems. Note that, we assume that the user of this framework have the safety goal(s) defined for the subject system. As seen in the figure, the framework contains six different steps. The first three of these steps are performed during design time and the rest of the steps are performed repeatedly during runtime. The framework steps are performed as follows:

1. In light of assumptions made previously, as the first step of the framework, the behavioural model of the system is developed as a state machine. To do so, analysts require knowledge of the architecture and both nominal and failure behaviour of the studied system. Digital Dependability Identities (DDIs) [20] can be used to encapsulate this behavior into a machine-readable format.
2. Once the state machine is formed, per the second step of Fig. 1, analysts must identify the safety status of the system in each of the previously identified states with respect to the safety goal(s) defined earlier. Based on the state machine, per-state actions are defined to assure safety of the overall system operation. In other words, as a particular state depicts a distinct operational context for the system, actions are defined to reduce or eliminate unacceptable i.e. unsafe risk of operation under that context. How such actions should be processed in general depends on the specific application. For instance, some actions may be provided as recommendations to human operators, others may be input for automated controls.
3. The third step involves developing an executable model used at runtime to estimate the operational state of the system. To develop such an executable model, the first task is to identify necessary conditions that must be verified at runtime to ascertain the system state. Once such conditions are known, these conditions must be formulated in a verifiable format using parameters known at design time and parameters that can be monitored during system operation. The monitoring data based on these parameters includes internal system data, external data received from other collaborating systems, and environmental conditions. In this paper, we utilise the modelling capability of Bayesian Networks (BNs) to formulate such an executable model. In the BN model, leaf nodes are variables representing different parameters necessary to learn about the state of the system. The root node evaluates the current state of the system based on the leaf nodes. Note that, if multiple states could be evaluated from one BN, then multiple root nodes can be

included. Alternatively, it is also possible to separate the executable model into several BNs when different state evaluations are needed. In this paper, we assume that each of the smaller participating subsystems to the larger system operate based on the principle of self-safety with group-awareness. This means that each subsystem aims to ensure its own safety in the context of the whole system's operation, based on the subsystem's own data and data received from others. For this reason, each such subsystem contains executable model(s) (i.e. BN model(s)) to evaluate its own state.

4. During operation, each subsystem monitors its own data and data collected from other systems, and provides runtime input to the BN model(s). In the context of a BN model, this involves setting evidence on the leaf nodes of the appropriate BNs.

5. In the next step of Fig. 1, whenever new evidence is provided to the BN, the model is executed automatically to update the knowledge about the current state of the system's operation.

6. Once the current system state is known, appropriate actions can be selected for the current state from the predefined set of actions. As actions are predefined to assure system safety, proper execution of the actions should guarantee the safe operation of the system from any state, providing development assumptions hold. However, even if recommended actions are not executed properly, the executable model can revise the earlier recommendation by accounting for the new situation. In the worst case scenario, if the subsystem's safe operation cannot be guaranteed in the context of the larger system, then the operation can be suspended.

4   Illustrative Example

In this section, we use an abstract vehicle platooning system (see Fig. 2) example to demonstrate the proposed approach. For illustration, an already formed, stable platoon scenario with two vehicles, a leader and a follower, is assumed. Each vehicle is equipped with sensors and other components to detect frontal obstacles and communicate with other vehicles and roadside infrastructure. For brevity, we consider all communication channels adequately secure, hence, security issues

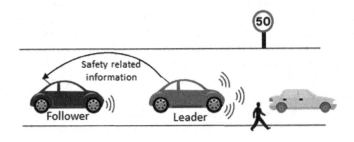

Fig. 2. Platoon with two vehicles

are not considered in this use case. Moreover, we consider that both vehicles can operate in either Cooperative or Adaptive Cruise Control (CACC/ACC) mode. In CACC mode, each vehicle collaborates with other vehicles to provide safety guarantees. In the absence of collaboration (ACC mode), vehicles rely only on their own components to drive safely.

In our illustration, we assume that two vehicles are driving in CACC mode. For effective platooning, the follower vehicle always attempts to maintain the minimum distance from the leader such that inter-vehicle distances should not increase downstream from leader to followers. This concept is also known as 'string stability', [22]. Driving in close proximity to the leader leads offers improved fuel efficiency, at the cost of increased risk of frontal collision. The aim of this use case is to show that the follower vehicle can ensure, through the proposed approach, that the risk of frontal collision with the leader in any of its operational modes is minimal. Towards this end, the follower vehicle must verify specific safety properties during runtime. Similar to the example provided in [14], we consider that to ensure safe and lawful driving the follower vehicle has to ensure the following conditions:

- Condition 1: $d \geq d_s$, where d is the distance from the front vehicle and d_s is the minimum safety distance.
- Condition 2: $Speed_{vehicle} \leq Speed_{limit}$, where $Speed_{vehicle}$ is the current speed of the vehicle and $Speed_{limit}$ is the speed limit of the road.

Therefore, the safety goal considered is **"avoid violation of the safe distance and legal speed limit"**. For the purposes of the study presented here, only a few factors are considered for the determination of d_{min}. In practice, there is a plethora of additional dynamic factors that affect this limit and will need to be accounted for. A more detailed analysis of the involved factors can be found in [17, p. 45].

Across all scenarios, if the above conditions cannot be satisfied, then the follower vehicle will take appropriate action based to achieve safety by satisfying the conditions. However, if any of the above conditions are not verifiable at runtime, then the proposed approach will recommend the vehicle switch to ACC mode until verification can be performed. Potential reasons for non-verifiability include the unavailability of one or more parameters required for verification or poor parameter detection quality by the vehicles.

Figure 3 presents the block diagram showing how safety is assured during runtime, from the follower vehicle's perspective. In the figure, the follower vehicle collects external runtime evidence from the leader and the roadside infrastructure via its communication interface. This evidence, coupled with the follower's internal parameters, are fed to its calculation unit. Within the calculation unit, the safety distance is calculated by accounting for different factors that may affect the vehicle's reaction capability. The specifics of the calculation are outside the scope of this paper. We consider the outcome of the calculation block available to the executable models created as part of the proposed framework.

The state machine of the behaviour of the follower vehicle in the context of the whole platoon is shown in Fig. 4. The state machine accounts for the differ-

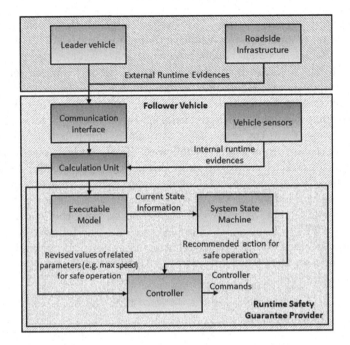

Fig. 3. Runtime safety assurance concept for the following vehicle

ent operational system contexts, with the follower vehicle being in six possible
operational states. To guarantee safety in each state, Table 1 shows the required
action in each state. That means a distinct safety guarantee is associated with
each state. In state S0, both conditions (distance and legal speed limit) are sat-

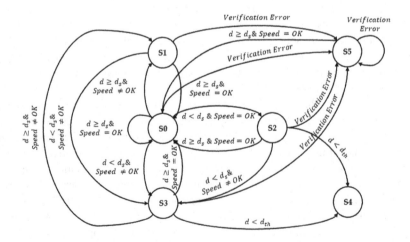

Fig. 4. State machine of the platoon system

Table 1. State with their description and associated actions

State	Description	Actions
S_0	The safety constraint is fulfilled and the vehicle is driving within the speed limit of the road	The state is safe, therefore continue driving
S_1	The safety constraint is fulfilled but the vehicle is driving outside the speed limit of the road	Decelerate to fall within the speed limit
S_2	The safety constraint is not fulfilled and the vehicle is driving within the speed limit of the road	Decelerate to increase distance with the front vehicle until safety constraint is fulfilled
S_3	The safety constraint is not fulfilled and the vehicle is driving outside the speed limit of the road	Decelerate to achieve safety distance and fall within speed limit
S_4	The safety constraint is not fulfilled, the vehicle is driving outside the speed limit of the road, and it is driving too closely	Brake to stop driving
S_5	Safety constraint and/or speed limit cannot be verified	Switch to ACC mode

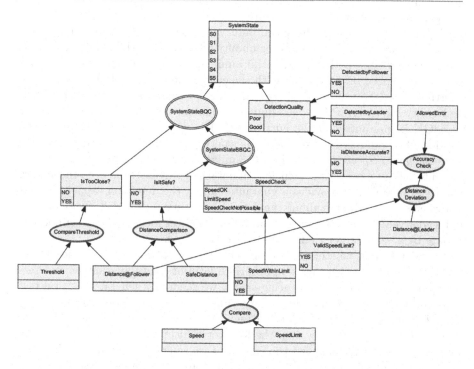

Fig. 5. BN model for deterministic estimation of system state

isfied, therefore no special action is needed in this state. However, in S2, the first condition is not satisfied, therefore the follower should decelerate to increase distance from the leader. We should note that the state machine's role is advisory rather than prescriptive or descriptive. This means that it is used as a guide for identifying recommended actions to transition to safe/safer states, rather than being actively executed.

To identify the current operational situation for the follower vehicle, we consider internal safety-related data from the vehicle itself and external data from the leader and the environment together in a unified BN model as shown in Fig. 5. Note that this model is defined at design time and evaluated at runtime. In this model, we combine both quantitative and qualitative safety parameters for runtime inference about system state. For instance, Speed, SpeedLimit, Distance@Follower, SafetyDistance etc. are quantitative parameters. On the other hand, DetectedbyFollower, DetectedbyLeader, 'ValidSpeedLimit?' are qualitative binary parameters. In the model, different nodes are responsible for guaranteeing different conditions. For instance, the SpeedCheck node guarantees compliance of the vehicle's speed with the legal speed limit. The SpeedCheck node receives input from two child nodes. The child node 'ValidSpeedLimit?' represents a certificate about the validity of the speed limit, which is shared either by other vehicles or by roadside infrastructure. As vehicles may drive very closely in a platoon, street signs could be missed due to the view being obstructed by nearby vehicles. Moreover, the speed limit varies based on location, therefore it is also necessary to have a guarantee about the liveness of the monitored speed limit. Another child node, SpeedWithinLimit, monitors the legality of the vehicle's current speed by comparing with the current speed limit. In the absence of a certificate on the validity of the speed limit, no guarantee is provided regarding legality. However, if the speed limit is validated, the internal safety property SpeedOK is guaranteed if the current speed is within the speed limit. If the speed limit is valid and is exceeded, the safety property LimitSpeed is set; this is equivalent to $Speed \neq OK$ in Fig. 4. Similarly, the node 'IsItSafe?' provides a guarantee about whether the vehicle is maintaining safe distance from the leader. The DetectionQuality provides a guarantee about the detection capacity of the two vehicles. A guarantee about the detection quality is provided if the follower and leader vehicle detect each other and the distances measured by them do not deviate by a value larger than a predefined threshold.

In order to test whether the approach can detect different scenarios based on the runtime inputs, provide appropriate level of safety guarantees and recommend proper actions for ensuring safety, we randomly generated several test cases and tested the executable model of Fig. 5. Out of these test cases, Table 2 shows 6 different test cases ($C1$ to $C6$) which lead the executable model to provide six different guarantees, i.e., the follower vehicle was detected to be in six different states. Figure 6, shows the first test case where the system was detected to be in $S0$, meaning a guarantee is provided about 'complete' safety i.e. safe distance and legal speed. On the other hand, in case **C2**, the system state is estimated as **S2**, meaning the system is violating the first safety constraint, thus **LimitSpeed** guarantee is provided in this case.

Note that, in the above test cases it was assumed that the values of the parameters are deterministic and their values are known with certainty, as a

Table 2. Results of runtime verification of safety guarantees

Parameters	C1	C2	C3	C4	C5	C6
Distance@Follower (m)	6.0	4.0	6.0	1.8	4.2	5.5
Distance@Leader (m)	6.2	3.9	5.9	1.9	4.4	6.2
Safe distance (m)	5.0	5.0	5.0	5.0	5.0	5.0
Too close distance (m)	2.0	2.0	2.0	2.0	2.0	2.0
Allowed error in distances (m)	0.5	0.5	0.5	0.5	0.5	0.5
Speed (miles/h)	48	47	37	37	77	48
Speed limit (miles/h)	50	50	30	30	70	50
Validity of speed limit	Yes	Yes	Yes	Yes	Yes	No
Leader detected by follower	Yes	Yes	Yes	Yes	Yes	Yes
Follower detected by leader	Yes	Yes	Yes	Yes	Yes	Yes
State estimated	**S0**	**S2**	**S1**	**S4**	**S3**	**S5**

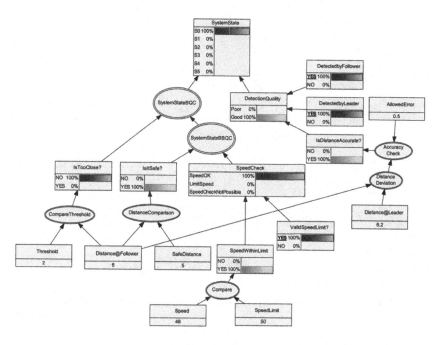

Fig. 6. Case 1 (C1) as shown in Table 2

result, using the model in Fig. 5, the system states were estimated deterministically. However, in practice, we may be uncertain about the parameter values. In such cases, to address parameter uncertainty, we propose to use a probabilistic version of the executable model. As an example, we present a probabilistic version of system estimation in Fig. 7. In this example, the inputs to the BN model are probabilities instead of deterministic binary values. For instance, the node

SpeedWithinLimit represents that there is an 80% chance that the speed of the vehicle is within limit and 20% of chance of exceeding it. Similarly, all other root nodes of the BN model represent probabilistic values for different parameters. As a result of using such probabilistic values for the inference process, unlike the deterministic model, the system states are estimated with probabilistic rather than absolute guarantees. For instance, in the case of Fig. 7, the system was estimated to be in states S0 to S5 with 53%, 13%, 6%, 1%, 0%, and 26% probability, respectively. As S0 state has the highest probability, it could be said that the system is most likely in state S0. Thereby, a (probabilistic) safety guarantee for this state can be provided and actions for this state can be executed. The simplistic rule applied is that the state with the highest probability is selected. However, there may be cases where two states both have (approximately) the highest probability. To resolve such cases, predefined rules can be applied for choosing state. For instance, the more safety-critical state can be chosen in the case of ties.

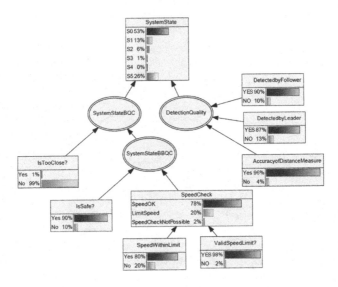

Fig. 7. An example of probabilistic system state estimation

5   Conclusion

In this paper, we present a conceptual framework for addressing the issue of safety under uncertainty in open adaptive systems. Our approach builds upon previous work on runtime certification, through the use of design-time dependability artifacts such as safety contracts, state machines and Bayesian Networks.

Artifacts are deployed at runtime alongside a monitoring framework for observing system and environmental state. Thus, runtime knowledge is utilised to maintain safety properties or recover from unsafe situations.

The work presented here is part of a larger effort, the DEIS research project. As part of our ongoing research, we aim to integrate our proposed framework with the concept of the DDI. DDIs aim to support modularity, composition, seamless exchange and evaluation of the associated dependability artifacts at runtime. DDI integration offers an avenue for implementing the approach in a larger systematic, top-down, traceable development framework. Such a framework provides justified confidence in the assurance of dependability-critical properties of CPS. Further avenues of investigation include linking the proposed approach with ConSerts. By combining modular and conditional certification with probabilistic reasoning and runtime monitoring, a larger section of the development lifecycle could be supported via relevant model-based techniques. Further, an assumption of our current approach is that the actions for mitigating safety risk defined from each system state have deterministic outcomes. A more robust framework would ideally be capable of deciding on actions with uncertain effects as well.

Acknowledgements. This work was supported by the DEIS H2020 Project under Grant 732242.

References

1. Arnold, A., Point, G., Griffault, A., Rauzy, A.: The AltaRica formalism for describing concurrent systems. Fundam. Inform. **40**(2), 109–124 (2000)
2. Bergenhem, C., Shladover, S., Coelingh, E., Englund, C., Tsugawa, S.: Overview of platooning systems. In: Proceedings of the 19th ITS World Congress, Vienna, Austria, 22–26 October 2012 (2012)
3. Bittner, B., et al.: The xSAP safety analysis platform. In: Chechik, M., Raskin, J.-F. (eds.) TACAS 2016. LNCS, vol. 9636, pp. 533–539. Springer, Heidelberg (2016). https://doi.org/10.1007/978-3-662-49674-9_31
4. CCAV: Connected and autonomous vehicles: market forecast. Technical report, Centre for Connected and Autonomous Vehicles; UK Department of Transport (2017). https://www.gov.uk/government/publications/connected-and-autonomous-vehicles-market-forcecast
5. Cheng, B.H.C., et al.: Using models at runtime to address assurance for self-adaptive systems. In: Bencomo, N., France, R., Cheng, B.H.C., Aßmann, U. (eds.) Models@run.time. LNCS, vol. 8378, pp. 101–136. Springer, Cham (2014). https://doi.org/10.1007/978-3-319-08915-7_4
6. Dolginova, E., Lynch, N.: Safety verification for automated platoon maneuvers: a case study. In: Maler, O. (ed.) HART 1997. LNCS, vol. 1201, pp. 154–170. Springer, Heidelberg (1997). https://doi.org/10.1007/BFb0014723
7. Fagnant, D.J., Kockelman, K.: Preparing a nation for autonomous vehicles: opportunities, barriers and policy recommendations. Transp. Res. Part A: Policy Pract. **77**, 167–181 (2015)

8. Feiler, P., Rugina, A.: Dependability modeling with the architecture analysis & design language (AADL). Technical report, Software Engineering Institute, Carnegie Mellon University, July 2007

9. International Electrotechnical Commission: IEC 61508: Functional Safety of Electrical/Electronic/Programmable Electronic Safety-related Systems, ed. Technical report, International Electrotechnical Commission, Geneva, Switzerland (1997)

10. ISO: ISO 26262: Road vehicles - functional safety. Technical report, International Organization for Standardization, Geneva, Switzerland (2011)

11. Kabir, S., Papadopoulos, Y.: Applications of Bayesian networks and Petri nets in safety, reliability, and risk assessments: a review. Saf. Sci. **115**, 154–175 (2019)

12. Kabir, S., et al.: A model-based extension to HiP-HOPS for dynamic fault propagation studies. In: Bozzano, M., Papadopoulos, Y. (eds.) IMBSA 2017. LNCS, vol. 10437, pp. 163–178. Springer, Cham (2017). https://doi.org/10.1007/978-3-319-64119-5_11

13. Kabir, S., Walker, M., Papadopoulos, Y.: Dynamic system safety analysis in HiP-HOPS with Petri nets and Bayesian networks. Saf. Sci. **105**, 55–70 (2018)

14. Mueller, S., Liggesmeyer, P.: Safety assurance for emergent collaboration of open distributed systems. In: IEEE International Symposium on Software Reliability Engineering Workshops, pp. 249–256. IEEE (2016)

15. Östberg, K., Bengtsson, M.: Run time safety analysis for automotive systems in an open and adaptive environment. In: SAFECOMP 2013-Workshop ASCoMS (Architecting Safety in Collaborative Mobile Systems) of the 32nd International Conference on Computer Safety, Reliability and Security, p. NA (2013)

16. Papadopoulos, Y., et al.: A synthesis of logic and bio-inspired techniques in the design of dependable systems. Annu. Rev. Control **41**, 170–182 (2016)

17. Reich, J.: Systematic engineering of safe open adaptive systems shown for truck platooning. M.Sc. thesis, Technical University of Kaiserslautern, Kaiserslautern, Germany (2016). https://doi.org/10.13140/RG.2.2.27809.61283

18. Rushby, J.: Runtime certification. In: Leucker, M. (ed.) RV 2008. LNCS, vol. 5289, pp. 21–35. Springer, Heidelberg (2008). https://doi.org/10.1007/978-3-540-89247-2_2

19. Schneider, D., Trapp, M.: Conditional safety certification of open adaptive systems. ACM Trans. Auton. Adapt. Syst. (TAAS) **8**(2), 1–20 (2013)

20. Schneider, D., Trapp, M., Papadopoulos, Y., Armengaud, E., Zeller, M., Höfig, K.: WAP: digital dependability identities. In: 2015 IEEE 26th International Symposium on Software Reliability Engineering (ISSRE), pp. 324–329. IEEE (2015)

21. Stoller, S.D., et al.: Runtime verification with state estimation. In: Khurshid, S., Sen, K. (eds.) RV 2011. LNCS, vol. 7186, pp. 193–207. Springer, Heidelberg (2012). https://doi.org/10.1007/978-3-642-29860-8_15

22. Swaroop, D., Hedrick, J.K.: String stability of interconnected systems. IEEE Trans. Autom. Control **41**(3), 349–357 (1996)

23. Tsugawa, S., Jeschke, S., Shladover, S.E.: A review of truck platooning projects for energy savings. IEEE Trans. Intell. Veh. **1**(1), 68–77 (2016)

24. Whittle, J., Sawyer, P., Bencomo, N., Cheng, B.H.C., Bruel, J.: RELAX: incorporating uncertainty into the specification of self-adaptive systems. In: 17th IEEE International Requirements Engineering Conference, pp. 79–88, August 2009

AI in Safety Assessment

Clustering Environmental Conditions of Historical Accident Data to Efficiently Generate Testing Sceneries for Maritime Systems

Tim Wuellner[1]([✉]) [iD], Sebastian Feuerstack[1] [iD], and Axel Hahn[2] [iD]

[1] OFFIS e.V. - Institute for Information Technology, Oldenburg, Germany
{tim.wuellner, sebastian.feuerstack}@offis.de
[2] University of Oldenburg, Oldenburg, Germany
axel.hahn@uni-oldenburg.de

Abstract. Vessels are getting more and more equipped with highly-automated assistant systems that benefit from the use of machine learning. Such trained safety-critical systems demand for new means of Verification and Validation (V+V). Their complex decision making process is hidden and traditional system analysis and functional testing is no longer possible as the testing space becomes too large to test. Scenario-based V+V performed in a simulation environment is a promising approach to tackle these challenges, triggering potential system malfunctions and covering as much as possible of the problem space.

The authors propose a data-driven method to identify relevant sceneries, which describe states of a system in a scenario by a set of parameters. These states are derived from accident reports, summarizing the most critical situations a vessel and its automated assistant systems might be confronted with. By a chain of several methods, such as Principal Component Analysis and K-Mean Clustering the authors show that the value space of scenery parameters to be tested can be reduced and clusters can be identified that define equivalence classes of accidents. These clusters can then be partitioned depending on their probability distributions and open up a (reduced) space for random sampling of testing sceneries.

The authors tested the method focusing on a weather-related parameter set of 1700 accidents in 2016 and 2017 that were retrieved from three different sources. Results show, that the first three principal components of the environmental parameters explain over 90% of the original variance and can be divided into 13 clusters. The authors then manually identified those accidents of a different data pool from 2013–2015 for that weather conditions were reported as the main cause of the accident and found the majority of them (61%) within the clusters and further 23% already in close distance. The more accidents are considered as input for the method the better would be the cluster fitting.

Keywords: Scenario-based testing · Principal component analysis · K-Mean Clustering · Latin Hypercube · Ship accidents

© Springer Nature Switzerland AG 2019
Y. Papadopoulos et al. (Eds.): IMBSA 2019, LNCS 11842, pp. 349–362, 2019.
https://doi.org/10.1007/978-3-030-32872-6_23

1 Introduction

New assistance systems that incorporate machine learning algorithms and thus trained data are being developed to support the crew on board. The Verification and Validation (V+V) of these new kinds of systems is a challenge. Traditional approaches such as functional testing are not capable of inspecting the behavior of a system that hides its complex decision making processes within its trained structures [1]. Scenario-based V +V has been proposed, e.g. in the automotive sector, to tackle this new challenge [2]. There, scenarios are used to test a system within a simulative environment. But a challenge remains: How to identify those scenarios that represent an entire bunch of critical situations and therefore cover broad parts of the enormous space to test?

One current approach is to involve experts to identify testing scenario catalogues that represent and cover to the best of their knowledge the most critical situations a vessel can be imagined in [3].

To extend these scenarios the authors propose a data-driven approach based on automatically deriving information from investigation reports and structured databases. In order to reduce the complexity of our approach for this contribution, the authors decided to exclude the consideration of the evolution of an accident over time and instead focus on data that the authors assume remains stable over the evolution of an accident. Such data is for instance data that is related to environment, such as wind, wave period, and current for instance. Environmental effects are also one of the four most common contributing factors that lead to accidents, according to the "Annual Overview of Maritime Casualties and Incidents 2018" from EMSA. In the final outlook the authors present how other factors, such as machine defects or misunderstandings in communication can be addressed by this method as well, but for the sake of brevity they are out of scope for a detailed discussion in this work.

The paper is structured as followed: First, an introduction to scenario based V+V is given and the used terms are introduced in Sect. 1.1, which is followed by an overview of relevant work in Sect. 1.2. Section 2 presents the main contribution of this work, which is the method for the generation of sceneries, a concrete value setting for relevant scenario parameters. Afterwards, in Sect. 3, this method is applied and evaluated in a use case that focuses on environmental parameters corresponding to historical accidents. Finally, the results are discussed in Sect. 4.

1.1 Scenario-Based Verification and Validation (V+V)

Scenario-based V+V defines a type of test procedures aiming at testing new systems or systems of systems within a simulative environment. Ulbrich et al. [4] proposed a definition of the term "scenario" (c.f. figure 1): "A scenario describes the evolution over time of elements of scenes within a sequence of scenes, starting with an initial scene." Hence, an integral part of scenarios are scenes. These scenes are composed of "dynamic elements", "scenery" and "self-representations of actors and observers". According to Ulbrich et al. [4], the scenery describes, amongst others, environmental conditions and static objects. This definition forms the basis for this use case and is also adopted in the maritime domain, where e.g. Shahir et al. [5] used vignette generators in order to describe time varying traffic conditions as a composition of different basic traffic situations.

This contribution focuses on the efficient identifications of relevant sceneries to be used within a scenario-based V+V approach. The current state of the method does not consider the evolution of time and space, which is also essential but out of scope for this work. Nevertheless, the authors briefly discuss at the end how we think that "dynamic objects" and the changes of environmental conditions ("sequence of scenes") can be covered by the presented method.

1.2   Related Work

First attempts in scenario-based testing were made by Schuldt et al. [6], using combinatory procedures for systematic test case generation in a simulative environment. The approaches for scenario-based testing that the authors are aware of, typically depend on a database that aggregates historical information about relevant scenarios to test. These relevant scenarios can consist of critical situations like near collisions [7] or even accidents [8]. Youssef and Paik [9] also use historical grounding accidents as a database to examine grounding parameters. In addition, they applied Latin Hypercube Sampling in order to conduct a qualitative risk assessment of these accidents, but in contrast to the study presented here, they focused on hazard identification without the use in scenario based V+V. Esnaf et al. [10] analyzed the spatial distribution of ship accidents in the Bosporus by the use of two different (fuzzy) clustering algorithms, revealing the key factors and locations, where accidents and incidents mostly occur, which can be seen as a possible preliminary work in order to identify relevant parameters for the presented work

Lema et al. [11] analyzed the circumstances during ship accidents using K-Mean-Clustering and Elbow Method with a result of 15 different clusters of typical situations, also using investigation reports like the authors do here as the foundation for their study. They found that human errors leading to accidents are often coexisting with specific ship conditions or adverse environment conditions, which is within the line of the presented work in the way, that even accidents caused by humans should be included in the data basis, since these mistakes often are triggered by other parameters.

In the maritime domain the environmental impact on ship safety is one of the most common contributing accident factor according to the "Annual Overview of Maritime Casualties and Incidents 2018" from EMSA and intensively discussed: Zhang and Li [12] give an overview of wave related accident causes. High waves [13], the presence of swell [14] to enhance parametric rolling [15], wind [16, 17], currents [18] and dangerous shoals [19] are often discussed accident causes. Erol et al. [20] stated that poor weather conditions can increase the severity of accidents.

Accident analysis is also being performed in other safety-critical domains. Caliendo and Parisi [21] applied a principal component analysis (PCA) on road and environment related variables in order to remove redundant variables within car accident data resulting in an explanation of about 90% of the variance by the use of six principal components from originally eight variables. Golob and Recker [22] also applied a PCA to identify independent variables within car accident data. These approaches motivated us to integrate their approach in our method and to also apply a PCA for dimension reduction, which has so far to the best of our knowledge not being applied in the maritime domain to process accidents.

In the following section the authors propose a method for data-driven scenery generation followed by a use case (Sect. 3) that applies the method for generating maritime environmental sceneries to be used within a scenario-based V+V process.

2   A Method for Data-Driven Scenery Generation

As shown in Fig. 1, the method is organized into the following subsequent steps: (1) *Data Preparation*, to identify for each accident of a given accident database the concrete values of a pre-set set of relevant parameters; (2) *Dimension reduction*, to reduce the dimensionality of the parameters without losing significant variance; (3) *Clustering*, to obtain equivalence classes of accidents and finally (4) *Sampling*, to choose the most relevant sceneries for testing with the highest probability first. In the following, each step and its corresponding sub-sets are presented in detail.

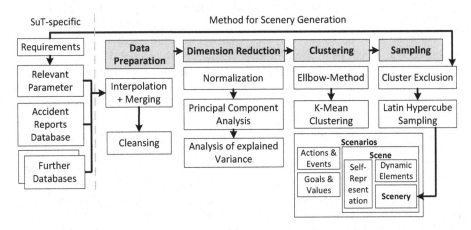

Fig. 1. Schematic process diagram of the proposed method for the generation of sceneries for a specific system under test (SuT)

Data Preparation. The present process is based on historical accident report data for that SuT relevant parameters are identified. Concrete data like e.g. detailed weather or current information needs to be retrieved from further databases based on the exact location and time of the accident. Since the resolution in terms of time and space of these annotated data is often different interpolation techniques like e.g. "Nearest-Neighbor" or "Linear Interpolation" are applied. If an accident location or time is not covered by any of the parameters, this accident is excluded from the further procedure.

Dimension Reduction. At this step, for each accident, multiple parameters are available. Each parameter represents one dimension of the data. Since the parameters differ in coverage of range and units, a normalization must be carried out. Besides that, the following clustering uses Euclidean Distance as the metric for the separation of clusters, which should not be affected by each parameter's range. The normalization of an arbitrary parameter v is done using following formula:

$$v_{norm} = \frac{v - \min(v)}{\max(v) - \min(v)} \tag{1}$$

where $\min(v)$ represents the minimum value of v and $\max(v)$ the maximum, respectively. After normalization, the problem remains, that data with multiple dimensions is difficult to cluster [23]. Therefore, it is necessary to find a small number of parameters, which represent the characteristics of the data best and use these parameters for the subsequent clustering. In addition, correlation between parameters can be exploited to reduce the number of dimensions. This can be done by a Principle Component Analysis (PCA) [24]. In general, PCA is a coordinate transformation, where each dimension consists of a linear combination of all original parameters. These new dimensions are called "principal components" (PC) and correspond to the eigenvectors of the data's covariance matrix. By selecting a smaller number of PCs than the number of original parameters, a dimension reduction is achieved. In order to find the right number of PCs to cover most of the variable space, the explained variance of each PC is calculated by dividing the variance of the ith PC V_i from the total variance of the data V_{tot}. If the explained variance of a reduced number of PCs is over 90%, remaining PCs are excluded from the process.

The result of the PCA is a reduced dimensionality of the data, where each dimension is represented by one PC. Each PC in turn, is a linear combination of all parameters, consequently not the amount of parameters, but the variance of some parameters is reduced by a small quantity. The extracted PCs are the ideal metric for clustering, since these cover the largest percentage of characteristics of the original data.

Clustering. Often, the SuT requirement specification enables to further reduce the sampling space of sceneries. Restrictions of the SuT, such as for instance a requirement that restricts a docking pilot assistant system to perform reliable only in port areas with a maximum wave height of 0.5 m, further limits the sample space, since stormy conditions don't need to be included in the sceneries for conforming to this requirement. Clustering partitions data while respecting given limits.

For determining the optimum number of clusters, k_o, the elbow method [25] is used. The elbow method internally iteratively applies K-Mean Clustering [26] that requires a predefined number of clusters for clustering. If the number of clusters is too small, the exclusion of a cluster might result in uncovered parameter spaces. Therefore, a minimum number of four clusters and a maximum of 50 is used. Within each iterative usage of K-Means, the sum of squared errors (SSE) between each data point and the corresponding cluster centroid is calculated. The elbow identifies then k_o for that an increase in the amount of clusters does not longer significantly decrease the SSE. Afterwards K-Mean Clustering is performed using k_o as the amount of clusters.

It's important to understand that the PC data is used for the generation of clusters. Each cluster therefore represents a specific condition, which is characterized by a combination of the original parameters. Thus, the clustered data is still in form of PCs, in order to limit the dimension of clusters not only for visualization purposes, but also to restrict the space for sampling.

Sampling. Clusters define not only the limits of the entire sampling space, but also for each condition class. A naïve sampling approach would be random parameter sampling. If one takes instead the distribution of the accident data within each cluster into account, those sceneries which occur more frequently than others would be the most probable scenery samples.

In order to consider the probability of accidents, Latin-Hypercube-Sampling (LHS) [27] is used. During LHS, the probability density function (PDF) of the specified number of PCs within each cluster is generated. Then, the number n of intervals of each PC needs to be set at one's own discretion. The PDF is now divided into n intervals, where each interval spans over a probability interval of $1/n$. The advantage of LHS is, that the slope of the PDF is higher at regions with more data points. In combination with the equal distribution of the PDF based on probability p, the probability intervals correspond to smaller data ranges where the number of data points is high. The partition into n probability dependent intervals is performed for each of the PCs, which cumulative explain 90% of V_{tot}, resulting in an irregular grid with n intervals in each dimension. Subsequently within each grid cell one combination of scenery parameter is selected randomly. Since this parameter combination, is a point in principal component space, a retransformation into the original data space is achieved by the following equation:

$$v_d = \mu + v_{pca} \cdot \theta \qquad (2)$$

with v_d being the parameters in original data space, μ its mean, v_{pca} the parameters in principal component space and the PCA coefficients θ. In addition, the normalization made before the PCA (see Eq. 1) needs to be reversed as well.

The partition into intervals by the use of LHS is performed for each PC and represents the main result of this use case. The random generation of concrete sceneries within each interval is trivial and therefore not elaborated here.

3   Generating Maritime Environmental Sceneries

The presented approach is used to generate scenery sampling spaces for a maritime assistance system, affected by environmental conditions. First, insights into the data basis are given, followed by the results for each step shown in Fig. 1.

3.1   Data

Several sources for maritime accidents are available. Here, the authors use longitude, latitude and time information of three accident databases: HELCOM[1] for the Baltic Sea, MARSIS[2] for coastal regions close to Canada and GISIS[3] covering inter alia global open ocean accidents. In order to gain knowledge about the environmental conditions, data was acquired from the ERA5 Reanalysis [28], ETOPO1 [29] and

---

[1] helcom.fi, last checked 5/15/19.

[2] bst-tsb.gc.ca, last checked 5/15/19.

[3] gisis.imo.org, last checked 5/15/19.

CFSv2 [30]. Detailed information about the environmental datasets are listed in Table 1.

Table 1. Information about environmental datasets, including spatial (Δx) and temporal (Δt) resolution

Data source	Type	Δx	Δt	Variables
ERA5	Reanalysis	$0.5° \times 0.5°$	1 h	Wind speed u_w Wave height h_s Period of swell T_s Period of wind waves T_w
CFSv2	Forecast System	$0.5° \times 0.5°$	6 h	Current speed u_c
ETOPO1	Global Relief Model	$0.17° \times 0.17°$	–	Bathymetry d

3.2 Results

First, environmental data was assigned to the accidents by using a nearest neighbor method in space and time. From originally 2600 Accidents in the time between 2016 and 2017, approximately 1700 Accidents were remaining after data cleansing. A major amount of accidents was excluded due to missing values of oceanographic parameters near the coast, caused by the low resolution of the CFSv2 and ERA5 data sources. The data was then used to perform a PCA. By analyzing the explained variance of each PC, a dimension reduction from originally six parameters to three PCs could be achieved. These three PCs jointly explain 90% of the variance of the initial data. Afterwards the Elbow method provided the o-ptimum number of clusters k_o. By analyzing the SSE of the clustered data as described above, a k_o was determined visually (see Fig. 2). In order to confirm this rather subjective approach, the Calinski-Harabasz index [31] was applied as well. Both methods lead to $k_o = 13$.

The determined k_o was used subsequently to cluster the data in principal component space by applying K-Mean Clustering. The results of this method are shown in Fig. 3.

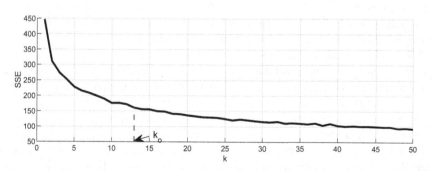

Fig. 2. SSE of different amount of clusters k. Optimum number of clusters k_o is found at $k_o = 13$, since a further increase of k doesn't decrease the SSE sufficiently.

The distribution of accidents ranges from 25 accidents in cluster C10 to 231 accidents in cluster C5, with a median of 126 accidents per cluster. Clusters represent different equivalence classes, e.g. C10 incorporates heavy sea states with significant wave heights of more than 8 m and wind speeds of more than 20 m/s.

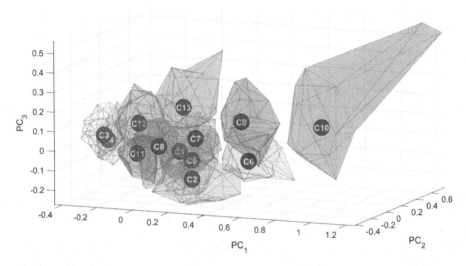

Fig. 3. Results from cluster analyzes. Big dots represent the cluster centroids of the respective cluster indicated by the white text within. Data is shown in principal component space consisting of three PCs.

Another cluster of heavy sea state is given by C9. As seen in Fig. 5, C9 is associated with e.g. significant wave heights from 3 to 4 m and a wind speed up to 16 m/s. Like in C10, the period of swell is higher than in the remaining data. In order to get a better understanding of the cluster's data ranges in the original data space, a transformation using Eq. 2 from the principal component space into original data space was performed (see Fig. 4). For this transformation, only the first three PCs were used, losing approximately 10% of the original variance of the data, but keeping a small amount of dimensions within the principal component space.

The last step within our concept is the sampling using LHS. LHS is performed on every cluster within the principal component space of the first three PCs. This approach allows a sampling of six different parameters by effectively sampling only three PCs. For each of the three PCs the cumulative probability density distribution was generated, and their respective intervals determined. For each cluster, this procedure results in an irregular gridded space, where each grid cell will be sampled by one random PC value. The underlying density distribution ensures that grid cells with higher probabilities are of smaller size and therefore these data ranges are sampled more. In order to get an idea of how these cluster dependent grids are arranged, Fig. 5 represents the grid generated by LHS of cluster C5, prescribing a partition into ten intervals.

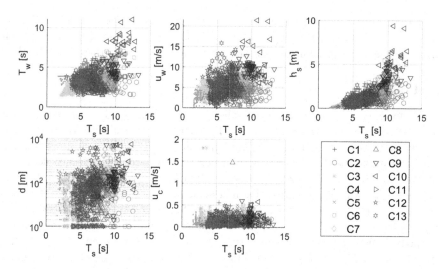

Fig. 4. Transformation results from principal component space into original data space using only three PCs. Different clusters are represented by different colors and marker shapes. Bathymetry d (bottom left) is shown on a logarithmic grid.

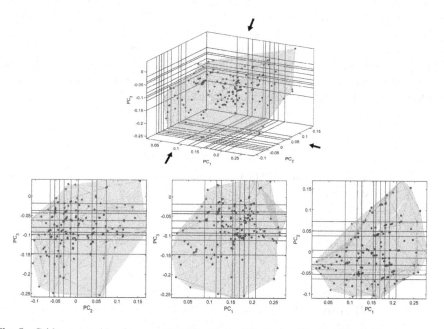

Fig. 5. Grid generated by the use of LHS for cluster C5. Each grid cell will provide one random PC combination as a V+V scenery. At the top, the whole three dimensional sampling space is shown. The bottom represents views from different angle, indicated by arrows. Left: View on PC_3/PC_2 plane. Middle: View on PC_3/PC_1 plane. Right: View on PC_2/PC_1 plane

After the generation of the irregular grid, each grid cell can be sampled randomly. Afterwards, the sample consisting of three PC values is transformed into the original data space and serve in the form of sceneries as the basis for scenario based V+V.

3.3 Evaluation

In order to make statements about the validity of the obtained clusters, investigation reports from the Transportation Safety Board of Canada were analyzed. The aim was to find accidents, which were affected by environmental conditions. To ensure, that these accidents were not part of the procedure, which created these clusters, only accidents from 2012 to 2015 were analyzed, resulting in 22 different accidents. Location and time of the accidents was obtained from the investigation reports, environmental data was gathered from the same sources as described in Sect. 3.1. After data cleansing and removing those for which no environmental conditions could be gathered, 13 accidents remained for the analysis. For each accident, the Euclidean Distance to all cluster centroids was calculated. The centroid closest to the accidents defines the most similar cluster. Afterwards, the Minimum Bounding Box (MBB) for the respective cluster was built, and it was analyzed, if this accident is located within the MBB. The MBB defines the data range in each dimension of the cluster, thus, this corresponds to the space covered by the respective LHS.

As a result of this evaluation, 8 of 13 accidents were located within a MBB, the remaining 5 accidents all were located very close to the borders of the MBB. In order to express this closeness, the nearest point of the cluster was found and the distance to the respective centroid was calculated. The proportional distance D_{prop} was built by dividing the distance from the accident outside the MBB to the centroid and the distance from the closest point to this accident to the centroid. Results, including accident ID and environmental conditions are listed in Table 2.

Table 2. Results of the evaluation

Accident	Cluster	MBB	D_{ratio}	Conditions
M15P0347	7	–	12%	Breaking Waves
M15C0006	9	–	33%	Wind, cross current
M15A0045	9	✓		Wave
M14P0014	4	✓		Visibility
M14C0219	12	✓		Tide, Darkness
M14C0193	9	✓		Ebb Tide Current
M14A0051	9	✓		Ice, Wind
M13N0014	13	✓		Wind, Visibility, Swell
M13N0001	9	–	24%	Wind, Wave
M13M0102	9	–	41%	Cross Tides, Wind, Wave
M13L0185	3	✓		Wind, Wave, Visibility
M12W0062	9	✓		Swell, Wind
M12W0054	1	–	17%	Cross Tides, Swell

More than 60% of the environment related accidents used for evaluation can be found within a respective cluster (C3, C4, C9 and C13). Another 23% (M15P0347, M13N0001 and M12W0054) are located close to the existing clusters C1, C7 and C9.

4 Discussion

The authors propose a data-driven method based on historic data for deriving sceneries that capture the constant part of a scenario within a scenario-based V+V to evaluate the performance of new safety critical systems like assistance systems. In a use case the method was applied to generate a sample space for environmental conditions based on maritime accident reports from multiple sources, which identify critical situations.

The extent of these clusters defines the value space of parameters for the scenery and therefore minimized the computing effort of simulations. Since clustering of multidimensional data is difficult caused by the sparseness of the data, a principal component analysis was applied for dimension reduction. The PCA transformed the original data in a smaller amount of PCs, but reduced the variance of the original parameters value spaces by less than 10 and without losing parameters. After the transformation, LHS has been used to generate partitions within each of the cluster in the principal component space for the subsequent random generation of parameter configurations. These then can be transformed back to the original data space for scenario based V+V consisting of all original parameters and covering all historical accidental conditions.

The use case applied the proposed method to generate sceneries representing environmental conditions during ship accidents and can be improved in several aspects. A data driven-method depends on the availability of data. According to the "Annual Overview of Maritime Casualties and Incidents 2018" from EMSA over 45% of the maritime accidents happen in port areas. Close to the coast, the resolution of the available data is coarse and the oceanographic grid assumes land cells instead of ocean cells. The same problem was observed for bathymetry, resulting in negative values close to the coast, indicating land values. A finer resolution of oceanographic data by dedicated wave and current simulations could solve this problem.

Another aspect regarding bathymetry is that depths of up to 6000 m do not have an impact on the ship's maneuverability. According to Reynolds [32] the impact of the ground is negligible, if the water depth is greater than five times the draught of the ship. Assuming that the largest class of ships is the Suezmax with a draught of 20.1 m, this corresponds to a maximum water depth to be considered of approx. 100 m. On the other hand, deep sea scenery could be of interest, when testing e.g. Autonomous Underwater Vehicle (AUV) instead of assistance systems for ships. In this case, deep sea sceneries might be important for the AUV's resilience against high pressure. This example shows the advantage of our approach. In the case of testing an assistance system for ships, deep sea clusters can be excluded from the scenery generation process as shown in the "Sampling" block of Fig. 1. This also reveals that the selection of parameters for scenery generation highly depends on the SuT. Since for this use case the focus was put on efficiently sampling based on a given parameter set it was assumed that input parameters for the scenario based V+V are pre-defined. The parameter selection is SuT dependent and its selection out of scope of this contribution.

For the evaluation purposes only a small amount of environment affected accidents were available, since only those for that the environment was clearly stated as the accident cause were selected. Nevertheless over 60% of these selected accidents were covered by the clusters that were generated by a different accident report data set. Even the accidents not covered were close to the existing clusters as seen by D_{prop} in Table 2. However, cross currents are not represented well. Hence, more accidents caused by cross currents should be included in the historical data and the direction of currents in different depths, as well as information about the direction of swell and wind waves might be crucial for safety at sea, but must be proven in future studies.

The environment affected accidents are represented by clusters: C3, C4, C9, C12 and C13 (and additionally almost by C1 and C7). This indicates that these clusters define environment related accident sceneries, but due to the small amount of accidents available for evaluation, this statement must be treated with caution. The remaining clusters might represent different accident causes, but this must be proven in future studies as well. Another important aspect is the dimension reduction by the percentage of explained variance criterion. According to Hair [33], the necessary amount of explained variance varies among the fields of science from 60% in social science to 95% in nature science. Jolliffe and Cadima [34] stated that 70% of explained variance is a common although subjective cut-off point and in addition, the number of principal components is often cut-off after two components due to the better possibility of visualization. Here, we are able to represent over 90% of variance using three PCs. Depending on the possible test effort, which is limited by time and compute power, the explained variance can be increased by adding the remaining principal components resulting in a potential increase of the search space. This raises the question of whether the remaining 10% of variance represent critical situations considered important for the subsequent V+V procedure. Additionally, more variables like wavelength, relation of wave period and natural frequency of the ship and the wave spectrum should be included as well. This will increase the dimensionality of the sceneries and potentially confirm the benefits of the dimension reduction.

As mentioned before, the proposed method has the potential to cover traffic sceneries and even dynamic aspects of V+V scenarios as well. This can be achieved by expressing traffic sceneries by a new type of parameter set, including e.g. distance between participating ships, relative bearing between them and others. Parameters describing the ship condition (e.g. failure rates of machines and sensors) can also be associated to the accidents. Dynamic aspects of e.g. environmental conditions can be simplified by analytical functions, whose parameters can be included in this method, too. Especially for the last aspect further research is needed and can be the focus for future studies.

Acknowledgement. This research is supported by the state of Lower Saxony as part of the project Architecture and Technology – Development – Platform for Realtime Safe and Secure Systems (ACTRESS).

References

1. Maurer, M., Gerdes, J.C., Lenz, B., Winner, H.: Autonomes Fahren: Technische, rechtliche und gesellschaftliche Aspekte. Springer, Heidelberg (2015). (in German). https://doi.org/10. 1007/978-3-662-45854-9
2. Brinkmann, M., Böde, E., Lamm, A., Maelen, S.V., Hahn, A.: Learning from automotive: testing maritime assistance systems up to autonomous vessels. In: OCEANS 2017 – Aberdeen, pp. 1–8 (2017). https://doi.org/10.1109/oceanse.2017.8084951
3. Lamm, A., Hahn, A.: Detecting maneuvers in maritime observation data with CUSUM. In: 2017 IEEE International Symposium on Signal Processing and Information Technology (ISSPIT), pp. 122–127. IEEE, Bilbao (2017). https://doi.org/10.1109/isspit.2017.8388628
4. Ulbrich, S., Menzel, T., Reschka, A., Schuldt, F., Maurer, M.: Defining and substantiating the terms scene, situation, and scenario for automated driving. In: 2015 IEEE 18th International Conference on Intelligent Transportation Systems, pp. 982–988. IEEE, Gran Canaria (2015). https://doi.org/10.1109/itsc.2015.164
5. Shahir, H.Y., Glässer, U., Farahbod, R., Jackson, P., Wehn, H.: Generating test cases for marine safety and security scenarios: a composition framework. Secur. Inform. 1 (2012). https://doi.org/10.1186/2190-8532-1-4
6. Schuldt, F., Reschka, A., Maurer, M.: A method for an efficient, systematic test case generation for advanced driver assistance systems in virtual environments. In: Winner, H., Prokop, G., Maurer, M. (eds.) Automotive Systems Engineering II, pp. 147–175. Springer, Cham (2018). https://doi.org/10.1007/978-3-319-61607-0_7
7. Lamm, A., Hahn, A.: Towards critical-scenario based testing with maritime observation data. In: 2018 OCEANS - MTS/IEEE Kobe Techno-Oceans (OTO), pp. 1–10. IEEE, Kobe (2018). https://doi.org/10.1109/oceanskobe.2018.8559045
8. Pütz, A., Zlocki, A., Bock, J., Eckstein, L.: System validation of highly automated vehicles with a database of relevant traffic scenarios. In: 12th ITS European Congress, p. 8 (2017)
9. Youssef, S.A.M., Paik, J.K.: Hazard identification and scenario selection of ship grounding accidents. Ocean Eng. 153, 242–255 (2018). https://doi.org/10.1016/j.oceaneng.2018.01.110
10. Esnaf, S., Koldemir, B., Küçükdeniz, T., Akten, N.: Fuzzy cluster analysis of shipping accidents in the bosporus. Eur. J. Navig. 6 (2008)
11. Lema, E., Papaioannou, D., Vlachos, G.P.: Investigation of coinciding shipping accident factors with the use of partitional clustering methods. In: Proceedings of the 7th International Conference on Pervasive Technologies Related to Assistive Environments - PETRA 2014, pp. 1–4. ACM Press, Rhodes (2014). https://doi.org/10.1145/2674396.2674461
12. Zhang, Z., Li, X.-M.: Global ship accidents and ocean swell-related sea states. Nat. Hazards Earth Syst. Sci. 17, 2041–2051 (2017). https://doi.org/10.5194/nhess-17-2041-2017
13. Guedes, S.C., Bitner-Gregersen, E.M., Antão, P.: Analysis of the frequency of ship accidents under severe North Atlantic weather conditions. In: Conference: Design and Operation for Abnormal Conditions, vol. 2, pp. 221–230 (2001)
14. Tamura, H., Waseda, T., Miyazawa, Y.: Freakish sea state and swell-windsea coupling: numerical study of the *Suwa-Maru* incident. Geophys. Res. Lett. 36, L01607 (2009). https://doi.org/10.1029/2008GL036280
15. Bruns, T., Lehner, S., Li, X.-M., Hessner, K., Rosenthal, W.: Analysis of an event of "Parametric Rolling" onboard RV "Polarstern" based on shipborne wave radar and satellite data. IEEE J. Ocean. Eng. 36, 364–372 (2011). https://doi.org/10.1109/JOE.2011.2129630
16. Ueno, M., Kitamura, F., Sogihnara, N., Fujiwara, T.: A simple method to estimate wind loads on ships. In: Advances in Civil, Environmental, and Materials Research, pp. 26–30 (2012)

17. Heij, C., Knapp, S.: Effects of wind strength and wave height on ship incident risk: regional trends and seasonality. Transp. Res. Part D: Transp. Environ. **37**, 29–39 (2015). https://doi.org/10.1016/j.trd.2015.04.016

18. Gluver, H.: Ship Collision Analysis: Proceedings of the International Symposium on Advances in Ship Collision Analysis, Copenhagen, Denmark, 10–13 May 1998. Routledge, London (2017)

19. Simonsen, B.C., Hansen, P.F.: Theoretical and statistical analysis of ship grounding accidents. J. Offshore Mech. Arct. Eng. **122**, 200 (2000). https://doi.org/10.1115/1.1286075

20. Erol, S., Demir, M., Çetişli, B., Eyüboğlu, E.: Analysis of ship accidents in the Istanbul Strait using neuro-fuzzy and genetically optimised fuzzy classifiers. J. Navig. **71**, 419–436 (2018). https://doi.org/10.1017/S0373463317000601

21. Caliendo, C., Parisi, A.: Principal component analysis applied to crash data on multilane roads. In: Proceedings of Third International SIIV Congress, vol. 1, pp. 1–7 (2005)

22. Golob, T.F., Recker, W.W.: Relationships among urban freeway accidents, traffic flow, weather, and lighting conditions. J. Transp. Eng. **129**, 342–353 (2003). https://doi.org/10.1061/(asce)0733-947x(2003)129:4(342)

23. Steinbach, M., Ertöz, L., Kumar, V.: The challenges of clustering high dimensional data. In: Wille, L.T. (ed.) New Directions in Statistical Physics, pp. 273–309. Springer, Heidelberg (2004). https://doi.org/10.1007/978-3-662-08968-2_16

24. Hotelling, H.: Analysis of a complex of variables into principal components. J. Educ. Psychol. **24**, 498–520 (1933). https://doi.org/10.1007/978-3-642-04898-2_455

25. Thorndike, R.L.: Who belongs in the family? Psychometrika **18**, 267–276 (1953). https://doi.org/10.1007/BF02289263

26. Hartigan, J.A., Wong, M.A.: Algorithm AS 136: a K-Means clustering algorithm. Appl. Stat. **28**, 100 (1979). https://doi.org/10.2307/2346830

27. Owen, A.B.: Orthogonal arrays for computer experiments, integration and visualization. Stat. Sin. **2**, 439–452 (1992)

28. Copernicus Climate Change Service: ERA5: Fifth generation of ECMWF atmospheric reanalyses of the global climate. Copernicus Climate Change Service Climate Data Store (2017)

29. Amante, C., Eakins, B.W.: ETOPO1 1 arc-minute global relief model: procedures, data sources and analysis. NOAA Technical Memorandum NESDIS NGDC-24 (2009). https://doi.org/10.7289/v5c8276m

30. Saha, S., et al.: The NCEP climate forecast system version 2. J. Clim. **27**, 2185–2208 (2014). https://doi.org/10.1175/JCLI-D-12-00823.1

31. Calinski, T., Harabasz, J.: A dendrite method for cluster analysis. Commun. Stat. **3**, 1–27 (1974)

32. Reynolds, J.: Ship-turning characteristics in different water depths. Safety at Sea International, no. 90 (1976)

33. Hair, J.F. (ed.): Multivariate Data Analysis. Pearson, Harlow (2014)

34. Jolliffe, I.T., Cadima, J.: Principal component analysis: a review and recent developments. Philos. Trans. R. Soc. A: Math. Phys. Eng. Sci. **374** (2016). https://doi.org/10.1098/rsta.2015.0202

Pattern-Based Formal Approach to Analyse Security and Safety of Control Systems

Inna Vistbakka[1(⊠)] and Elena Troubitsyna[1,2]

[1] Åbo Akademi University, Turku, Finland
inna.vistbakka@abo.fi
[2] KTH – Royal Institute of Technology, Stockholm, Sweden
elenatro@kth.se

Abstract. Increased openness and interconnectedness of safety-critical control systems calls for techniques enabling an integrated analysis of safety and security requirements. Often safety and security requirements have intricate interdependencies that should be uncovered and analysed in a structured and rigorous way. In this paper, we propose an approach that facilitates a systematic derivation and formalisation of safety and security requirements. We propose the specification and refinement patterns in Event-B that allow us to specify and verify system behaviour and properties in the presence of both accidental faults and security attacks and analyse interdependencies between safety and security requirements.

1 Introduction

Modern industrial control systems are rapidly becoming increasingly open and interconnected. Reliance on networking technologies offers a number of business benefits – flexibility, possibility to integrate new components and subsystems, remote control and diagnostics – just to name a few. However, the networked control systems are also becoming vulnerable to security threats. Security vulnerabilities can be exploited to undermine safety, e.g., by tampering with sensor data or hijacking the controlling functions.

Traditionally safety and security engineering have been considered to be two separate disciplines with different sets of methods and tools. Security analysis is typically data-centric, i.e., it focuses on determining the impact of security attacks on the system data flow. In contrast, safety analysis is concerned with defining the impact of failures on system functioning. Moreover, safety and security goals might result in the orthogonal functional requirements that are hard to resolve at the implementation level. Hence, there is a clear need for the modelling techniques that enable a formal reasoning about safety and security interdependencies at the early stages of the system development. In this work, we present a formal approach that allows the designers to uncover the implicit security requirements that are implied by the explicit system-level safety goals.

© Springer Nature Switzerland AG 2019
Y. Papadopoulos et al. (Eds.): IMBSA 2019, LNCS 11842, pp. 363–378, 2019.
https://doi.org/10.1007/978-3-030-32872-6_24

To analyse the intricate interdependencies between the requirements, we rely on formal modelling in Event-B [1]. Event-B is a rigorous approach to correct-by-construction system development by refinement. System development usually starts from an abstract specification that models the most essential system functionality. In the refinement process, the abstract model is transformed into a detailed specification. While refining the system model, we can explicitly represent both nominal and failure behaviour of the system components as well as define the mechanisms for error detection and recovery. We can also explicitly represent the effect of security vulnerabilities such as tampering, spoofing and denial-of-service attacks and analyse their impact on system safety.

In our previous works [17,18], we investigated the possibility to combine a traditional safety analysis approach and data flow analysis, while in [19] we studied application of Event-B and its refinement technique to uncover the interdependencies between safety and security. In the current paper, we extend and generalise our approach. We propose specification and refinement modelling patterns in Event-B to analyse security and safety requirements of control systems. These patterns capture the dynamic nature of safety and security interplay, i.e., they allow the designer to analyse the impact of deploying the security mechanisms on safety assurance and vice versa. An illustration of the proposed patterns is described in the formal development of a water treatment control system.

2   Safety and Security Interplay in Control Systems

In this section we discuss a generic architecture of a networked control system. We use the four-variable model of software-controlled systems proposed by Parnas [8]. This model (shown in Fig. 1) defines the dependencies between the controlled physical process, input and output devices, and controller. The system goal is to maintain a physical process within the predefined safety bounds. The input device (sensor) measures the value of the controlled parameter that characterises the physical process. Then the controller reads this measurement as an input and computes the output – the state of the actuator. According to this state, the actuator affects the behaviour of the controlled physical process.

By applying the four-variable model, we derive two main types of requirements that should be implemented to guarantee system safety. The first type is the fault tolerance requirements. Since both sensors and actuators can be unreliable, to cope with their failures, either the system should contain redundancy or the controller should be able to put the system in a failsafe state. Moreover, the controller should consider the sensor imprecision. The second type of the requirements is correctness. We should guarantee that the controller output preserves the safety boundaries of the monitored physical process.

To address a connectivity of modern control systems, the four-variable model can be extended to take into account the impact of malicious attacks on the communication channels. Figure 2 presents our proposal to extend the four-variable model to define a generic architecture of a networked control system.

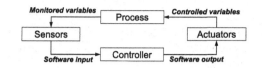

Fig. 1. The four-variable model

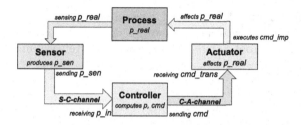

Fig. 2. Architecture of a control system and involved data control cycle

Let us discuss the behaviour of a networked control system and its components as well as a flow of the involved data. The controlled parameter, characterising the physical process, is denoted by p_real. The sensor senses the value of p_real and produces p_sen. Since, the sensor has a certain imprecision, i.e., the reading p_sen does not exactly match p_real. The measured value p_sen then is transmitted over the network to the the controller. In general, the transmission channel between the sensor and the controller *S-C-channel* might be untrusted, i.e., it might be a subject of security attack. Then the value that is received by the controller p_in might be different from p_sen.

The controller checks the reasonableness of the received p_in. It decides to use it as the current estimate of p_real or ignore it. The value p that the controller adopts as its current estimate of the process state should pass the feasibility check, i.e., should coincide with the predicted value and the freshness check, i.e., should be ignored if the transmission channel is blocked due to a DOS attack. If the controller ignores the received value p_in, it uses the last good value and the maximal variation of the process dynamics to compute p.

The value of p is then used to calculate the next state of the actuator that affects the controlled process. The command from the controller to the actuator is transmitted over a network. In the similar way, the transmission channel *C-A-channel* might be attacked. Hence, the command cmd_trans received by the actuator might be different from the command cmd send by the controller. Upon receiving the command cmd_trans the actuator applies it, which should result in the desirable change of the process state.

For our generic control system, we can define the main safety requirement as the following predicate: $Safety = p\_real \leq safe\_threshold \lor stop = TRUE$. It means that the controlled process shall be kept within the safety bounds while the system is operational; otherwise, a safe shutdown should be executed. While designing a networked control system, our goal is to proof its *Safety*.

Traditionally, the design of a safety-critical software-intensive control system relies on specific assumptions and properties of the domain as well as properties of the controlling software [19]. During the design of such a system we should prove the following judgement:

$$(\textbf{\textit{ASM, DOM, SW}}) \vdash Safety,$$

Here **ASM, DOM** and **SW** stand for assumptions, domain and controlling software properties, respectively. Next we will discuss these three types of properties that suffice to proof *Safety* for our generic control system.

- **ASM** – assumptions:
  A1. $p\_sen = p\_real \pm \Delta_1$
  A2. $p = p\_sen + \Delta_2 \wedge \Delta_2 = k\Delta_3$
  A3. $(stop = FALSE \wedge cmd\_trans = cmd) \vee stop = TRUE$

The assumption **A1** means that the sensor measurements are sufficiently precise and unprecision is bounded, where Δ_1 is its maximal imprecision value. The assumption **A2** states that the controller always adopts a measurement of the value of the process parameter that either coincides with p_sen, i.e., $k = 0$, or is calculated on the basis of the last good value and Δ_3 – the maximal possible increase of the value p_real per cycle ($\Delta_2 = k\Delta_3$, where k is the number of cycles). This assumption implies both safety and security requirements. Firstly, we should guarantee that the channel *S-C-channel* is tamper resistant and the sensor is spoofing resistant. Secondly, we should ensure that the controlling software checks the validity of the input parameter and ignores it, if the check fails. The assumption **A2** also implies that, in case of an attack on the channel *S-C-channel*, the system continues to function for some time by relying of the last good value. The assumption **A3** means that if a failure or an attack on the channel *C-A-channel* is detected then the system is shut down. It means that the system should have some (possibly non-programmable) way to execute a shutdown in case the channel *C-A-channel* becomes unreliable.

- **DOM** – domain properties:
  D1. $cmd = INCR \Rightarrow p\_real_{c+1} \geq p\_real_c$ (for any system cycles c and $c + 1$), while system is operational.
  D2. $cmd = DECR \Rightarrow p\_real_{c+1} < p\_real_c$, while system is operational
  D3. $max|(p\_real_{c+1} - p\_real_c)| = \Delta_3$
  D4. $failsafe=TRUE \Rightarrow p\_real_{c+1} \leq p\_real_c$, while system is shut down.

The property **D1** states that an execution of the command *incr* results in the increase of the value p_real. The property **D2** is similar to **D1**. The property **D3** states that the maximal possible increase of p_real per cycle is known and bounded. **D4** stipulates that when the system is put in the failsafe state, the value of the physical parameter does not increase.

- **SW** – controlling software property
  S1. $p\_est + \Sigma_{i=1}^3 \Delta_i \geq safe\_threshold \wedge stop=FALSE \Rightarrow cmd = DECR$

Here, the software property **S1** corresponds to the safety invariant that controller should maintain: the controller issues the command *decr* to the actuator if at the next cycle the safe threshold can be exceeded.

Straightforward logical calculations allow us to prove

$$(A1, \ A2, \ A3, \ D1, \ D2, \ D3, \ D4, \ S1) \vdash Safety.$$

Our system level analysis has demonstrated that both safety and security aspects are critical for fulfilling the system-level goal of ensuring safety. Hence, both these aspects should be explicitly addressed during the system development. It is easy to observe, that we had to define a large number of requirements even for a generic high-level system architecture. To facilitate a systematic requirements derivation, we propose to employ formal development framework Event-B.

3   Modelling and Refinement in Event-B

Event-B [1] is a state-based framework that promotes the correct-by-construction approach to system development and formal verification by theorem proving. In Event-B, a system model is specified using the notion of an *abstract state machine*. It encapsulates the model state, represented as a collection of variables, and defines operations on the state, i.e., it describes the dynamic behaviour of a modelled system. A machine has an accompanying component, called *context*, which includes user-defined sets, constants and their properties given as axioms.

The dynamic behaviour of the system is defined by a set of atomic *events*. Generally, an event has the following form:

$$e \ \widehat{=} \ \mathbf{any} \ a \ \mathbf{where} \ G_e \ \mathbf{then} \ R_e \ \mathbf{end},$$

where e is the event's name, a is the list of local variables, G_e is the event guard, and R_e is the event action. The guard is a predicate over the local variables of the event and the state variables of the system. The guard defines the conditions under which the event is *enabled*. If several events are enabled at the same time, any of them can be chosen for execution nondeterministically.

In general, the action of an event is a parallel composition of deterministic or non-deterministic assignments. A deterministic assignment, $x := E(x, y)$, has the standard syntax and meaning. A non-deterministic assignment is denoted either as $x :\in S$, where S is a set of values, or $x : |P(x, y, x')$, where P is a predicate relating initial values of x, y to some final value of x'. As a result of such an assignment, x can get any value belonging to S or according to P.

Event-B employs a top-down refinement-based approach to system development. Development typically starts from an abstract specification that nondeterministically models the most essential functional requirements. In a sequence of refinement steps, we gradually reduce nondeterminism and introduce detailed design decisions. In particular, we can add new events, split events as well as replace abstract variables by their concrete counterparts, i.e., perform *data refinement.* When data refinement is performed, we should define *gluing invariants* as a part of the invariants of the refined machine. They define the relationship between the abstract and concrete variables.

The consistency of Event-B models, i.e., verification of well-formedness, invariant preservation and correctness of refinement steps, is demonstrated by discharging a number of verification conditions – proof obligations. The Rodin platform [2] provides an automated support for formal modelling and verification in Event-B. It automatically generates the required proof obligations and attempts to discharge (prove) them automatically.

4   Pattern-Based Development of a Control System in Event-B

In this section, we present a generic methodology for the refinement-based development of control systems that facilitates identifying implicit security requirements that should be fulfilled to satisfy system safety. To support such development of a control system in Event-B, we define a set of Event-B specification and refinement patterns that reflect the main concepts of the safety-security co-engineering discussed in the previous section. Such patterns represent generic modelling solutions that can be reused in similar developments.

4.1   Specification and Refinement Patterns

Control Cycle Modelling Pattern. This pattern corresponds to the initial Event-B specification. To formulate this pattern, we introduce an abstract type $PHASES = \{PROC, SEN, TO\_CONTR, CONTR, TO\_ACTUA, ACTUA\}$ defining all stages of a control cycle. Moreover, a variable *phase* $\in PHASES$ abstractly models a current stage of a control cycle.

The abstract model (given in Fig. 3) represents the overall behaviour of the control system by a set of events modelling the phases of a control cycle. In the initial model, we also abstractly specify an occurrence of faults. The event **FailureDetection** non-deterministically models the outcome of the error detection. A reaction on errors is abstractly modelled by the event **FailSafe**.

Physical Process Modelling Pattern. The objective of this modelling pattern is to explicitly introduce the behaviour of the environment – introduce dynamics of the controlled process. While defining this pattern, we should ensure that the domain properties **DOM**, discussed in the Sect. 2, are formalised.

We define the behaviour of the physical process characterised by the variable *p_real*. We also model the dependencies between the actuator state and the expected range of *p_real* value. The abstract function *process_fnc* (formulated in the model context) is used to specify our knowledge about the process:

$$process\_fnc \in \mathbb{N} \times ACTUATOR\_STATES \rightarrow \mathbb{N}.$$

```
Process ≙
  when  phase=PROC ∧ stop=FALSE          C_A_Chan ≙
  then  phase:=SEN                         when  phase=TO_ACTUA ∧ failure=FALSE ∧
  end                                            stop=FALSE
Sensor ≙                                    then  phase:=ACTUA
  when  phase=SEN ∧ failure=FALSE ∧       end
        stop=FALSE                       Actuator ≙
  then  phase:=TO_CONTR                     when  phase=ACTUA ∧ failure=FALSE ∧
  end                                            stop=FALSE
S_C_Chan ≙ ...                              then  phase:=PROC
  when phase=TO_CONTR ∧ failure=FALSE     end
  then  phase:=CONTR                     FailureDetection ≙ ...
  end                                    FailSafe ≙
Controller ≙                               when  phase=CONTR ∧ failure=TRUE ∧
  when  phase=CONTR ∧ failure=FALSE ∧            stop=FALSE
        stop=FALSE                          then  stop:=TRUE
  then  phase:=TO_ACTUA                    end
  end
```

Fig. 3. Events of the *Control Cycle Modelling Pattern*

This function takes as an input the previous value of the process as well as the actuator state and returns a next predicted value of the process. We also formulate the properties of the process dynamic depending on the actuator state:

$$\forall n \cdot n \in \mathbb{N} \Rightarrow process\_fnc(n \mapsto ON) \geq n, \ \forall n \cdot n \in \mathbb{N} \Rightarrow process\_fnc(n \mapsto OFF) \leq n.$$

When the actuator state is ON, the value of *p_real* should increase. Correspondingly, while the actuator state is OFF, the value of *p_real* should decrease. We formulate these properties in the model context. Thereby we formalize the properties *D1* and *D2* discussed in Sect. 2. Moreover, the following constraint in the context formalises the property *D3*:

$$\forall n \cdot n \in 0 .. p\_max + delta3 \Rightarrow process\_fnc(n \mapsto ON) \leq safe\_threshold$$

It requires that, if the process state is currently in the safe range $[0..p\_max + delta3]$, it cannot exceed the critical range within the next cycle, i.e., the safety gap between *p_max* and *safe_threshold* is sufficiently large.

We then refine the abstract event **Process** and model the changes of the physical process:

```
Process refines Process ≙
  when  phase=PROC ∧ stop=FALSE
  then  phase:=SEN
        p_real:=process_fnc(p_real ↦ act_state)
  end
```

Sensor Behaviour Modelling Pattern. In this pattern we specify normal and faulty sensor behaviour as well as a detection of a sensor failure. In the refined machine, we introduce a variable *p_sen* to model the value of the physical variable measured by the sensor. It can be affected by the sensor imprecision or failures, thus our goal is also to specify the assumption *A1*.

The event **Sensor_Normal** models the behaviour of the sensor by assigning to the variable p_sen any value from the range $[p\_real - delta1 \ldots p\_real + delta1]$. Here $delta1$ is the maximal imprecision value for the sensor introduced as a model constant. The event **Sensor_Failure** models the sensor failure. In case of a failure, the sensor produces the reading that is out of the expected range.

```
Sensor_Normal refines Sensor ≙
   when  phase=SEN ∧ failure=FALSE ∧ stop=FALSE
   then  phase:=TO_CONTR
         p_sen :∈ p_real − delta1 ... p_real + delta1
   end
Sensor_Failure refines Sensor ≙
   when  phase=SEN ∧ failure=FALSE ∧ stop=FALSE
   then  phase:=TO_CONTR
         p_sen : | p_sen′ ∈ ℕ ∧ p_sen′ ∉ p_real − delta1 ... p_real + delta1
   end
```

Sensor's Data Transmission Modelling Pattern. This pattern aims at modelling sensor reading communication to the controller. We introduce the variable p_in denoting the value of the sensor measurement received by the controller as an input. It might differ from the p_sen value due to possible security attack on the channel $S\_C\_Channel$. We then refine the abstract event **S_C_Chan** by two more concrete events, modelling the normal and abnormal cases of data transmission, where we assign to p_in different outcomes.

```
S_C_Chan_Normal refines S_C_Chan ≙
   when  phase=TO_CONTR ∧ failure=FALSE ∧ attack_s_c=FALSE
   then  phase:=CONTR
         p_in := p_sen
   end
S_C_Chan_Failure refines S_C_Chan ≙
   when  phase=TO_CONTR ∧ failure=FALSE ∧ attack_s_c=TRUE
   then  phase:=CONTR
         p_in : | (p_in′ ∈ ℕ ∧ p_in′ ≠ p_sen ∧ p_in′ ∉ p_real − delta1 ... p_real + delta1)
   end
```

Moreover, to abstractly model a possible attack on the channel $S\text{-}C\text{-}channel$, we define a variable $attack\_s\_c \in BOOL$ indicating whether the system is under attack. The attack can happen anytime while transmitting the sensed data to the controller and is modelled by the event **Attack_S_C_Chan**. We use this abstraction to represent the results of the security monitoring.

At this refinement step, we prove the property that describes the effect of the attack on $S\_C\_Channel$: $attack\_s\_c=FALSE \land phase=CONTR \Rightarrow p\_in=p\_sen$.

Controller Behaviour Modelling Pattern. The goal of this pattern is to uncover a detailed specification of the controller behaviour (and also specify **SW** assumption). In this refinement step, we refine the abstract event **Controller** to represent different alternatives that depend on the received sensor reading.

We model the procedure of computing the current estimate p. The controller either accepts the current input or relies on the last good value, or calculates a new value p on the basis of the last good value and the maximal possible increase per cycle. The computed value of p is used to calculate the output – the next state of the actuator, i.e., update the variable cmd.

The output of the controller – the next state of the actuator – depends on the value of p adopted by the controller as the current estimate of the process state. Upon receiving the input p_in the controller checks its reasonableness. If the check is successful then p obtains the value of p_in. Then the controller proceeds by checks whether p exceeds p_max or is in the safe range $[0..p\_max]$. These alternatives are modelled by the events **Controller_normal_DECR** and **Controller_normal**, correspondingly.

If the input does not pass the reasonableness check, the controller calculates the value of the process parameter using the last good input value and the maximal possible increase of the value p_real per cycle $delta3$. Then, the controller checks whether p exceeds p_max and computes the output. These alternatives are covered by the events **Controller_retry_DECR** and **Controller_retry**, correspondingly. Here the variable $retry$ is introduced to model the number of retries before the failure is considered to be a permanent and system is shut down. The behaviour of the controller preserves the following invariants:

$$phase = TO\_ACTUA \wedge p > p\_max \Rightarrow cmd=DECR,$$

$$phase = TO\_ACTUA \wedge p \in 0..p\_max \Rightarrow cmd=INCR \vee cmd=DECR.$$

They postulate that the controller issues the command $DECR$ if the parameter p is approaching the critically high value. If the controlled parameter is within the safety region then the controller output might be either $DECR$ or $INCR$.

```
Controller_normal_DECR refines Controller ≘
  when  phase=CONTR ∧ failure=FALSE ∧ stop=FALSE ∧
        p_in = process_fnc(p ↦ act_state) ∧ p_in > p_max
  then  phase:=TO_ACTUA
        p := p_in
        cmd := DECR
        retry := 0
  end
Controller_retry_DECR refines Controller ≘
  any  p_new, delta3
  where  phase=CONTR ∧ failure=FALSE ∧ stop=FALSE ∧
         p_in ≠ process_fnc(p ↦ act_state)  ∧ retry ≤ 2 ∧ delta2=(retry+1)*delta3 ∧
         p_new ∈ p-delta3 ... p+delta3 ∧ p_in > p_max
  then  phase:=TO_ACTUA
        p := p_new
        cmd := DECR
        retry := retry + 1
  end
```

Controller's Command Transmission Modelling Pattern. The goal of this modelling pattern is to introduce into the Event-B model a transmission of the command issued by the controller to the actuator as well as introduce an abstract representation of the attacks and the system reaction on them.

We construct this pattern similarly to *Sensor's Data Transmission Modelling Pattern*. We add several new variables and events into the refined system specification, (e.g., $attack\_c\_a$, the events **Attack_C_A_Chan**, **C_A_Chan_Normal**, **C_A_Chan_Failure**). According to the assumption **A3**, if an attack on the channel C-A-$channel$ has occurred then the controller output would differ from the command received by the actuator. Safety cannot be ensured if an attack on the channel *C-A-channel* is detected and hence the system should be shut down.

We formulate and prove the following property, that describes the effect of the attacks on the controller output: $attack\_c\_a{=}FALSE \wedge phase{=}ACTUA \Rightarrow cmd{=}cmd\_trans$.

Actuator Behaviour Modelling Pattern. Our last refinement pattern focuses on modelling the behaviour of the actuator. We assume that the actuator can fail during performing its function. Then the impact produced by the actuator on the process might also deviate from the one associated with the command *cmd*. We define by the variable *cmd_imp* the state of the actuator produced on the process and assign to it different outcomes depending on the actuator behavior. We refine our abstract event **Actuator** and model different alternatives.

As a result of this refinement step, we arrive at a sufficiently detailed specification to define and prove the following safety invariant: $p\_real \in 0..safe\_threshold$.

Actuator_Normal refines **Actuator** $\widehat{=}$
   when *phase=ACTUA $\wedge$ failure=FALSE $\wedge$ stop=FALSE $\wedge$ attack_c_a=FALSE*
   then   *phase:=PROC*
            cmd_imp := cmd
   end
Actuator_Failure refines **Actuator** $\widehat{=}$
   when *phase=ACTUA $\wedge$ failure=FALSE $\wedge$ stop=FALSE $\wedge$ attack_c_a=TRUE*
   then   *phase:=PROC*
            cmd_imp :$\in$ CMD \ {cmd}
   end

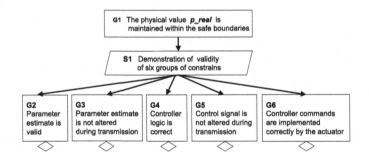

Fig. 4. Decomposition of top-level safety goal

4.2 Construction of Evidences for Safety Case

Safety-critical systems should be developed in such a way that their safety is also demonstrable, i.e., it can be convincingly argued that the system is acceptable safe. The safety argument – a *safety case* explicitly defines the safety requirements and justifies why the design adequately implements them. Goal Structuring Notation [5] has became a popular form of representing a safety case.

It explicitly describes how the safety goals are decomposed into subgoals until claims can be supported by the direct evidences.

During our formal modelling we derive and verify safety and safety-related security requirements, then the artifacts collected during the development can be used in the safety case construction. Next we briefly demonstrate how to construct the evidence justifying the safety goal associated with a control system using different specifications and proofs constructed during the system development. The detailed guidelines for constructing the safety cases from the formal specification in Event-B are described in our previous work [12].

Figure 4 depicts a part of the resulting safety case for our generic networked control system. Rectangles contain definitions of goals, parallelograms show the definitions of the strategies, while circles represent solutions. Lets consider the goal **G4** (Fig. 5): "The controller logic is correct". It is considered in the context of formal modelling in Event-B with Rodin platform tool (**C1**). To support that claim **G4** holds, we state a strategy **S4** to be used in solution of a goal. Namely, we need to define constrains over constants as axioms. Moreover, we have to model the controller actions as well as define the safety invariant and prove it preservation during system execution. Consequently, we further decompose the goal **G4** into three subgoals and define the solutions that support the claims.

Next we will demonstrate how the proposed pattern-based refinement process can be applied to development of a water treatment control system [13].

5   Case Study: Water Treatment Control System

In this section, we overview a water control system [13] and briefly discuss how to develop an Event-B specification of this system and uncover the mutual interdependencies between safety and security requirements. While our modelling, we will rely on the generic development patterns presented in Sect. 4.

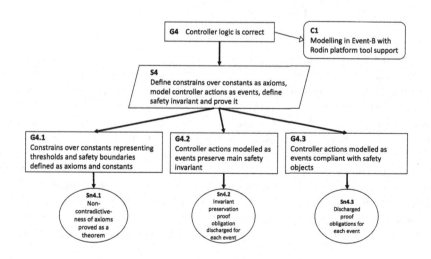

Fig. 5. Decomposition of G4 safety goal

5.1   Case Study Description

We consider a minimal set up in Modern Industrial Control System – a water treatment system [13]. The water treatment system (WTS) is a control system that adjusts the quantity of water in the tank to maintain it within the predefined safety bounds. The system consists of the following main components (depicted in Fig. 6): motorized inflow valve, a tank, a pump, a sensor to measure the quantity of water in the tank, Programmable Logic Controller (PLC) and a central supervisory control system (SCADA).

The system performs the following global scenario. An inflow valve let passage of water into a tank through a pipe. A tank is equipped with a sensor which measures the level of the water inside the tank. Then the sensor communicates its reading to PLC. When the level of the water reaches a certain upper (lower) threshold, PLC communicates to the motorized inflow valve to close (open) and to the pump to start (stop). The sensor and actuators (pump, valve) operate by receiving and sending analog signals. PLC converts the analog signals into digital signals. The digital signals are then exchanged between PLCs and SCADA.

The main hazard of the system is associated with overflow of water in the tank. The main safety goal of WTS is then to keep the level of the water WL_real inside the tank within the predefined boundaries: $0 \leq WL\_real \leq WL\_max\_crit$.

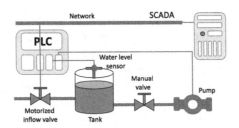

Fig. 6. Water treatment system

Since WTS is an example of the networked system then it could threaten to increase vulnerability to malicious attacks. In general case, we assume that the attacker's goal is to cause a water burst in the tank. Therefore, while reasoning about the behaviour of such a system, we should also reason about the impact of security threats on its safety. The analysis presented in Sect. 2 shows that safety cannot be guaranteed when the controller-actuator channel is attacked. Then WTS should include an additional component – a manual valve – that should be placed in the systems architecture. The behavior of the manual valve is the same as the inflow valve. The only difference is that the manual valve can only be manually operated, i.e., cannot be operated using network messages. Such a non-programmable component can put the system in the failsafe state to guarantee safety. Next we present an abstract Event-B specification of WTS.

5.2 Event-B Development of the Water Treatment System

We design the Event-B specification of WTS incrementally, i.e., by gradually unfolding system functionality and architecture. Our development relies on the generic development presented in Sect. 4. Due to space limits, we only highlight the most important modelling solutions of the development.

Initial Specification. We start with an initial model of WTS where we define its cyclic behaviour. By following the guidelines defined in Sect. 4, we introduce an abstract representation of the control cycle and the corresponding phases.

The event WaterTank models the changes of the water level parameter wl_real while charging. WLSensor event models the estimation of this parameter (that is defined by wl variable). The event PLC specifies the PLC actions (i.e., sending the command to open or close valve and to stop pump). The events TransmReadings and TransmCommands model transmission of the corresponding sensor readings and controller commands, correspondingly. Finally, Actions event models the required actions upon receiving the commands from PLC.

First Refinement. At this step we elaborate on the dynamics of the controlled process, i.e., define the changes in the water level wl_real.

Second Refinement. Here we model the behaviour of the sensor and unfold the value of the physical variable wl_sen measured by the sensor. Since this value can be affected by the sensor imprecision or failures, we address it in our model.

Third Refinement. We model the transmission of the sensor reading to PLC.

Fourth Refinement. This step aims at introducing a detailed specification of the PLC logic. We define the control algorithm, i.e., model the behavior of the controller. The controller calculates the commands to be send to the valve and pump using the current estimate of the water level.

At each control cycle, the PLC controller receives the current estimate of the water level from the sensor. The controller checks whether the water level is still in safe range and sends commands continue to open valve or close valve and stop the pump. The decision to continue water supply can be made only if the controller verifies that the water level at the end of the next cycle will still be in the safe range $[0 \dots wl\_max\_crit]$.

We refine the abstract events of the previous refinement step to represent different alternatives of PCL behaviour. At this stage we can formulate correctness of the WTS logic by the following invariants:

$$phase = TRANSM \wedge wl \geq wl\_max \Rightarrow signal{=}STOP,$$
$$phase = TRANSM \wedge wl < wl\_max \Rightarrow signal{=}CONT.$$

The invariants postulate that the WTS issues the signal to stop when the parameter wl is approaching the critically high value (wl_max_crit), and vice versa. To give the system a time to react, WTS sends the stopping command to the actuators whenever the value wl breaches the predefined value wl_max.

Fifth Refinement. We model signal transmission issued by PCL to the valve and the pump. Here we model different cases of the nominal and abnormal signal transmission (including DOS attack, security failure, etc.). We incorporate into the model architecture a certain mechanism that would allow the system to transmit the signal in a secure way. In particular, we add a new component – security gateway – between the WTS and the external actuators. It could control the network access according to predefined security policies and can also inspect the packet content to detect intruder attacks and anomalies.

Sixth Refinement. Finally, we elaborate on the behaviour of the actuators. Upon receiving the command from PCL, the valve closes and the pump starts or valve opens. As a result of the last refinement step, we arrive at a sufficiently detailed formal specification to define and prove the desired system level property: $wl\_real \in 0 .. wl\_max\_crit$.

6   Related Work and Conclusions

In recent years, co-engineering of security and safety requirements has received increasing attention by researchers [10,16,20]. The possible integration of safety and security techniques has been addressed by adaptation conventional techniques for analysing safety risks to perform a security-informed safety analysis [4,14]. Proposed techniques provide the engineers with a structured way to discover and analyse security vulnerabilities that have implications on system safety.

Formal analysis of safety and security requirements interactions has been addressed in works [6,11]. However, most of the works focus on finding and demonstrating conflicts between safety and security. In contrast, in our work, we treat the problem of safety-security interplay at a more detailed level. We analyse the system architecture, investigate the impact of security failures on system functioning and system safety. Such an approach allows us to study the dynamic nature of safety-security interactions. Ponsard et al. [11] study how Goal-Oriented Requirements Engineering can support co-engineering to address the safety and security dimensions in cyber-physical systems.

In the work [3] distributed MILS approach is presented to support a powerful analysis of the properties of the data flow using model checking and facilitates derivation of security contracts. Since our approach enables incremental construction of complex distributed architectures, it would be interesting to combine these techniques to support an integrated safety-security analysis throughout the entire formal model-based system development.

The four-variable model proposed by Parnas has also been adopted in work [9]. The authors show application of this model in the development of safety-critical systems in industry. They show how this model helps to define the behaviours of, and the boundaries between, the environment, sensors, actuators, and controlled software. Similarly, in our work four-variable model allows us to derive the behaviour of controller that is acceptable from the safety point of view. However, we also employ formal modelling technique to uncover mutual interdependencies between safety and security.

Similar to our work, a model-based approach for the formalization of system requirements, and their early validation with respect to system design has been proposed in [15]. This work introduces a bottom-up design approach as opposed to the top-down approach that used in Event-B. The emphasis is on property preservation through gradual composition of models derived from patterns (architectures) rather than on refinement and generation of model invariants and constraints such as in the Event-B.

The approach to integrate the modelling with UML, formal methods and the actual implementation for developing security-critical applications is discussed in [7]. However, the authors do not consider safety aspect of the modelled system.

In this work, we have proposed a formal approach enabling derivation and formalising safety and security requirements using correct-by-construction development paradigm. Our proposed approach allows us in a systematic manner to derive the constraints that should be imposed on the system to guarantee its safety even in presence of the security attacks. Our approach has relied on modelling and refinement in Event-B.

The approach presented in this work generalises the results of our experience with formal refinement-based development in the Event-B conducted in the context of verification of safety-critical control system [17–19]. The results have demonstrated that the formal development significantly facilitates derivation of safety and security requirements. We have also observed that the integrated safety-security modelling in Event-B could be facilitated by the use of external tools supporting constraint solving and continuous behaviour simulation. Such an integration would be interesting to investigate in our future work.

References

1. Abrial, J.R.: Modeling in Event-B. Cambridge University Press, Cambridge (2010)
2. Abrial, J., Butler, M.J., Hallerstede, S., Hoang, T.S., Mehta, F., Voisin, L.: Rodin: an open toolset for modelling and reasoning in Event-B. STTT **12**(6), 447–466 (2010). https://doi.org/10.1007/s10009-010-0145-y
3. Cimatti, A., DeLong, R., Marcantonio, D., Tonetta, S.: Combining MILS with contract-based design for safety and security requirements. In: Koornneef, F., van Gulijk, C. (eds.) SAFECOMP 2015. LNCS, vol. 9338, pp. 264–276. Springer, Cham (2015). https://doi.org/10.1007/978-3-319-24249-1_23
4. Fovino, I.N., Masera, M., Cian, A.D.: Integrating cyber attacks within fault trees. Reliab. Eng. Syst. Saf. **94**(9), 1394–1402 (2009). https://doi.org/10.1016/j.ress.2009.02.020
5. Kelly, T.P., Weaver, R.A.: The goal structuring notation - a safety argument notation. In: DSN 2004, Workshop on Assurance Cases (2004)
6. Kriaa, S., Bouissou, M., Colin, F., Halgand, Y., Pietre-Cambacedes, L.: Safety and security interactions modeling using the BDMP formalism: case study of a pipeline. In: Bondavalli, A., Di Giandomenico, F. (eds.) SAFECOMP 2014. LNCS, vol. 8666, pp. 326–341. Springer, Cham (2014). https://doi.org/10.1007/978-3-319-10506-2_22

7. Moebius, N., Haneberg, D., Reif, W., Schellhorn, G.: A modeling framework for the development of provably secure e-commerce applications. In: ICSEA 2007, p. 8. IEEE Computer Society (2007). https://doi.org/10.1109/ICSEA.2007.7

8. Parnas, D.L., Madey, J.: Functional documents for computer systems. Sci. Comput. Program. **25**(1), 41–61 (1995). https://doi.org/10.1016/0167-6423(95)96871-J

9. Patcas, L.M., Lawford, M., Maibaum, T.: Implementability of requirements in the four-variable model. Sci. Comput. Program. **111**, 339–362 (2015)

10. Paul, S., Rioux, L.: Over 20 years of research into cybersecurity and safety engineering: a short bibliography. In: Safety and Security Engineering, vol. VI, p. 335 (2015)

11. Ponsard, C., Dallons, G., Massonet, P.: Goal-oriented co-engineering of security and safety requirements in cyber-physical systems. In: Skavhaug, A., Guiochet, J., Schoitsch, E., Bitsch, F. (eds.) SAFECOMP 2016. LNCS, vol. 9923, pp. 334–345. Springer, Cham (2016). https://doi.org/10.1007/978-3-319-45480-1_27

12. Prokhorova, Y., Laibinis, L., Troubitsyna, E.: Facilitating construction of safety cases from formal models in Event-B. Inf. Softw. Technol. **60**, 51–76 (2015). https://doi.org/10.1016/j.infsof.2015.01.001

13. Rocchetto, M., Tippenhauer, N.O.: CPDY: extending the Dolev-Yao attacker with physical-layer interactions. In: Ogata, K., Lawford, M., Liu, S. (eds.) ICFEM 2016. LNCS, vol. 10009, pp. 175–192. Springer, Cham (2016). https://doi.org/10.1007/978-3-319-47846-3_12

14. Schmittner, C., Ma, Z., Smith, P.: FMVEA for safety and security analysis of intelligent and cooperative vehicles. In: Bondavalli, A., Ceccarelli, A., Ortmeier, F. (eds.) SAFECOMP 2014. LNCS, vol. 8696, pp. 282–288. Springer, Cham (2014). https://doi.org/10.1007/978-3-319-10557-4_31

15. Stachtiari, E., Mavridou, A., Katsaros, P., Bliudze, S., Sifakis, J.: Early validation of system requirements and design through correctness-by-construction. J. Syst. Softw. **145**, 52–78 (2018). https://doi.org/10.1016/j.jss.2018.07.053

16. Troubitsyna, E., Laibinis, L., Pereverzeva, I., Kuismin, T., Ilic, D., Latvala, T.: Towards security-explicit formal modelling of safety-critical systems. In: Skavhaug, A., Guiochet, J., Bitsch, F. (eds.) SAFECOMP 2016. LNCS, vol. 9922, pp. 213–225. Springer, Cham (2016). https://doi.org/10.1007/978-3-319-45477-1_17

17. Troubitsyna, E., Vistbakka, I.: Deriving and formalising safety and security requirements for control systems. In: Gallina, B., Skavhaug, A., Bitsch, F. (eds.) SAFECOMP 2018. LNCS, vol. 11093, pp. 107–122. Springer, Cham (2018). https://doi.org/10.1007/978-3-319-99130-6_8

18. Vistbakka, I., Troubitsyna, E.: Towards a formal approach to analysing security of safety-critical systems. In: EDCC 2018, pp. 182–189. IEEE Computer Society (2018). https://doi.org/10.1109/EDCC.2018.00040

19. Vistbakka, I., Troubitsyna, E., Kuismin, T., Latvala, T.: Co-engineering safety and security in industrial control systems: a formal outlook. In: Romanovsky, A., Troubitsyna, E.A. (eds.) SERENE 2017. LNCS, vol. 10479, pp. 96–114. Springer, Cham (2017). https://doi.org/10.1007/978-3-319-65948-0_7

20. Young, W., Leveson, N.G.: An integrated approach to safety and security based on systems theory. Commun. ACM **57**(2), 31–35 (2014). https://doi.org/10.1145/2556938

Author Index